The Nature of Grief

The Nature of Grief is a ground-breaking and provocative new synthesis of material from evolutionary psychology, ethology and experimental psychology on the process of grief. It steps outside of the psychiatric and psychoanalytic perspectives that have dominated grief research for so long, and argues that grief is not an illness or a disorder but a natural reaction to losses of many kinds.

John Archer identifies grief as a common experience throughout all human cultures that has evolved from simpler versions in animals. Human grief is built upon these primitive reactions, but involves higher-level mental processes that attribute meaning to the events and feelings experienced. Differences in grieving depend on differences between the types of relationship involved, and these are considered in terms of evolutionary psychology and attachment theory. This use of Darwinian and attachment theory has made it possible to integrate a large amount of research on individual differences which would otherwise have been unrelated to theory.

The Nature of Grief also considers the cultural and historical context of contemporary ideas about grief, discusses literary, biographical and other non-scientific writings, and includes a wide-ranging, comprehensive and up-to-date review of research. It will be of interest to developmental and clinical psychologists and all those in the caring professions.

John Archer is Professor of Psychology at the University of Central Lancashire. His previous publications include *Male Violence* (1994), *Ethology and Human Development* (1992) and *Human Aggression: Naturalistic Approaches* (1989, edited with K. Browne).

The Nature of Grief

The evolution and psychology of reactions to loss

John Archer

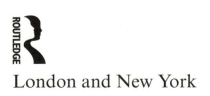

London and New York

First published 1999
by Routledge
11 New Fetter Lane, London EC4P 4EE

Simultaneously published in the USA and Canada
by Routledge
29 West 35th Street, New York, NY 10001

Typeset in Times by RefineCatch Limited, Bungay, Suffolk
Printed and bound in Great Britain by
Biddles Ltd, Guildford and King's Lynn

British Library Cataloguing in Publication Data
A catalogue record for this book is available from the British Library

Library of Congress Cataloging in Publication Data
Archer, John, 1944–
    The nature of grief : the evolution and psychology of reactions to
    loss / John Archer.
        Includes bibliographical references and index.
        1. Grief.   2. Bereavement – Psychological aspects.   Death –
        Psychological aspects.   4. Loss (Psychology)   I. Title.
    BF575.G7A73   1998
    155.9′37 – dc21   98–20134

ISBN 0–415–17857–6 (hbk)
ISBN 0–415–17858–4 (pbk)

Contents

Illustrations

Figures

Tables

Preface

This book draws upon evolutionary psychology, ethology and psychology to consider grief from two perspectives: first as a process which shares certain common features, and second as something that is variable under different circumstances.

The commonality of grief reactions among different people and under different circumstances can be understood in terms of John Bowlby's attachment theory, which was inspired by ethological research. Bowlby's evolutionary speculations, and those of Colin Murray Parkes, can now be extended to link up with the modern Darwinian thinking that underpins evolutionary psychology. To complement the attachment and evolutionary perspectives, which provide a broad framework for the origins and general form of grief, I have added two other features. The first is a detailed general description of what grief entails, thus following Niko Tinbergen's view that the first step in understanding a phenomenon is to have an adequate description of it. I have also sought to understand the mental and emotional processes involved in the process of grief by drawing upon psychological research. By doing so, it is possible to evaluate many common beliefs that have grown up from outside the realms of empirical research, and have been maintained in writings on grief from Freud to the present day.

This book also examines variations in grief, and in doing so is guided by evolutionary psychology and attachment theory. Theories based on the process of natural selection can be used to predict variations in the intensity of grief following the loss of different categories of relationship. The main variables considered are kinship, age and sex. Attachment theory often makes parallel predictions, and in addition indicates that different styles of relating to others may predict different forms of grieving.

This consideration of individual differences guided by Darwinian thinking and by attachment theory makes it possible to integrate a large amount of research which would otherwise have been unrelated to theory. To keep the book to a manageable length, it was not possible to consider all of the many influences on the nature and course of grief. There are, therefore, no separate treatments of traumatic grief, or the impact of forewarning, or the influence of sociocultural variables such as mourning rituals, social support, and religious beliefs on grief. I have also omitted consideration of the grief-like reactions that often occur when a person loses a way of life or a bodily part or function. These important topics deserve detailed discussion. Their omission stems from a decision to concentrate on the evaluation of individual differences that can be understood from the vantage point of evolutionary psychology, kinship, age and sex.

The perspective outlined above provides a commentary on grief research that adopts a radically different voice from that found in other contemporary books on the subject. It also differs in other ways. Most current research concerns American citizens, and people living in similar modern western states. I have wherever possible introduced a cross-cultural and historical dimension to the picture obtained from this narrow research base. In particular, I have examined cultural differences from the perspective of Triandis' distinction between individualistic and collectivist cultures. It is worth noting that the US is perhaps the most individualistic society on earth and most of the research evidence comes from there.

Another way in which this book provides a distinctive voice is that I acknowledge that many of the findings and insights found in academic research have parallels in older and contemporary writings by poets, novelists, playwrights and biographers. In this respect the British psychologist Alexander Shand was far-sighted: in 1914, he devised a series of hypotheses about grief, which he called 'the laws of sorrow', from many of the great classical authors. Shand's insights have been largely neglected, in favour of Freud's speculations on grief published at about the same time. I have given Shand the place I think he deserves in the history of writings about grief. I have also argued that Freud's influence handicapped grief research with a rigid framework which remained largely untested until recent times.

Many people have helped me over the years in the preparation of this book. In particular, I would like to thank: the University of Manchester for granting me a Simon Fellowship, and Tony Butterworth, Pat Bateson and Tony Gale for supporting my application; Norman Birbeck for library assistance and finding references; Vivian Ward, my editor at Routledge, for providing practical assistance and encouragement; Colin Murray Parkes, Nancy Segal and Eric Salzen for comments on parts of the manuscript; Peter Young, Alan Roff and Paul Pollard for providing a supportive environment at the University of Central Lancashire; and my wife Odile for her continued love and support.

I would like to dedicate the book to the memory of my father who died on 19th February 1993, and to all those who are struggling to come to terms with the loss of a loved one.

John Archer
January 1998

Acknowledgements

I would like to thank the following for permission to quote excerpts from material for which they hold the rights:

Curtis Brown Group Ltd, London, for *The Memorial* and *A Single Man* (US rights) by Christopher Isherwood (on behalf of the Estate of Christopher Isherwood. Copyright Christopher Isherwood).

Doubleday, New York, for *Black Dogs* by Ian McEwan (US and Canada).

Faber & Faber Ltd, for *A Grief Observed* by C.S. Lewis (excluding US), and *Amongst Women* by John McGahern.

HarperCollins Publishers (UK), for *C.S. Lewis: A Biography* by A.N. Wilson, *The Things They Carried* by Tim O'Brien (excluding US), and *Reach for the Sky* by Paul Brickhill.

HarperCollins Publishers (US), for *The Unbearable Lightness of Being* by Milan Kundera and *A Grief Observed* by C.S. Lewis.

Little Brown (UK), for *The Moral Animal* by Robert Wright (UK and Commonwealth excluding Canada).

Macmillan, for *The Last Enemy* by Richard Hillary.

Pantheon Books, for *The Moral Animal* by Robert Wright (US and Canada).

The Regents of the University of California for *Death Without Weeping: Mother Love and Child Death in North-East Brazil* by Nancy Scheper-Hughes.

Random House UK Ltd., for *A Single Man* by Christopher Isherwood (non-US rights), and *Black Dogs* by Ian McEwan (UK and Commonwealth excluding Canada).

Random House US, for *Shrapnel in the Heart* by Laura Palmer.

Research Press for *Parental Loss of a Child* by T.A. Rando.

Rogers, Coleridge & White, for *Black Dogs* by Ian McEwan (US and Canada).

Viking-Penguin, for *The Ghost Road* by Pat Barker, *The Time of My Life* by Denis Healey, *Darwin* by A. Desmond and J. Moore, and the translation of *The Iliad* by E.V. Rieu.

In all other cases where excerpts have been quoted, every effort has been made to contact the copyright holders, but without success in some cases. If proper acknowledgement has not been made, the copyright holder should contact the publishers.

1   Introduction

What is grief?

Every perturbation is a misery, but grief is a cruel torment, a domineering passion: as in old Rome, when the Dictator was created, all inferior magistracies ceased, when grief appears, all other passions vanish. It dries up the bones, saith Solomon, makes them hollow-ey'd, pale and lean, furrow-faced, to have dead looks, wrinkled brows, shriveled cheeks, dry bodies, and quite perverts their temperature that are mis-affected with it.

(Robert Burton, 1651, *The Anatomy of Melancholy*: 225–6, 1938 edn)

Approaches to the understanding of grief

The aim of this book is to provide an understanding of the process of grief, the reaction to loss. We normally think of grief as occurring in the context of bereavement, the loss of a loved one through death, but a broadly similar reaction can occur when a close relationship is ended through separation, or when a person is forced to give up some aspect of life that was important. I shall concentrate on examining the general features of grief in the context of losing a close relationship.

I begin by considering three different ways in which grief has been understood by those who have studied it in the past. It has variously been described as a natural human reaction, as a psychiatric disorder and as a disease process. Robert Burton's description at the beginning of this chapter reveals all three aspects: it is a natural reaction or 'passion', yet it produces mental suffering and afflicts physical health. All three statements contain some element of truth, but the first one is perhaps the most useful for understanding the meaning and origins of grief.

Grief can be described as a natural human reaction, since it is a universal feature of human existence irrespective of culture, although the form and intensity its expression takes varies considerably. It also occurs widely in other social mammals and in birds, for example after loss of a parent, offspring or mate. Animals and young children show similar responses to temporary separations and permanent losses. Two types of reaction are shown under these circumstances, active distress and passive depression. These can also be identified in extended and modified form in the grief of adult humans, indicating that this has probably originated and developed from these simpler reactions.

Seeking medical help to alleviate the state of mind which follows bereavement has a long history, depression (melancholy) being acknowledged as a common and serious consequence of grief. Robert Burton described grief as a 'cruel torment'. The nineteenth-century physician Benjamin Rush recommended bleeding, purges and opium for grief (Rush, 1812). More recently, it has been said that the study of grief has been hijacked by psychiatry. Certainly, the best-known pioneering studies were carried out in a psychiatric framework (Lindemann, 1944). The first scientific descriptions were obtained from people who had suffered bereavement under traumatic circumstances, or who had sought psychiatric help to overcome problems associated with grief. Two broad types of reaction were described: one, associated with a sudden and traumatic death or a dependent relationship, involved intense and prolonged grieving; the other, associated with the suppression of painful thoughts or with an ambivalent relationship, involved delayed grief.

While the study of grief from a psychiatric vantage point was undoubtedly necessary in view of the mental suffering such cases involved, it did distort the descriptions of grief that resulted. Both community-based and cross-cultural studies were necessary to redress the balance and to emphasise the range of reactions shown and their social context.

The present-day relation of grief to psychiatry is ambivalent. Whilst a large proportion of studies are still carried out by psychiatrists, grief itself has not – and never has been – classified as a psychiatric disorder.[1] Yet grief experienced under traumatic circumstances would be classified as a post-traumatic stress disorder; and intense and exaggerated forms of grief reactions, such as severe depression or pronounced panic or anxiety, can lead to a psychiatric diagnosis (Kim and Jacobs, 1993; Prigerson *et al.*, 1994). Although a number of terms have been applied to the different forms of abnormal grief, there is some confusion in their use amongst experts (Middleton *et al.*, 1993).

A recent trend has been toward including forms of grief referred to as 'complicated' (Marwit, 1996; Prigerson *et al.*, 1994; Rando, 1992–3), 'traumatic' (Prigerson *et al.*, 1997a) or 'pathological' (Horowitz *et al.*, 1993) as diagnostic categories, which are seen as distinct from a major depressive episode or anxiety state resulting from bereavement (Prigerson *et al.*, 1997c). These forms of grief do not resolve with time and therefore require psychiatric intervention. Yet their descriptions (Horowitz *et al.*, 1993; Prigerson *et al.*, 1995) appear not to be qualitatively different from the typical grief reaction. There is the added problem, realised in some earlier writings

---

1 DSM-IV (American Psychiatric Association, 1994) classifies bereavement under 'Other Conditions that may Be a Focus of Clinical Attention' and concentrates on symptoms that are not characteristic of normal grief. These appear to be exaggerations or prolongations of aspects of 'normal' grieving.

on grief (Eliot, 1932; Volkart and Michael, 1957) that attempts to define normality in the grieving process are beset by the problem of cultural relativity.

Broadly speaking, the psychiatric framework emphasises the human suffering grief involves, and therefore provides a useful balance to viewing it simply as a natural reaction.

Robert Burton also emphasised the adverse consequences of bereavement for health, and referred to examples of historical figures who died of grief, such as the Roman Emperor Severus. In recent times, more systematic comparisons have indicated high morbidity and mortality amongst bereaved people. This, and the general recognition of the importance of psychological suffering in generating physical disorders, has led to grief being described as a disease process. Examples can be found among those who study grief and among lay persons. Engel (1961) advocated this view in a paper entitled 'Is grief a disease?'. Bartrop *et al.* (1992) referred to bereavement as a 'toxic life event for the vulnerable'. In a BBC Radio 4 programme on personal experiences of grief (10th November 1992), the British Conservative politician Lord Hailsham said: 'One thing you've got to realise is that grief is an illness'.

We should treat this statement with some caution. Deaths and deterioration in health shown during bereavement are not necessarily the *direct* result of the grief process. On the one hand, there is clear evidence that separation reactions in animals give rise to a physiological stress reaction which is associated with suppression of the immune system (Chapter 4). On the other, among bereaved people such direct stress-induced effects on health are difficult to separate from indirect effects caused by a change in life-style, such as altered nutrition and drug-intake, and increased attention paid to physical ailments which were in existence before the bereavement. There may be other influences which lead to married couples having similar illness patterns and dying close to one another in time, such as selective pairing of similarly healthy or unhealthy people, or sharing common health hazards (M.S. Stroebe *et al.*, 1981–2; M.S. Stroebe and W. Stroebe, 1993).

Having said this, there are now several prospective studies showing increased mortality for bereaved spouses compared with matched non-bereaved controls (Young, Benjamin and Wallis, 1963; Parkes, Benjamin and Fitzgerald, 1969; Helsing and Szklo, 1981). This is particularly (or perhaps only) the case of widowers (M.S. Stroebe and W. Stroebe, 1993; M.S. Stroebe, 1994a). However, a prospective study which divided the sample by age and sex (Smith and Zick, 1996) found that the elevated risk was confined to younger widowers experiencing an unexpected death. There is also evidence to suggest that mortality is increased in the case of bereaved kin (M.S. Stroebe, 1994a).

These findings, together with the existence of a plausible physiological mechanism (Irwin and Pike, 1993), generally support the case for a link between bereavement and mortality (Middleton and Raphael, 1987; Rogers and Reich, 1988; M.S. Stroebe and W. Stroebe, 1993; W. Stroebe and M.S.

Stroebe, 1992), and to some extent justify Engel's (1961) portrayal of grief as a disease process.

Overall, it is fair to say that although grief is a natural human reaction, the mental suffering involved has linked it with the psychological problems that come under the domain of psychiatry, and these can lead to a deterioration of physical health, highlighted by considering grief as a disease. It is therefore understandable that grief has been studied largely within a psychiatric and medical framework. I shall argue that this focus has held back our overall understanding of the processes involved, since it is narrow in scope and has been dominated by one way of looking at grief, originating from psychoanalysis.

Instead, a synthesis of three perspectives is used to consider grief as a natural human reaction. First, evolutionary psychology provides an understanding of how grief arose through the process of natural selection, and also enables us to understand variations associated with kinship, age and sex. The evolutionary approach is limited to one type of explanation, that concerned with the origins of a phenomenon through natural selection. The older biological approach to the study of animal behaviour, ethology, was broader in that evolutionary function was one of four types of explanation applied to the study of behaviour (Tinbergen, 1963). This perspective enables us also to examine the mechanisms underlying the grief process, in terms of their origins in non-human animals, using interspecies comparisons, in particular involving the process of attachment. I shall also adopt another feature of the ethological approach, which is to provide a detailed description of a phenomenon before theorising about it. This is applied to an examination of the features of human grief. It is apparent from the description that a full appreciation of human grief must involve mental processes. This leads us beyond a view of grief based in ethology to a consideration of relevant areas of human psychology. From these, we can construct an overall understanding of human grief in terms of its immediate causes, its changes over time and its eventual resolution. We can also use psychological research to understand more fully some of the mental processes characteristic of grief.

Grief as a product of natural selection

The evolutionary approach to human behaviour, which is becoming an important part of modern psychology, provides a fundamentally different way of looking at the process of grief from that found in psychiatry, medicine or conventional psychology. First, it poses the question of how grief originated through the process of natural selection, in other words its contribution to reproductive success, or 'fitness'. Second, such reasoning can be extended to ask how, from the viewpoint of natural selection, we should expect grief to vary according to relationships which differ in terms of the fundamental biological variables of kinship, sex and age.

The answer to the first question is not straightforward. In general terms, we should expect natural selection to result in psychological dispositions which enhance an individual's chances of surviving and reproducing in its natural environment. We have already seen that grief involves a number of features – ill-health, depression, distress – which are likely to detract from this. Therefore, how can we reconcile the existence of grief with the workings of natural selection? The key to answering this question is to appreciate that any solution to an evolutionary problem has to fit in with the way the organism works already, and must not impose too great a cost on other adaptive responses. Organisms are generally well adapted for their environments, but any particular set of reactions which contributes to this adaptation may prove maladaptive under a particular set of circumstances.

The evolution of grief can be viewed from this perspective, in terms of trade-offs with other adaptive features. Bowlby (1980a) proposed that a psychologically distressing reaction to separation from a loved one is generally useful because it motivates the individual to seek reunion. Those occasions when it is useful in this way greatly outnumber those when it is not because the loved one has died: thus, grief (which is itself not adaptive) arises as a by-product of the broadly similar reaction to separation (which is adaptive).

Parkes (1972) proposed a related view, that grief is a consequence of the way we form personal relationships. These involve representations of the loved one which affect every aspect of our lives, and which are resistant to attempts to change them. This motivating aspect of close relationships shows itself in terms of wanting to maintain contact and as jealousy, mechanisms which go back a long way in evolutionary history. But they have one drawback. The emotional and motivating responses which are essential for maintaining the relationship when the other is alive (felt as love) also operate when the loved one is no longer there (felt as grief): that is, when, in functional terms, they are futile. Grief, then, is the cost we pay for being able to love in the way we do. This view implies that grief will vary according to strength of the lost relationship.

This evolutionary analysis helps us to understand what sort of process grief is. A further application of evolutionary principles to grief concerns the way in which it varies under different circumstances. We are here considering the relative benefits of certain types of relationships. Evolutionary theorists have concentrated on the impact of kinship, sex and age on the value of particular classes of relationships. This type of reasoning can be applied to grief reactions in an indirect way via Parkes' view that the intensity of grief will vary according to the strength of the relationship. Evolutionary theory provides reasons why certain classes of relationships – between parents and offspring, for example – should in general be stronger, and hence more resistant to change, than others. It also provides a clear basis for understanding the impact of age, both in relation to the bereaved and the deceased, and enables us to examine sex differences in grieving in a new light.

Grief from the viewpoint of ethology

As indicated above, the evolutionary approach provides only one type of explanation. Ethology is a way of studying the behaviour of animals which is rooted in the evolutionary approach and in an appreciation of the way animals behave in the natural world (Tinbergen, 1951, 1963; Hinde, 1970, 1982). The same general approach has also been applied to studying aspects of human behaviour (Archer, 1992a; Hinde, 1982). It is relevant to the study of grief in a number of ways. First it involves an appreciation of not just why certain types of behaviour have originated through natural selection (as evolutionary psychology does) but also of their evolutionary history. This is studied through a comparative approach, whereby universal features of human behaviour are compared with similar features in non-human animals (and in some cases very specific aspects such as smiling and laughing, traced back to possible antecedents). The roots of grief in the animal world were recognised in Charles Darwin's writings on comparative psychology (Darwin, 1872), which formed one of the bases for the emergence of ethology in the 1930s and 1940s. Although not systematically studied from a comparative perspective by ethologists, the scattered material on grief in animals was later discussed in several reviews of grief (Bowlby, 1961; Pollock, 1961; Averill, 1968), and there are further descriptions of animal grief in more recent studies.

Ethology involves several different types of explanation of behaviour, including the evolutionary. But it is recognised that there is no direct line from the genes to behaviour, and therefore it is also important to study the mechanisms through which evolutionarily important forms of behaviour are controlled. The mechanisms underlying the reactions to the loss of a loved one are those controlling the way relationships originate and are maintained. Bowlby (1969) described these in terms of the concept of attachment, which refers to biologically important relationships in non-human and human animals. Bowlby's theoretical writings on attachment drew upon the ethological concept of a behavioural system, which refers to the organised system that controls a pattern of instinctive behaviour. In making this link, Bowlby viewed attachment as involving a form of instinctive behaviour which is essentially similar in different animals (including humans). Within this framework, grief was the by-product of a set of mechanisms which would set off the urge to search for and seek proximity with a loved one who is missing. In this sense grief is a reaction to a deficit, representing the disruption of a goal-directed organised system.

One other aspect of the ethological approach is relevant to the approach to grief taken in this book. Referring to the way that human psychology had developed up to that time, the pioneering ethologist Niko Tinbergen (1963) criticised the omission of a preliminary natural history phase, which was present in ethological studies of animal behaviour. He viewed psychologists as having been too ready to generate and test theories without much prior

description of the phenomena they were considering. Only by prior description, Tinbergen argued, could one fully appreciate the important questions to
be asked and choose appropriate measures when testing them. I shall apply
this general point to grief by seeking to construct a detailed description of it
(in Chapter 5). In doing so, it becomes apparent that theorising about human
grief derived only from attachment theory is limited.

Grief as a psychological process

We saw in the previous section that the ethological concept of the behavioural
system can aid our understanding of the organisation of human grief.
Nevertheless, it can take us only part of the way towards a full understanding of human grief. This is because grief involves a rich array of feelings
and thoughts, which go beyond the separation reactions occurring in
animals. There are higher-order mental processes, such as intrusive thoughts,
hallucinations, feelings of a change in identity, and defences against the distressing aspects of grief. For a full appreciation of human grief, we have to
turn to those branches of psychology that can inform us about mental
processes.

Several theorists have provided an overall conceptual framework for
understanding the way the mental processes involved in grief are generated.
These frameworks complement the accounts derived from attachment rather
than replace them. Their main points are very similar, although the details
and the terminology are different. In all cases, the individual is said to possess
a complex representation of the loved one stored in the brain: these are
variously called 'working models' (Bowlby, 1969, 1973), 'stored memories
with expectancies of likely consequences' (Fisher, 1989), 'schema' (Horowitz,
1976; Horowitz *et al.*, 1993; Janoff-Bulman, 1989, 1993) or 'assumptive
worlds' (Parkes, 1971). In each case, there is a comparison process which
raises the alarm if perceptions from the outside world are substantially different from the central representations. Absence of effective feedback, through
the loved one no longer being there, will set off a major alarm reaction, aimed
ideally at regaining contact. Where this not possible, we have a futile
alarm reaction which continues and continues. This is essentially the view of
separation and grief reactions found in the writings of Bowlby, derived
from the ethological concept of a behavioural system.

However, the important additional aspects which are incorporated into
conceptual frameworks such as that of Parkes (1971) concern the way in
which the representations of the loved one are part of the person's sense of
self, and can themselves be changed – but only gradually and with effort – as
a result of experiencing the discrepant signals. This additional aspect enables
our understanding of grief to go beyond a simple reaction to a mismatch, so
as to incorporate the gradual changes in identity that occur on the way to the
resolution of grief. We can paraphrase this aspect in general terms as follows.

As a result of our life experiences, we develop complex sets of ideas about our identities. These ideas are intimately tied up with those aspects of life which are most important to us, such as close personal relationships, family, home, job, and cherished possessions and beliefs. They are highly emotionally charged and resistant to change, and are central to self-esteem. They not only govern the assumptions we make about ourselves and our personal worlds, but also enable us to make plans for the future, safe in the knowledge that our personal world is stable.

This feeling of stability is an illusion. One phone call or a few seconds on the motorway is enough to change someone's life. Death of a loved one may occur at any time, without warning. Established patterns of life may end abruptly as a result of accident or illness. Jobs and homes may be lost as a result of social forces outside our control. In all these cases, the external world changes suddenly and irrevocably. But the inner experience of what has been lost remains intact and cannot change either quickly or easily.

The process of changing the ideas we hold about our identity so that they match changes in the outside world is highly emotional and painful, and may take a long time to complete. It is this process which forms the essence of grief. Normally the term is used to refer to bereavement, the death of a loved one, a spouse or child, or close relative or friend. However, as indicated earlier, a similar process occurs whenever we are forced by circumstances to change any of the fundamental assumptions we hold about our personal worlds, and hence our identity. In this sense, individuals may go through a grief-like process under a number of diverse circumstances, such as when they lose a home, a job, or even a limb (Parkes, 1971).

The crucial feature in all this is that the person has lost an essential part of what has become, in terms of inner experience, part of his or her self. If someone has been pinning all his or her hopes on something happening – however unrealistic it may be – a grief-like reaction will be experienced if it fails to materialise. In this case, the loss will be all in the mind, rather than externally perceived by others.

This view of grief enables us to understand the central part played by a gradual change in a person's identity over time. This is superimposed on, and is derived out of, the more specific reactions to the loss, the fluctuating strong emotions, impulses and urges to act, and patterns of thought that dominate everyday life and routines. An emphasis on a gradual change in identity complements descriptions of grief which emphasise features such as separation distress and depression.

Psychological research in more specific domains can also aid our understanding of the particular mental processes that occur during the course of grief. These include the generation of intrusive thoughts of the deceased, seeking to suppress such distressing thoughts, the nature of hallucinatory experiences, and the conditions under which people attribute blame to others and themselves. So far, research in cognition and social cognition which might be relevant to these issues has only occasionally been applied to the study of grief. There is therefore no systematic account of how grief changes the way people think, although there is much that is potentially relevant to this topic.

An outline of the book

In the remainder of this book, the three approaches – the evolutionary, the ethological and the psychological – will be used to provide an understanding of the nature of grief, and its major variations. We begin in Chapter 2 by outlining the historical background to contemporary scientific accounts of grief, which are largely based on studies of people living in modern, technologically advanced societies, mainly from a psychiatric and medical perspective. In Chapter 3 I discuss how this view of grief might be supplemented by considering less systematic accounts of grief from other times and in other cultures, and from people expressing the experiences of grief in ways other than through the scientific and medical traditions. Anthropological, historical, personal, literary and other artistic sources are briefly examined in this chapter.

Throughout the other chapters, which concentrate on scientific evidence, I try not to lose sight of the contributions from these other sources, both in challenging the sometimes narrow scope of scientific research (which is mainly obtained within modern western societies), and also to provide a wider description than can be derived from the more systematic sources.

Chapter 4 concerns the biological context of grief. The principal concern of the first part of the chapter is attachment theory. Through this concept we can understand the significance of parallels with human grief found in the animal kingdom. I shall argue that there is a crucial difference between the grief of animals and of humans, which arises from animals lacking a concept of death. Chapter 4 also contains a fuller exposition of the ways in which grief might have resulted from natural selection. Theories which view grief as adaptive are contrasted with the approaches introduced above, that grief can be considered in terms of a maladaptive reaction which involves a trade-off between its costs and the benefits of other reactions which are related to the grief response.

In Chapter 5, specific reactions which make up the overall process of grief are described in detail, mainly from research on spousal bereavement. This enables us to consider all the component parts of the grief reaction. Some of these have arisen from separation reactions known from studies of animals and children, considered in Chapter 4. Others represent ways in which humans seek to avoid these distressing feelings and thoughts, and others are derived from the impact of the loss on feelings of identity, and the changes in identity which occur over time.

Following this analytic approach to the grief process, Chapter 6 concerns more holistic views, examining first such issues as whether it is useful to refer to the intensity of grief, and changes over time, before going on to consider two conceptual frameworks that have been applied to the grief process, one derived from both behavioural studies and attachment theory, and the other a coping-based framework, the Dual Process Model, proposed by M.S. Stroebe and Schut (1995).

These models raise the question of what constitutes recovery from, or resolution of, grief. In Chapter 7, this question is considered in relation to several more specific issues, such as whether concepts of resolution are determined by cultural values, and whether resolution of grief is inevitable. The possible mechanisms through which resolution is achieved are then discussed, in relation to the concept of grief work, before considering the part played by forming a new relationship in the resolution of grief.

In Chapter 8, I consider the way in which grief affects people's thought processes. Although there is little research directly addressing this question, there is research on several aspects of cognition and social cognition which can be applied to it. This concerns, for example, the generation of the intrusive thoughts about the deceased that bereaved people experience, and perceptual illusions such as apparently hearing or seeing the deceased. There is also research on the types of mental coping strategies that are likely to be associated with a more positive outcome, and on the ways in which people make causal attributions for events such as a loss, and the impact of these on the outcome of grief.

The remaining chapters are concerned with variations in the grief response, from the perspective of evolutionary theory. In Chapter 9, I consider the various evolutionary principles which may enable us to understand the origins of variations in social behaviour according to differences in kinship, age and sex. I also consider the few existing studies which have sought to apply these principles to grief and consider some complications in making exact predictions about individual differences on the basis of evolutionary principles.

One of these complications is the indirect way in which grief is related to fitness, that is, evolutionary success, through the relationship with the deceased. In Chapter 10, the nature of the relationship with the deceased is considered, to assess the view, derived from attachment theory, that intensity of grief follows the closeness of the relationship. An evolutionary approach that has linked differences in attachment style to environmental variations, and hence to alternative ways of enhancing fitness, is then introduced as a way of linking attachment styles to fitness.

In Chapter 11, I discuss the death of a son or daughter, which is the most important form of loss from the viewpoint of natural selection. This form of loss is considered at different stages in the life of the offspring. The topics covered are, therefore, miscarriage (including induced abortion), stillbirth and neonatal death (including sudden infant death); death of a child and of grown-up sons or daughters. Again, the research is considered in terms of evolutionary principles, notably reproductive value, and in terms of the proximal mechanisms based on variations in attachment.

In Chapter 12, I continue the theme of kinship and age differences, first considering death of parents during childhood and adulthood, again in relation to changes in evolutionary principles and attachment. I also cover the loss of other relatives, such as a brother or sister, and grieving for a friend, a partner and a non-human companion, from the same perspectives.

In Chapter 13, I examine research on variations in grief associated with age and sex differences, in relation to the evolutionary considerations outlined in Chapter 9, and differences in attachment discussed in Chapter 10.

Chapter 14 contains a summary of the main conclusions that can be derived from applying a synthesis of evolutionary, ethological, and psychological perspectives to grief.

2 The historical background to grief research

An excellent observer, in describing the behaviour of a girl at the sudden death of her father says she "went about the house wringing her hands like a creature demented, saying 'It was her fault;' 'I should never have left him;' 'If only I had sat up with him'" &c. With such ideas vividly present before the mind, there would arise, through the principle of associated habit, the strongest tendency to energetic action of some kind.

As soon as the sufferer is fully conscious that nothing can be done, despair or deep sorrow takes the place of frantic grief. The sufferer sits motionless, or gently rocks to and fro; the circulation becomes languid; respiration is almost forgotten, and deep sighs are drawn.

(Charles Darwin, 1872, *The Expression of the Emotions in Man and Animals*: 79–80, 1904 edn)

Pre-1900 accounts of grief

Robert Burton's *The Anatomy of Melancholy* was published in 1651. As its title indicates, it was a treatise on the nature of melancholy, or depression as it is now called. In several places Burton discussed bereavement and other forms of loss, illustrated by an extensive knowledge of history, literature and the medicine of the time. His general description of grief was outlined in the first chapter. He also noted the association between certain features of grief and mental and physical well-being: for example, confiding feelings and thoughts in others was seen to have beneficial effects (Chapter 7). Burton was also concerned with other types of loss, such as liberty, occupation and status, subjects which were not taken up again until relatively recently (Parkes, 1971; Archer and Rhodes, 1987, 1993, 1995).

There are a number of other references to grief in historical sources from Stuart and Tudor England (Cressy, 1997; Laurence, 1989). Grief was viewed as potentially fatal in the seventeenth century, a number of physicians listed grief among their patients' symptoms, and it was widely believed that grief could make people mad. An analysis of mortuary bills from the seventeenth century indicated that grief was listed as the cause of death in a significant number of cases.

The American physician Benjamin Rush (1812) included a short section on grief in his book on 'the diseases of the mind', noting its immediate and long-term characteristics, and its increased risk of mortality. He also outlined a variety of remedies, both physical and 'moral'. These included administering opium, encouraging crying, and in cases of great emotion, bleeding and purges, which were generally advocated for physical ailments at that time (Rush, 1794).

In his book on emotional expressions, Charles Darwin (1872) carefully described the mechanics of weeping, and followed this with an account of the expressions associated with grief and depression. These involved the raising of the inner ends of the eyebrows, to produce a puckered fold in the middle, and furrows on the forehead (Figure 2.1), accompanied by the drawing down of the corners of the mouth. It is interesting to compare Darwin's description with a portrayal of the same emotion in the work of LeBrun (1698), whose purpose was to enable painters to represent the emotions, but who portrayed these in a static and stylised way. Nevertheless, the same features are apparent in the eyebrows and mouth (Figure 2.2).

As indicated in the opening quotation, Darwin also noted that grief involves an active frantic form and a passive depressive one, a distinction which has been maintained in writings about grief up to the present day. Darwin also described the outward expression of grief in a number of monkeys and apes. His descriptions were important in that they alerted later writers, notably John Bowlby and James Averill, to the occurrence of grief in other animals, and hence to its biological origin and significance (Chapter 4).

Figure 2.1 Photographs from Darwin (1872) showing facial expressions associated with grief in adult and child.

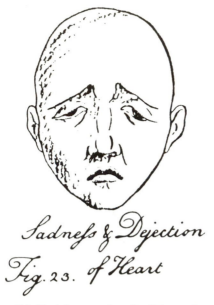

Sadness & Dejection

Fig. 23. of Heart

Figure 2.2 Facial expression signifying sadness and dejection, from LeBrun (1698).

Shand's *Foundations of Character*

Despite such earlier contributions, the first extended discussion of the psychology of grief is found in a book on instincts and emotions written by the British psychologist A.F. Shand (1914, 1920). Shand (Figure 2.3) referred to grief in terms of 'the laws of sorrow'. In the absence of empirical research, these 'laws' were illustrated by works of poetry and literature. Shand's account is remarkable because he described many of the features of grief that are now familiar from modern research. He also pre-dated some important theoretical developments in other areas of psychology: for example, he outlined the link between frustration and aggression later elaborated by Dollard *et al.* (1939); Shand's 'system of the sentiments' included a hierarchical organisation of behaviour, very similar to that proposed by ethologists in the 1940s, and later transferred to human attachment (Bowlby, 1969; Archer, 1992a); he even recognised the importance of negative feedback, now regarded as a widespread principle in the control of behaviour (Carver and Scheier, 1982; Powers, 1978).

Shand used the work of 'the great dramatic poets' because he regarded them as good observers of human emotions. He described four types of grief reaction, one active and directed aggressively to the outside world, another depressive and lacking energy, a third suppressed through self-control, and a fourth involving frenzied activity. He wrote that the depressive alternative is how all prolonged grief turns out, possibly mixed with anger. He therefore provided a simple description of the main features of

Figure 2.3 Photograph of A.F. Shand taken in the 1930s.

Source: Reproduced by kind permission of the British Psychological Society, from the BPS Grace Rawlins Visual Archive

grief, together with an acknowledgement of its individual variations and changes over time.

Shand described many other aspects of grief, such as the importance of social support, the continued tie to the deceased, and the additional distress caused by sudden death. His ideas were clearly ahead of his time. Yet his book only had limited impact on later research. Becker (1932–3) summarised Shand's 'laws of sorrow' in a psychology journal, and illustrated them with case histories from his own work. But, as far as I know, Shand's writings on grief had little influence after this time. His contributions were acknowledged and apparently valued in Bowlby's (1980a) book on loss. Nevertheless, they were not really used by Bowlby: Shand was cited far fewer times than was Freud, who had long since become the dominant influence on grief research and theory. A survey of experts in this area carried out in the late 1980s showed that the psychodynamic framework was endorsed as one of the two most useful models for conceptualising grief (Middleton *et al.*, 1993).

Freud's *Mourning and Melancholia*

Freud (1913) outlined his general approach to grief in *Totem and Taboo*, where he tried to explain why fear of the spirits of the dead was so widespread in traditional societies (see Chapter 3). Of mourning (i.e. grief), he wrote that it 'has a very distinct psychic task to perform, namely to detach the memories and expectations of the survivors from the dead' (ibid.: 96, 1938 edn). He subsequently elaborated this statement in *Mourning and Melancholia* (Freud, 1917), where he stated that much psychiatric illness was an expression of pathological grieving, a view which was later shared by Bowlby (1980a).

Freud proposed that when a loved 'object' ceases to exist, the person becomes conscious of the loss. Reality demands that the libido – the emotional attachment – be withdrawn from that 'object', but this is both very difficult and very painful. The pain may become so intense that the bereaved person turns away from reality and clings to the object by refusing to believe it is no longer there. However, reality is gradually accepted and the withdrawal of libido gradually carried out, at the expense of time and 'cathetic' energy. ('Cathexis' is the concentration of mental energy in one channel.) During this process, the existence of the loved object is psychically prolonged. Every memory and expectation in which the libido is bound to the lost object is brought up and is hypercathetic – that is, mental energy must be used to sever the link and thereby set free the specific energy that is bound up with it.

Divested of its psychoanalytic jargon, Freud's account contains a number of important features which influenced later descriptions of and assumptions about the nature of grief. Foremost among these is the view that grief is an active process involving the struggle to give up the emotional and internal attachment to a love-object, a process which takes up much time and energy (later called 'grief work'). Other features derived from Freud's account include the initial denial of reality, followed by a gradual withdrawal of the inward attachment to the lost person. This involves a very vivid mental 'set' for that person: not only are they thought about a lot, but perception of events and planning of actions is very much influenced by an awareness of them.

Freud derived his theoretical account of grief before the time he experienced a number of personal losses: his 27-year-old daughter died in 1920, and his grandson in 1923 (Horacek, 1991). In 1929, when replying to a letter from Ludwig Binswanger, who had just lost a son, he acknowledged that grief is in some senses inconsolable (Freud, 1929).

Freud's theoretical analysis of grief influenced several further psychoanalytic descriptions, the first being that of Abraham (1924). He described working off the traumatic effects of a loss by the unconscious process of introjection of the loved object, i.e. incorporation into the self. He also maintained Freud's distinction between normal and pathological grief, and the importance of conflicting feelings about the lost object in generating pathological grief. The later writings of Deutsch (1937) and Klein (1940), also maintained the emphasis on libido and mental energy found in both Freud's and Abraham's work. As indicated at the end of the last section, the psychoanalytic framework continues to be very influential in writings about grief to this day.

Early twentieth-century studies of grief

In addition to these psychoanalytic writings, there were a few passing references to grief in the psychological and psychiatric literature. For example, in his questionnaire study of crying, Borgquist (1906) referred to grief as a principal cause of sobbing or prolonged crying. He also used cross-cultural and historical material to address issues such as self-mutilation following bereavement, and the possible cathartic effect of crying. A rather more fleeting reference to grief is found in a later article on crying (Lund, 1930).

Amongst psychiatric sources, Mapother (1926) referred to grief as an important cause of depression, and described aspects such as the selective memory of events associated with the loss, and the control of perception by memories of the deceased, which were elaborated in later research (Chapters 5 and 8).

In 1930, the American sociologist Thomas D. Eliot wrote that family research on widows and orphans had centred around their economic adjustment, neglecting the psychological impact of bereavement. The topic had been left to poets, composers, artists and 'seers' (the contribution of the former being amply demonstrated by Shand). Eliot (1930) pleaded: 'Is there not room for a mental hygiene of grief?' (p. 114).

He subsequently set out to study the responses of families to bereavement (Eliot, 1932). Although primarily concerned with family interactions, he also described several features of grief which have become familiar from later studies, for example shock, disbelief and anger (Chapter 5). He referred in passing to Shand, but not to Freud. He proposed four categories of adjustment following bereavement, ranging from a total failure to adjust, such as suicide or continued obsession with the loss, to conspicuous success, such as forming a new relationship or creating constructive memories of the deceased. His categories are an interesting early contribution to the question of what constitutes effective adjustment following bereavement (Chapter 7). Eliot's research was extended in a PhD thesis by Fulconer (1942) who studied 72 bereaved adults during the first six weeks of grief, by a case-study method. Fulconer described the progress of grief – even during this short time – in terms of five stages, thereby anticipating a popular approach in later writings (see later section). Eliot published further articles on bereavement, including one after the Second World War on recovery from war bereavement (Eliot, 1946). In an account of 'acute war neuroses', Sargant and Slater (1940) also referred to cases of traumatic grief following the evacuation of Dunkirk.

The Coconut Grove fire study

The earliest well-known empirical study of grief was carried out by Lindemann (1944). He followed Freud in his description of grieving as an active process, referring to it as 'emancipation from the bondage to the deceased', readjustment to the changed environment, and the formation of new relationships. Lindemann saw problems arising when people held back from 'grief work' – the mental struggle necessary to obtain release from attachment to the deceased. He also envisaged problems for those who found this process unbearably painful. Lindemann extended his analysis to anticipatory grieving, which he identified as occurring when a loved one was expected to die.

Lindemann's account was based on an empirical study of 101 people, some of whom were patients undergoing psychiatric treatment. The sample contained the following: (i) psychoneurotic patients who had lost a relative during the course of treatment; (ii) relatives of patients who had died; (iii) relatives of people killed in the Second World War; (iv) bereaved victims and close relatives of the dead from a fire which killed nearly 500 people at a Boston nightclub, the Coconut Grove, following a Harvard–Yale football match in 1942.

Lindemann interviewed each patient, allowing feelings to emerge unprompted. The interviews were recorded and analysed in terms of what were referred to as 'symptoms', and also changes in mental state throughout the interview. A picture of acute grief was established, involving waves of distress accompanied by bodily symptoms associated with strong emotion, such as tightness in the throat, emptiness in the stomach and extreme tension. Lindemann also described the sense of unreality and preoccupation with thoughts of the deceased experienced by bereaved people.

This pioneering investigation of the experiences of bereaved people had a strong influence on later research on grief, and directly led to the first research on a grief-like process following another form of loss (Fried, 1962). It was, however, rooted in a psychiatric approach to grief and by modern standards suffers from a number of methodological defects which, to be fair, also beset many later clinically based studies. Lindemann reported neither how soon after the death the first interview was carried out, nor the time period over which the interviews extended. No specific method of analysis was apparent from his paper, and no statistical analysis was given. The study involved a poorly selected sample and the resulting descriptions were liberally interspersed with the author's interpretations. He appeared to rely heavily on the evidence from the Coconut Grove fire survivors (Cobb and Lindemann, 1943), even though these were only 13 in number. In these cases, additional problems are posed by the traumatic nature of the bereavement, which involved sudden death, mutilation of the bodies and public attention. These are all known to produce different and more severe reactions than death occurring under more straightforward circumstances (Rynearson, 1987;

Hodgkinson and Stewart, 1991). Since the participants were hospital patients, their social circumstances were also different from those of bereaved people living in the community.

In the years following Lindemann's study, there were no further extensive studies of bereavement. A few clinically based accounts described particular features of grief, such as somatic illnesses, idealisation of the deceased, pre-occupation and guilt, but not in any detail (Brewster, 1950; Stern, Williams and Prados, 1951; Wretmark, 1959). Such studies were limited because they did not provide a detailed description and were based on small clinical samples. There was also an interesting article on bereavement from the viewpoint of cross-cultural psychiatry (Volkart and Michael, 1957), which made a number of points that echo modern discussions of issues such as abnormal grief and grief work, emphasising the importance of not restricting our consideration of grief to its expression within one culture.

British studies of community samples, 1958–65

The first study of bereavement among community samples was published in the UK in 1958. Marris, a psychologist by training who was attached to the London Institute of Community Studies, interviewed 72 young or middle-aged women whose husbands had died during the previous two years. The interview covered not only grief but also its social context, for example economic circumstances, mourning customs, remarriage and family relationships. Excerpts were used to describe particular grief responses, together with a numerical account of their frequency. These included involuntarily behaving as if the husband were still alive, wanting to escape, restlessness, insomnia, hostility, withdrawal and physical symptoms indicative of deteriorating health.

Marris provided a more organised and systematic description of the typical pattern of grief than had appeared up to then, since he based it on a more representative sample, and avoided the clinical slant of Lindemann's study (the Institute of Community Studies being more concerned with the social context of widowhood). The main methodological limitations lay in the single interview, and a restricted quantitative analysis. Information is therefore limited to providing a list of features that occur in some people at some time following bereavement. Marris' interpretations of his findings involved modifications of Freud's view: for example, he maintained a belief in the cathartic expression of grief, and linked this with the existence of mourning rituals. Marris (1974) later used his findings to derive a more general theory of loss.

Hobson (1964) interviewed 40 widows from a small town in the Midlands of England. All had been bereaved over 6 months previously, most had been married for over 10 years and their ages ranged from 25 to 58 years. Again, they were interviewed only once, at varying times after their bereavement, thus enabling only a general picture to be formed. Physical symptoms such as migraine, ulcers, asthma, chest pains and skin complaints were prevalent, as was a general feeling of tiredness and being remote from reality. Hobson confirmed many of the psychological reactions found by Marris (and in later studies), such as a sense of the husband's presence nearby, hostility – particularly to medical personnel – and little interest in outside events. She also emphasised the widows' social position. Financial problems were coupled with a reluctance to accept or seek help, and ways of relating to those outside the family were lacking, leading to loneliness. In the part of East London where Marris carried out his study, there appeared to have been more community support. This echoes modern studies showing the importance of having a supportive environment and the impact of social institutions that surround bereavement in different cultures.

Gorer (1965) described the grief reactions of a sample of 80 people, aged 18–80 years from throughout the UK, consisting not only of widows and widowers but also people bereaved in other ways. Again, this involved a single interview, which in some cases was carried out up to 5 years after the death. Some assessment of changes over the course of grief was made through a rather haphazard cross-sectional analysis which was rendered less reliable by much of the information being derived retrospectively. Statistical analysis was also weak.

Like Lindemann, Gorer was interested in the clinical manifestations of grief, particularly when it was incomplete or arrested. He identified two types which were apparently intense and permanent. He aptly termed the first of these 'mummification', since the bereaved kept his or her home and life routines exactly as they were before the death. The second was called 'despair', the person becoming emotionally flat and living in comparative isolation. Gorer also noted that grieving could be minimised, or even absent, for example through holding religious beliefs that questioned the permanence of death. He was able to compare grief following the loss of various sorts of relationship, and he identified death of an adult offspring as producing the most severe reaction, which he described as more or less permanent grieving. However, in view of reservations about the analysis, and the relatively small numbers experiencing this form of bereavement, his conclusion should be treated with caution, although some later evidence is consistent with it (Chapter 12).

One very important aspect of the approaches adopted by Marris and Hobson and Gorer was their inclusion of the social context of the bereaved person. In doing so, they took up an important theme from the earlier work of Eliot, omitted from Freud's and Lindemann's clinically based accounts.

Parkes' interview studies

During the 1960s, several influential theoretical articles were published on the processes of grief, by Pollock (1961) and Averill (1968) in the US, and Bowlby (1960a,b, 1961) in the UK (Chapter 4). Under Bowlby's direction, the British psychiatrist Colin Murray Parkes began research on bereavement in the early 1960s. It was clinically based to begin with, but subsequently a detailed longitudinal study of a community sample was undertaken. This marked the beginning of a sounder empirical basis for a description of grief.

The clinical study (Parkes, 1964b, 1965, 1972) was concerned with atypical patterns of grief, and involved detailed reports of 21 bereaved patients (mostly women), supplemented with case notes from a larger sample, obtained from two London hospitals. Most were interviewed after beginning their treatment, around 17 months after the death.

The community sample comprised 22 London widows who were interviewed over the 13 months following their bereavement (Parkes, 1970, 1972). The information was described verbally and was also quantified, so that changes over time, and the association between grief reactions could be investigated. The study provided a detailed description of the grief process (Chapter 5). Nevertheless, it had its limitations. The sample was relatively small, involving only widows, and the time period was restricted to 13 months.

These limitations were remedied by Glick, Weiss and Parkes (1974) and Parkes and Weiss (1983), who used a larger sample of both sexes from Boston (US), interviewing them four times after their bereavement, at 3 weeks, at 8 weeks, around 13 months, and 2 to 4 years. Parkes and Weiss investigated the influence of the suddenness of the death and the relationship with the deceased on subsequent grieving. Their methods were more complex than in previous studies, involving wide-ranging interviews on the nature of the marriage and the circumstances of the death and including rating scales to assess health, depression and prior marital discord. Comparisons were also made with a matched non-bereaved sample.

Parkes' contributions are important because he provided a sound description of grief (Chapter 5) and because he began the difficult task of investigating variables affecting the nature and course of grief. While these studies were being undertaken, research on grief became established in other parts of the English-speaking world. In 1970, the journal *Omega*, dealing with all aspects of research on death and dying, was first published. Studies carried out in Boston, St Louis and Sydney, whose main focus was on marital bereavement and health, began to be reported at around the same time (Maddison and Walker, 1967; Maddison and Viola, 1968; Clayton, Halikas and Maurice, 1972). Pioneering studies of grief following the death of a child or infant were also undertaken then (see Bowlby, 1980a, for a review).

Questionnaire measures of grief

Parkes' research had its roots in a clinical tradition which emphasised case studies and in-depth interviews (although he did also use rating scales). Modern North American researchers of grief have developed a preference for standardised questionnaires rather than detailed interviews. The first rating scales covered physical and psychological health (Maddison and Walker, 1967; Maddison and Viola, 1968; Clayton *et al.*, 1972); established question-naires for depression, anxiety and psychological well-being were introduced later (Vachon *et al.*, 1982a,b; Zisook, Shuchter and Lyons, 1987a).

A more recent development is the construction of specific bereavement questionnaires (Jacobs, 1987; Raphael, 1995). The Impact of Events Scale measures intrusive thoughts and avoidance of thinking about the loss. It was developed for assessing the impact of a wider range of traumatic events (Horowitz, 1976; Horowitz *et al.*, 1980), but can be used for grief (Levy, Martinkowski and Derby, 1994). A second scale was devised by Jacobs *et al.* (1987, 1987–8) by adding items covering bereavement to an established depression scale, so as to form 38 items, measuring numbness and disbelief, sadness, loneliness and crying, searching for the deceased, and distressing feelings of yearning.

The Texas Inventory of Grief (Faschingbauer, DeVaul and Zisook, 1977) is a very brief (7-item) scale, consisting of the central aspects of grief, notably preoccupation with the deceased, pining and crying, as well as identification and an inability to accept the death. Zisook, DeVaul and Click (1982) used items drawn from their clinical experience and from studies of normal and atypical grief to form a 58-item expanded version of the original Texas Inventory of Grief. A shorter revision of this scale (Faschingbauer, Zisook and DeVaul, 1987) provided a subscale involving present feelings (13 items) and one involving those at the time of the death (8 items).

The Grief Experience Inventory, or GEI (Sanders, 1980; Sanders, Mauger and Strong, 1985), is a widely used scale. It is modelled on a well-known personality inventory, the Minnesota Multiphasic Personality Inventory (MMPI), and consists of 135 true or false items designed to assess feelings, symptoms, experiences and behaviour. The complex nature of grief is recog-nised, with nine subscales representing anger, despair, guilt, social isolation, loss of control, rumination, depersonalisation, bodily symptoms and death anxiety. Three other scales assess responding in a socially desirable way, as a further reliability check. A number of different studies of bereaved volunteers have been undertaken, to produce norms for these scales. The same people show reasonably consistent scores on different occasions (i.e. it shows test–retest reliability). Unfortunately, the GEI is limited through only having 'yes' or 'no' responses permitted to each item, and through the authors pre-selecting nine grief scales, to provide totals based on numbers of 'yes' scores for each one. This method loses most of the information potentially available from the 135 questions, and effectively reduces it to a 9-item scale. This criticism does not apply to other less widely used scales, such as the Response to Loss Instrument (Deutsch, 1982), the Revised Grief Experience Inven-tory (Lev, Munro and McCorkle, 1993), the Inventory of Complicated Grief (Prigerson *et al.*, 1995), the Core Bereavement Items (Middleton *et al.*, 1996; Raphael, 1995), and the Perinatal Grief Scale (Toedter, Lasker and Alhadeff, 1988). These are more carefully validated questionnaires, which are internally consistent (Table 6.1), and their underlying dimensions are known (Chapter 6).

One general point about these scales is that their usefulness, and indeed their structure, depends on the range and type of items placed on them, the people filling them out, and the time since the loss. Rating scales are most useful in studying those issues where it is convenient to have a single measure of the intensity of grief, for example whether grief following death of a son or daughter varies with the age and sex of the parents and offspring (Fish, 1986; Chapters 9 and 11). They are less useful for providing a description of grief, for which detailed interviews are better suited (Chapter 5). In Chapter 6, we return to rating scale measures in relation to the question of whether it is useful to consider grief as a single entity or whether there are clear-cut subgroupings.

Established beliefs about the grief process

There are more general articles and books on the subject of grief than there are detailed empirical studies. Interpretations and speculations abound in these accounts. There is in fact an abundance of established folklore which goes way beyond the evidence. This is partly because the way in which grief is usually portrayed originated in an essentially interpretative discipline (i.e. psychoanalysis). It is also because of the urgent need for those working with bereaved people to have guidelines and concepts to help them make sense of their clients' and patients' experiences. It is therefore not surprising that, in the years before detailed studies were available, concepts derived from Freud's writings should survive untested (and later become established dogma) to some extent among researchers and more widely among those working with the bereaved (Middleton *et al.*, 1993; Wortman and Silver, 1987; van den Bout, Schut and M.S. Stroebe, 1994).

In another context, Bowlby (1980b) wrote that within psychoanalysis, 'hypotheses, unchecked by independent data, have run wild' (p. 650). I would argue that Bowlby's comment applies to beliefs held by practitioners, and to many of those who have studied grief. This view is supported by several recent attempts to look anew at some of the established concepts about grief. Shackleton (1984) provided a detailed examination of the main theories of grief, finding them generally logically incoherent and lacking in empirical support. Wortman and Silver (1989) have referred to assumptions held by researchers, laypersons and professionals about how others should respond as 'the myths of coping with loss'. Although M.S. Stroebe, van den Bout and Schut (1994) have convincingly argued that these 'myths' are not widely held by researchers, a study of Dutch practitioners (general practitioners, clergymen and social workers) indicated that they were widely endorsed by this sample (van den Bout, Schut and M.S. Stroebe, 1994). The specific beliefs Wortman and Silver considered were: that every bereaved person necessarily shows distress or depression; that absence of these reactions indicates pathological grieving; that recovery always occurs given time; and that 'grief work' is necessary for recovery. (Van den Bout *et al.*, 1994, added some further common beliefs to the list, such as the notion of fixed stages, discussed in the next section.) These so-called myths will be discussed at appropriate points in this book. A general conclusion from Wortman and Silver's article, and the responses to it by M.S. Stroebe and her colleagues, is that we need to examine critically many of the assumptions which have been made about the grief process.

The stage or phase view of grief

One of these assumptions, which was not on the list of 'myths', but is discussed elsewhere by Wortman and Silver (1987, 1992), is the concept of 'stages', or 'phases'. This is perhaps more widely believed than the other so-called myths, and it has implications for how grief is approached and considered. In many writings on grief it has been accepted that an orderly progression occurs through distinct periods which can be identified and described by particular features (Averill, 1968; Bowlby, 1980a; Bowlby and Parkes, 1970; Engel, 1964; Fawzy, Fawzy and Pasnau, 1991; Seitz and Warrwick, 1974; Pincus, 1976; Pollock, 1961; Raphael, 1983; Volkan, 1981). There are some variations in the precise stages or phases, but the most widely quoted are those of Bowlby or Kubler-Ross.

Bowlby's phase account was originally (Bowlby, 1961) based on an analogy with young children's reactions to separation (Bowlby, 1960a), a much shorter process lasting a matter of days. Initially, three stages were suggested, protest, despair and detachment, an initial one of numbness and disbelief being added later to form the four phases for adult grief described by Bowlby and Parkes (1970) and by Bowlby (1980a), shown in Table 2.1. Engel (1964) described four stages which were rather similar to those of Bowlby and Parkes.

The initial phase is one of numbness and disbelief, the second consists of anxiety and anger, the third a depressive reaction, and the final one involves

Table 2.1 The four phases of grief

1 NUMBNESS and DISBELIEF: A phase of numbness that may be interrupted by outbursts of distress and/or anger.

2 YEARNING and SEARCHING: Accompanied by anxiety, and intermittent periods of anger. Viewed as lasting for months or even years.

3 DISORGANISATION and DESPAIR: Feelings of depression and apathy when old patterns have been discarded.

4 REORGANISATION: Recovery from bereavement.

Source: Modified from Bowlby 1980a

acceptance. Some accounts of abnormal grief (Volkan, 1981) conceive of it as being arrested at an early stage and unable to progress.

Although Kubler-Ross (1969, 1971) developed her stage view in relation to the process of dying, based on interviews with terminally ill patients, it seems that the inspiration for this formulation came from an earlier version of Bowlby and Parkes' stage view of grief (Parkes, 1995). Kubler-Ross's stages were later applied by others to the grief process (Seitz and Warrwick, 1974; Herman, 1974; Goldberg, 1981–2; Freeman, 1984). There were five stages – denial, anger, bargaining, depression and acceptance. Most are self-explanatory, except for bargaining which represents attempts to say to oneself 'Maybe if I do this, everything will turn out all right'. Not surprisingly, Kubler-Ross's stages bear some similarity to those of Bowlby, and they have been very influential in nursing and counselling, applied both to dying patients and the bereaved (Wortman and Silver, 1987, 1992).

Both accounts were put forward before the time when prolonged, detailed follow-up studies of bereaved people had been undertaken. It is now apparent from such studies (Parkes, 1970, 1972; Barrett and Schneweis, 1980; Elizur and Kaffman, 1982; Lund, Caserta and Dimond, 1986, 1993; Prigerson *et al.*, 1996b; Shuchter, 1986; Shuchter and Zisook, 1993) that with the possible exception of the initial reaction (shock and disbelief) the process of change through time is much more of a mixture of reactions which wax and wane in relation to outside events and may be delayed, prolonged or exaggerated according to the person's mental state and circumstances (Chapter 6). Many of those who have adopted the phase view have also sought to qualify it. In fact, Bowlby himself wrote, 'These phases are not clear cut, and any one individual may oscillate for a time back and forth between any two of them' (Bowlby, 1980a: 85).

Sanders (1989) also sought to recognise the limitations and yet still retain the phase view in some form. She viewed phases as representing 'a cluster of responses that one could expect to encounter during that particular period of grief'. She admitted that they overlapped and that there were regressions. The five specific phases Sanders suggested were shock, awareness of the loss, conservation (involving withdrawal), healing and renewal. These were different from those of Bowlby and Kubler-Ross. Sanders emphasised that they were to be viewed only as guidelines, rather than in the rigid terms that writers such as Kubler-Ross had used them. Such caveats are well meaning, but they tend to become forgotten in secondary sources and by students and practitioners looking for clear guidelines to the grief process (for example, the stage view was endorsed by practitioners in the study by van den Bout *et al.*, 1994).

In a personal account of grief (see Chapter 3), C.S. Lewis expressed his feelings about the way grief changed in the following terms 'For in grief nothing "stays put". One keeps on emerging from a phase, but it always recurs. Round and round. Everything repeats. Am I going in circles, or dare I hope I am on a spiral?' (Lewis, 1961: 46).

He also described grief as 'like a long valley, a winding valley', one in which you are likely to encounter 'the same sort of country you thought you had left behind miles ago' (p. 47).

In view of reservations about the phase or stage view, and because longitudinal studies provide little or no evidence to support it, several commentators have argued that it is misleading for practical purposes (Archer and Rhodes, 1987; Archer, 1991b; Brasted and Callahan, 1984; Bugen, 1977; Clegg, 1988; Lund *et al.*, 1993; Shackleton, 1984; Silver and Wortman, 1980; van der Wal, 1989–90; Wortman and Silver, 1987, 1992; Wortman, Silver and Kessler, 1993). Instead, the evidence is more compatible with several intermingled reactions which, although broadly changing over time, do not show a smooth progression (see Chapter 6). Another important reservation is that the experience of grief differs between individuals and is more susceptible to outside influences than is acknowledged by the stage view (Rosenblatt, 1983; Wortman and Silver, 1992; Wortman *et al.*, 1993). Such considerations are also important for linking individual differences in grief to a wider body of psychological research on stress and coping (W. Stroebe and M.S. Stroebe, 1987a,b, 1992; Wortman *et al.*, 1993). For these various reasons, grief is not considered in terms of supposed stages in the present book, although the stage view is considered further in Chapter 6, in relation to conceptual frameworks for the grief process.

Conclusions

In this chapter I have traced the history of research on grief from early writings of physicians, psychiatrists and psychologists to the more empirical basis of today's accounts of the subject. It was apparent that the psychoanalytical framework has had an important influence on later theoretical concepts applied to the grief process, particularly the notion of grief work. The influence began with Freud's *Mourning and Melancholia* and progressed through the works of Lindemann to the more recent writings of John Bowlby. Bowlby also introduced the concept of stages early on in his writings on grief. An important general point about these theoretical concepts is that they arose from a psychoanalytically driven framework for grief before the time when empirical evidence was available to test them.

Research on grief has led to a clear description of its main aspects and to an understanding of the many variables which influence its variability under different circumstances. Yet it has only fairly recently begun to test empirically such widely established theoretical concepts as grief work and stages.

Looking back over the history of research on grief, it seems that the dominant influence of *Mourning and Melancholia* overshadowed other earlier writings, such as those of Shand and Eliot, to the detriment of the development of the understanding of grief. Shand's laws of sorrow would have made a sounder basis for empirical research than that provided by Freud's depiction of grief. Having said this, it is clear that the subject of bereavement has now become part of mainstream psychology, and that concepts which were once accepted without question are being tested by empirical evidence.

3 Accounts of grief from other sources

> I shall use the term 'psychology' and 'psychologist' to denote the scientific varieties; but in so doing, I shall imply no disrespect for the achievements in this sphere of poets and biographers and writers of romance. The wise psychologist will regard literature as a vast storehouse of information about human experience, and will not neglect to draw from it what he can.
>
> (William McDougall, 1923, *An Outline of Psychology*: 9)

Introduction

The research tradition outlined in Chapter 2 is located in modern western societies in the twentieth century. It therefore needs to be placed into a wider context by considering accounts of grief from other times and from other cultures. This can be achieved first by looking at historical and anthropological sources, and second by considering the depiction of grief in poetry, literature and other personal accounts, and in the arts generally. As we noted in the previous chapter, Shand (1914, 1920) illustrated his pioneering writings on grief with quotations from the great novelists, poets and playwrights. In the remainder of this book, I shall also seek to use such illustrative sources, although I have the benefit of modern systematic research which was not available to Shand. My use of this 'vast storehouse of information about human experience' will therefore supplement the research rather than replace it, the only option available at the time Shand was writing.

Historical sources

There are some general descriptions of grief in previous centuries which have been derived from literary sources and from diaries written by ordinary people in western societies (Messer, 1990; Smith-Rosenberg, 1975; Saum, 1975; Steele, 1977). Rosenblatt (1983) made a more specific assessment of whether twentieth-century ideas about grief are consistent with reports of death and separation in the nineteenth century. Since the feelings were recorded as they were experienced, there could be no question of the writer being influenced by beliefs held in the twentieth century about the nature of grief.

Unfortunately, the information used in Rosenblatt's study was seldom in a form suitable for testing twentieth-century theories about grief, and for distinguishing between alternative interpretations (Archer, 1987). Nevertheless, his book provides fascinating descriptive material, much of which is clearly relevant to issues raised in modern discussions of grief. For example, the diaries indicated that grief waxes and wanes intermittently, rather than progressing through stages (see Chapters 2 and 6) or smoothly progressing towards recovery (Chapter 7).

Grieving over the death of a child was found to be intense even at a time when infant mortality was very high, contrary to other writings which have suggested that parents accepted such losses readily (Laslet, 1968; Lloyd, 1982; Parkes, 1986). Although he was explicitly dealing with an earlier historical period, Stone (1977) also advanced this view in an influential book on family and social life from 1500 to 1800. He argued that, in western Europe, affective bonds between family members were only found from the mid-eighteenth century onwards when child mortality dropped. Before this time, Stone suggested, the death of an infant or young child, and indeed a spouse, was so common that people did not enter into deep relationships with them: consequently, children would have been neglected and marriages were lacking in love and affection. Only when mortality generally declined did loving relationships begin to develop between family members. A variation on this theme, but coming from a different ideological background, was the argument by the anthropologist Scheper-Hughes (1992) that modern childhood and family roles are 'inventions' coinciding with modernity and the demographic transition. She even gave qualified endorsement to the claim that mother love is a 'bourgeois myth', of relatively recent invention.

As I have already indicated, Rosenblatt's analysis came from a slightly later period in the US. Nevertheless, there is abundant other evidence from personal historical records that parents did love their children in former centuries, and showed grief when they died. This is shown in diaries and autobiographies from the sixteenth to the eighteenth centuries in both Britain and the US (Laurence, 1989; Macfarlane, 1979; Pollock, 1983; Smart, 1993), and from evidence from sources such as letters and church court cases (Cressy, 1997; Silverman, 1997). Smart pointed out that examples of parental grief can even be found in Stone's book for those historical times when, according to him, it was not supposed to occur. Cressy (1997) concluded that most of the evidence indicates that love and grief were widely felt in Tudor and Stuart England, despite 'mortality rates that a modern society might find numbing' (p. 393).

Stone's thesis also appears implausible to anyone familiar with the origins of affective relationships in the animal world. Social animals show a strong distress reaction to both separation and death of an offspring, parent or mate (Chapter 4). In reviewing Stone's book, Macfarlane (1979) also pointed out that there are many anthropological records of societies with both high infant mortality and love for children and, as Stone himself admits, there is no historical association between mortality rates and the degree of familial affection. Yet there is clear evidence from the observations by Scheper-Hughes (1992) of mothers in Brazilian shanty-towns that emotional indifference does occur in the case of death of their very young children, in circumstances where the infant mortality rate is high. This is not, however, the same as the complete emotional indifference to children argued by Stone. As indicated in Chapter 10, Scheper-Hughes' observations can readily be reconciled with modern attachment theory (Chisholm, 1996) which emphasises different forms of attachment under different environmental conditions.

Macfarlane (1979) also countered Stone's view by arguing that there is no evidence that people consciously work out expectations of mortality and tailor their emotional attachments accordingly. Modern studies of people's beliefs about what is likely to happen to them do show that positively biased assumptions are widespread (Taylor and Brown, 1988, 1994), even in the face of clear evidence to the contrary (Janoff-Bulman, 1993). In other words, people do not believe that misfortunes will apply to them.

However, the studies showing that positive illusions are widespread involved people from western societies with a background of an expectation of low mortality. The mothers Shepher-Hughes studied lived in a society where there was great uncertainty about life and death, where women had learned the reality of infant death from an early age. They therefore come from a very different background from that of the typical participant in North American studies of positively based assumptions. For the Brazilian shanty-town mothers, positive illusions may be absent. Instead, there may be emotional indifference in the face of infant mortality arising from the more gradual or delayed formation of an attachment to the offspring. This, in turn, is related to a pragmatism in making ethical decisions fostered by high rates of infant mortality. Under exceptional circumstances which also involve high mortality, such as the Black Death and other plagues (Thompson, 1985), and in concentration camps (Kaminer and Lavie, 1993), it seems that personal relationships become unemotional and apathetic. Whether this is also attributable to the absence of attachment bonds developing, or whether it represents a form of emotional numbing in the face of losses too great to bear is not entirely clear from the present evidence.

The debate amongst social historians and anthropologists about the universality of mother love is paralleled by a similar one concerning romantic love. Again, there is on the one hand the belief that it is confined to Euro-American culture, linked with modernism and the rise of individualism. In contrast, this view has been challenged by some historians (Cressy, 1997) and by evolutionary social scientists. Jankowiak and Fischer (1992) examined a world-wide sample of the ethnographic record and found clear evidence of the existence of romantic love in 88.5 per cent of 166 cultures across all parts of the world. On this basis, they suggested that it is a universal or near-universal phenomenon, and argued against the view that it is a product of western culture.

Ethnographic sources

Rosenblatt, Walsh and Jackson (1972, 1976) analysed patterns of grief across different cultures by examining ethnographic accounts of many different societies. Their research, together with other studies of specific cultures, is considered in Chapter 4, in relation to whether grief is a universal human reaction.

Ethnographic sources undoubtedly provide a considerable amount of material on grief, but this has, until recently, seldom been related to psychological issues. It has more often been used to study rituals and beliefs surrounding death. In some cases, there are interesting parallels with findings from modern studies of grief in western societies. For example, the widespread notion of a good or bad death (Jankofsky, 1981–2; Lévi-Strauss,1973), found in former times (Figures 3.1 and 3.2) and in traditional cultures today, parallels findings from modern research on the impact of sudden and traumatic deaths (Parkes and Weiss, 1983; Rynearson, 1987). Generally, a good death is a prepared death whereas a bad death is untimely or unprepared. Modern research shows the additional problems faced by the bereaved when death is sudden and occurs in traumatic circumstances.

The single most important message we can obtain from even a cursory examination of material from other societies and from other times is the difference in the significance of and approach to death from what is understood and taken for granted today in western secular societies. In the traditional world, and in former centuries in Europe and North America, life is often seen as a preparation for the afterlife (Figure 3.3), and death has a spiritual meaning as a transition to this afterlife, which has to be facilitated by the appropriate rituals (Eliade, 1977; Goss and Klass, 1997).

The importance of the afterlife, and of aiding progress to it through appropriate acts and ceremonies, probably had their greatest impact in the ancient Egyptian civilisations. Elaborate beliefs in the afterlife were reflected in their art, architecture, technology and laws, and are familiar to us today through the artefacts associated with burial practices, such as pyramids and other tombs, mortuary temples (Figure 3.4), and elaborately constructed and provisioned burial chambers which include sarcophagi and mummies (Spencer, 1982). This is an extreme example of the sort of belief which took root in many civilisations, and is still widespread today. In many parts of the industrialised world it is, however, giving way to a more secular and scientific view of death. Accompanying this is a more private, and indeed hidden, view of death, since the older communal rituals have less impact without the beliefs on which they were based.

An influential distinction between the way different societies view their social relations is individualism versus collectivism (Triandis, 1995). In individualistic societies, loosely linked individuals view themselves as independent entities, largely motivated by their own preferences and needs. Priority is given to personal goals over those of others and social relationships are seen

Figure 3.1 'Death on a Desert Island' by Thomas Rowlandson, from his series 'Dreadful Deaths', pencil and watercolour 1791. This illustrates the concept of a bad death prevalent in former times and in many parts of the world today.

Source: Reproduced by permission of the Victoria and Albert Museum Picture Library

Figure 3.2 'Death in a Riding Accident' by Thomas Rowlandson, from his series 'Dreadful Deaths', pencil and watercolour 1791, again illustrating the concept of a bad death.

Source: Reproduced by permission of the Victoria and Albert Museum Picture Library

in instrumental terms. In collectivist societies, closely linked individuals see themselves as part of a whole, and are motivated by norms and duties to the group. Priority is given to communal goals rather than personal ones and there is an emphasis on the connectedness of people and their obligations to others.

The more private view of death can be linked with the individualistic view of social life in western countries, whereas a view of death as part of traditional communal belief-systems is associated with a collectivist outlook. Triandis (1995) illustrated this difference in outlook with a number of examples, including the following two related to death. As an example of an act characteristic of an individualistic outlook, Triandis refers to a subordinate in England not mentioning to his supervisor that his father has died. In contrast, a national survey in Korea found that 40 per cent of employers sent condolences for the death of a parent-in-law. These two examples illustrate different assumptions about the private and the public nature of death. When considering research on grief from western societies, it is worth remembering that these are largely individualistic in outlook, whereas most of the world is collectivist (Triandis, 1995). Some of the implications of this distinction are explored in other chapters. One is that the breadth of relationships will be far narrower in a collectivist society. The reaction to the loss of a crucial

Figure 3.3 'The Bad Man at the Hour of Death', after Francis Hayman, first published 1783. This illustrates the belief that life is a preparation for the afterlife: in this case an unprepared life leading to dread at the moment of death.

Source: Copyright © British Museum. Reproduced by permission.

Figure 3.4 Queen Hatshepsut's mortuary temple, Deir el-Bahri (West Bank, Luxor, Egypt), eighteenth dynasty, c. 1498–1483.

Source: Photograph by the author, 1994

relationship is therefore likely to be more intense since the deceased will have occupied a more central and exclusive role in the life of the bereaved (see Chapter 10). A second implication of Triandis' distinction is that in a collectivist society people will be surrounded by others for most of the time, so that the time for private reflection about the deceased and for dwelling on reminders will be minimal (Lofland, 1985). A third is that there will be more pressure from relatives to replace the lost spouse or child in a collectivist society (Chapter 7).

Grief in literature, religion and biography

Whether a person lives in an individualistic or a collectivist society, the experience of bereavement generates a need to communicate thoughts and feelings to others, to review past events and above all to make these events part of a meaningful pattern. As Harvey *et al.* (1992: 108) put it: 'The search for meaning surrounding significant others' deaths consumes a period of time and degree of emotional energy that are of staggering proportions'. These needs (further discussed in Chapter 7) may be channelled into both the public sources associated with the mourning rituals of collectivist societies, or they may lead to more private means of expression, including the generation of the many literary works concerned with grief.

Long before modern psychologists and psychiatrists began to study grief, novelists, poets and playwrights described many of the features that would be recognised by contemporary researchers. Their writings stretch back to the ancient world, including the Old Testament and ancient Greek literature. Freedman (1970: 340) remarked that grief was 'one of the most compelling of literary subjects in the landscape of human experience', indicating that Homer had provided some vivid descriptions in the *Iliad* and *Odyssey*, for example Achilles' intense grief for Patroclus, his venting of the resulting anger in his treatment of Hector's body, and the grief of Hector's father Priam, resulting in the meeting with Achilles when they weep together for their respective losses (Rieu, 1950).

Poetry is perhaps the ideal medium for expressing the emotions of grief. It 'opens a window into our emotions and struggles' (Higginson, 1996: 12), and enables the deepest, most painful experiences to find expression. The themes of grief and loss are to be found in the poetical heritage of most languages, so that it is only possible to refer to a few well-known examples here. Most will be taken from English literature (for two contemporary anthologies of poems associated with bereavement and death, see Benson and Falk, 1996, and Duffy, 1996).

A number of Shakespeare's plays and sonnets portray aspects of grief and loss known from modern research, and they are therefore used to provide illustrations of points raised in this book. In the works of Shand (1920) and Becker (1932–3), poetry and prose were used extensively to illustrate psychological principles, Shand referring to the dramatic poets as 'great psychologists'. As Chiles (1982) commented, it is the method not the subject matter which makes psychology a young science. There have, however, been few systematic examinations of literary texts for grief-related themes in the way that Rosenblatt attempted for historical sources (Freedman, 1970).

One exception is Chiles' analysis of Tennyson's famous poem 'In Memoriam A.H.H.', written on the sudden death of his friend Arthur Hallam. Chiles identified several features apparent in scientific studies of grief, such as the tendency of current losses to bring back previously unresolved losses, and guilt, anger, the anniversary reaction, and the need for self-expression (Chapter 5). Only enthusiastic application of Kubler-Ross's stages of dying (see Chapter 2) marred Chiles' analysis.

Until recently, beliefs about death were intimately connected with religious beliefs which are practically universal in the traditional world. Feelings of grief were often associated with a dialogue with God, either testing or reaffirming the person's faith. The book of Job in the Old Testament is perhaps the most famous example. Tennyson began his poem 'In Memoriam A.H.H.' by reaffirming his faith in God:

> Strong son of God, immortal Love,
> Whom we, that have not seen Thy face,
> By faith, and faith alone, embrace,
> Believing where we cannot prove;

Thine are these orbs of light and shade;
Thou madest Life in man and brute;
Thou madest Death; and lo, Thy foot
Is on the skull which Thou hast made.
     (Tennyson, 1850; in Jump, 1974)

An internal dialogue about God can be seen in the contemporary personal account of bereavement by the Christian writer C.S. Lewis (1961). His clear description of the experience of grief is intermingled with a questioning of the role of God in so much suffering. The test of his faith lies not in ceasing to believe in God, but in coming to believe in a malign God – can He really be a 'Cosmic sadist'?

Lewis' spare and honest prose provides a stark contrast with one eighteenth-century tradition of accounts of personal grief, referred to as 'consolation literature' (Douglas, 1975). Usually written by clergymen who had experienced the death of one or more children, they were a combination of personal accounts and what was sometimes termed 'mourning manuals'. One which was written by a prominent New York clergyman (Cuyler, 1873) stimulated many thousands of letters from other bereaved people who had been comforted by his words. An earlier book, by the New England minister Nehemiah Adams, described the overwhelming grief he and his wife experienced after the death of their daughter Agnes: the couple spent a great deal of time at Agnes' grave, discussing with other bereaved parents the possibilities of heavenly reunion (Adams, 1857a). A companion book (Adams, 1857b) speculated on the death of children in God's plan. Nehemiah Adams experienced a further bereavement soon afterwards when his 19-year-old daughter died following an illness. His third book (Adams, 1859) recounted the events and sorrow surrounding Catherine's death, and the book's dedication – 'to every father having a daughter in heaven' – reflects both the sadness and commonplace of child mortality at that time.

War has often provided the impetus for portraying the feelings aroused by so much death, horror and waste. The realistic descriptions found in the poetry of Walt Whitman, describing the American Civil War, and in the British poems of the First World War, provide a stark contrast to the patriotic propaganda used to induce young men to fight. Rupert Brooke wrote in 'The Dead':

These hearts were woven of human joys and cares,
Washed marvellously with sorrow, swift to mirth.
The years had given them kindness. Dawn was theirs,
And sunset, and the colours of the earth.
These had seen movement, and heard music; known
Slumber and waking; loved; gone proudly friended;
Felt the quick stir of wonder; sat alone;
Touched lovers and furs and cheeks. All this is ended.
     (Brooke, 1921)

Poetry provides an ideal medium for expressing the feelings of grief. However, the close association of grief with human relationships makes it also an inevitable part of works of prose. The following examples represent a personal selection. They mostly come from English language sources over the last hundred years, but in other chapters I shall use a wider range of literary sources as illustrations.

In *The Californian's Tale* (Mark Twain, 1893) the narrator tells of being invited into a man's house, being shown around and told a lot about his young wife. When asked where she is, the man says that she has gone to visit her relatives and will be back at nine o'clock on Saturday, a few days hence, and he invites the narrator to stay and meet her. When Saturday evening comes, a few friends arrive to drink and await the woman's return. As the time approaches, the host becomes more agitated and the friends drug his drink and put him to sleep. As they are about to go, the narrator asks them not to because he will not know the man's wife. They turn and tell him that she has been dead for 19 years, captured by Indians on the way back from visiting her relatives. Every year on the anniversary, a (now dwindled) band of sympathetic friends help the man to maintain the illusion. This story portrays an extreme version of a general tendency towards being unable to accept the reality of the death. It is more likely to happen in circumstances like those described in the story, when no body was found and there were no witnesses to the death (Chapter 5).

In Louisa M. Alcott's sequel to *Little Women*, entitled *Good Wives* (Alcott, 1903), she described the despair and grief of the young woman Jo after the death of her sister Beth. Jo cries out for her to come back and imitates her ways. In contrast to *The Californian's Tale*, here we have descriptions of some of the more usual aspects of grief (again found in contemporary research: see Chapter 5).

Grief following the death of a homosexual partner (Chapter 12) was the subject of Christopher Isherwood's novel *A Single Man* (Isherwood, 1964), in which he described not only the personal feelings but also the way in which this sort of grief is commonly unrecognised by others, including the partner's family, since the relationship is not acknowledged.

Susan Hill's novel *In the Springtime of the Year* (Hill, 1974) is an account of the grief of a young woman whose husband was killed while working, and illustrates how grief can accentuate the barriers already present between a widow and her dead husband's family. In this case, both the mother and the widow sought to possess the memory of the deceased but in different ways that were not understood by the other. The novel describes the personal feelings of grief (Chapter 5), their variation in different individuals, and their place in the wider social context.

Bagley (1990–1) discussed three contemporary autobiographical German novels, in which daughters of fathers whose earlier life coincided with the Nazi era describe the impact of their fathers' deaths on their own grief and their sense of identity. All three books (*Mitteilung an den Adel*, *Lange*

Abwesenheit and *Der Vater*) were written shortly after the father's death and show themes of preoccupation and identification with the deceased, guilt and anger, which are familiar from systematic studies of bereavement (Chapter 5). They also show some more specific reactions, such as the difficulty in accepting the reality of the death which is often associated with a sudden death (investigated in the context of loss of a spouse by Parkes and Weiss, 1983): in *Der Vater*, it is only when the narrator sees the announcement of her father's death in the newspaper that it becomes real to her.

In all three writings there is a description of ambivalent feelings towards the father and initial feelings of hostility displayed shortly after the death, which were replaced later by a more positive and idolised picture of the deceased. Parkes and Weiss (1983) also investigated the impact of a conflict-ridden marital relationship on subsequent grieving. They too found that initially negative feelings predominated, but that as time went by these were replaced by a more positive view of the deceased associated with stronger feelings of grief than was apparent for people whose marriages had been less conflict-ridden. However, as indicated in Chapter 10, some other findings are difficult to reconcile with these.

Grief in film

The rapid development of electronic communication during the twentieth century has meant that audio-visual images now provide major alternatives to the printed page as avenues of self-expression. There are many examples of the portrayal of grief in film. Here I shall confine myself to three examples from contemporary English-dialogue films, again reflecting a personal selection.

Nicholas Roeg's *Don't Look Now* is an enigmatic film, based on a short story by Daphne du Maurier, and set in Venice. It concerns a couple whose young daughter had drowned near their house in England and who are shortly afterwards staying in Venice, where the husband (Donald Sutherland) is an architect restoring an old church. Several aspects of their behaviour show features of grief familiar from research. These include: intermittent flashbacks to the drowning; the attraction for the wife (Julie Christie) of spiritualism (in the form of two middle-aged English women); the markedly different ways in which the husband and wife seek to come to terms with the loss, leading to conflict; and the husband repeatedly 'seeing' the red shiny raincoat worn by the daughter when she died.

Hallucinations connected with bereavement are portrayed as apparitions in two other films. In *Ironweed*, Francis (Jack Nicholson), who accidentally killed his baby many years before, is continually haunted by apparitions from his past. In *Truly, Madly, Deeply*, the ghost of the dead lover (and his film-buff friends) is more metaphorical, depicting Nina's continued attachment to him: when she begins a new relationship the ghosts disappear. This film skilfully uses the apparently real presence of the dead lover (Alan Rickman) interwoven with many realistic aspects of grief displayed by Nina (Juliet Stephenson), to depict the complexities produced by an interaction between continuing an attachment to the past, the pain of grief, and opportunities for the future. These themes are discussed in Chapters 5 to 7.

Shadowlands, originally a television play by Bill Nicholson, is better known as Richard Attenborough's film of the same name starring Anthony Hopkins and Debra Winger. This purports to tell the story of the later years in the life of C.S. Lewis, the religious and children's writer, and author of *A Grief Observed*, although as Lewis' biographer remarks, it retells the story 'without too much regard for empirical evidence' (Wilson, 1990: 306). The play and film nevertheless depict the experience of impending loss, which has been termed 'anticipatory grief' in research-based writings, and the way this forces 'Jack' Lewis to face up to his love for Joy, the American woman who has been his friend for some years and is now diagnosed as having cancer. A major theme in the whole film is the relationship between the happiness of love and the pain of loss, a topic of central concern when considering the evolutionary function of grief (Chapter 4). Lewis' actual time of grief – the subject of *A Grief Observed* – is only briefly covered in the film, but the closing sequence reiterates the link between love and loss.

Grief in the visual arts

From the viewpoint of a psychological study of grief, the written word is the most useful medium for portraying the thoughts, feelings and behaviour that are involved. However, for enabling the dead to live on in memory, the visual arts have been used from the earliest times to provide elaborate tombs, representations in religious buildings, and commemorative statues and paintings. Llewellyn (1990) has provided a description of the different ways in which the visual arts have been used in relation to death in England from 1500 to 1800. The use of commemorative objects, such as jewellery or small pictures of the deceased (*memento mori*) to sustain their memory, is just one way in which such artefacts have become incorporated into the process of grieving. Death-bed portraits (Figures 5.1 and 5.2) were a common form from the Renaissance onwards in western Europe, and later in North America (Lloyd, 1982). They were later largely replaced by photographic records of the deceased (Figures 11.2 and 11.3; Ruby, 1988–9). A related tradition, found in nineteenth-century North America, was the use of the corpse to paint a likeness of the person as if they were still alive (Lloyd, 1978–80). These were commissioned by the families for use in mourning, and this distasteful work was necessarily undertaken by commercially less successful artists.

The visual arts can also be used as a medium for directly expressing the feelings of grief in a way that parallels the written word. Researchers interested in death and bereavement have only just begun to examine systematically the visual arts for such themes (Pacholski, 1986a; Llewellyn, 1990).

Lloyd (1982) provides some background on the way such paintings can be

transferred from tragedy to melodrama. In 1872, Charles Willson Peale portrayed the body of his infant daughter on her deathbed, following an established tradition. Three years later he enlarged the picture to include the
child's mother weeping over her, basing her facial expression on drawings
from LeBrun's famous book on emotional expressions (see Chapter 2, Figure
2.2), and the general position of mother and child on representations of the
Madonna watching over the sleeping Christ Child. The painting therefore
incorporated stylised elements to fill in details of the mother's grief at this
later time. Peale's sons went further in painting the face of a young woman
bereaved in the Mexican War of 1848 (Figure 3.5), based on earlier stylised
depictions of the bereaved mother of Christ; the other son painted a family
scene depicting receipt of news of a family member's death in the Civil War:
again, the expression harps back to early stylised religious paintings and
strikes us today as exaggerated melodrama.

These examples illustrate a theme applicable to all sorts of depictions of
grief, that expression and exploration of true feelings can be replaced by the
tear-jerking melodrama whatever the medium, be it a country and western

Figure 3.5 Face of a young woman bereaved in the Mexican War of 1848, by
Rembrandt Peale, entitled 'Pearl of Grief'.

Source: Reproduced by permission of the Milwaukee Art Center Collection

ballad, a poem, or an oil painting. In all cases, it is likely that archetypal images which are removed from the artist's or writer's own experiences and feelings are used as substitutes for the expression of personal feelings. In this way the image will have the widest possible appeal at the expense of individual creativity. Nowhere is this more apparent than when patriotic depictions rather than personal images are used in times of war. This applies to the paintings of the Peale sons described above, and even to recognised poetry such as Lawrence Binyon's 'For the Fallen', which deals with death on a large scale from the vantage point of patriotic ritual mourning:

> With proud thanksgiving, a mother for her children,
> England mourns for her dead across the sea.
> Flesh of her flesh they were, spirit of her spirit,
> Fallen in the cause of the free.
>
> Solemn the drums thrill: Death august and royal
> Sings sorrow up into immortal spheres.
> There is music in the midst of desolation
> And a glory that shines upon our tears.
>
> (Binyon, 1921)

Such patriotic obscenities express what Wilfred Owen described as 'the old lie', and contrast markedly with the realistic descriptions of war provided by Whitman, Owen, Brooke and others (cf. the excerpt from Rupert Brooke's 'The Dead' quoted above).

Grief in music

Music has also been used to express the emotions associated with grief, often to accompany the expression of feelings in words. Various forms have become established through history as appropriate for mourning the dead in western cultures, and other traditions have equivalent types of music. For example, the requiem developed in the context of Christian mourning services. Laments and dirges form more general ways of expressing sorrow with words and music.

There are a number of specialist forms which can be called 'the music of mourning' (Pacholski, 1986b). The dirge is slow, mournful and doleful, with a march-like thread to it, and is associated with burial. It often involves setting to music earlier poetry: for example Stravinsky used Dylan Thomas' 'Do Not Go Gentle Into That Good Night' for his memoriam for the poet. A lament refers to a wide range of musical and poetic forms which mark the end of a person's life. Similar ritual leave-taking chants, such as the Irish keening, were once widespread across Europe and into Asia, but are now preserved mainly in the more traditional cultures. An elegy is a more formal piece of music marking the loss of someone, and is widely represented in the works of the major composers (Pacholski, 1986b). There are a number of other more specialised forms of mourning music in the western European tradition, such as the planctus – a medieval song of lamentation – and the lamento – a tragic or mournful aria.

The Requiem Mass was derived from the funeral customs of the early Christians, and developed through solo voices, chorus and orchestra (Robertson, 1967). At first there was not a specific mass for the dead, but the requiem developed to emphasise the rest, sleep and peace of death – which did not have a finality for the early Christians, because of a strong belief in resurrection. The modern form was derived from the original plainsong which became set in polytonic versions from the fifteenth century onwards (Pacholski, 1986b). In recent times, the requiem has become more formalised with works by the great classical composers using it to set dramatic and poetic works to music: for example, Elgar's *Dream of Gerontius* and the work of poets such as Wilfred Owen and Walt Whitman were used in First World War requiems. More recent requiems include Penderecki's *Dies Irae*, which commemorated Auschwitz victims, and modified an earlier plainsong form, *The Dies Irae,* used in requiems since the thirteenth century (Pacholski, 1986b).

The fusion of words and music is characteristic of folk and popular music, which have always involved themes of thwarted love and separation. Indeed, Klinger (1977) remarked that 'a large part of folk music consists of complaint by losers and compassion for losers' (p. 151). An interesting musical and lyrical form in this respect is the blues, which arose among African-Americans before the First World War (Charters, 1961), and has more recently become integrated into modern popular music. The blues communicates a depressive and sorrowful mood. Again, it seems that expression of such feelings, whether they come from grief, thwarted love or some other misfortune, helps to raise the singer's spirits (Ellis and Dick, 1992). A notable example is the work of the religious singer Blind Willie Johnson whose recordings date back to 1927 in Dallas, Texas. The song 'Motherless Children' is described as 'almost a cry of pain' (Charters, 1961), and reflects Johnson's loss of his own mother at the age of seven. With its refrain 'Nobody treats you like mother will', it indicates the special difficulties involved in losing a mother, from the viewpoint of her protective role. The opening words 'Motherless children have a hard time' refer not to their emotional difficulties, although those are implied throughout the song, but to the loss of a crucial role, which no one, even a father or a sister, can replace. The distinction between the impact of the loss of a specific person and of the role they fulfilled is emphasised in Hofer's two-process theory of grief described in Chapter 4.

Widely selling popular music has usually dealt with themes of grief and thwarted love in a melodramatic way, rather like the paintings described in the previous section. Nevertheless, this does not stop them being of interest for the study of bereavement. One form of teenage popular music which explicitly used the theme of bereavement was the 'coffin song' of the early 1960s (Denisoff, 1972). Typically, it involved the interruption of a – usually doomed – teenage love affair by sudden death.

There were two interesting aspects to this genre. The first was the recurrent theme of being reunited with the dead lover. The voice from the grave says 'Tell Laura not to cry/My love for her will never die' in 'Tell Laura I Love Her'; the singer in 'Ebony Eyes' says he will be reunited with his girlfriend killed in a plane crash. Themes of continued attachment to the deceased are an important feature of grief (Chapter 5), but in the coffin song this is used to elevate the fragile teenage relationship to a permanent status (Denisoff, 1972). The second interesting aspect is the fragility itself, which is often portrayed as being due to interfering parents. 'Patches' is a wonderful example of this: the parents isolate the teenage boy from his lower-class girlfriend who then commits suicide by drowning. The boy reasserts his independence by vowing to follow Patches into death: 'It may not be right/But I'll join you tonight/Patches, I'm coming to you'!

Although we can cite these specific examples, the majority of Anglo-American popular music concerns the break-up of relationships rather than bereavement – i.e. the pain and misery of rejection. Apart from the coffin songs, there are few serious popular songs involving death, and these are mostly of relatively recent origin.

The advent of the singer-songwriters of the 1960s, some of whom used their lyrics in an expressive and confessional manner, led to the exploration of the issues of separation and loss in a deeper and more serious manner. These concerns then filtered through into rock music lyrics, such as those of 'Box of Rain' by the Grateful Dead (1972), which was written at a time when several of the band had lost their fathers. Two other striking examples are by Lou Reed and Eric Clapton. Lou Reed's 'Magic and Loss' (1992) is explicitly about the feelings aroused by the terminal illness and death of two of his close friends (Reynolds, 1992). An earlier Lou Reed song ('Halloween Parade') concerned the decimation of the gay community in New York by AIDS. Eric Clapton wrote and performed songs about the death of his 5-year-old son in 1991, notably 'Tears in Heaven' (Spencer, 1992), which was later recorded on his album *Unplugged* (1992). This particular song was played at the funeral of a 2-year-old boy from Merseyside (James Bulger) on 1st March 1993, whose murder by older children produced shock and outrage within that area and in Britain generally. To these two examples can be added many more portraying the pain of relationship break-up in the works of songwriters such as Joni Mitchell and Bob Dylan (notably 'Blood on the Tracks' in 1975 and 'Time Out of Mind' in 1997).

Midway between the deliberate melodrama of the coffin song and genuine expressions of personal experiences of grief comes the most famous contemporary popular song about grief, 'Candle in the Wind', sung by Elton John at Princess Diana's funeral in 1997. Rewritten (by Elton's songwriter) specially for the occasion of the funeral, the record was subsequently bought by millions of people. The strange phenomenon of mass grieving for public figures is discussed in Chapter 12.

Conclusions

I began this chapter with a quotation from the early twentieth-century psychologist, William McDougall, which included the statement that 'The wise psychologist will regard literature as a vast storehouse of information about human experience'. In relation to grief, we have seen that this comment can be extended beyond literature to other forms of art, such as music, painting and film. All these forms of expression can be viewed as having a dual role, first as personal expressions of the emotions and thoughts of grief, and second as part of McDougall's 'vast storehouse' of information about grief. In the previous chapter we noted the rather narrow basis of the twentieth century research tradition which has contributed to the scientific account of grief. In constructing a full picture of the experience of grief, I shall endeavour to make use of the artistic sources to supplement what has been written from a scientific viewpoint. In this sense, literary sources, as well as biographical accounts, provide part of the natural history of grief, which from the ethological perspective (Chapter 1), is a necessary first step when studying any phenomenon.

I began this chapter by considering some historical and contemporary cross-cultural accounts of reactions to bereavement. These also provide an important contribution to the study of grief, because they (like many older literary sources) enable the view of grief obtained from contemporary psychiatric and psychological sources to be assessed in terms of its applicability at other times in history and in different cultures. As I show in later chapters, there is both cross-cultural similarity and diversity in grief reactions.

4   The biological context of grief

> Now it seems to me that love of some kind is the only possible explanation of
> the extraordinary amount of suffering that there is in the world. I cannot
> conceive of any other explanation. I am convinced that there is no other, and
> that if the world has indeed, as I have said, been built of sorrow, it has been
> built by the hands of love, because in no other way could the soul of man, for
> whom the world was made, reach the full stature of its perfection.
>
> (Oscar Wilde, 1905, *De Profundis*: 59)

Introduction

Oscar Wilde realised that there was a connection between love and suffering.
He saw it as the way in which the Creator was able to raise up the human soul
to a higher level. This view of suffering assumes that it is necessarily ennob-
ling, and that it is part of the Creator's divine plan. Modern evolutionary-
based accounts also view the suffering of grief as a consequence of love, but
as a by-product of the way we build up a close relationship with the person
concerned. One particularly influential biologically based perspective concerned with close relationships is attachment theory, which also has much to
say about what happens when a relationship is ended either by separation or
bereavement. I begin this chapter by examining grief from the perspective of
attachment theory, concentrating on the issue of similarities and differences
between separation reactions in children and responses to bereavement in
adults, which were crucial for the early theoretical writings of John Bowlby. I
then examine the evidence that grief is a universal human reaction, and
whether there are similar processes in other animals. This leads to a biologically based theory of the grief process which originated from research on
animals. Finally, I examine the puzzling issue of the evolutionary origin of
grief, which was introduced in Chapter 1.

Attachment theory

Two of the most influential theorists on the subject of grief, John Bowlby and
Colin Murray Parkes (see Chapter 1), were both strongly influenced by evo-

lutionary biology as well as being rooted in psychoanalytic theory (Bowlby, 1960a, 1961; Parkes, 1972, 1986, 1996). Although a biological perspective is shared with other major accounts (Averill, 1968; W. Stroebe and M.S. Stroebe, 1987a), Bowlby's approach is distinctive in that it involved a broader theory of the making and breaking of emotional bonds, known as attachment theory.

Bowlby's theory of attachment was initially applied to the emotional bond between a young child and its mother or caregiver. Central to his view of attachment is the concept of a biological system, derived from the early work of the Dutch ethologists Gerard Baerends (1941) and Niko Tinbergen (1942, 1951), elaborated by Baerends (1976). This was foreshadowed by Shand (1920), who described the 'systems of the sentiments' as involving greater systems such as love, which organised and directed the lesser systems (i.e. anger, joy, fear and sorrow), so as to fulfil the function of the greater system. For example, Shand said that if the object of love is present, the lesser system for joy is activated; if there is interference with this, anger results; if there is physical separation, sorrow results.

The ethologists viewed each specific biological system as a functional entity that controls some instinctive form of behaviour, such as nest-building or parenting. Each one has an overall goal, for example to build a particular type of nest or to ensure the well-being of the young. This controls and organises a series of lesser activities (Archer, 1992a). Bowlby (1958, 1969) realised that emotional attachments between young and their parents formed such a system. Thus there is an overall goal of maintaining the relationship ('set-goal'), which at first amounts to keeping in physical proximity with the parents, and later is replaced by knowledge that they are nearby (Bowlby, 1980b: 651; Marvin, 1977). This overall goal directs and integrates specific activities such as smiling, waving, and running to the parents, and – in their absence – searching for them and crying.

Bowlby's view of attachment was very different from that held by the social-learning theorists and psychoanalysts of the time: they saw children's emotional bonds to their parents as developing from an association with rewards such as food or warmth, through a process known as associative learning or, in colloquial terms, 'cupboard love'. Instead, Bowlby (1969) traced the development of the child's tie with its parents (or caregiver) from an innate tendency for the infant to respond to the parents' social signals, and for the parents to respond to the infants' signals, through a subsequent process of exposure learning. This refers to the way in which humans and other animals develop preferences for people, places and things as a result of constantly being with them. No inducements – or reinforcements – are needed for this form of learning: being there is sufficient. The formation of attachments is also likely to be facilitated by the quality of the interactions between parent and child.

In the previous paragraph I referred to parents in general, and even to non-parental caregivers. Bowlby himself was usually more specific, referring to the mother as the child's primary caregiver. The crucial role of the mother was incorporated into his controversial theory of 'maternal deprivation'. In this, he argued that the child's bond to its mother is particularly important for ensuring later psychological well-being, a theory which was to prove particularly controversial (Morgan, 1972; Rutter, 1972). We should note that as a result of concern with this issue, Bowlby (1973) turned his attention to the short- and long-term consequences for the child of separation from the attachment figure, in this case the mother. The immediate response is an emotional reaction which was viewed as being similar to adult grief (Bowlby, 1960b, 1980a): as was noted in Chapter 1, Bowlby described both childhood separation and adult grief in terms of the same 'phases' (Chapter 2). He clearly stated that children were capable of showing grief reactions as soon as they had developed attachment relations (around the end of the first year). This was in contrast to various analytically oriented theorists who insisted that mechanisms such as reality testing and partial control of the id by the ego were necessary for grieving. Indeed, some went even further and insisted that 'true' mourning does not occur until adolescence (Chapter 12; Volkan, 1981). Such speculations are not supported by empirical studies, which show that the behavioural and emotional reactions to loss indicative of grief occur following separation even at very young ages.

Bowlby viewed the loss of any significant attachment figure as resulting in grief. He used the term 'affectional bonds' (from Harlow and Harlow, 1965) to describe biologically significant social ties whose severance results in grief. Ainsworth (1989) later sought to distinguish this term from attachment. She described affectional bonds as long-lasting and characteristic of the individual (as opposed to relationships which involve both partners); attachment was viewed as a form of affectional bond which involved security and comfort, i.e. it applied mainly to child-to-parent relationships but also to sexual partners and sometimes to siblings. In contrast, the affectional bond which involved caregiving was viewed as distinct from that involving security and comfort (attachment in Ainsworth's definition).

Although Bowlby (1969) did distinguish the caregiving system of the parents from the security-seeking system of the offspring, in his subsequent writings (Bowlby, 1980a: 39–41) he seems to have used the terms attachment and affectional bonds more or less synonomously. More contemporary theorists have argued that attachment is an appropriate term for relationships with either or both the components of security and caregiving. Weiss (1988, 1991), for example, referred to the parent-to-child bond as attachment. He argued that both here, and in relationships between sexual partners, behaviour serving the attachment system – in this case proximity-seeking and caregiving – is initiated by any threat to the relationship. This widening of the concept of attachment enables it to apply to all forms of affectional bond. It also enables common features which follow the severance of different types of bonds to be understood.

Other discussions of this issue in relation to adult attachment (Berman and

Sperling, 1994; Feeney and Noller, 1996) have also concluded that the care-seeking and the caregiving systems are combined, in that most relationships between adults contain both. Berman and Sperling (1994) viewed caregiving as an integral part of, and an outgrowth from, the care-seeking system. Similar emotional experiences underlie both aspects. A similar view was taken by Mason (1997), and by Field (1996), who emphasised multiple attachments to a variety of figures at different stages of the lifespan, for example parents and other adult relatives during childhood, sexual partners and children during adulthood, and friends, partners and grandchildren during later life. Again, the term attachment is used to denote any form of emotionally based bond whose severance leads to separation distress (i.e. what Ainsworth referred to as an affectional bond).

Attachment theory, used in this broad sense, highlights responses characteristic of loss or separation, enabling them to be distinguished from other forms of emotional distress. Behaviour associated with seeking to regain attachment with the lost person consists of pining, preoccupation, yearning, searching and calling. These all capture the central and specific components of grieving (Parkes, 1970; Jacobs *et al.*, 1987–8; Sanders, 1989). They are often referred to collectively as 'separation anxiety' or 'separation distress', after the term used in studies of separation in children (Parkes, 1970, 1972, 1985, 1988; Jacobs *et al.*, 1987–8; Berman, 1988; Sanders, 1989). The essential experience involves a feeling of losing a safe haven or source of emotional security, and the loss of control and uncertainty that this engenders. This experience motivates the individual to direct his or her activities towards being reunited. The general emotional disturbance which accompanies these reactions, involving features such as anxiety, depression, high sympathetic nervous system activity, and sleep loss has been referred to as a background or non-specific response (Parkes, 1985), since it is also found in other distressing circumstances.

Reactions to separation and death in children

The implications of attachment theory are that a core reaction (separation anxiety or distress) occurs whenever an animal, child or human adult is separated from or loses an attachment figure. In the case of animals, young children and some mentally handicapped adults (Conboy-Hill, 1991), the reaction will be the same for a temporary separation as it is for a permanent one involving death.

During the course of their first few years of development, human children gradually become able to substitute mental representations of their parents for their continual physical presence (see above). However, it is only at around the age of 5 years that some understanding of death as a permanent separation begins to emerge.

Investigation of the development of the concept of death in childhood began with the pioneering studies by Anthony (1940) in London and Nagy

(1948) in Hungary. Anthony was concerned with the mental health implications of children's understanding of death at a time when western Europe was living under the shadow of war. She used several methods to explore not only conceptual changes in the understanding of death, but also the links with anxiety, hostility and guilt. She concluded that in young children's fantasies, death meant departure or disappearance. She also found, from an analysis of responses to the word 'dead' among a sample of 3–13-year-olds that children younger than 7 or 8 years had markedly limited conceptions of its meaning, consistent with the Piagetian analysis of the development of conceptual thought (see below).

Using the method of asking children to tell her about several words including death, Nagy (1948) found that children younger than about 5 years of age regard death as reversible and like separation or sleep. At these ages, children attribute life and consciousness to the dead, and they mix up departure and death. As Bowlby indicated, it is the separation that produces the sorrow in young children. Both Anthony (1940) and the later more systematic study of Koocher (1973) have linked this level of understanding of death with Piagetian concepts of pre-operational thinking and egocentricism. At the younger ages, children attribute life-defining functions to dead things (what Piaget called 'animism'), and they think that certain individuals will not die (Speece and Brent, 1984). There is also confusion between 'inanimate' and 'dead', both of which are seen as different from 'living' (Carey, 1985). Diary records and transcriptions of 3-year-olds' questions and conversations about death (Carey, 1985) show how difficult it is for them to understand the concept, despite a lively curiosity about it (cf. Menig-Peterson and McCabe, 1977–8). They seek to understand death in terms of what dead people do, or what it must feel like to be dead, and any adult answers to such questions are incomprehensible, since these are based on a view of death as a biological process. It seems clear that such confusions reflect the children's chronological age and level of conceptual thinking (Carey, 1985; Jenkins and Cavanaugh, 1985–6),

A vivid illustration is the following quotation from the novel *Black Dogs* by Ian McEwan. It involves a conversation between a 4-year-old and a 7-year-old on the way to their grandmother's funeral:

> Alexander, our four-year-old, was aghast that we were planning to put his granny, of whom he was very fond, in a wooden box and lower her into a hole in the ground and cover her with earth. 'She doesn't like that,' he said confidently. Harry, his seven-year-old cousin, had the facts. 'She's dead, stupid. Stone cold dead. She doesn't know anything about it.' 'When is she coming back?' 'Never ever ever ever. She's in heaven, stupid.' 'When is she coming back? Granddad? When is she, Granddad?'
> (McEwan, 1992: 63).

Between the ages of 5 and 7 years, most children come to understand the irreversibility of death. According to Speece and Brent (1984), they also understand that it involves lack of functioning and is universal. At these ages and up to about 9 years, children attribute death to outside agencies (Nagy, 1948; Carey, 1985), such as a person or God, often as a punishment for wrongdoing. These beliefs are likely to affect the way children grieve, for example blaming themselves for a sibling's death (Rosen, 1984–5). They are also reminiscent of beliefs about outside agencies causing death, commonly held throughout the traditional world. In many ways, such attributions are never far away from adult beliefs in modern western societies. Many people show a readiness to blame others or themselves for a death, even when it is unreasonable to do so (Chapter 8).

Although there is a consensus that the child develops from viewing death as reversible to realising that it is a permanent state, there is also considerable variability according to the samples and the methods of inquiry used in particular studies (Speece and Brent, 1984; Carey, 1985; Stambrook and Parker, 1987). There is some evidence that experiences with death, religious beliefs and what children are told about death, also affect their ability to understand it (Stambrook and Parker, 1987; Anthony and Bhana, 1988–9). Experience with death may facilitate the understanding that it is irrevocable; being told that the deceased has 'gone to Jesus' or gone away will not facilitate it, whereas religious beliefs that stress the finality of death will do so (Anthony and Bhana, 1988–9). It is interesting to note that an analysis of the concept of death in books for 3–12-year-olds in the US (Bailis, 1977–8) showed that it was portrayed as temporary in most of them. None of the 40 books sampled said that death was the end of all existence.

The scientific view, that death is an inevitable biological process restricted to biological organisms, is understood by about 9–10 years of age (Nagy, 1948; Carey, 1985). Carey emphasised that this does not replace the earlier ways of understanding death but that it provides an additional framework. Therefore, although separation anxiety forms a prototype for the grief reaction, it originates before the concept of death has been understood. It changes with age so as to incorporate new ways of understanding the meaning of death. Even in adulthood, the grief reaction will be a complex mix of the separation reaction, a readiness to attribute death to an outside agency and the rational view that it is a natural biological process.

Thus, in one sense separation reactions of children are similar to the grief reactions of adults. Yet, in another they are very different. Studies of developmental changes also emphasise the totally different conceptual levels on which adults and older children are operating compared to younger children – and to animals. Knowledge of the reason for the separation, and its likely implications, produce a different pattern of reactions to bereavement and to temporary separation in adult humans. Yet in young children reactions to these two types of event are similar.

Is grief universal in humans?

One of the implications of viewing grief from the viewpoint of the biologically based theory of attachment is that we should expect it to it occur
throughout the human species, since it is deeply rooted in pre-human evolution. Before going on to explore the evidence for grief processes in animals,
let us consider the evidence for grief being a universal reaction in the human
species.

Following their discipline's emphasis on cultural differences (Brown, 1991),
anthropologists have typically been interested in the cultural patterns associated with mourning, rather than the process of grief itself. Therefore, the
information relating to this question has been collected during the course of
research carried out for different aims, thus limiting its usefulness. Nevertheless, most available cross-cultural evidence supports the view that grief is a
universal feature of human beings, although there are wide variations in the
nature, extent and duration of grief reactions in different cultures. These can
be related to differences in wider cultural beliefs about life and death, and
about the expression of emotions (Goss and Klass, 1997; Wikan, 1988).

Rosenblatt *et al.* (1976) examined accounts of grief in a wide variety of
cultures using the Human Relations Area Files. These are documented
accounts which can be used as source material for cross-cultural comparisons. Examining the expression of emotions during bereavement in different
cultures is limited by not distinguishing between private expressions of grief
and culturally prescribed mourning (Williams and Morris, 1996). Nevertheless, Rosenblatt *et al.* did report that the general reactions – crying and
distress, anger and aggression – were similar to those reported in western
societies. However, there were also reactions less familiar to us, notably self-
injury and fear of the dead (Chapter 5). Crying and self-injury were more
common among women and anger directed outwards was more common
among men. Rosenblatt *et al.* suggested that cultural habits and rituals
tended to encourage or reduce particular aspects of the grieving process, a
view which was shared by other writers (Averill, 1968; W. Stroebe and
M.S. Stroebe, 1987a).

W. Stroebe and M.S. Stroebe (1987a) discussed whether grief is a universal
human characteristic, and concluded from the admittedly limited ethnographic accounts that there are no instances where loss is greeted with
emotional indifference. Examining one specific aspect of grief, crying, the
Stroebes concluded that this is a universal response despite cultural differences which sometimes drastically curtail grief and in other cases prolong
it. Nevertheless, there are enormous differences in the cultural traditions
surrounding mourning, which can be seen in the following examples.

The Balinese show cheerfulness where western observers would expect
sorrow, including after a bereavement (Wikan, 1988, 1990). Yet they do
cry under such conditions and view crying as a natural response to tragedy.
The key to understanding their predominant reaction of cheerfulness and

laughter lies in the belief that sadness and anger are detrimental to good health and happiness: contriving to be cheerful under such circumstances is seen as inducing inner happiness to replace sadness. It is also viewed as having social repercussions since, in Bali, to express sadness is to induce it in others.

Among the indigenous North American people, the Navajo, the accepted time for mourning is limited to four days, and only during this time is the expression of grief and discussion of the deceased condoned (Miller and Schoenfeld, 1973). After this period, the bereaved person is expected to return to everyday life, not to show grief and not to speak of the deceased or the loss. This restriction is connected with fear of the dead person's spirit, and belief in the power of ghosts to harm (as is common in traditional societies).

Abbreviated grief reactions also occur in some other cultures. In the ancient mid-American Maya civilisation, grieving was reported in their literary sources to be expressed openly and intensely but to last a matter of days rather than months (Steele, 1977). Pressure was brought to bear to limit the overt expression of grief. Again, this was part of an elaborate set of myths and rituals which controlled people's behaviour concerning death, dying and bereavement. The rituals specified clearly how the bereaved and their families were to respond, and were enforced by social pressures.

Although in these last two accounts mourning is controlled by established beliefs and customs, it is another matter whether the feelings and experiences of grief itself are also controlled. In one case, however, it does seem that customs and beliefs may genuinely mitigate – but not abolish – grief. Ablon (1971) described the pattern of grief in the Samoan community living on the US west coast as characterised by a more rapid and less painful recovery than was apparent in the US generally. This occurred even when the loss had occurred under traumatic circumstances, in particular a fire which had occurred at a Samoan community dance. It appeared from respondents' accounts that they did suffer less than European North Americans, and this was related to several aspects of Samoan culture: first, the network of social, religious and financial support which was present as soon as someone died; second, the extended family system which resulted in multiple attachments, and enabled vacant roles to be readily occupied by others; and third, personal attitudes, which involved both a stoical approach to misfortune and a fatalistic Christian faith, involving acceptance of God's will as irreversible fate.

Ablon quoted one widow as saying that Samoans did not grieve or worry like Americans. Nevertheless, it would be a mistake to take this completely at face value. The three features just described combine to mitigate grief, and the culture discourages a show of emotion and encourages acceptance of fate; however, this does not mean that grief is not felt at all, and indeed other widows did indicate their distress to the researcher, for example reporting apathy, depression and a feeling of isolation.

In the previous chapter, I referred to the study of Brazilian shanty-town mothers by Scheper-Hughes (1992). This is interesting in the present context because she found an absence of grief under circumstances where we should expect it, i.e. by a mother for her dead infant. Yet this lack of sorrow contrasted with clear signs of grief in response to other losses, such as an older child or lover, indicating that the lack of grief for an infant is associated with a lack of a strong attachment in the first place. In cultures where emotional ties are dispersed between many members of the extended family, we should also expect a lesser degree of grief for the death of any one member than is the case with the modern western nuclear family (Volkart and Michael, 1957). Among the Trobriand Islanders studied by Malinowski (1926), it is the dead man's brother and maternal relatives, rather than his wife, who are seen as bereaved: this follows the rules of matrilineal kinship, whereby the man's wife remains a stranger to his relatives.

We can agree with W. Stroebe and M.S. Stroebe (1987a) that there is substantial variation in the cultural rules surrounding mourning, and in all cultures grief is channelled along specific lines. Mourning rituals can be seen as solutions to the problems posed by the process of grief, itself an innate reaction which seems to be universally felt even though its manifestations are extremely varied. Averill (1968) drew an analogy with sexual feelings, which are a human universal, yet are channelled within each society by elaborate sets of social rules. We can, therefore, conclude that grief is a characteristic human reaction but that its form varies greatly as a result of circumstances and the cultural traditions within which it operates. Eliot (1932), one of the earliest researchers to appreciate the cultural context of grief, described it as follows: bereavement is linked with affective attachments, and it produces an individual and family crisis of a sort for which there have been ample precedents in the history of a cultural group, so that beliefs and rituals will have grown up to deal with it.

Grief in animals

Having shown that grief is a universal human reaction, evidence for similar processes in other social animals is now assessed. We need to look for reactions similar to the separation reactions of young children. The reason for this is that, of all the animal species, only humans of a particular developmental age can understand the significance of death, and therefore respond differently to bereavement and to separation.

Let us first consider the evidence for this statement. Because many humans show an initial inability to accept the death of a loved one (Chapter 6), we cannot be completely sure that behaviour apparently inconsistent with the finality of death indicates that animals cannot understand its implications. Nevertheless, observations from several primate field studies do strongly suggest a pattern of behaviour very different from that shown in all present-day human societies.

In a study of yellow baboons in Kenya, Altmann (1980) observed that mothers carried around their dead infants for some time, gradually leaving the dehydrating or rotting corpse for longer periods while foraging, until it was abandoned altogether. Similarly, Schaller (1963) observed a gorilla mother carrying its dead baby around for four days before abandoning the decaying carcass. Van Lawick-Goodall (1968) observed chimpanzee mothers carrying their dead infants, but these seemed to be abandoned after a day or less. In contrast, all known human cultures have methods of treating, or disposing of the dead body. Archaeological evidence locates the beginnings of burial practices to the Neanderthals, over 60,000 years ago (Pfeiffer, 1969). If this is correct, it would have arisen comparatively late in hominid evolution.

This line of evidence is supported by studies of the mental processes of other animals, which so far indicate that the conceptual level necessary for understanding death has not been achieved, even by chimpanzees (Chapter 10 in Archer, 1992a; cf. Allen and Hauser, 1991).

If this argument is correct, the essential difference between human and animal grief will be determined by the availability or not of the meaning of death. This difference was expressed in a poem by J.C. Squire, entitled 'To a Bull-dog', which concerned his own and his dog's reactions to the death of their friend Willy in the First World War:

> But now I know what a dog doesn't know,
> Though you'll thrust your head on my knee,
> And try to draw me from the absent-mindedness
> That you find so dull in me.
>
> And all your life you will never know
> What I wouldn't tell you even if I could,
> That the last time we waved him away
> Willy went for good.
>
> (Squire, 1921)

It has long been known that animals show behaviour indicative of grief, or as I have argued, separation distress. Darwin (1872) described monkeys such as macaques, as 'weeping' through grief, and he later outlined the general effects of grief on outward expressions. Between Darwin's time and the 1950s there have been a number of scattered accounts of grief in animals (Bowlby, 1961; Pollock, 1961; Averill, 1968). Most are anecdotal or unsystematic observations. For example, Konrad Lorenz described jackdaws and geese frantically searching and calling when they had lost a mate. They also showed depressive behaviour, such as a lack of interest in social contacts. Lorenz described the distress shown by a dog which had lost its owner: its behaviour suggested searching, some aggression and agitation. Similar reactions have been reported among primates.

Bowlby (1961) concluded that although such reports were scrappy and unsystematic, a general picture emerged which corresponded to that of grief in humans. Adults, children and social animals all show protest and hostility in response to the loss of an attachment figure. Later, behaviour becomes reorganised in relation to another figure. Averill (1968) reached a similar conclusion, and identified a need for more controlled laboratory studies of grief in animals. Few such studies have been carried out, and deliberately inducing grief in animals would now be regarded as ethically unacceptable or at least questionable (Archer, 1990), in terms of the scientific knowledge it is likely to produce (Archer, 1986b; Bateson, 1986; Driscoll and Bateson, 1988).

Nevertheless, since both grief and separation reactions are equivalent in animals, we can examine the many studies of the reactions of young primates to separation from a parent as a further source of evidence about grief in animals. Ethological research on loss of an imprinted relationship has involved birds such as ducks and geese (Hoffman *et al.*, 1966; Lamprecht, 1977); laboratory research has involved guinea pigs (Ritchey and Hennessy, 1987), rats (Hofer, 1984, 1996), and primates (Mineka and Suomi, 1978; Field, 1996). Typically, all these young animals show distress, calling and increased activity after separation from their parents.

The research on primates, pioneered by Harlow, is perhaps the best known and most extensive. It was primarily concerned with the consequences for long-term psychological well-being of the loss of, or separation from, a parent figure early in life. The purpose of the research was to provide an animal model for human conditions which are difficult to study directly (Hinde, 1983; Archer, 1992a). However, the research also investigated the immediate reactions to separation shown by young primates such as rhesus monkeys. The typical features involved two types of reaction, one active and the other passive. The first consists of the whimpering, crying and calling noted by Darwin, accompanied by signs of prolonged active protest (Seay, Hansen and Harlow, 1962; Kaufman and Rosenblum, 1967, 1969; Levine *et al.*, 1987; reviews by Bowlby, 1973; Mineka and Suomi, 1978). The second involves withdrawal, an inactive depressive response which is accompanied in some species by secretion of the hormone cortisol from the adrenal cortex (Levine *et al.*, 1987; Wiener *et al.*, 1990). Similar reactions have been described in separated human children (Kaufman and Rosenblum, 1967; Bowlby, 1973; Hollenbeck *et al.*, 1980; Field and Reite, 1984; Field, 1996).

These two reactions have been widely described as representing the first two of Bowlby's three phases (Bowlby, 1961, 1973). Nevertheless, detailed studies of brief separations by Robert Hinde's research group (Spencer-Booth and Hinde, 1971a,b) show considerable variation and overlap in these reactions, so that it is probably best to view them as interrelated reactions with different time-courses and probably with different causes (Archer, 1992a). There are also species differences: for example, more pronounced reactions have been found in squirrel monkeys than in rhesus macaques (Levine *et al.*, 1987) and in pigtail in than bonnet macaques (Laudenslager, Boccia and Reite, 1993). In pigtail macaques, physiological responses associated with the autonomic system (sleep disturbances, decreased heart rate and temperature) accompany depressive behaviour (Reite *et al.*, 1981), as they do to a lesser extent in bonnet macaques (Reite, Kaemingk and Boccia, 1989). Laudenslager *et al.* (1993) reported that measures of immune functioning co-varied with the time spent in a slouched, withdrawn posture by macaque infants.

When separated from a sexual partner or their peer group, adult primates show calling, distress and depressive reactions, which are comparable with those shown by young primates separated from their parents (Mineka and Suomi, 1978). Separation reactions also occur in adult birds which have lost a sexual partner. For example, Butterfield (1970) studied the reactions of zebra finches. When an adult is separated from its mate, the male shows increased activity and the female calls loudly. Under natural conditions, their chances of being reunited are increased by these reactions.

The reactions of a young animal separated from its mother and an adult separated from its mate are similar because both involve the loss of a biologically important relationship. As indicated earlier, Harlow and Harlow (1965) referred to these relationships as 'affectional systems', and their list included relationships between infants and mothers, sexual partners, siblings or young peer companions, and between fathers and infants. Modern evolutionary thinking about animal behaviour enables this list to be summarised as being all those relationships that are important for overall (or 'inclusive') fitness (Dawkins, 1976; Archer, 1991a). It includes those in the Harlows' list, together with other relationships based on kinship or mutual benefit ('reciprocal altruism': Trivers, 1971).

There is, therefore, abundant evidence that reactions essentially similar to those shown by humans occur in social animals which have lost or been separated from a social companion with whom they have an evolutionarily important relationship. Although most experimental research has concentrated on separation in young primates, there is sufficient evidence from other types of relationship and other species to suppose that the reactions are widespread in those social animals that form relationships based on individuality. In other words, grief will occur in species where there are prolonged relationships involving individual recognition, based on parental care, kinship or mutual benefit.

A two-process theory of grief

Several times in the previous section, I have referred to the two different types of reaction to separation found in young primates. This distinction was made in many of the earlier writings, such as those of Darwin (1872), Shand (1920), Becker (1932–3) and Engel (1962). Engel argued that organisms show two basic but opposite responses to what he called 'unpleasure', an active pattern seeking to achieve needs through an external object, and a conservative pattern in which activity is reduced. Klinger (1975, 1977) viewed the two responses as part of a sequence of disengagement, with depression occurring when active responses have proved unsuccessful.

Instead of being sequential reactions in the same overall process, Hofer (1984) argued that the two reactions represent different processes. He extended this two-process view to form a specific theory of grief. Reviewing his own work on the behavioural and physiological consequences of maternal separation in rat pups, and that of other researchers on primates and humans, Hofer argued that the two reactions to separation differ not only in their behavioural and physiological characteristics but also in their antecedents. They are controlled by different aspects of the environment, the distress reaction being a response to loss of a significant individual, and the despair reaction occurring to deprivation of stimuli important for influencing behavioural and physiological regulation derived from the lost relationship. Hofer was able to prevent the active distress reaction from occurring in rat pups, by presenting a familiar companion or the mother, even if she were anaesthetised and unresponsive. This did not, however, prevent the more slowly developing physiological changes and behavioural inactivity usually associated with maternal separation. Hofer found that these constituted a series of independent reactions each controlled by particular aspects of the mother–pup relationship, which he termed 'regulators': for example, growth hormone stimulation was controlled by tactile contact with the dorsal surface, and noradrenaline increase by body warmth (Hofer, 1984).

Hofer used these findings, and others from non-human primates, to generate a theory that all relationships provide such 'regulators' and that there are two types of reaction to separation. In young animals, these were viewed as separate but overlapping phases (but see the reservations about phase views expressed in Chapter 2). In adult human bereavement, the two reactions are extended in time and are interwoven with one another. Adult human grief can therefore be viewed in terms of the same two basic responses – an active one to the specific loss, and a passive depressive response to deprivation of the regulators provided by that class of relationship. The first process involves features such as distress, searching, preoccupation and aggression. The second includes features such as lack of sleep and appetite, and depressed mood, which Hofer referred to as a chronic background disturbance (as did Parkes, 1985). Hofer pointed out the similarity between this background disturbance and reactions to sensory deprivation: he argued that during bereavement there is a deprivation of accustomed stimuli and often self-imposed restriction of activities. He also argued that aspects of the habitual social environment control regulation of physiological processes, such as biological rhythms.

Hofer applied these considerations to grief by suggesting that relationships provide hidden regulators built up over a long period of time through a network of reminders and expectancies. These are broken down after the loss of the person providing the regulators, and are only gradually replaced by new relationships. If correct, Hofer's theory has some similarities to Jahoda's (1979, 1982) view of unemployment, that employment provides a number of latent functions, for example stimulating activity and providing social contacts, and that many of the reactions to unemployment can be viewed as reactions to the deprivation of these latent functions.

Hofer's theory, which is consistent with more recent psychobiological research on attachment and separation (Field, 1996; Hofer, 1996), also has important implications for how we view readjustment or recovery from bereavement. Most writers, influenced by the psychoanalytic foundations of the study of grief, view it in terms of a single process of change through time. Thus depression is seen as forming a later part of the same sequence as the active responses (Klinger, 1975, 1977; Bowlby, 1980a). In analytically influenced writings, this process is also viewed as essentially inwardly directed, with no short cuts being possible. If, however, the grief process involves two different reactions, to deprivation as well as a reaction to the specific loss, this opens the possibility that the deprivation reaction can be forestalled by establishing another satisfactory relationship of the same sort: this would be remarriage in the case of spousal bereavement or having another baby in the case of perinatal bereavement. Thus Hofer's theory has important implications not only for how we view grief in theoretical terms, and also for how we evaluate practical strategies for aiding recovery from grief. It is therefore important to test the theory in future studies of grief. This topic is considered further in Chapter 7 in relation to the resolution of grief.

The function of grief

So far we have seen that grief is a universal reaction in human beings, and that a similar process occurs in response to both separation and loss of affectional bonds in social animals. The widespread occurrence of grief reactions in humans and other social animals would at first sight seem to indicate that it is a reaction which was favoured by natural selection in social animals. However, when we look at what the process of bereavement involves for the individual, it appears to be maladaptive. It is associated with physiological stress, leading to poor health, and increased risk of mortality, loss of appetite, loss of weight, depression, increased alcohol and drug consumption, and a loss of sexual interest and functioning. This raises a basic dilemma for explaining the origin of grief through the process of natural selection (Averill, 1968).

Some researchers (Tobach, 1970; Littlefield and Rushton, 1986; Izard, 1991) have implied or stated that grief is adaptive. It is therefore worth considering in more detail the evidence for the maladaptive nature of grief, in terms of its effects on the stress responses and the ability to resist disease. In Chapter 1, I referred to Engel's (1961) characterisation of grief as a disease process, and the increased mortality following bereavement. M.S. Stroebe and W. Stroebe (1993) concluded that the available evidence generally shows that mortality is higher among bereaved people than controls, and that this is either more pronounced for men than for women (Young *et al.*, 1963; Helsing and Szklo, 1981; Gallagher-Thompson *et al.*, 1993) or only applies to men

(Smith and Zick, 1996). The causes of death include heart disease, cancer, various forms of violent deaths including suicide, and cirrhosis of the liver.

Many of these deaths can be seen as being mediated directly or indirectly by the depressed state following bereavement (whereas others may be secondary consequences of the loss: see M.S. Stroebe, 1994a). Some, for example coronary heart disease and cancer, can be linked with physiological stress reactions induced by bereavement.

There is also evidence of increased somatic symptoms among bereaved compared with control samples (Parkes and Brown, 1972; Windholz, Marmar and Horowitz, 1985; Gallagher-Thompson *et al.*, 1993) and for more pronounced negative health consequences when the grief reaction is particularly intense (Prigerson *et al.*, 1997a). A larger body of evidence demonstrates a link between bereavement or separation and stress reactions. Overall, studies show an increase in adrenocortical secretion following bereavement (Biondi and Picardi, 1996; Goodkin *et al.*, 1996), but there are individual variations, so that greater increases tend to be associated with more distress. Hofer *et al.* (1972) showed that adrenal cortical secretion increased in parents whose children had died of leukaemia, and that individual increases paralleled the parents' emotional distress. Jacobs (Kim and Jacobs, 1993) found that although serum cortisol levels were not elevated following death of a spouse or associated with greater distress, urinary cortisol values were associated with greater psychological distress. When human infants were separated from their mothers, those with higher levels of separation anxiety showed increased cortisol levels (Tennes, Downey and Vernadakis, 1977).

Fredrick (1976–7, 1982–3) argued that such increases in adrenal cortical secretion would, if maintained over a period of time, suppress the protective responses of the immune system. Since then, a number of studies have investigated changes in the immune system following separation in animals (Coe *et al.*, 1987; Hojat and Vogel, 1987; Laudenslager, 1988; Laudenslager *et al.*, 1993). Laudenslager (1988) concluded that there was good evidence to support changes in immunomodulation accompanying maternal separation in monkeys, and that similar changes are apparent in the case of human bereavement (Schleifer *et al.*, 1983). Laudenslager argued for the value of animal models because of the difficulty of separating the effects of grief from associated changes such as increased drug consumption and altered nutritional intake in humans. Evidence from controlled human studies (Goodkin *et al.*, 1996; Kemeny *et al.*, 1995) has shown that changes in immunomodulation (in particular, lower natural killer cell activity) occur following bereavement, and in some studies these are associated with depression (Herbert and Cohen, 1993; Irwin and Pike, 1993). There is also evidence of a decline in sperm quality following death of a close family member (Fenster *et al.*, 1997)

Responses to loss and separation are, therefore, maladaptive, in terms of their effects on mortality and morbidity. Further features – such as reduced motivation for feeding, sexual behaviour and other activities which directly or indirectly enhance fitness – would further disadvantage a grieving individual, in terms of competition for survival and reproduction. The essential evolutionary question is why such individuals were not replaced by others who did not show such fitness-depleting characteristics. Why did social animals not simply respond to a dead mate or offspring with emotional indifference, and carry on with their other activities?

One suggestion (Averill, 1968; Averill and Wisocki, 1981; Izard, 1991) is that grief enhances group cohesion. It is, however, apparent that this reasoning, which regarded grief as having evolved for 'the good of the species', is a group-selectionist one. This way of thinking was characteristic of evolutionary speculations in both psychology and biology before the writings of Hamilton, Maynard Smith and Williams became widely known in the mid-1970s (Dawkins, 1976; Archer, 1986a, 1991a). They introduced a more precise way of thinking about how natural selection works, which emphasised that individuals (or, more precisely, their genes: see Cronin, 1991; Dawkins, 1976) were favoured by selection, not groups or species.

Bowlby (1980a) and Parkes (1972, 1986) both offered answers to the dilemma of why such a maladaptive feature as grief should have evolved, and in their case the suggestions are compatible with selection acting at the level of the gene (for most purposes this would coincide with the individual). Bowlby viewed grief within the wider context of attachment theory: in particular, he argued that it was connected to the evolution of separation reactions. Consider again the mated pairs of zebra finches observed by Butterfield (1970). When separated, the female calls and the male is active in searching: in functional terms these responses immediately make sense in terms of aiding reunification (hence in the long run promoting pair-bonding and the rearing of offspring). But had one of the pair died, such responses could not be seen as adaptive: persistent searching would not then enhance fitness.

Why does the zebra finch – and indeed any other social animal – not have two responses, one for separation and the other for death? Bowlby's answer to this question was that separation is much more common than death in animals under natural conditions, and that mechanisms controlling the reactions are not sufficiently flexible to apply to one and not the other. Therefore the maladaptive response to bereavement is the price to pay for the overall much more frequently used separation reaction. The costs involved in grief can therefore be viewed as a trade-off with the overall benefits conferred by separation responses.

One further point is that animals would not be able to tell whether separation or death had occurred in such cases. Where death occurred out of view of the other – for example by predation – there would, of course, be no way of telling for humans and non-humans alike; Price (1972) and Badcock (1990) both make the point that such cases of 'missing' would be particularly common for males in evolving hominids. However, even if death were witnessed, I argued earlier that animals do not possess a concept of death as an irreversible change, thus further closing off the possibility of evolving appropriate responses to death and separation. I also indicated that recognition of death probably arose fairly late in human evolution, making the evolution of a separate response to separation and death unlikely even in the human case.

Badcock (1990) offered the additional suggestion that grief might be adaptive in those cases where the lost loved one did return: it would enable the relationship to be continued, rather than leaving the returning individual to find that his or her place had already been taken by another. A similar view was expressed by Shand (1914: 333) when he wrote that 'the bond which joy alone forms with an object would in its absence be quickly dissolved, were there no sorrow to reinforce it'.

A slightly different way of viewing the evolution of the grief reaction is in terms of the way that biologically important relationships are maintained (Parkes, 1972). The mechanisms involved in forming such relationships include principles such as an initial attraction to physical features and exposure learning. Once established, the individuals concerned will have formed a stable representation of the other, which ensures that they react to changes perceived as affecting the stability of the relationship: if this arises from a third party, reactions such as jealousy (Daly, Wilson and Weghorst, 1982) will occur and, if it arises from separation, reactions such as distress and protest will result. Therefore grief reactions are seen as the by-product of the way in which biologically important close personal relationships are maintained. The central representation of the other cannot be changed overnight, and furthermore is resistant to attempts to do so. In this sense, grief exerts adaptive costs, and these form a trade-off with the much greater benefits of being able to form close relationships. Grief is 'the cost of commitment' (Parkes, 1972). Charles Darwin summed up this view in a letter to his cousin, Charles Fox, whose wife had died in childbirth a year before:

> Strong affections have always appeared to me, the most noble part of a man's character and the absence of them an irreparable failure; you ought to console yourself with thinking that *your grief is the necessary price for having been born with* (for I am convinced they are not to be acquired) *such feelings.*
>
> (Darwin, 1843; italics added).

In this explanation, the emphasis is placed more on the necessity of having the mechanisms which result in grief, because they facilitate the maintenance of relationships, rather than on the widespread usefulness of separation reactions themselves. The two are, however, connected and they may be viewed as differing only in emphasis.

Although these two explanations are the most plausible ones, it is worth mentioning others which are less credible. One is that grief is adaptive because it evokes help or sympathy (Tobach, 1970; Crawford, 1989; Izard, 1991). As Tobach put it: 'The expression of grief presents a strong attractive stimulus to other individuals' (p. 352). She went on to suggest that this would facilitate the formation of new bonds. Such explanations emphasise the importance of sadness and distress for communication with companions. However, there is no indication that such feelings are accentuated when potential helpers are around, or indeed that they are attractive to others. In fact, in non-human primates very obvious signs of grief are greeted with apparent indifference by social companions (Seyfarth and Cheney, 1992). In the human case, it would seem that sadness is strongest when the person is alone (Nesse, 1991).

An alternative adaptive hypothesis is that of Thornhill and Thornhill (1989). They began with a suggestion from Alexander (1986) that 'mental pain', i.e. frustration and distress, must serve some function. This deduction was based on an analogy with physical pain, whose function was seen as drawing the animal's attention to some physical injury. However, even for physical pain the assumption that it must necessarily be functional is problematic, and many forms of pain clearly do not serve any apparently useful purpose (Melzack and Wall, 1982). Similarly, in the case of mental suffering, it is an act of faith rather than an empirically verified conclusion that this must always confer a selective advantage (cf. similar assumptions made about grief discussed above).

Thornhill and Thornhill's hypothesis covers 'mental pain' in general, and they argued that it represents an adaptation designed to detect and cope with social problems that had, in evolutionary history, reduced an individual's fitness. However, they emphasised different adaptive functions for different contexts of mental pain. For example, they argued that the suffering following rape victimisation serves to focus attention on events surrounding the rape, promoting their avoidance in the future. In the case of grief, such a response would be inappropriate. Instead, they argued that it represents a display of commitment to biologically important bonds, notably those concerned with reciprocity and nepotism. In other words, this is another variant on the social cohesion explanation, albeit one which is firmly rooted in individual selection. The Thornhills did, however, say little about why this should, in general, be advantageous: they were more concerned with arguing that variations in grief intensity follow the relative importance of the particular relationship for fitness.

Another – more promising – suggestion concerning the overall adaptive significance of grief was offered by Klinger (1975) within the context of an incentive-motivation theory of frustration (Chapter 6). He was concerned with the process of disengagement following not only losses but also other forms of frustration and disappointment. He described the sequence of a vigorous initial reaction, followed by depression, and finally disengagement from that particular goal, thus paralleling frameworks suggested for separation. He viewed depression as part of an overall process of disengaging from pursuing impossible goals and being able to switch attention to other activities. If such actions are guided by internal representations of incentives, it will be necessary to have these mechanisms in order to prevent being locked on to inappropriate incentive-related cues.

From this viewpoint, grief can be seen as a more prolonged and complex disengagement process necessary where there are a series of related 'goals' associated with a biologically important attachment. This is perhaps another way of saying that grief is the 'cost of commitment', the downside of being attracted to anything whether great or small. But it is more than that. It proposes a crucial role for depression in stopping people pursuing impossible or unproductive goals. If correct, those who show little or no signs of a sad mood whatever the circumstances would spend a lot of their time in useless pursuits which others would have given up a long time ago (Nesse, 1991). In everyday life, a mild sad mood would be important for routinely disengaging from unproductive activities. As far as I am aware, this has not been tested.

Klinger's hypothesis presupposes that the reaction to loss is a single rather than a dual process, as Hofer (1984) argued. It also assumes that reactions to major losses are simply larger-scale versions of minor disappointments. However, there are likely to be important differences between the two cases. Even if a mildly depressive mood were adaptive for disengaging from minor disappointments, it would not necessarily follow that a more prolonged period of depression was adaptive for disengaging from a major loss. Again, there would be the implication that people who did not show depression would remain preoccupied with the loss, and those who were readily depressed would disengage more rapidly. Overall, the evidence suggests the opposite – that depression is associated with more preoccupation and lack of adjustment (Chapter 6).

In summary, therefore, the alternative suggestions regarding the adaptive significance of grief are on balance less plausible than Bowlby's separation argument and Parkes' cost of commitment. These remain the most likely reasons, albeit indirect ones, for the evolutionary origins of grief.

Conclusions

In this chapter I have ranged over a variety of issues concerning the biological origin and significance of grief. I have argued that grief is a universal human characteristic, whose central features are similar to the reactions of other social animals to separation and loss. These involve two processes, one consisting of active distress, searching and anger, which is called separation distress or separation anxiety, and the other an inactive depressed state. In adult humans, these processes have been incorporated into a more complex set of reactions involving a change in personal identity. In non-human animals and young children, there is an inability to understand death as a biological event, so that reactions to death and separation are equivalent.

Hofer has argued that the two processes, separation distress and the depressive state, are controlled respectively by the absence of the specific individual and deprivation of that type of relationship. If correct, this 'two-process' theory of grief would have far-reaching implications, since most of the other theories of grief assume that it is a single process of change through time.

Central to an understanding of the biological significance of grief is its link with attachment, the formation and maintenance of an emotional bond to another individual. Either because separation distress is useful in the context of temporary separations, or because the bond cannot be severed suddenly, grief occurs following death of a loved one despite its being maladaptive for survival and procreation. It is, as Parkes realised, 'the cost of commitment'.

5 The grief process
An analytic approach

I tell you, hopeless grief is passionless;
That only men incredulous of despair,
Half-taught in anguish, through the midnight air
Beat upward to God's throne in loud access
Of shrieking and reproach. Full desertness
In souls as countries, lieth silent-bare
Under the blanching, vertical eye-glare
Of the absolute Heavens. Deep hearted man, express
Grief for thy Dead in silence like to death –
Most like a monumental statue set
In everlasting watch and moveless woe
Till itself crumble to the dust beneath.
Touch it; the marble eyelids are not wet:
If it could weep, it could rise and go.
                 (Elizabeth Barrett Browning, 1883, 'Grief')

Introduction

In Elizabeth Browning's sonnet, we again see the distinction between two primary grief reactions, active distress and passive despair, which was described in the previous chapter. Browning contrasted the 'shrieking and reproach' of active grieving which she viewed as aiding recovery, with passive despair, which she saw as a barrier prolonging and setting grief. Active distress and depression are important aspects linking adult human grief with the reactions of animals and young children. But in adults, grief goes beyond the straightforward emotions of separation distress to include thought processes and experiences surrounding these emotions, which in turn transform separation distress into a more complex set of reactions. In addition, adult humans show various ways in which they seek to minimise or avoid the psychological pain of grief. Their sense of self and identity is also profoundly affected by the experience of bereavement, and shows a gradual change throughout the process of grief.

All these aspects of grief are described in this chapter, from the analytic approach of viewing them as specific reactions. Perhaps the best existing description of the grief process – which is based on studies of spousal bereavement – is that of Parkes (1970, 1972, 1986, 1996). He also used the analytic approach of breaking down grief into its constituent parts, such as alarm, searching, mitigation, anger, guilt, and gaining a new identity (Parkes, 1964a, 1972). Although he used the stage or phase approach in earlier work, some of his later writings (Parkes, 1988) question this, and emphasise more the usefulness of describing grief in terms of its specific features, or 'components'. These were divided into two categories (Parkes, 1985, 1986): episodic reactions such as anger and searching, and a general background disturbance, involving features such as anxiety and feelings of depression – a distinction reminiscent of the two-process view of grief described in the previous chapter.

Sources of information about grief

In this chapter I am largely following Parkes' approach to the description of grief, both in terms of the level of the categories used, and in terms of their specific content. The information comes mainly from studies or accounts of spousal bereavement, with a tendency for widows to be over-represented. The ideal for such studies would be a detailed description of people's experiences of grief and how these change over time. Unfortunately, few existing studies fulfil both criteria. Many of the older studies, such as those of Lindemann and Marris (Chapter 2) contained the detail but were only snapshots, involving single interviews. Of nine studies of bereavement following death of a spouse listed by Bowlby (1980a: 83), only three involved more than one interview. Clayton, Desmarais and Winokur (1968) interviewed three times during the 13 months following bereavement; studies by Parkes (1970, 1972, 1986, 1996) and Parkes and Weiss (1983) both involved more descriptive detail and a more extensive timespan.

Since Bowlby's review, a number of other longitudinal studies have been carried out. They include two larger-sample investigations in San Diego by Zisook, Shuchter and their colleagues, who used both interview and questionnaire methods. The results have been presented in a number of books and papers (study 1: Shuchter, 1986; Zisook and Shuchter, 1986; Zisook, Shuchter and Lyons, 1987a; study 2: Shuchter and Zisook, 1993; Zisook, Mulvihill and Shuchter, 1990; Zisook, Shuchter and Lyons, 1987b). A second project was the Tübingen longitudinal study (W. Stroebe, M.S. Stroebe and Domittner, 1988; W. Stroebe and M.S. Stroebe, 1992, 1993) which concentrated on depression and other health-related measures. A third was that of Vachon *et al.* (1982a,b) in Toronto, which involved predictors of distress rather than a detailed description of grief. Four other studies were specifically concerned with older people in different parts of the US (Faletti *et al.*, 1989; Gallagher-Thompson *et al.*, 1993; Lund, Caserta and Dimond, 1989a, 1993; van Zandt, Mou and Abbott, 1989), and another is the Baltimore Bereavement Project (Levy, Derby and Martinkowski, 1992, 1993; Levy *et al.*, 1994), which examined bereavement over 18 months in spouses of cancer patients. Further studies have been carried out in Pittsburgh (Prigerson *et al.*, 1994, 1996b, 1997a), Goteborg (Grimby, 1993), Brisbane (Middleton *et al.*, 1996), Melbourne (Kissane *et al.*, 1996a,b) and Sydney (Bartrop *et al.*, 1992). To this list we can also add those which involved limited follow-ups of the same sample (Cleiren, 1993; Jacobs *et al.*, 1987; Sanders, 1979–80).

Perhaps the most forward-looking and sophisticated study is that initiated by Wortman and her colleagues (Wortman *et al.*, 1993) which involved a large representative sample of the general US population, who were followed up three years later. Since this produced a substantial number of bereaved respondents at the second interview it was uniquely possible to make within-individual comparisons before and after bereavement. This study is considered further in Chapter 10.

In terms of providing a descriptive base, the studies of Parkes, and subsequently Shuchter and Zisook's San Diego studies are the most useful. The Californian group confirmed many of Parkes' initial findings with a larger sample, and documented changes over time. Nevertheless, the impression is that the additional longitudinal studies have not added appreciably to Parkes' description, in some cases because they have simply confirmed his accounts, and in others because they have used more limited measures, such as depression inventories and general health questionnaires, or limited rating-scale measures of grief (Chapter 2).

Therefore, Parkes' accounts will be used extensively in this chapter, with the San Diego and other studies mentioned above forming a supplementary source, along with a wide variety of specific descriptions of grief from sources such as case studies, ethnographic accounts, and literary and biographical sources. Parkes' two main studies were one carried out in London, concerned with the 'normal' pattern of grief in a sample of 22 younger and middle-aged widows, who were interviewed during the 13 months following their husbands' death; and a second carried out in Boston (Glick *et al.*, 1974; Parkes and Weiss, 1983), which involved a sample of both men and women, extending over four years.

There follows an account of grief broken down into its constituent parts, before considering, in Chapter 6, how these are organised together.

Numbness and disbelief

Numbness and disbelief are common initial reactions to bereavement. Eliot (1946) described disbelief (or 'denial') as 'one's natural defense', remarking that it is only a temporary buffer from reality. On occasions, it may take the form of a complete and consistent refusal to acknowledge the death at all, even to the extent of keeping the body in the house for weeks, months or even years, in some cases making crude attempts at preservation (Gardner and Pritchard, 1977). Accounting for such actions, one man said of his mother: 'I couldn't accept that she'd died. I wanted things to go on the same' (ibid., p. 25).

These cases strike us as gruesome and bizarre, but they can be viewed as extreme manifestations of an initial natural response to bereavement, to disbelieve its reality. This was a common way of reacting to the news of the husband's death among the London widows studied by Parkes (1970). He reported statements such as 'It doesn't seem real' or 'I can't believe it's happened'. However, the apparent calm of this reaction could be interrupted at any time by an outburst of intense emotion, and was preceded by an initial outburst of great distress in some cases: 16 of the 22 widows had difficulty accepting that their husband was really dead, and this persisted later from time to time as denial. Zisook *et al.* (1987b) reported that 85 per cent of the widows from the second San Diego study reported some disbelief by 2 months after the loss, but only 26 per cent rated these feelings as 'extreme'. In a personal account of grief following the sudden death of his young wife, Lichtenberg (1990) said that he was only just beginning to realise that she was dead 2 months afterwards.

In cases where the circumstances of the death are unclear, and there is no body (as often happens in wartime), the sense of disbelief may be prolonged, kept alive by the remotest possibility that the person has survived (Golan, 1975). The rituals of the funeral seem to serve an important function in countering the tendency to foster such hopes and maintain disbelief.

Numbness is an alternative initial reaction to news of the loss. In Parkes' London study, it was described by just under half the sample (10) and lasted from a day to a week in five cases. Shuchter (1986) found that 29 per cent of the respondents in the first San Diego study reported experiencing numbness 1 month after the loss, with a decline thereafter (Shuchter and Zisook, 1993).

Although numbness is an initial and transient state, some form of disbelief may be prolonged in the form of an inability to accept the loss: over half of the sample of London widows Parkes studied said there were still times when they had difficulty believing in the reality of their husband's death a year after it had occurred.

Numbness and disbelief correspond closely to the Freudian notion of psychological defences, which includes denial, repression and dissociation. In contrast to the original emphasis on psychopathology, Parkes (1972, 1986) and Janoff-Bulman (1993) have emphasised the adaptive role of denial in buffering the person from the full emotional impact of what has happened (cf. Kaminer and Lavie, 1993, for a similar view of repression). Janoff-Bulman (1993: 99) argued that denial enables the person to 'confront the threatening experience in smaller, manageable doses'. Writing of his own experience as a hostage in the Lebanon, Brian Keenan stated that 'Denial gives time for a temporary retreat from reality, time for our internal forces to regroup and to regain strength, to begin to deal with the loss that has been forced upon us' (Keenan, 1992: 31).

Anger and aggression

An alternative way of resisting what is unacceptable is to fight it, and an initial expression of anger has been observed among bereaved people. Marris (1958) described one widow physically attacking the doctor who brought the news of her husband's death. Writing of perinatal death, Peppers and Knapp (1980) mentioned several examples of violent responses, including a father who plunged his fist through the hospital wall. In Lindsay Anderson's film *This Sporting Life* (1963), Frank Machin (Richard Harris) shows a similar reaction when he hears that the woman he loves is dead: at first he says 'No, she isn't' and then he smashes a spider on the hospital wall with his fist.

Anger is also likely to flare up periodically throughout the grieving process, and is a widespread reaction to grief in many different cultures (Rosenblatt *et al.*, 1972, 1976). In Parkes' London study, expressions of anger, of sufficient intensity to be commented upon, were admitted some time during the first year of grief but only by a minority of respondents. In subsequent studies, the proportion reporting anger during the first 2 months after the death has varied from 12 per cent (Shuchter, 1986) to about a third (Glick *et al.*, 1974; Zisook *et al.*, 1987b). However, an observational study of bereaved people discussing the deceased 6 months after the loss, found that 60 per cent of them expressed anger in their facial expressions (Bonanno and Keltner, 1997).

In a minority of cases, anger may be associated with acts of extreme violence. Examples can be found in literature from ancient times: in *The Iliad*, Achilles cuts the throats of 12 highborn Trojan youths, to vent his anger at the death of Patroclus (Rieu, 1950, book XXII). More recently, in Laos, men who had lost their whole families through death or separation carried out indiscriminate grenade attacks, which killed and maimed people almost at random (Westermeyer, 1973). In February 1992, a grief-stricken off-duty Belfast (RUC) policeman went to a local Sinn Fein headquarters and killed several people before shooting himself (Bowcott, 1992). In his account of the Vietnam War, O'Brien (1990) described his platoon's reaction to the sudden loss of one of their men from a sniper's bullet:

> After the chopper took Lavender away, Lieutenant Jimmy Cross led his men into the village of Than Khe. They burned everything. They shot chickens and dogs, they trashed the village well, they called in artillery and watched the wreckage.
>
> (O'Brien, 1990, 1991 edn: 14)

Since anger forms one of the reactions involved in separation distress (Chapter 4), it can be regarded as a basic emotional response to loss. The initial response of an outburst of pronounced aggression – including the extreme example just cited – may represent a way of mitigating the unbearable mental pain engendered by the loss. In the same book, O'Brien described an act of apparently wanton cruelty inflicted on a water buffalo by one of his men (Rat Kiley) after his buddy had been killed. The writer described the other men's reactions thus:

> Nobody said much. The whole platoon stood there watching, feeling all kinds of things, but there wasn't a great deal of pity for the baby water buffalo. Curt Lemon was dead. Rat Kiley had lost his best friend in the world. Later in the week he would write a long personal letter to the guy's sister, who would not write back, but *for now it was a question of pain.* He shot off the tail. He shot away chunks of meat below the ribs . . .
>
> (O'Brien, 1990, 1991 edn: 17. Italics added)

The same connection between an irrational violent act and the need to block out overwhelming mental pain was made by the Russian novelist Gogol (1842) in describing an act of self-injury following bereavement (see following section). It is also known from animal experiments that rats subjected to electric shocks show indications of a lesser degree of physiological stress if they have attacked another animal immediately after the shock rather than trying to escape (Williams and Eichelman, 1971; Conner, Vernikos-Danellis and Levine, 1971). Possibly a similar adaptive response occurs – at least in the short term – with severe psychological pain.

Although anger can be viewed as a basic emotional response to separation and loss, in the case of adult human grief, its form and intensity will be subject to attributional processes seeking to make sense of the loss. It may be directed at people who bring home its reality, or those who remind the person of the loss when she is struggling to put it out of her mind (for example, other happily married couples: Hobson, 1964). Anger, or prolonged bitterness, may be directed at someone who is seen as responsible for the loss, such as the hospital, a nurse, a doctor, or even God (Parkes, 1972, Glick *et al.*, 1974; Hobson, 1964). Zisook *et al.* (1987b) found that 35 per cent of their second San Diego sample showed some anger towards the doctors 2 months after the death. Alternatively, the dead person may be blamed, perhaps for being care- less or not looking after his health (Chapter 4), or for 'abandoning' the bereaved (Lichentenberg, 1990). The young widow in Susan Hill's novel *In the Springtime of the Year* screamed out in resentment, 'Why did you have to die?' (Hill, 1974: 14).

Anger and bitterness will have both personal and social consequences. Often, bereaved people realise the irrational and unfair nature of their anger and feel guilty about it afterwards. Their angry reactions may drive away well- meaning people offering help and may lead to social isolation. Those widows who expressed the most anger in Parkes' London study tended to be more socially isolated than those who expressed less (Parkes, 1970). Here, it is difficult to tell whether this is cause or effect. But in a study concerning anger among patients with severe and chronic breathing disorders, Lane and

Hobfoll (1992) found that higher levels of anger produced both immediate and delayed increases in anger among those residing with them and providing them with social support. In a study measuring participants' responses to a series of vignettes portraying patients suffering from depression, anorexia and obesity under various circumstances, Schwarzer and Weiner (1991) found that anger directed at the person concerned was the best predictor of an unwillingness to provide social support.

In an earlier report of their cross-cultural study, Rosenblatt *et al.* (1972) considered how different societies dealt with anger and aggression resulting from grief. One common solution was the use of specialists who provide rituals for the bereaved. By doing so, Rosenblatt *et al.* suggested, they can not only provide advice and assistance but also reduce frustrations, interpret emotions and promote responses other than aggression. Indeed, their findings support this in that there was a significant negative association across different societies between the use of such ritual specialists and measures of aggression following bereavement.

Rosenblatt *et al.* commented that dealing with such anger and aggression becomes a problem for a society in that, if unchecked, they can lead to high mortality, injury and disruptions of personal relations. Indeed, the extreme acts of violence considered earlier in this section would support this view. They further speculated that two common customs, isolation or seclusion of the bereaved and setting them apart by altering their appearance, for example through clothing or facial appearance, could also have originated from the same need to deal with their potential for anger and aggression. One problem with this explanation is that such seclusion applies more to widows than to widowers, yet of the two they have the lesser tendency towards violence (Rosenblatt *et al.*, 1976).

Guilt, self-blame and self-injury

Another reaction which involves the attribution of responsibility is self-blame or guilt. Parkes (1972, 1986) found that 13 of the 22 widows he interviewed reported self-reproach at some time during the first year. This ranged from simply asking 'What could I have done?' to blaming themselves for some specific act of commission or omission which might have caused or contributed to their husband's death. Alternatively, they looked back over the relationship and felt regret or guilt about something that they had not done for him, or something they wished they had not done. These are both examples of counterfactual ('if only') thinking, which Davis *et al.* (1995) found could be – but was not necessarily – associated with guilt following bereavement (see Chapter 8).

Compared with Parkes' study, Shuchter (1986) found that a smaller proportion (27 per cent) of the first San Diego sample reported guilt 1 month after the bereavement, declining to 10 per cent at 10 months, and rising to double this value at 13 months (perhaps associated with a renewal of grieving at the anniversary of the death). Miles and Demi (1983–4) reviewed 12 different studies of bereavement and found considerable variation in the frequency of guilt. Its incidence varied from none at all in a small-scale study of Japanese widows (Yamamoto *et al.*, 1969), to 58–69 per cent in studies involving sudden traumatic deaths. A more recent study (Weinberg, 1994) also found a much higher proportion of self-blame among people bereaved by an event such as a motor vehicle crash or suicide than by illness.

Miles and Demi (1983–4) outlined five possible sources of guilt, and looked for evidence of these among a sample of bereaved parents attending a seminar on guilt at a national meeting for bereaved parents in the US. The two most common categories, both reported by 54 per cent of the 28 parents, were about the cause of death and whether it could have been prevented, and about deficiencies in their role as a parent. Other forms of guilt were rare in this sample. Similar findings were reported in a later study of a larger sample, involving death of a child by suicide, accident or disease. The two categories of guilt found in these studies of parental grief correspond well to those found by Parkes for widows. Again, they involve counterfactual thinking.

One other form of guilt that is often found among people who survive an accident or disaster, or who have lost their comrades in combat, is survivor guilt, a feeling that someone who has been killed is more worthy of having survived than they are (Glover, 1984; Thompson, 1985).

A more extreme form of hostility directed towards oneself occurs in the form of self-injury. As W. Stroebe and M.S. Stroebe (1987a) pointed out, it is a response with which we are relatively unfamiliar in western cultures. Yet is it widely reported in the Old Testament and in writings from many ancient cultures, as well as in many present-day traditional cultures (Borgquist, 1906; W. Stroebe and M.S. Stroebe, 1987a). In their cross-cultural survey, Rosenblatt *et al.* (1976) found that self-injury occurred in 32 out of the 78 societies studied: in 18 there were no sex differences, but in another 12 it was women who were more likely to injure themselves. Borgquist's earlier account of historical and ethnographic studies of self-injury also indicated that it was more prominent in (but not confined to) women. It included what to us would be extreme examples, such as widows from some native North American tribes cutting off a finger, and Biblical accounts of mutilations of the nose, brow and ears, which were then forbidden by the law of Moses.

Nevertheless, examples of self-injury can be found in western cultures, if not at the present time, in historical and literary accounts from former centuries. Edmund Spenser wrote:

> She wilfully her sorrow did augment,
> And offered hope of comfort did despise;
> Her golden locks most cruelly she rent,

And scratched her face with ghastly dreriment;
Ne would she speke, ne see, ne yet be seene,
But hid her visage and her head downbent.
(Spenser, 1596, *The Faerie Queene*)

In the novel *Dead Souls*, Gogol (1842) described the hero as dashing his head against the wall, and tearing his hair out. Similarly, after the bombing of an Iraqi air-raid shelter in the 1991 Gulf War, one report described boys overcome with grief in the hospital courtyard beating their heads against a wall until they bled, screaming 'Gone! Gone!' (Rojo, 1991). Gogol described his character as 'enjoying the pain by which he strove to deaden the unquenchable torture of his heart'. This suggested motive is different from the one often put forward in anthropological and psychological discussions of self-injury, that it is related to self-blame and guilt (W. Stroebe and M.S. Stroebe, 1987a). Gogol's interpretation was that physical pain is being used to try to blot out the mental pain. It may well be the motive for an initial response of this sort, serving the same psychological function as a feeling of numbness. More prolonged self-injury is, in many cultures, complicated by the action being a socially accepted way of responding to grief, particularly for women (Rosenblatt *et al.*, 1976).

Distress and anxiety

The typical background emotional state found early in bereavement is one of great distress, which Parkes (1972) described as anxiety verging on panic, a desperate feeling of not knowing what to do next, or of wanting to run away. Associated with this is high arousal and an inability to concentrate or to sleep (Hobson, 1964; Clayton *et al.*, 1968; Parkes, 1970; Glick *et al.*, 1974). However, great distress is not a consistent state: at first there are pangs of grief, episodes when the dead person is strongly missed and the bereaved sobs aloud for them. The active form of crying that we refer to as sobbing is especially characteristic of bereavement, and can be distinguished from a more passive form of tearfulness which is associated with tender feelings (Darwin, 1872; Williams and Morris, 1996). Bereavement is the principal circumstance which evokes this form of sobbing, as indicated by cross-cultural surveys (Borgquist, 1906; W. Stroebe and M.S. Stroebe, 1987a) and questionnaire studies of when people say they would cry (Lombardo *et al.*, 1983; Williams and Morris, 1996).

These episodes of overt distress and sobbing begin a few hours or days after the loss and reach peak severity within 5–14 days (Parkes, 1972). Gradually, over the months that follow, such episodes usually become less common and the degree of emotional disturbance is reduced (Shuchter, 1986), but they can be precipitated by something that brings the loss to mind. In some cases, however, there is a delayed emotional response to the loss (Parkes and Weiss, 1983), so that these responses begin some time afterwards.

Shackleton (1984) has questioned Parkes' characterisation of the emotional state of grief as anxiety on the grounds that reactions such as sighing and yawning, which do occur, are not associated with anxiety, whereas others, such as sweating and tremor, which do not occur, are normally associated with anxiety. However, evidence for high levels of anxiety following bereavement has been found using standard scales of state anxiety (Bartrop *et al.*, 1992; Porritt and Bartop, 1985; Rubin, 1981, 1991–2), other scales (Grimby, 1993; Sable, 1989), and clinical assessments based on the DSM-III[1] diagnostic criteria for anxiety states (Jacobs *et al.*, 1990). It is clear from these studies that anxiety is significantly higher among bereaved than non-bereaved samples up to 6 months after the death (Bartrop *et al.*, 1992), and that the clinical criterion for an anxiety disorder is commonly reached (Jacobs *et al.*, 1990). Anxiety disorders are associated with severe grief and depression.

Prigerson *et al.* (1996b) found that measures of anxiety were distinct from those of other aspects of grief and from depression among a sample of 56 older bereaved people followed up at 6, 12 and 18 months after the loss. Earlier levels of anxiety predicted depression later in the study.

Measures of anxiety include nervousness, fearfulness, tenseness, panic, restlessness, and signs of high sympathetic nervous system activity (cf. Goodkin *et al.*, 1996). They are comparable to the emotional reaction accompanied by distress calling which is the primary response to separation in animals and children (Chapter 4). Other evidence (Kim and Jacobs, 1993; Laudenslager *et al.*, 1993) indicates that this is associated with neuroendocrine changes indicative of stress. Although Parkes did not carry out any physiological measurements in his London study, it was clear that most of the widows showed signs of high sympathetic nervous system activity, such as restlessness, muscular tension, dryness of the mouth, loss of interest in food, digestive disturbances, palpitations, and the inability to sleep. It was often reported that feelings were centred on a lump in the pit of the stomach. Headaches and other pains, irritability and complaints of poor health were also common. Shuchter (1986) also found high frequencies of restlessness, tension, tearfulness and sleeplessness a month after bereavement in the first San Diego study, consistent with other findings (Glick *et al.*, 1974). Writing of his own experience of grief, C.S. Lewis commented:

> No one ever told me that grief felt so like fear. I am not afraid, but the sensation is like being afraid. The same fluttering in the stomach, the same restlessness, the same yawning. I kept on swallowing.
>
> (Lewis, 1961: 7)

He later added that it was more like suspense than fear, suggesting a state at least similar to anxiety. It is, anyway, a highly aroused, active form of

---

1 American Psychiatric Association (1980).

distress, so that the bereaved may feel that they are exhausted from grieving (cf. Hill, 1974: 69).

Yearning and preoccupation

Separation distress involves the feelings of sorrow, mental pain, anxiety and anger which have already been described. In adult human grief, these are strongly linked with the mental experience of preoccupation, which is probably an elaboration of the more basic reactions of yearning and pining, these less elaborated mental states involving missing the deceased strongly, and being part of separation distress (Parkes, 1988). They are experienced early in the grief process as episodes when a feeling of pining surges up inside the person, producing pangs of grief, often resulting in an outburst of sobbing (see previous section).

Throughout grieving, the central cognitive feature is an obsession or preoccupation with thoughts of the deceased. Yet at the same time these intrusive thoughts are deeply distressing and painful. In his London study, Parkes (1970) found that preoccupation was most prevalent between 1 and 5 months after the loss, although even at 13 months most of the widows still spent much of their time thinking about their husband. A similar pattern was found by Shuchter (1986) in the first San Diego study.

Parkes found that preoccupation was associated with a clear visual image of the deceased and a sense of his or her presence nearby. Shuchter found that a clear visual image was reported by 27 per cent of the sample 1 month after the loss but this percentage declined over subsequent three-monthly interviews.

Preoccupation with thoughts of the deceased forms part of a more general topic in psychology known as intrusive thought processes (or 'stimulus-independent thought'), and the possible relevance of experimental studies to the generation of these patterns of thought is discussed in Chapter 8. One aspect of the methodology often used in such studies may prove useful in further investigating preoccupation in the context of grief. At present, the extent of such intrusive thoughts is assessed by retrospective self-reports and questionnaire ratings. They might, however, be assessed more accurately by using the method of consciousness-sampling, in which people are given a periodic bleeper signal which acts as a prompt for them to report the content of their thoughts at the time (Singer and Kolligian, 1987). This experience-sampling methodology has been extended to studies outside the laboratory. It has, for example, been used to investigate the moods, fantasies and activities of teenagers as they go about their daily lives over a period of several weeks, and the activities, motivations and feelings of young people at work and leisure (Haworth and Hill, 1992).

Preoccupation is often associated with the need to mentally relive times which were shared, and to go over the circumstances of the loss, particularly if it was sudden or traumatic. Parkes has aptly referred to this as the 'obsessive review', and Hobson (1964) described widows dwelling on happy times, pouring over wedding photos and other mementos. Along with the need to think about events from the past is the urge to talk about them again and again. Some bereaved people fulfil this need by writing, for example in the form of letters to the deceased, or poetry or essays (Lattanzi and Hale, 1984–5; see Chapter 7). Many works of literature have arisen from this need. In 'In Memoriam A.H.H.', Tennyson indicated the beneficial effects of writing about grief, with the following words:

> But, for the unquiet heart and brain,
> A use in measured language lies;
> The sad mechanic exercise,
> Like dull narcotics, numbing pain.
>   (Tennyson, 1850; in Jump, 1974)

From the writings of medieval poets and playwrights, to present-day clinical and psychological reports, there is a consensus that expressing feelings of grief in words is therapeutic. Perhaps the most famous quotation is from *Macbeth*. Malcolm tells Macduff, whose wife and children have been killed by Macbeth:

> Give sorrow words: the grief that does not speak
> Whispers the o'er-fraught heart, and bids it break.
>   (Shakespeare, 1623a, IV, iii, 209)

Likewise, Spenser wrote in *The Fairie Queene*, 'He oft finds med'cine who his griefe imparts'. These and many other quotations (Becker, 1932–3) indicate a consensus that it is advantageous to express the feelings and thoughts of grief in words. Research now indicates that talking or writing about painful thoughts is associated with more positive moods, lower depressive mood, and fewer health-related symptoms at a later time (Lepore *et al.*, 1996; Pennebaker, 1988, 1997; Chapter 7).

Shand (1920) and others (Becker, 1932–3; Epstein, 1993) have distinguised between this sharing of feelings with others, and the expression of the emotion itself. Tennyson clearly had the second of these in mind when he wrote in 'The Princess':

> Home they brought her warrior dead:
> She nor swoon'd, nor utter'd cry:
> All her maidens, watching, said,
> 'She must weep or she will die'.
>   (Tennyson, 1847; in Jump, 1974: 72)

In contrast to this often repeated belief in the efficacy of 'ventilating' emotion, Shand argued that control over the expression of the emotion would – up to a point – help to diminish it: uncontrolled emotion becomes difficult to stop, as Dostoyevsky indicated in *The Brothers Karamazov*:

> The sort of relief which these lamentations produce is artificial and serves only to deepen the wound the heart has suffered, as one irritates an ulcer by touching it. It is a dolefulness that does not want consolation: it feeds upon itself.
>
> (Dostoyevsky, 1880)

This is very different from the assumption that emotional expression must be cathartic, which is apparent in most psychoanalyically derived views of grief. These contain an assumed hydraulic view of emotional expression, which holds that blocking it causes a pressure to build up which is then transferred into an abnormal reaction. This belief has even been incorporated into a behaviourist view of grief by Ramsay (1977). However, it was challenged by another behaviourist, Shackleton (1984), who argued that the experience of emotional distress is punishing rather than cathartic. This view is consistent with evidence that pronounced emotional distress early in the course of grief predicts poorer recovery (Chapter 7), and with the views of Dostoyevsky, Shand and Becker, referred to above.

It is also supported by a careful contemporary study by Bonanno and Keltner (1997), who carried out systematic observations of the facial expressions of bereaved people at around 6 months after their loss, and obtained further measures of grief, health and well-being at 14 and 25 months after the loss. They found that a greater expression of negative emotions such as anger, contempt, disgust and fear at 6 months was associated with more severe grief and poorer health later on. This association held up even when the initial levels of self-reported intensity of emotional experience and of grieving were controlled. In other words, the expression of negative emotions in the face had a separate mediating influence on later distress, over and above any association it might have because it was simply reflecting the early intensity of grief.

We should therefore be careful to distinguish, as Shand and the others have, between the uncontrolled expression of emotional distress, which seems to predict a poorer outcome, and the sharing and expression of thoughts and feelings with others, which seems to predict a better one. Since sharing of emotions through conversation may often be accompanied by emotional expressions such as crying, it is easy to see how the two can overlap, and why they have very often been considered as the same process (as, for example, in the grief work hypothesis, considered in Chapter 7).

Associated with preoccupation with the deceased and the urge to search (see later section) is a loss of interest in other aspects of life, such as work, leisure interests, family, personal appearance, friends and food (Shuchter and Zisook, 1993; Rosenbloom and Whittington, 1993). Whether this is a direct consequence of attention and interests being directed elsewhere, or whether they are part of an overall depressed state (see later section) is not clear. Possibly both are contributing factors.

Illusions, hallucinations and ghosts

Sometimes sights or sounds are misinterpreted as the deceased being present. In other cases, the bereaved person believes that the deceased has actually visited them. In Christopher Isherwood's novel *The Memorial*, Lily, who was bereaved in the First World War, prays that her husband will appear to her, after her widowed friend had described seeing her own husband at the top of the stairs.

> Several days passed. And then, one evening, as she was coming up the staircase from the hall to dress for dinner, she saw Richard standing in front of her. It was getting rather dark, as he appeared, strangely distinct, within the archway of the corridor. He was as she had last seen him, on his last leave, a slightly bowed figure in the British Warm and frayed tunic, his mild eyes wrinkled like his father's, but prematurely, with his deeply lined forehead and large fair moustache. There he was. Then he was gone.
>
> (Isherwood, 1932, 1988 Methuen edn: 61).

This description is in accord with research findings. Hobson (1964) reported widows hearing, seeing and sensing the presence of their husbands, and imagining them coming through the door. Parkes (1972) referred to common examples of 'hearing' the dead person's footsteps on the stairs, or 'seeing' them in the street. Over half of a sample of Californian widows studied by Ball (1976–7) experienced the presence of, or thought they saw or heard their dead husband (see also Glick *et al.*, 1974; Shuchter and Zisook, 1993). Similarly, Rees (1971) found that 39 per cent of a sample of 363 bereaved people from mid-Wales said they had felt the presence of the deceased, 14 per cent said they had seen them, 13 per cent had heard them, and 2 per cent said they had felt their touch. Grimby (1993) reported figures of around 50 per cent for feeling the presence of the deceased, 30 per cent for hearing them, and 26 per cent for seeing them, among a sample of people in their seventies in Sweden, at 1 month after the loss. In a study of bereaved children, almost half of the sample reported that they had heard the dead parent speaking to them (Silverman and Worden, 1993).

Rees (1971) investigated the relationship between proneness to these phenomena, which he collectively called 'hallucinations' and a variety of other variables. He found that higher occupational status, older age and a happier marriage were associated with greater reported frequency of hallucinations. However, the inclusion of the sense of the deceased's presence (which was by far the most common form) within this category makes interpretation problematic. A sense of presence is more widespread and is related to aspects of mitigating the loss and to identification with the deceased, which are discussed in later sections.

These reports of having seen or heard the dead spouse all come from modern western cultures, where there are few encouragements to view them as anything other than mistaken interpretations. Indeed, to think otherwise is often viewed as a sign of insanity. However, in many traditional cultures, people believe that the dead return as spirits or ghosts. We might expect such beliefs to encourage different attributions of 'seeing' the deceased.

Hallucinations of the presence of the deceased have been studied among bereaved Hopi women, living on a reservation in north-west Arizona (Matchett, 1972). In their culture, apparitions are tolerated but are not part of the cultural beliefs surrounding mourning. They come to the woman when she is in a darkened room with outside stimuli limited. It is well known that conditions of low stimulation facilitate hallucinations (Chapter 8), the most extreme being sensory deprivation (Bexton, Heron and Scott, 1954). Nevertheless, being alone and quiet at night may be enough for an active troubled mind. In the excerpt quoted at the beginning of this section, Lily saw her husband 'as it was getting rather dark'.

The Hopi women's hallucinations were clear enough to be reported in great detail – even to be struggled with physically – but they were still regarded as outside the usual definition of reality: the women often argued with the apparition about its existence! None of the women were psychotic or had a history of psychiatric problems. Matchett regarded these hallucinations as a way of mitigating the psychic pain, and in the study of Grimby (1993) most respondents said that these experiences were pleasant. In this respect, they are like the reassuring pretence that the deceased is nearby, described by Rees (1971), Parkes (1972) and others.

However, hallucinations may get out of hand, and induce fear, particularly when coupled with established beliefs about the malevolent nature of spirits of the dead. In their cross-cultural survey, Rosenblatt *et al.* (1976) found fear of ghosts in 84 per cent of the societies they examined. A study of children's grief found that 81 per cent felt that the dead parent was watching them and about 70 per cent of these were frightened by this feeling (Silverman and Worden, 1993). In *Totem and Taboo*, Freud (1913) attributed such widespread fears to the projection of unconscious hostility towards the deceased. They are more likely to arise from the general inability of human beings to understand and accept the reality of death.

Although belief in apparitions is, on the surface, largely absent from modern western cultures, we do not have to look too far back for examples of such visits from the dead. The use of apparitions as specific dramatic characters is of course well known from Charles Dickens' *A Christmas Carol*, when Scrooge is visited by the ghost of his former partner, and in several of Shakespeare's tragedies. The viewer expresses doubts about the vision's reality, yet converses with it, and may be fearful of it. For example, in *Julius Caesar*, when Caesar's ghost enters Brutus' tent, he says:

How ill this taper burns!- Ha! who comes here?
I think it is the weakness of mine eyes
That shapes this monstrous apparition.
It comes upon me. - Art thou anything?
Art thou some god, some angel, or some devil,
That mak'st my blood cold, and my hair to stare?
Speak to me what thou art.
(Shakespeare, 1623b, *Julius Caesar*, IV, iii, 275–81)

Anniversaries and reminders

Rosenblatt (1983) has emphasised the ability of events such as birthdays and anniversaries, and reminders, such as people, places and things associated with the deceased, to rekindle thoughts of the deceased, together with the feelings of distress and sadness which accompany them. In Shelley's poem 'Adonais', written on the death of Keats in 1821, he wrote:

Ah, woe is me! Winter is come and gone
But grief returns with the revolving year
(Shelley, 1821)

It is well known that anniversaries of the death – particularly the first one – are a difficult time for bereaved people, a time they often view pessimistically in terms of a set-back in their recovery, and when past events are recollected clearly and painfully (for example, see personal accounts of grief such as that of Lichtenberg, 1990). Researchers studying grief have specifically avoided follow-up interviews at this time, locating them at 13 months instead (Parkes, 1970; Parkes and Weiss, 1983; Shuchter, 1986).

Because reminders prove painful, some bereaved people deliberately avoid them: for example, Shuchter (1986) found that 23 per cent of the first San Diego study did so 1 month after the loss, and 19 per cent at 4 months. Avoidance of reminders would be one way of mitigating the pain of grief (see later section), but both experimental and clinical evidence suggest that it does not help the resolution of grief (see Chapters 7 and 8).

Although unexpectedly coming across something that was associated with the deceased may also prove a painful reminder, some people deliberately surround themselves with such objects in order to maintain a sense of the presence of the deceased. This has often been associated with prolonged or suspended grief, referred to as 'mummification' (Chapter 1). Shand (1920) commented that wanting to be shut away with recollections of the lost person, and being resistant to consolation, also stemmed from the desire to hang on to the attachment. Parkes and Weiss (1983) have linked this reaction to a highly dependent relationship with the deceased (Chapter 7).

In a study of patients exhibiting this form of grief, Volkan (1972, 1981) described their use of 'linking objects', which were associated with the deceased, and were jealously protected by the bereaved, exerting a fascination for them. The objects consisted of items worn by the deceased, paintings or photographs of them, personal possessions, or objects nearby when the death occurred. Volkan saw them as ways of keeping alive the link with the deceased, and distinguished them from mementos of the deceased in general: linking objects were invested with magic and symbolism.

From a different perspective, linking objects can be viewed as another aspect of seeking to maintain attachment, which is more commonly shown in the urge to search (see next section). Klass (1988) provided further instances in his study of parental grief (Chapter 11), for example the use of the child's stuffed toys.

During the eighteenth and nineteenth centuries, specially constructed mourning objects were used to maintain memories of the deceased. The *momento mori* tradition involved the incorporation of tiny strands of hair into jewellery such as rings, which were distributed to friends and other mourners (Llewellyn, 1991). Often they incorporated earlier symbols of death such as skulls or skeletons.

Memories of the deceased were also sustained by pictures, which were often small enough to be carried in a pocket or bag. The deathbed painting by Van Dyck of Sir Kenelm Digby's wife (Figure 5.1), who died suddenly at a relatively young age in 1633, was used in this way by her bereaved husband (Llewellyn, 1991). He kept it with him at all times, carrying it around his apartment at Gresham's College where he became a recluse. He said 'This is the only constant companion I now have'. A year later, he arranged for a permanent monument to be constructed in London, with a Latin inscription translated as 'The pleasure is in loving a living wife; the dead one, I revere'. (Llewellyn, 1991: 33). In other cases, pictures of the deceased made while still living, were also used as private reminders: Figure 5.2 shows a painting by John Greenhill of Mrs Jane Cartright in mourning clothes (which represent the mourning of her husband William after her death).

Deathbed paintings (and death masks) provided ways of maintaining a feeling that the deceased is nearby. Portrayal of the dead became more widespread with the advent of photography in the nineteenth century, at least in the US. Post-mortem photography was socially acceptable and publicly acknowledged (Ruby, 1988–9); such services were advertised, and images were publicly displayed in frames and albums. In the twentieth century, it gradually became a more private affair, to be maintained mainly within families who had suffered a stillbirth or infant death (Ruby, 1988–9).

In an early account of widowhood from a cross-cultural perspective, Cochrane (1936) noted the practice of carrying around part of the dead husband's body in some cultures: this ranged from his hair and loin-cloth among the Bekana of New Guinea to his skull in the Andaman Islands, and even his penis in Bali. Similarly, one interpretation of the separation of parts of the body, particularly the head, found in ancient Egyptian burials from the

Figure 5.1 'Venetina Stanley, Lady Digby, on her death bed' by Anthony Van Dyck, 1633.

Source: Reproduced by permission of the Governors of the Dulwich Picture Gallery

earliest dynasties, was that relatives kept the head, and perhaps other parts, for a while as reminders of the deceased (Spencer, 1982); the separated part would be placed in the tomb with the rest of the body at a later time.

Although these practices may appear unusual and even distasteful by present-day western standards, they can be understood as one of many possible ways of maintaining or creating reminders of the deceased, and perhaps mitigating their loss. In the present day, bereaved people may keep personal reminders such as clothing instead (Shuchter and Zisook, 1988, 1993; Silverman and Worden, 1993).

The urge to search

Perhaps the most notable motivational feature of grief is the urge to search. This can also be viewed as part of separation distress and can be understood in terms of the link between grief and the process of attachment (Chapter 4), but it may be a puzzling and distressing feeling for a bereaved person to experience.

Figure 5.2 'The last wife of Mr. Cartright' by John Greenhill, before 1676.

Source: Reproduced by permission of the Governors of the Dulwich Picture Gallery

Parkes (1970, 1972) argued that many of the features described so far, such as preoccupation, a clear visual image, illusions, restlessness and also the use of linking objects, are all closely associated with a strong urge to search for the dead person, i.e. are part of separation distress (Parkes, 1988). This view is supported by the pattern of correlations between the various features reported by Parkes (1970). Pining, in particular, was viewed as the persistent and obtrusive wish for the lost person to return: it is accompanied by an unpleasant emotion because it is the subjective component of the urge to search for a lost loved one. Similarly, Averill (1968) argued that the emotions of grief could be best understood in motivational terms, in that the unpleasant feelings associated with being separated motivate the person to search and seek to be reunited.

Although searching is obviously irrational in the case of bereavement, it is, according to this view, a more general impulse which makes sense in cases of temporary separation from a loved one, and of other losses which are potentially retrievable (see Chapter 4, and Bowlby, 1980a). Consequently, the same impulse is felt even when, objectively speaking, it makes no sense.

The urge to search may be manifest in several different ways. Literally walking around looking for the lost loved one was reported in Parkes' London study. In other cases, the urge is felt but action is deliberately suppressed. Calling for the lost person was reported by some of the widows in Parkes' study.

More generally, there is a feeling of being drawn to places and objects associated with the dead person. Tennyson described the feeling in the following words:

> So find I every pleasant spot
> In which we two were wont to meet,
> The field, the chamber and the street,
> For all is dark where thou art not.
> (Tennyson, 1850, 'In Memoriam A.H.H.'; in Jump, 1974)

Attention becomes directed to those parts of the familiar environment most closely associated with the lost person, such as places and possessions (see previous section). For example, a widow may experience the urge to hurry home because her husband would be waiting for her. Or she may frequently gaze at his chair, or feel strongly drawn to the cemetery or to his grave.

The attraction of spiritualism and seances for many bereaved people can also be seen in this light, but these interests are not usually maintained. In *The Ghost Road*, Pat Barker wrote of a spiritualist meeting towards the end of the First World War: 'Too many widows. Too many mothers looking for contact with lost sons' (Barker, 1995: 77).

Suicidal ideas may be expressed, death being seen as a means of being reunited with the deceased. As Shand (1920) pointed out, many poets portrayed the dead as calling out to the living. A particularly good example is contained in the following lines:

> O that I were where Helen lies!
> Night and day on me she cries;
> Out of my bed she bids me rise,
> Says, 'Haste, and come to me!'
> (Anon., 'Helen of Kirconnell'; Quiller-Couch, 1919).

A similar attraction is described in Edgar Allen Poe's 'Annabel Lee', and in the 1960s 'coffin song' (Chapter 3), 'Endless Sleep',[2] in which the bereaved hears the deceased calling from the sea.

Mitigating or avoiding grief

A further important aspect of the grief process concerns the regulation or suppression of the source of psychological distress. This begins with the reactions of numbness and disbelief discussed earlier. To differing degrees, and in different ways, thought patterns which lessen the experience of grief are maintained as time goes on. One of these is a continuation of the initial sense of unreality, but seldom is such disbelief complete. Parkes (1972) remarked that one of the commonest ways of gaining comfort is the pretence that the lost person is really nearby, in the next room or just around the corner, which is often associated with a strong mental image or set for the lost person. In other cases, there is a more consistent feeling that the deceased is always nearby, perhaps associated with a belief that they continue to live in some form. In his book, *The Last Enemy*, Second World War fighter pilot Richard Hillary recalls a conversation with the grieving fiancée of his friend who was killed in action. She said:

> 'I *know* that everything is not over for Peter and me. I know it with all the faith that you are so contemptuous of. We *shall* be together again. We are together now. I feel him constantly close to me . . . Peter lives within me. He neither comes nor goes, he is ever-present. Even while he was alive there was never quite the tenderness and closeness between us that there is now.'
>
> (Hillary, 1942: 137, 1956 edn)

This example takes us beyond a temporary pretence that the deceased is nearby, to a consistent feeling that he or she is always nearby, or has actually become part of the bereaved person ('Peter lives within me'). In this sense it overlaps with a feeling of identification with the deceased, which is discussed in the next section.

Recovery of the lost person may also occur in dreams (Shuchter and Zisook, 1988, 1993). The widows interviewed by Hobson (1964) reported vivid dreams of their husbands. In Parkes' London study he most often found that such dreams were happy ones, although there was usually something present to indicate that all was not well. These sorts of dreams were also reported in the personal account of grief by Lichtenberg (1990). Tennyson alluded to them and to the disappointment felt upon awakening in the following lines:

2 Jody Reynolds (© Johnstone-Montei Inc. Elizabeth Music BMI).

Tears of the widower, when he sees
A late-lost form that sleep reveals,
And moves his doubtful arms, and feels
Her place is empty, fall like these;
(Tennyson, 1850: 'In Memoriam A.H.H.'; in Jump, 1974)

A different way of lessening the impact of grief is deliberately to avoid pain-ful thoughts associated with the loss. As indicated above, this may involve avoiding people and situations that act as reminders, and also putting away photographs and personal belongings. It is widely believed that if this is carried too far, or goes on for a long time, it will restrict the areas of life with which the person feels capable of dealing. Shutting out painful or unresolved conflicts may enable a person to function with a lower level of distress in the short term, but it is usually considered that doing so precludes any progress or personal growth in what have effectively become emotional no-go areas. This is the basis of the widely held concept of 'grief work', derived from a psychoanalytical model of grief (introduced in Chapter 2, and assessed in more detail in Chapter 7).

A superficially similar, but theoretically very different approach lies behind behaviourally based therapies that have been applied to people who avoid grieving (Gauthier and Pye, 1979; Lieberman, 1978; Ramsay, 1977). Based on a theoretical model derived from phobias (Shackleton, 1984; Rachman, 1974), it is assumed that the distressing properties of the avoided stimuli are maintained by the continued avoidance. Therefore, the aim of the therapy is to confront these stimuli, thus allowing extinction of the negative emotions associated with them to occur. Although based on learning theory principles, the approach of encouraging (or sometimes forcing) people to confront emo-tionally charged but avoided areas from their past is one which is shared with – and is usually more characteristic of – psychoanalytic and humanistic methods. However, the theoretical reasons for doing so are very different. The behaviourist approach views emotional expression as punishing – and there-fore the less that it occurs the better – whereas psychoanalytical and human-istic approaches view it as cathartic, and therefore to be encouraged.

Identification

Identification is a term derived from Freudian psychoanalytic theory which describes ways in which one person's sense of identity is defined by the presence of a significant other. It describes a sense in which someone wants to be like another person. In relation to grief, Freud (1913) originally specified that identification of the ego with 'the abandoned object' (i.e. person) was narcissistic (i.e. unhealthy). The concept of identification has since been developed in a number of psychoanalytic accounts up to the present time (Klass, 1987–8). Klass himself followed Volkan (1981) in arguing that identi-fication enables a healthy representation of the deceased to occur, serving as a transition to being able to attain complete independence. Bowlby (1980a) relegated identification to a minor role in grief, so that phenomena which might be viewed in this way were seen in terms of maintaining attachment (Klass, 1987–8). Parkes (1972) described a number of aspects of loss as identification phenomena, but it is clear that this was intended to be descriptive rather than to represent adherence to a Freudian viewpoint.

The clearest examples of identification phenomena following bereavement are for a physical pain to develop in the same part of the body as in the deceased's (Parkes, 1972; Faschingbauer *et al.*, 1977), or for the bereaved to adopt the deceased's interests, likes and dislikes.

Some inner feelings can also be described in the same way. These are perhaps best illustrated by the following remark from a widow in Parkes' London study who said 'My husband's in me right through and through. I can feel him in me doing everything' (Parkes, 1986: 107). John McGahern's novel, *Amongst Women*, concerns the changing family ties between an old Irish Republican (Moran) and his daughters. Just after the father's funeral, the author describes the way in which his daughters felt supported by a continued identification with their father:

> But as the small group of stricken women slowly left the graveyard they seemed with every step to be gaining in strength. It was as if their first love and allegiance had been pledged uncompromisingly to this one house and man and that they knew that he had always been at the living centre of all parts of their lives. Now not only had they never broken that pledge but they were renewing it for a second time with this other woman who had come in among them and married him. Their continual homecomings had been an affirmation of its unbroken presence, and now, as they left him under the yew, it was as if each of them in their different ways had become Daddy. 'He may be gone home but he'll always be with us,' Maggie spoke for all of them. 'He'll never leave us now.'
>
> (McGahern, 1990: 183)

This description indicates a feeling akin to that involved with the sense of the presence of the deceased, and with experiencing a strong visual image. Those aspects of grief have been linked with preoccupation and continued attachment (Parkes, 1972, 1986), rather than with identification in its Freudian sense. An alternative interpretation is that identification phenomena are related to mitigation reactions involving pretending that the deceased is nearby. Both views of identification phenomena differ from the psychoanalytically derived one referred to above, i.e. that identification is itself an important process for the resolution of grief (Klass, 1987–8). This provides one way of seeking to describe the complex changes in a person's identity when he or she undergoes a major loss. In the absence of empirical evidence linking identification and resolution of grief, the view that identification is part of continued attachment to the deceased would seem the most plausible.

However, if identification is combined with a strong element of pretence, it may be better thought of as a way of mitigating or avoiding the reality of the loss.

Changes in self-concept

In Chapter 1, I referred to the grief process as involving a change in identity. Widows in Parkes' London study described their feelings as initially involving a 'loss of self'. This was often felt physically, in terms of a wound or a void or something being cut off. In a series of interviews with people who had experienced losses of various kinds (Brown, 1986), a man who had earlier lost a leg described the similarity between the feeling of grief (when his wife died) and his experience of loss after his leg had been amputated. A similar case is also mentioned in the book on parental grief by Klass (1988). This feeling of physical loss can be understood as a subjective consequence of the internalisation of the personal world which is at the heart of all emotional attachments that people build up (Chapter 1). When something is missing from this personal world, the bereaved person may feel physically incomplete.

The initial feeling of loss of self can be viewed as the subjective manifestation of the incomplete nature of the old self, which is no longer appropriate for the changed circumstances. Many other aspects of a person's self-definition will no longer be accurate in terms of the outside world. The bereaved person will have to change conceptions of the self which are associated with, for example being married, not being alone, being part of a two-parent family and being a sexual partner. Gradually, she or he will become able to adopt new roles: for example, a widow who fulfilled the traditional role of housewife may become, as a single person, the family administrator and wage-earner. However, it is the change in self-concept accompanying these external changes that is widely regarded as being crucial for the resolution of grief, and which is considered in the next two chapters.

Hopelessness and depression

The biphasic reaction found in separated young animals (Chapter 4) involves active distress accompanied or followed by despair and depression. The stage or phase view of grief (Chapter 2) holds that they succeed one another in time. However, feelings of hopelessness and depression occur throughout the grief process (Clayton *et al.*, 1972; Middleton *et al.*, 1997; Parkes and Weiss, 1983; Prigerson *et al.*, 1996b; Shuchter, 1986; Zisook *et al.*, 1987a), rather than being confined to when separation distress has burnt itself out (see Chapter 6). Shand (1920) regarded a depressive, inactive response to bereavement as one of four types of sorrow, varying in terms of their energy and degree of self-control. If we suppose that these variations also occur within individuals, so that both energetic and inactive responses are intermingled during the earlier parts of the grief process, the presence of depressive reactions throughout can more readily be understood.

When bereaved people are compared with matched samples of married people, the proportion showing clinical levels of depression are considerably higher among the bereaved, although significant differences may be confined to soon after the loss (Zisook and Shuchter, 1991; Shuchter and Zisook, 1993; Gallagher-Thompson *et al.*, 1993; Lund *et al.*,1989).

Briscoe and Smith (1975) compared the backgrounds of a sample of people showing clinical levels of depression following bereavement with those of depressive in-patients who did not have a background of loss, and with another sample who showed depression following divorce. The bereaved sample showed fewer prior incidences of depression than the in-patients and, surprisingly, than the divorced sample. This study suggests that death of a marital partner does indeed act as a precipitating event for depression in people who would not otherwise be prone to it. The findings for the divorced sample indicate that their depressive state may have been part of a longer history of relationship difficulties, or of being depression-prone in a variety of circumstances.

These studies are based on the Beck or Zung depression scales or DSM III criteria (American Psychiatric Association, 1980). Studies involving comparisons between the depression scores of bereaved and matched control samples indicate higher values among bereaved people during the first 2–3 years overall (Lund *et al.*, 1989; W. Stroebe and M.S. Stroebe, 1992, 1993; Thompson *et al.*, 1989) or at specific times following bereavement (2 weeks and 6 months: Bartrop *et al.*, 1992; 1 and 6 months: Jacobs *et al.*, 1987; 14 months: Parkes and Brown, 1972; 2–4 months and 10–12 months: van Zandt *et al.*, 1989). In all these cases, there was a decline in depression with the time since the loss: in the last study, levels were similar to those of controls 2–3 years after the loss (van Zandt *et al.*, 1989). In contrast, Lehman, Wortman and Williams (1987) found that people who had lost a spouse or a child in an motor vehicle crash 4–7 years before still had substantially higher depression levels than a control sample.[3]

Bereaved people also show specific reactions indicative of depression, such as loss of appetite, insomnia (Parkes and Brown, 1972; Ball, 1976–7), loss of interest in television and news, and difficulty concentrating (Clayton *et al.*, 1968; Shuchter and Zisook, 1993).

Conclusions

In this chapter I have adopted an analytic approach to describing the various reactions associated with grieving. Such detailed description is an important

---

3 Effect sizes (i.e. differences between the means, in terms of the overall standard deviation) were approximately .8 to .9 for the Schedule for Affective Disorders Scale, a value which is characterised as a large effect (Cohen, 1977).

first step towards understanding the process of grief as a whole. As the ethologist Niko Tinbergen (1963) commented, psychology has often missed out
the descriptive natural history phase which is characteristic of other sciences.
The cost of doing so is the generation of theory based on limited evidence or
premature experimentation using rather restricted measures. We can certainly
find examples of the first of these in bereavement research, the stage view
being a primary one. The tendency in US research to rely on depression scales
or simplified rating scales to measure grief could be seen an example of the
second.[4]

However, mere description is not enough, as Tinbergen himself was the
first to recognise. In order to inform the question of how the various aspects
of the grief process fit together, we require evidence on their association with
one another and how they change over time. As we shall see in the next
chapter, such evidence is at present fragmentary. Yet there is no shortage of
theoretical speculation about how the specific reactions do fit together. This
topic is considered in the next two chapters, Chapter 6 examining the process
of grief from a holistic perspective and Chapter 7 examining the nature of the
resolution of grief.

4 In Chapter 7 I argue that the appropriateness of such measures depends on the aims of the
study.

6 The grief process
Holistic views

Gallagher's numbness continued. In the days that followed the news of Mary's death, he worked furiously on the road, shovelling without pause in the drainage ditches, and chopping down tree after tree whenever they had to lay a corduroy. He would rarely halt in the breaks they were given every hour, and at night he would eat his supper alone and curl into his blankets, sleeping exhaustedly with his knees near to his chin . . . Gallagher showed no sign of his grief except that he became leaner and his eyes and eyelids were swollen as if he had been on a long drinking bout or had played poker for forty-eight hours at a stretch.

(Norman Mailer, 1949, *The Naked and the Dead*, 1992 edn: 285)

Introduction

This excerpt describes one of the initial reactions many people show to a bereavement, an apparent numbness and inability to take in what has happened. The writer says that Gallagher showed no signs of his grief, meaning that he did not show active distress or obvious depression, which are generally regarded as signs of grief. However, the descriptions of grief encountered in the previous chapter certainly included numbness, along with other ways of avoiding the distress of grief. Nevertheless, as we shall see later in the present chapter, when examining the *process* of grief, it may be useful to separate reactions which maintain and encourage confrontation with the loss from those that involve avoidance or mitigation of the loss.

We can start this enquiry about the process of grief by distinguishing several conceptual groupings among the specific reactions described in the previous chapter. The first two consist of derivations from the separation reactions of young children and animals – active and passive distress. Into the first we can obviously place distress and anxiety, and anger and aggression, along with guilt and self-blame which are derived from these; also yearning and the urge to search, together with preoccupation, identification with the deceased, a sense of their presence, illusions and hallucinations, which can be viewed as derived from the urge to search (Bowlby and Parkes, 1970). The second separation reaction is equivalent to depression, and a lack of interest in other areas of life. A third grouping is the one referred to above, the various ways of avoiding or mitigating the reality of the loss, including the initial numbness and disbelief (and possibly the sense of the presence of the deceased). A fourth one consists of the impact of grief on the experience of self, and changes in the person's sense of identity throughout the grief process. In this chapter we are mainly concerned with the first three of these, since the last one is bound up with notions of recovery from, or resolution of, grief, and is discussed separately in Chapter 7. We begin by examining views which have implied a unity in the overall reactions of grief, to assess whether we do indeed have to look for a more complex organisation underlying the process.

Grief as an intervening variable

When experimental psychologists have studied particular types of motivation, such as hunger, sexual arousal or aggression, they have commonly used the term 'intervening variable' to denote an internal state which mediates a disposition to act in a particular way (Hinde, 1970: 194–202; 1974: 23–31). If a man threatens, shouts and raises his fist when someone contradicts him, when he is kept waiting, and when a member of his family interrupts his favourite television programme, it is useful to link these events together in terms of an intervening variable, such as aggressiveness or anger. In this example, we are describing a longer-term disposition as well as a temporary motivational state. Thus the concept of intervening variable can be extended to refer to dispositional characteristics.

Generally, intervening variables are useful in grouping certain responses which tend to occur together but may occur in a range of circumstances. These are assumed to be affecting a single internal characteristic, the intervening variable, which affects the various responses. Although grief has not explicitly been regarded as an intervening variable, this view is implicit whenever researchers have sought to measure the *level* or *intensity* of grief through a simple rating scale. There is a hidden assumption that the specific reactions vary together and therefore that a single intervening variable ('grief') underlies them.

Some of these rating scales have been poorly constructed when judged by the established criteria for psychological scales (Chapter 2). Others include only a few items. This trend reached its logical conclusion in the study by Littlefield and Rushton (1986) who assessed the level of grief among various relatives after the death of a child by asking them to rate their grief severity along a 7-point scale.

Despite the simplification involved, the assumption that grief can be treated as an intervening variable, implicit in this approach, may be useful for providing a shorthand description of differences between individuals and under different circumstances. No one is going to argue with the general proposition that some people grieve more strongly than others, or that loss of a spouse generally causes more intense grief than loss of a distant relative. If we are dealing with such clear-cut differences, it is easy to rank people along a single dimension. But as soon as we become interested in the different ways in which people grieve, and in the variety of reactions shown to grief, this simple approach breaks down unless, that is, we can establish that the variety *is* accurately summarised as a single variable. To find out whether this is so, we need to know how the various grief reactions are associated together.

Correlations are the initial statistical tool for deciding whether responses vary together, and hence whether it is useful to regard them in terms of an intervening variable. When there are many responses, more complex techniques are necessary. One statistic which is commonly used to measure whether items on a rating scale are related to one another is the coefficient alpha (Allen and Yen, 1979): the nearer to 1.0 it is, the more closely the items are associated together. However, there is a distinction between interrelatedness of items and their forming a single dimension: the first is necessary, but not sufficient, for the second (Cortina, 1993). With a large number of items, the coefficient alpha can be high even if there is more than one underlying dimension. In order to examine this possibility, it is necessary to use techniques such as factor analysis which group together associated items, and hence make order out of a large number of intercorrelations such as those found among questionnaire items.

It is a general finding that when the common grief reactions are incorporated into a questionnaire, they show a high coefficient alpha (see Table 6.1). Consistent with this, Parkes and Weiss (1983) found that ratings on a wide range of outcome measures, such as guilt and anger, anxiety and depres-

Table 6.1 Summary of studies involving questionnaire measures of grief and the value for coefficient alpha (internal consistency) of the scale

Study	Alpha
Beutel *et al.* (1995)	.89
Bierhals *et al.* (1995–6)	.93
Deutsch (1982)	.95
Faschingbauer *et al.* (1987)	.86
Hogan (1988a, 1990)	.88
Hunfeld *et al.* (1993)	.80
Jacobs *et al.* (1987)	.84
Lev *et al.* (1993)	.93
Middleton *et al.* (1996)/Burnett *et al.* 1997	.91
Potvin, Lasker and Toedter (1989)	.95
Prigerson *et al.* (1995)	.94
Raphael (1995)	.85
Theut *et al.* (1989)	.88/.91/.84/.83*
Toedter *et al.* (1988)	.95

* For prenatal and postnatal loss in mothers (first two figures) and fathers (in third and fourth figures)

sion and acceptance, were intercorrelated with one another. In other words, the different grief reactions are closely associated, giving some support to the notion of an overall intensity of grief.

To assess whether they form a single dimension, we need to examine the pattern of associations between individual measures. Although there are several studies reporting factor analyses of grief inventories, there are methodological problems with some of these which limit the conclusions that can be drawn from them. For example, one sample contained bereaved and non-bereaved alike (Jacobs *et al.*, 1987–8), leading to a very fragmentary series of factors accounting for little variance. In the case of the GEI (Chapter 2) the subscales were decided in advance by grouping items together according to their content (Sanders *et al.*, 1985), and the overall factor analysis was carried out on the totals from these scales, effectively reducing the number of items to nine. This procedure produced a single main factor accounting for a large proportion of the variance, which is consistent with the interrelatedness of different aspects of grief found in other studies (see above).

Some studies without such methodological limitations have found several dimensions underlying grief. Caserta, Lund and Dimond (1985) used a rating scale with a wide range of measures, not only of grief reactions (from Glick *et al.*, 1974) but also of stress, coping, health and adjustment. Five factors were found, one involving emotional shock (including numbness and disbelief, but also panic and a feeling of emptiness), a second anger, guilt and confusion, a third helplessness and withdrawal, a fourth aspects of confronting the loss, crying and learning new tasks, and a final one positive coping.

Lev *et al.* (1993) used a 22-item scale based on some aspects of Parkes' description of grief, and found four factors accounting for much of the variance from a large, mainly professional and female sample obtained by post from the US, UK and Australia. The first factor was concerned with identity and meaning, the second depression and anxiety, the third anger and guilt, and the fourth physical distress.

The Hogan Grief Reaction Inventory (Hogan, 1988a) contains 61 items covering a variety of reactions found at different times after bereavement. Factor analysis showed at least six factors (Hogan, personal communication 1992), comprising despair, panic behaviour (i.e. anxiety symptoms), personal growth (i.e. signs of resolving grief), blame and anger, feeling detached, and disorganisation (i.e. difficulty concentrating and doing things).

Burnett *et al.* (1997) factor-analysed scores from a 76-item bereavement questionnaire, and found seven factors, representing specific aspects of the grief process, such as preoccupation, the sense of the deceased's presence, dreams, acute separation reactions, and the impact of reminders: each of these formed coherent groupings. Three of them (preoccupation, acute separation and reminders) were regarded as central or core aspects of grief: when grouped together, they formed a coherent whole with a high coefficient alpha (see above).

Other studies (Middleton *et al.*, 1997; Prigerson *et al.*, 1994, 1995, 1996a,b) have found a single factor identifying the core bereavement items, which is distinct from measures of depression and anxiety measured on standard scales. We should note that although depression and anxiety items load as separate factors, the scale scores are still closely related to one another. In a study of perinatal grief, Toedter *et al.* (1988) found a factorial distinction between items described as active grief, those representing difficulties coping, and those described as despair, measured at 6–8 weeks after the death. (We should note that despair was not equivalent to depression, which was more closely associated with coping difficulties: Potvin *et al.*, 1989.)

Prigerson *et al.* (1996b) further provided a more sophisticated factor analysis of their longitudinal study of older bereaved spouses at 6, 12 and 18 months after the loss. They used Confirmatory Factor Analysis, which involves testing the data for its closeness of fit to specified theoretical models. In this case, at all three times after the loss, the responses better fitted a model which viewed core grief reactions, depression and anxiety as separate (as opposed to one which grouped all three together or grouped depression or anxiety together with grief). We should, however, note that all three factors were associated with one another (as indicated by their high correlations): therefore, the separation of the three factors indicates that depression or grief are influenced by events other than bereavement (as we should expect), and not that grief, depression and anxiety are completely separate reactions. This is borne out by the additional finding that grief scores at 6 months predicted depression at 18 months when depression scores at 6 months were controlled.

Parkes' London study provided a detailed account of the diversity of grief reactions, but it involved neither the questionnaire format nor the sample size necessary to undertake a factor analysis. Nevertheless, it is possible to obtain an indication of the way in which some responses were grouped together from correlations between the overall scores (obtained from rating scales). These showed that the following were closely related (Parkes, 1986, Table 7): first, a clear visual memory of the deceased, a sense of his presence, preoccupation and, to a lesser extent, tearfulness and avoidance of reminders; second, irritability and anger, difficulty in accepting the loss, restlessness, tension, and social withdrawal at the first interview. These two groupings can be characterised as continued yet painful attachment to the deceased, and an aggressive reaction in the face of the loss. Parkes (1970) also reported that a single index of overall distress, including depression, was relatively unrelated to the first grouping outlined above. In other studies, depression has been found to be significantly correlated with either guilt and anger combined (Parkes and Weiss, 1983) or with guilt (Gass, 1987; van der Wal, 1988).

It appears from these studies that there is little overall consistency in the dimensions revealed by factor analysis or by examination of the intercorrelations, except perhaps with regard to the separation of anger and guilt in some cases, and anxiety and depression in others. This is perhaps not surprising in view of the variety of items placed on the different scales, the different samples used and the varied times since the loss at which the measures were taken. The search for a set of underlying dimensions for grief will always be limited by these considerations.

Grief as a behavioural system

The intervening variable approach considered in the previous section involved simplifying grief along a single dimension. It arises from a long tradition in psychology of seeking simple-outcome measures and attributing them to changes in a single internal state. Attachment theory is, as indicated in Chapter 4, derived from a different tradition, that of ethology – animal behaviour studied from a zoological perspective. Ethological approaches to motivation have regarded it as a more complex process, involving an overall goal, in pursuit of which there can be a variety of specific responses. These specific responses may vary according to the individual and the circumstances, and may form alternatives to one another. There is therefore flexibility in the means through which a particular end is pursued.

We have already seen (Chapter 4) that attachment was described in these terms by Bowlby (1958, 1969): the overall goal is to maintain the relationship, and separation or loss produces a set of reactions directed to this end. On this view of attachment, we would not expect the separation reactions, or the grief responses derived from them, to reflect an underlying single dimension, or even necessarily a consistent set of underlying dimensions. Indeed, researchers looking at human behaviour from an ethological perspective (Blurton Jones, 1972; Blurton Jones and Leach, 1972) have criticised psychologists for being too ready to assume that we can find 'measures of' processes such as attachment, i.e. that they must necessarily reflect intervening variables. The empirical evidence on factor analyses of grief measures was consistent with this view.

Two further considerations are likely to make the process of grief even more complex. One, which was noted at the beginning of this chapter, is that grief responses extend beyond those that can be traced to separation reactions: for example, some are concerned with avoidance and mitigation. We would therefore need to consider these in addition to reactions understandable in terms of the attachment system. In a later section, I outline one recent attempt to do so. A second complication concerns the dynamics of the grief process, that it involves changes in the various reactions over time.

The stage or phase view of grief and evidence for changes over time

The best-known attempt to consider how grief changes over time is the stage or phase view introduced in Chapter 2, which portrayed grief as a temporally organised series of reactions: the first reaction represents most strongly denial or avoidance of the loss, the second active distress associated with yearning, the third despair and depression and the fourth resolution (Bowlby, 1960a, 1980a; Bowlby and Parkes, 1970). In this section, evidence for the changes over time portrayed by the phase view is examined from longitudinal studies. I consider mainly the London study of Parkes (1970, 1972), the two San Diego studies (Shuchter, 1986; Zisook *et al.*, 1987a,b, 1990; Shuchter and Zisook, 1993), the Goteborg study of Grimby (1993), and the Pittsburgh longitudinal study of Prigerson *et al.* (1996a,b), since they provide the most detailed information.

In relation to the first phase, Parkes found that numbness occurred in half his sample immediately after the loss, and was infrequent thereafter. Jacobs *et al.* (1987) reported that both numbness and disbelief declined from 1 to 6 months. Shuchter (1986) provided a figure for numbness of 29 per cent at 1 month, declining to 9 per cent at 4 months and lower thereafter. In the second San Diego study (Shuchter and Zisook, 1993), numbness was reported by 12 per cent at 2 months, and again declined, although 70 per cent endorsed 'It's hard to believe' at 2 months, declining to 49 per cent by 13 months. There is therefore a separation between numbness and disbelief in this study, if we accept 'hard to believe' as indicative of disbelief.

Looking at the reactions ascribed to the yearning and searching phase, yearning declined slightly from 2 to 13 months in the second San Diego study (77 per cent to 58 per cent). Preoccupation declined from 91 per cent in the first month to around 50 per cent after 13 months in Parkes' study, and from 63 per cent to 33 per cent over the same time period in the first San Diego study. Similar decreases were found for preoccupation by Burnett *et al.* (1997), and for yearning, preoccupation and searching by Prigerson *et al.* (1996b).

Shuchter reported a decline in a clear visual memory (68 per cent at 1 month; 40 per cent at 13 months; and 21 per cent at 49 months); so did Grimby (1993) for illusions and hallucinations (over 12 months), and Burnett *et al.* (1997) for the sense of presence (from 4–10 weeks). However, Parkes found consistently high reporting (77 per cent) of a clear visual memory over 13 months.[1]

Four studies have shown a steep decline in tearfulness: from 77 per cent at 1 month to 23 per cent at 13 months in Parkes' study; from 73 per cent to 42 per cent (13 months) to 17 per cent (49 months) in the first San Diego study (Shuchter, 1986; Zisook *et al.*, 1987a). Rating-scale measures declined by about .6 of a standard deviation over 12 months in the Goteborg study (Grimby, 1993) and by about 1.0 standard deviation from 6–18 months in the Pittsburgh study (Prigerson *et al.*, 1996b).

The San Diego study also found that guilt, a sense of the deceased's

---

1 This occurred despite a high overall correlation with preoccupation, which did decline over time, showing that whether two measures tend to be associated within individuals throughout the period of grieving does not necessarily indicate a similar temporal change.

presence, restlessness, and loneliness declined steeply and significantly from an initially high level (Zisook *et al.*, 1987a), although the first two were again maintained at a more constant level in the second study (Shuchter and Zisook, 1993). Similar declines were found by Grimby (1993) over the first year of bereavement. A more general measure of separation anxiety which excluded both numbness and disbelief, and also depression, was found to decline from 1–6 months by Jacobs *et al.* (1987). Prigerson *et al.* (1996b) found a fairly large decrease in anxiety from 6–18 months, although a smaller one was reported by Grimby (1993) over the first year.

Parkes noted that anger was most pronounced soon after the loss and occurred intermittently thereafter, but no figures were presented. Shuchter found the highest frequency of anger of 12 per cent at 1 month, and a fluctuating level of 4–8 per cent thereafter, ending with 8 per cent at 37 and 49 months. Unlike the other measures described so far, there was no significant decline in the proportion showing anger (Zisook *et al.*, 1987a). In the second study, anger was between 7 per cent and 11 per cent from 2 to 13 months. On the other hand, both Grimby (1993) and Prigerson *et al.* (1996b) did find a significant decline in anger or hostility.

The third phase is characterised by despair and depression. In the second San Diego study, a similar proportion felt helpless at both 2 and 13 months after the loss. Regarding depression, the San Diego studies, like the earlier one of Clayton *et al.* (1972), measured the proportion of the sample reaching clinical levels, and found it to be around a third 1 month after the death (Shuchter, 1986; Zisook *et al.*, 1990). Levels of about a quarter were maintained until 7 months, after which there was a general decline (Shuchter, 1986; Shuchter and Zisook, 1993; Zisook *et al.*, 1987b, 1990; Zisook and Shuchter, 1993). Over a 4-year period, the proportion showing depression declined more gradually than measures such as crying and preoccupation did in the first San Diego study (Shuchter, 1986; Zisook *et al.*, 1987a). Other studies of spousal bereavement which have measured mean *levels* on a depression scale also found a decline within the first 6 months, 12 months or 2 years after the death (Jacobs *et al.*, 1987; Grimby, 1993; Middleton *et al.*, 1997; W. Stroebe and M.S. Stroebe, 1993). Prigerson *et al.* (1996b) found a large decline (of over 1.0 standard deviation) in measures of depression from 6 to 18 months.

Other studies indicate variability in the extent of depression following bereavement: for example, two studies of elderly people (Lund *et al.*, 1986, 1989; Faletti *et al.*, 1989) found low proportions reaching clinical levels (5–17 per cent), and others involving death of a child or a traumatic accident found high levels of depression maintained for up to 7 years after the loss (Lehman *et al.*, 1987; Martinson, Davies and McClowry, 1991).

There is, therefore, agreement that numbness and distress show a fairly rapid decline (but see Prigerson *et al.*, 1996b), and that other reactions such as preoccupation and restlessness decline more slowly. Anger was a less common reaction, and it showed a fluctuating frequency. Depression showed highest levels early in bereavement and gradually declined in frequency, either during the first year or later. There are therefore clear indications of changes over time but these do not fall into a simple pattern, either of phases or stages, or even of steady declines in all measures. Possible reasons for not finding such simple patterns include the following: individual differences in grieving (Chapter 7); that grief is subject to control by outside stimuli and events (Rosenblatt, 1983; Wortman and Silver, 1992; Chapter 7); and the complex interplay between different sub-processes involved in grief (as suggested above).

Although the phase view clearly lacks empirical support, we should not be entirely negative about it. It does represent an attempt to capture the dynamic nature of the process of grief, albeit one which was premature because it was not derived from an empirical base. A purely descriptive view of grief, for example as a series of 'components' (Parkes, 1985), might imply (however unintentionally) that we are dealing with a set of independent reactions (van der Wal, 1989–90). The stage view does at least recognise that these various components must be organised into a whole. Nevertheless, having done so, it does not address the issue of what might be the principles underlying this organisation. In a sense, these are embodied in other concepts that can be traced back to Freud (1913, 1917), namely that the function of grief is to detach or disengage the person from emotional bonds with the deceased; and, furthermore, that this process involves actively confronting thoughts and feelings associated with the dead person.

A behaviourally based view of grief

We now examine what in a sense is a totally different approach to the process of grief, since it is derived from a behaviourist rather than a psychoanalytical background. Nevertheless, the same central thesis that confrontation provides the key to disengagement is to be found there too. Klinger (1975, 1977) linked the process of grief to the issue of how any animal becomes disengaged from situations which no longer provide reinforcements, or in Klinger's terminology, *incentives*, which means the power of stimuli to arouse a motivational state (Bindra, 1978). Klinger proposed that when any incentive is no longer present, there is a disruption of goal-directed behaviour of the sort described by those who studied the extinction of a learned response in laboratory rodents (Amsel and Roussel, 1952). First, there is renewed vigour and additional efforts to achieve the goal. The lack of success produces the state of frustration, which is accompanied by anger and aggression (Azrin, Hutchinson and Hake, 1966), and eventually by depression and disengagement from these goals. Klinger enlarged and expanded this formulation so that it applied more widely to include not only minor frustrations, but also more major disruptions, such as losses, which involve the cessation of many different sorts of incentives at once.

Looked at in this way, separation distress involves, first, continued and invigorated attempts to maintain the attachment (for example searching and calling) accompanied by emotional reactions (distress, anxiety and anger) generated by the failure of this enterprise to provide the reinforcements that were generated before. More importantly, these attachment-related responses come to wane over time by a process similar to the extinction of any learned response (Klinger, 1975). In this formulation, we have an account of a process which explains both the generation of the emotions of separation distress and the decline in its attachment-related aspects such as searching and preoccupation.

The role for depressive reactions in Klinger's scheme is that they represent a form of learned helplessness (Seligman, 1975) which follows an active phase. As indicated in Chapter 4, they are seen as necessary for disengaging from the former incentives before new ones can be learned. By characterising depression in this way, Klinger allied it with the phase view of grief. There is no evidence from studies of extinction in animals – the original source of Klinger's theory – to support this particular aspect of it. Animals do show brief periods of immobility following the absence of an expected reward (Andrew, 1972; Archer, 1974; Slater, 1972), and these can be regarded as prototypical depressive responses. However, the evidence from these studies shows that although there is a tendency for periods of immobility to increase during the extinction process, they are not confined to a specific phase.

Klinger's model can be readily modified on this particular point, so that depressive reactions are seen as part of an intermingled, rather than a temporally separated, set of responses. Furthermore, if a depressive reaction does provide a mechanism for disengaging from incentives, it would not necessarily be as effective as alternative ways of doing so, such as avoidance and distraction (discussed below). These direct the animal either away from the incentive or direct attention to something else, whereas a depressive response represents a more general disengagement from *any* form of responding.

As noted earlier, grief also includes reactions which involve avoiding or mitigating the psychological distress accompanying the loss. Although these were not considered in Klinger's account, studies of behaviour shown by animals during extinction indicate that they are strongly motivated to escape from the situation (Adelman and Maatsch, 1956; Guiton and Wood-Gush, 1967) and that they show switching of attention to alternative responses (McFarland, 1966a,b; Duncan and Wood-Gush, 1972). These responses could be regarded as prototypes for the motivation to seek to avoid painful reminders and thoughts during grief, and to seek alternative activities. In other behavioural accounts of grief (Shackleton, 1984), avoidance reactions have been regarded in terms of learned avoidance of the distressing stimuli associated with the loss, and in their extreme form they are viewed as potentially interfering with the process of disengagement, and hence with the resolution of grief (Chapter 7).

In the modified form outlined above, Klinger's behaviourally based model of grief has a number of attractions. First, it explains the generation of active separation distress: these are partly attachment-related responses being pursued with increased vigour, and partly emotional reactions generated by the absence of incentives associated with the attachment figure. Second, it can, in a modified form, also deal with depressive reactions: these are a generalised mechanism of disengagement, which applies both to the attachment figure, and to any potential new incentives. Third, it can be extended to understand the generation of avoidance and distraction responses, as being derived from more specific means of disengagement. Finally, it links all of these to the well-known process of extinction of a learned response: they can all be observed in prototypical form when an animal experiences absence of a habitual incentive.

Despite these strengths, the behaviourally based view has a number of limitations as a full account of adult human grief. One is the difference in scope between separation or loss of an attachment figure and extinction of a learned response. The former provides a whole range of specific incentives, whereas the latter is limited to a specific source. In Bowlby's (1969) account of the attachment process, he emphasised the need to view this as an integrated behavioural system controlled by an overall (or 'top-level') goal, which is to maintain or regain proximity with the attachment figure (Figure 6.1). Other more specific responses are subservient to the overall control mechanism. Thus, although there is a similarity between specific separation or grief reactions and those shown during extinction, the former can be viewed as being organised into a top-level system with the goal of regaining contact with the attachment figure, rather than being a series of disconnected reactions driven by its absence. It is indeed likely that the separation reactions are derived from those found to be shown during extinction of a specific response, but they have also become co-ordinated together in the service of a higher-order goal. One implication of this is likely to be the additional strength and persistence of responses to separation.

The behavioural view does not, of course, address the cognitive processes that are involved in the case of adult human grief. As indicated in the next chapter, these are important when considering the way an individual's grief progresses through time, and whether it is or is not resolved. For example, a common feeling is a need to find meaning in, or an acceptable account of, the loss. This may involve attributing responsibility in the form of blame or guilt, which therefore transforms the separation reaction of anger into a more directed response with its own set of goals. A purely behaviourally based view of grief would be unable to deal with this added complexity.

It can also be argued that cognitive processes provide the principal control in the case of adult grief, so that any theory using animal behaviour as a prototype is bound to be limited. Here we can identify a distinction between views of grief based essentially on extinction (Klinger, 1975) or on separation anxiety (Bowlby, 1980a) on the one hand, and those which emphasise the importance of cognitive restructuring (Marris, 1974; Parkes, 1972; Parkes and Weiss, 1983) on the other. In the second case, the emphasis is on an

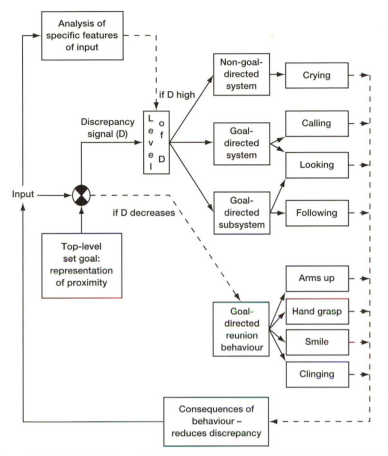

Figure 6.1 Simplified view of child-to-parent attachment behaviour viewed as a control-system. Whenever the input is different from the top-level goal of maintaining proximity with the attachment figure, a signal activates one or more of several possible subsystems which provide alternative or complementary ways of retaining proximity. Which one occurs depends on the circumstances, individual characteristics and age of the child. The usual consequence of such behaviour is to promote reunion with the parent, but more prolonged separation will produce more persistent and invigorated responses.

Source: From Archer, 1992a, p. 99, Figure 5.11; copyright John Archer

overall change in the person's self-concept throughout their grieving. Some accounts of the successful resolution of grief (Chapter 7) point to achieving a number of 'tasks' associated with this cognitive reconstruction process. If this is on the right lines, it would suggest that overall, grief is controlled by the need to construct a view of the self which incorporates the new reality and which assigns a different place and affectional status to the former relationship. This process can be seen as incorporating and being derived from the more automatic responses described by the behaviourally based view of grief described above.

The Dual-Process Model of grief

In the previous section, we noted that there were certain reactions which involved avoiding or mitigating the distress of grief and that these could also be traced to prototypical responses shown by animals during extinction. They ranged from an initial reaction of denying the reality of the loss or feeling unable to take in its implications, to feelings that the deceased is present nearby.

As indicated in Chapter 5, mitigation of grief has often been linked to the Freudian concept of defences (Parkes, 1972, 1986; Janoff-Bulman, 1993): when the limit of psychological pain is reached, the person withdraws psychologically from the situation producing the pain (i.e. from reality). Freud originally implied that defences were maladaptive, a block to positive mental health. Parkes and others considered that, in the case of bereavement, they could be viewed as ways of regulating the quantity of novel, unorganised and in other ways disabling information with which the person has to deal at any one time. He suggested that the various ways of mitigating grief may work like a valve or a lock, only allowing in what can be coped with at that time without mental anguish becoming uncontrollable.

This adaptive view of mitigation reactions may apply only up to a point. In both behaviourally based and cognitive restructuring views of grief, there is general acceptance that the main way in which people neutralise painful stimuli and thoughts associated with the loss is a series of interactions or confrontations with them, known as 'grief work' (see Chapter 7). However, this generates distress, which in turn will lead to avoidance and mitigation reactions. If these reactions become dominant, the person may never confront the loss. Methods of therapy have been designed to enable people who show extreme avoidance reactions to confront the loss (Chapter 5).

M.S. Stroebe and Schut (1993, 1994, 1995) have proposed a Dual-Process Model (DPM) of the grief process which incorporates this tension between approach and avoidance as its basic dimension. The central dynamic aspect of grief is portrayed as involving an oscillation between two processes, one of which is loss-oriented and the other restoration-oriented (Figure 6.2). By 'loss-oriented', they refer to facing grief, confronting stimuli and thoughts associated with the loss (i.e. 'grief work), and in the process gradually breaking the affectional bonds to the deceased. This is the approach part of the Dual-Process Model (DPM). The other – 'restoration-oriented' – part is not simply about avoidance. It concerns the way in which the person attends to other aspects of his or her life (coping with daily life, learning new tasks) instead of being concerned with the loss. In order to do so, it may be necessary actively to avoid thoughts and feelings associated with the loss, to deny aspects of it and to distract oneself from loss-related thoughts. In this model,

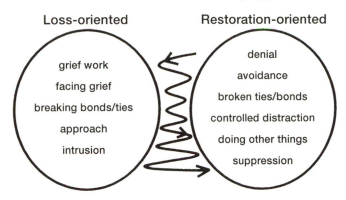

Loss-oriented   **Restoration-oriented**

grief work

facing grief

breaking bonds/ties

approach

intrusion

denial

avoidance

broken ties/bonds

controlled distraction

doing other things

suppression

Figure 6.2 The Dual-Process Model of coping with grief, showing loss-oriented and restoration-oriented styles of coping along with oscillation between them.

Source: From M.S. Stroebe, 1994, Figure 1; reproduced with permission of Margaret Stroebe

avoidance and mitigation are seen not merely as defences against psychological pain but as ways in which people are able to maintain essential activities and to restructure aspects of their lives. During the process, the person may be able to break away from habitual patterns which were bound up with the deceased, and hence break affectional bonds in a different way.

The DPM differs from most other views of grief, from Freud (1917) onwards, because it does not view a confrontation with thoughts and feelings associated with the loss ('grief work': Chapter 7) as *necessary* for its resolution. Stroebe and Schut proposed not only the alternative restoration-oriented coping style, but also that there is an oscillation between the two forms. Oscillation provides a central regulating mechanism in their model (Figure 6.2). Both coping styles are likely to have different sorts of costs, confrontation being physically and mentally exhausting and suppression requiring mental effort and perhaps also having consequences for health (Chapter 7). Oscillation between the two may enable the person to obtain the benefits of each and to minimise the costs of maintaining one strategy for too long. The process is also portrayed as time-related, being biased towards loss-orientation early in the grief process and restoration later on (M.S. Stroebe, 1994b).

There is little available evidence with which to assess the importance of oscillation between the two strategies for adjustment. A study by Powers and Wampold (1994) did find that a measure of the extent to which widows were able to engage in both grief-related and other activities predicted better adjustment when other variables were controlled. However, this study took both sorts of measures concurrently and therefore we can only regard the findings as an interesting starting-point in the evaluation of the importance of a balance between the two coping strategies.

M.S. Stroebe (1994b) suggested that there are two different processes underlying recovery, corresponding to the two coping styles. The first is habituation, involved in loss-orientation, and the second forgetting, involved in the restoration-orientation. As indicated earlier in this chapter, extinction is probably a better characterisation of the first. Perhaps learning of alternative responses is a better characterisation of the second. In the context of bereavement, the establishment of a new relationship would represent an extreme restoration-oriented strategy. Whether this by itself can lead to the resolution of grief is an interesting issue, which will be addressed in the next chapter.

Besides showing oscillation within a single individual, the uses of the two coping styles also differ between individuals. Wegner and Zanakos (1994) have investigated individual differences in the tendency towards suppressing unwanted thoughts and they found this to be a stable variable. Boden and Baumeister (1997) have found differences in the extent to which people can use pleasant thoughts to distract themselves from unwanted events. There are also sex differences in coping strategies (Chapter 13): typically, women are more inclined towards emotion-focused coping and men towards problem-focused coping. In the context of bereavement this is equivalent to loss-oriented and restoration-oriented coping (M.S. Stroebe, 1994b). Consistent with this, Schut *et al.* (1997) found that widows benefited more (in terms of showing a greater decline in distress) from a problem-centred therapy whereas widowers benefited more from an emotion-focused one.

In other cases, culturally induced variations or individual differences will bias individuals towards one or the other coping strategy. At the extreme, there may be such a bias towards one coping style that oscillation does not occur, producing obsessive rumination on the one hand or total avoidance on the other (M.S. Stroebe, 1994b). Another sort of complication – which has been most closely associated with traumatic stress – is for the oscillation process to be disturbed, so that the person has no apparent control over it.

The DPM provides us with a way of integrating some diverse features of the grief process, namely those aspects seemingly derived from continued orientation towards the deceased and those which involve avoidance or mitigation. It also provides an explanation for some puzzling existing findings, such as sex differences in coping strategies. Perhaps, most importantly, it provides an alternative to views of the resolution of grief based solely on confrontation with the loss. As indicated above, and discussed more fully in the next chapter, this mechanism has been at the heart of all existing attempts to characterise the process leading to resolution.

Conclusions

In this chapter, I first considered views of grief which involved simplifying it as a single entity or intervening variable. Evidence from rating-scale studies indicated that there was a measure of internal consistency among commonly used measures of grief. Therefore the use of such a simple measure can

provide a useful strategy for certain types of research, where it is only necessary to assess gross differences in the overall extent of grieving, for example
when examining differences according to the type of relationship (Chapters 9
and 10), or at different times throughout the grief process. However, detailed
studies of the pattern of associations between different grief reactions
revealed that there are several underlying dimensions, and that these are not
consistent across different samples and circumstances.

The main approach which sought to encompass the dynamic nature of the
grief process was the stage view, which, as indicated in Chapter 2, was put
forward before there was much evidence concerning changes over time. The
evidence now indicates that the characteristics of the supposed stages overlap
considerably and intermingle with one another. The time courses of specific
grief reactions differ considerably and these differences do not correspond
with the stage view.

I considered the behaviourally based model of loss proposed by Klinger,
and suggested a modified form of this. The essential starting-point was that
all situations which involve the absence of an expected reward or incentive
produce behavioural responses which can be regarded as the prototype of
grief. These involve the following: more vigorous attention to and approach
towards situations linked with the former incentive; emotional distress and
aggression generated by its absence; periods of immobility, representing disengagement from all responding; and reactions which produce escape from
the frustrating situation, or attention switched to other stimuli. In the case of
separation from, or loss of, an attachment figure it is suggested that these
responses become controlled by higher-order goals derived from the
behavioural system associated with attachment. In the case of adult human
grief, they have become further modified by cognitive process, principally the
overall meaning of the situation.

Both Klinger's behavioural model and views of grief derived from psychoanalysis emphasise confrontation with the loss as the essential process leading
to its resolution. In the Dual-Process Model of Stroebe and Schut, resolution
is viewed as being derived from the interaction – or rather the oscillation
between – two processes: one involves confrontation with loss-related situations; the second concerns other areas of life and is associated with those
processes which produce distraction from and avoidance of grieving. This
theory is novel, and important because it challenges the consensus that confrontation with thoughts and feelings about the loss provides the only path to
recovery from, or resolution of, grief. We discuss this consensus, the evidence
relating to it, and alternatives including the DPM, in the next chapter, on the
resolution of grief.

7   The resolution of grief

←thats a penis

O time! who know'st a lenient hand to lay
Softest on sorrow's wound, and slowly thence
(Lulling to sad repose the weary sense)
The faint pang stealest unperceived away;
On thee I rest my only hope at last,
And think, when thou hast dried the bitter tear
That flows in vain o'er all my soul held dear,
I may look back on every sorrow past,
And meet life's peaceful evening with a smile:
As some lone bird, at day's departing hour,
Sings in the sunbeam, of the transient shower
Forgetful, though its wings are wet the while:–
Yet ah! how much must this poor heart endure,
Which hopes from thee, and thee alone, a cure!
(William Lisle Bowles, 'Time and Grief', in Quiller-Couch, 1919: 579)

Introduction

What brings about the resolution of grief? According to the poet William Lisle Bowles, it is the passing of time, reflecting the phrase that time is a healer. It is commonly believed that it is not time itself that is the healer but some process which occurs during this time. As indicated in the previous chapter, most scientific and medical accounts are in no doubt as to what this process involves. The concept of grief work implies that a change over time leading to resolution can *only* be achieved through a long and difficult process of confronting thoughts of the loss, and that there are no easy routes or short cuts. Keeping thoughts of the deceased out of mind, whether by drugs, distraction or willpower, only delays the inevitable, which is to face up to the loss, to go over and over it in the mind and to unburden oneself by talking to others. Cobb and Lindemann (1943: 819) wrote: 'It seems that the grieving person can delay his grieving period but not avoid it.' Sanders (1989) stated that it is 'detrimental to try to quell the pain of grief'. While it is clear that grieving typically includes a process of repeatedly confronting painful thoughts, and involves a change over time towards resolution, there has been little investigation of whether the first of these two events causes the second. It is probably true to say that until recently few commentators have acknowledged that this might be an issue, so entrenched has been belief in the grief work hypothesis.

The Dual-Process Model (DPM) of M.S. Stroebe and Schut (Chapter 6) is important because it represents a challenge to the grief work hypothesis: both confrontation and an alternative process can play a part in the path towards resolution. The alternative process involves the person carrying on with and reconstructing his or her life. In the DPM, oscillation between the two processes is viewed as the optimum way for most people to achieve resolution, but wide variations between individuals are also envisaged.

There would therefore be circumstances in which people coped with grief predominantly by actively restructuring their lives, and in so doing distracted themselves from loss-related thoughts. It might, as M.S. Stroebe (1994b) suggested, involve gradual forgetting of memories associated with the deceased, through transferring attention to the learning of new activities. This opens the way for a possible alternative means of resolving grief which might have gone unnoticed under the dominant influence of the grief work hypothesis.

The trouble with this speculation is one implicitly recognised by the oscillation process of the DPM, that few alternative activities are sufficiently engaging to be strong enough distracters from loss-related thoughts and emotions. It usually requires much effort to distract oneself from the influence of the loss. Nevertheless, one situation which might provide a sufficient distracter from grief is the establishment of a new relationship of the same type. Remarriage is fairly common not long after a bereavement (at least for men) and in some societies replacement is obligatory. According to the grief work view, this should not help the process of resolution, but according to the DPM it could (although the model does not state that it necessarily would).

There are, therefore, three possible ways of achieving resolution: active confrontation or grief work; an oscillation between something like this and attending to other areas of life; and entering a new relationship or engaging in something sufficiently powerful to replace the memory of the lost loved one.

These alternatives all concern *how* the process of resolution is achieved. It is also necessary to consider *what* is achieved when grief is resolved. At first sight, the end-point of grief may seem fairly straightforward, but this may only be a consensus within modern western societies. Different cultures have different beliefs about the normality of continuing attachments to the deceased. A related issue concerns variations in the time taken to resolve grief. I shall examine both evidence for prolonged grief, and for short periods of grieving. The first questions the inevitability of resolution and the second challenges one assumption of the grief work hypothesis, that grief cannot or should not be foreshortened. One way of defining the end-point of grief is to specify what grieving has to accomplish for resolution to be achieved, in terms of a series of 'tasks'. This concept is closely related to that of grief work, in that the tasks are what has to be achieved and grief work provides the means for doing so

What is the resolution of grief?

The outcome of the process of grief is sometimes referred to as 'recovery' (Parkes and Weiss, 1983), but 'readjustment' 'adjustment', or 'resolution' are perhaps better terms. Recovery implies that the person returns to where they were, whereas resolution and readjustment acknowledge that they can never be the same as before. C.S. Lewis (1961) used the following analogy. He wrote that a person with appendicitis may be said to be 'getting over it', in that they return to more or less as they were before the operation. Someone who has lost a leg may only get over it in the sense that the stump heals, but not in the sense that he or she will ever be as they were before. Lewis said that he felt similar following his bereavement and would 'never be a biped again' (p. 43).

Eliot (1932) argued that the concept of adjustment following bereavement is relative to the values of the particular society. For example, in modern western society, suicide is viewed as an extreme failure to adjust, whereas in traditional Hindu society, failure to commit *suttee* – the ritual suicide of widows – would be viewed as maladjusted.

M.S. Stroebe *et al.* (1992) have argued that current western notions of adjustment emphasise the breaking of the ties with the deceased, viewing signs of continued attachment as problematic. They contrasted this with different patterns of grieving in other cultures such as the Balinese (see Chapter 4), and with the romantic ideal of seeking to sustain bonds to the deceased as an indication of the importance of the relationship and of one's own strength of character. Their final conclusion comes down in favour of making no value-judgements about different patterns of grief, but accepting that 'many forms of expression and behavioral patterns are acceptable reactions to loss' (p. 1211). A similar argument, derived from a consideration of grief within the context of ancestor worship in Japan, was advanced by Klass (1996).

Whilst agreeing that existing views of adjustment may have neglected cultural and individual variation, this position implies that there is no common end-point to the process of grief, and what counts as adjustment is being defined by cultural values. For the post-modernist, this may not pose a problem, but for a Darwinian view of human nature (Chapter 4) it does. There will always be the criterion of inclusive fitness by which to assess different patterns of behaviour. Although grief itself is a maladaptive process, from the viewpoint of lifetime reproductive success, there would have been selection pressures for some sort of return to previous levels of functioning in terms of maintenance activities and sexuality. The problem, as I outlined it in Chapter 4, is that the mechanisms enabling social attachments are insufficiently flexible for this process to occur quickly. Prolonged ties to the deceased would be maladaptive in terms of lifetime fitness, since they would hinder maintenance activities to other kin and renewed interest in replacing the lost relationship. Therefore, ideally, grief would involve a process of change through time. There may be individual variability but, from the Darwinian viewpoint, prolonged grief is maladaptive compared to a shorter period of grief followed by recovery of functioning.

Even Eliot (1932), who recognised that definitions of adjustment were relative to societal values, defined various outcomes in terms of success or failure. He classified adjustment into four categories, failure, partial failure, partial success and success. Failure included suicide or early death, seemingly[1] the most fitness-depleting outcome from a Darwinian viewpoint. He also viewed continued obsession with the deceased as failure (a view inconsistent with the argument of M.S. Stroebe *et al.*). Partial failure included self-blame or isolation, in line with evidence indicating that self-blame (Chapter 5) and lack of social support (Doka, 1989a; Stylianos and Vachon, 1993; Vachon *et al.*, 1982a) are associated with more pronounced distress. Success included integration of the memories of the deceased into the person's current life, with constructive memorials, or else entering into a new relationship. Eliot emphasised that combinations of categories could occur, so that success may be marred to some extent by self-blame.

Therefore, in answer to the question of what the resolution of grief involves, we can refer to returning to a normal level of functioning in everyday tasks, the absence of the distress associated with grief (memories of the deceased no longer being painful), and a change in identity to accommodate the new reality.

Variations in the time-course of grief

Variations in the time involved to resolve grief include, at the one extreme, cases where this is not achieved (see previous section) and, at the other, very short periods of grieving, which would seem to challenge the assumption, based on the grief work hypothesis, that grief cannot or should not be foreshortened.

As indicated in Chapter 6, it is certainly the case that *on average* people show a reduction in all sorts of indices of grief as time passes. However, this typical or average picture hides cases where grief has continued for years, and those where minimal levels of distress have occurred (Lund *et al.*, 1993; Rubin, 1991–2; Vachon *et al.*, 1982a, Wortman and Silver, 1989, 1992; Zisook and Shuchter, 1986). Levy *et al.* (1994) identified four or five different patterns in the changing levels of distress and depression bereaved people showed with time. Among these were consistently high and consistently low ones.

Bowlby (1980a) commented that there were many instances where people

---

1 But not necessarily: see Daly and Wilson (1994).

do not seem to achieve full resolution following spousal bereavement, and particularly that many widows never seem to fully recover the sense of well-being they experienced when they were married. Support for this view comes from the large-scale prospective study of Wortman *et al.*(1993), who found that it took bereaved spouses about a decade to approach non-bereaved controls on life-satisfaction measures, and about twice as long for depression to decline to control levels. However, these measures are likely in part to reflect chronic loneliness, missing a close personal relationship as opposed to missing the particular person: older people (Lund, 1989; Lund *et al.*, 1993), and particularly older widowers (Gallagher-Thompson *et al.*, 1993), are at risk in this respect. Hofer's two-process theory (Chapter 4) distinguished reactions to loss of a specific relationship from a response to deprivation of hidden 'regulators' provided by that type of relationship. Thus, if the social regulators provided by a marital relationship are not replaced, the deprivation-led aspects of process will continue for years. This can either be viewed as part of grieving or as a separate process.

Peppers and Knapp (1980) remarked that, following perinatal death, some mothers never completely resolved their grief, which is seen as being 'tucked away', experienced as a dull ache in the background, but ready to surface from time to time. This was referred to as 'shadow grief', and attributed to the lack of opportunity to express perinatal grief to sympathetic listeners.

Another explanation for prolonged grief is that it results from a particular coping style which involves the person constantly dwelling on the loss and its implications: 'rumination' (Martin and Tesser, 1996; Nolen-Hoeksema, 1996). It is distinguished from grief work because there is no progression. In terms of the DPM, it is an extremely loss-oriented strategy. It is ineffective in resolving grief, being associated with poorer longer-term adjustment following bereavement (Nolen-Hoeksema, McBride and Larson, 1997; Tait and Silver, 1989), and more generally with depression (Nolen-Hoeksema, 1987; Nolen-Hoeksema, Parker and Larson, 1994; see Chapters 8 and 13). Queen Victoria's prolonged grief for Prince Albert is an oft-quoted historical example of prolonged ruminative grief (see Chapter 10).

Prolonged grief may also occur when the circumstances surrounding the loss are such that they hinder or prevent its successful resolution. Sudden, unexplained or traumatic deaths (Wortman and Silver, 1987, 1989; Rynearson, 1987), and death of a child (Fish, 1986; Smith and Borgers, 1988–9; see Chapter 11), are all associated with a pattern of continuous grieving. When Charles and Emma Darwin's eldest daughter, Annie (Figure 7.1), died of a fever at the age of 10, Emma's reaction was described as follows:

> For Emma the wound never healed. She hoped 'to attain some feeling of submission to the will of Heaven', but it is doubtful whether she ever managed it. The small keepsakes she put away and cherished through the years – the childish notes, the half-finished woolwork, the locks of hair –

Figure 7.1 Annie Darwin, whose death at the age of ten affected Charles and Emma
  Darwin for many years afterwards, and illustrates the longlasting grief
  often experienced following the death of a child.

Source: Photograph courtesy of the British Heritage; obtained from Cambridge University
Library

were a constant reminder of her favourite daughter, wrenched away at
Easter.

(Desmond and Moore, 1991: 386)

Similarly, for Charles, the mental picture of his daughter was strongly evoked
even 30 years after her death, causing his emotions to 'overflow' (Desmond
and Moore, 1991: 651).

In both the case of traumatic deaths and the death of a child, problems of
resolution arise because the events are particularly resistant to incorporation
into the person's personal world. Explanations derived from studies of traumatic stress and victimisation (Hopkins and Thompson, 1984; Horowitz,
1976; Horowitz *et al.*, 1993; Janoff-Bulman and Frieze, 1983) emphasise the

difficulties caused by not being able to accept the traumatic event, which then sets up an alternating cycle of uncontrollable memories and extreme avoidance. This cycle is regarded as standing in the way of assimilating and coming to terms with the event.

The findings considered so far question the inevitability of the resolution of grief. At the other extreme are instances when people are resilient in the face of serious losses (Wortman and Silver, 1989). Studies reviewed in the next chapter indicate that a personality characteristic involving being able to meet the consequences of a loss in a determined and optimistic way is associated with lower distress following bereavement. A related characteristic, the degree to which the person sees purpose and order in life and seeks to pursue and obtain worthwhile goals, is also associated with a more positive outcome following bereavement and other major stressors.

Other reasons for resilience include strong religious beliefs[2] (Bohannon, 1991; Levy *et al.*, 1994) and social support (Levy *et al.*, 1994; McIntosh, Silver and Wortman, 1993; Vachon *et al.*, 1982a,b) provided by the family or community. Both of these were apparent in Ablon's (1971) study of the Samoan community in the west of the US (Chapter 4). It appeared from respondents' accounts that they suffered less and had shorter periods of grief than did European North Americans, and that this arose from social and financial support, having multiple attachments and a fatalistic attitude to death engendered by their religion. Although one respondent was quoted as saying that Samoans did not experience grief like European Americans did (Chapter 4), we should be cautious of this report for two reasons: first, it was made 5 years after the loss, at a time when most of the (female) respondents had remarried; second, it is likely to be heavily influenced by what Samoans thought the Samoan reaction to grief *ought* to be.

Other cross-cultural evidence on the shortening of the grief process is difficult to interpret. One often cited example (Chapter 4) concerns the Navajo native Americans, among whom mourning is limited to four days (Miller and Schoenfeld, 1973). After this, the bereaved person is expected neither to show grief nor speak of the deceased or the loss. The question raised by such examples is whether grief really is resolved by these prohibitions, or whether it emerges, albeit in a distorted form, at a later time. The original report suggested that pathological forms of grief did occur in the future, notably in the form of somatic problems and high levels of depression. However, the empirical basis for this was unclear. Other evidence for the existence of delayed grief of this sort is mixed: Sanders (1979–80) did report a pattern consistent with delayed grief in people showing 'compulsive optimism' (interpreted as suppression of emotional reactions), whereas other studies suggest that this is rare (Wortman and Silver, 1992; Middleton *et al.*, 1996).

---

2 These studies did find an association, although overall the findings are mixed.

There is, therefore, abundant evidence of prolonged, apparently unresolved grieving, and some evidence that certain coping styles and situational variables can dramatically reduce the period of grief. The cross-cultural evidence concerning whether cultural restraints on grief can be effective in shortening it was uncertain, since there remains the possibility that depressive and health-related problems surface later.

The 'tasks of grief'

Associated with the concept of grief work is the idea that there are specific tasks to achieve during grieving. The best known are those of Worden (1981) and of Parkes and Weiss (1983), although a third set was suggested by van der Wal (1989–90). The tasks define end-points, what resolution or steps on the way to resolution entails. In all three accounts, grief work is the proposed means to these ends. Although the tasks are not meant to be sequential, both Worden, and Parkes and Weiss viewed the first of their tasks as a necessary step for the others: according to Worden (1981), it is possible to have incomplete bereavement when only one or two of the tasks have been achieved.

The present discussion is confined to the two best-known sets of tasks, concentrating on the more straightforward three tasks suggested by Parkes and Weiss, but also referring briefly to Worden's four tasks. Neither set of tasks was derived from research evidence. Those of Parkes and Weiss were intended as a statement of the process of 'recovery' (resolution). Worden's were intended to be useful for the clinician dealing with bereaved people, and he emphasised their advantages over the phase view of grief.

Worden's first task involves accepting the reality of the loss, i.e. overcoming any tendencies to deny it, and the second involves working through the pain of grief. These are more restatements of grief work than of end-points to be achieved. His third and fourth tasks have more in common with those of Parkes and Weiss, emphasising a change in identity and emotional detachment from the deceased. They are more useful in specifying the end-points of grief.

The first task suggested by Parkes and Weiss is intellectual acceptance of the loss, the need to develop a satisfactory account of what has happened. This is regarded as necessary but not sufficient for later resolution. The other two tasks involve features that specify what resolution involves.

Although Parkes and Weiss provided only a brief outline, other evidence indicates that intellectual acceptance of a loss is particularly difficult in three sets of circumstances: first when there is room for doubt that the death has occurred, for example when no body has been found, in particular when the person is missing but presumed dead (Hunter, 1986; Vormbrock, 1993); second, where the circumstances are such that someone can readily be held responsible, for example in cases of murder, suicide or a motor vehicle crash (Rynearson, 1987; Masters, Friedman and Getzel, 1988; Range and Niss, 1990); third, where the circumstances are traumatic, and there are vivid memories of the event that become difficult to integrate with the person's usual expectations of life, again occurring in the cases of murder, suicide and accidents. Constructing an acceptable account of a loss will also depend on how the person characteristically views causal events in the world (Chapter 8).

There is some empirical support for a link between better adjustment and being able to find an acceptable meaning for the loss. Gallagher *et al.*(1989) reported that 3 months after a spousal bereavement, those older adults who viewed a search for meaning in the loss as more helpful had lower levels of grief. Among a sample of young adults who had lost a parent, those who were able to answer the question 'Why?' showed less intense grief than those unable to find an answer or who attributed the death to chance or to luck (Schwartzberg and Janoff-Bulman, 1991). McIntosh *et al.* (1993) reported that being able to find meaning in the sudden death of a child was associated with lower distress and higher well-being, and Powers and Wampold (1994) found comparable results among a sample of older widows. Similar associations have been found following other traumatic life events, for example among women who were incest victims during childhood (Silver, Boon and Stones, 1983), adult survivors of sexual assault (Harvey *et al.*, 1992) and stroke patients (Thompson, 1991).

These studies all involved concurrent measures of finding meaning and adjustment or distress, so that we cannot necessarily conclude that it is the lack of meaning that impedes adjustment. It could be that higher levels of distress produce difficulties finding a meaning, or that both result from more intense grief.

A finding by Downey, Silver and Wortman (1990) raises the question of whether it is necessary to develop an acceptable account of the loss: 45 per cent of parents bereaved by sudden infant death were not concerned with attributing responsibility for the death 3 weeks after it had happened. Those who attributed the death to the actions of themselves or others (i.e. producing an unacceptable account which blames the self or others) showed higher levels of distress, but these initial attributions did not predict subsequent changes in distress. These findings suggest that attributional processes and distress are linked because they both reflect the overall strength of grief, and that initial attributions do not predict later adjustment. In the studies reviewed above on meaning and distress, these two measures may similarly be associated because they both reflect the intensity of grief, and not because an adequate account leads to lowered distress.

Parkes and Weiss' second task is emotional acceptance of the loss, which is achieved when reminders are no longer painful and distressing. This is generally seen as the outcome of repeated confrontation with thoughts associated with the loss, i.e. grief work. It is important to recognise that it is the reminders and thoughts of the deceased ceasing to be painful that is important, and not that the person ceases to think about the deceased. In answer to the question 'What would indicate your grief recovery has taken place?', bereaved students mostly replied that it would be when they could think or talk about the death without getting upset (Balk, 1991b). Dembo, Leviton and Wright (1956) expressed the same point by stating that adjustment occurs when positive features from the lost relationship can be incorporated into the person's present life, and the past can be viewed with tenderness rather than pain. This implies a change in the relationship with the lost person, in other words a redefinition of attachment rather than detachment.

In a study of older widows and widowers, Moss and Moss (1984–5) found that the continuing tie with the deceased proved supportive in many cases. It was maintained, despite a deep sense of loss and recurrent feelings of grief, in the form of welcome memories and associations with everyday activities which were once shared. These memories still served as a focus for care and affection towards the deceased. Moss and Moss emphasised the normality of this tie: it formed 'a nourishing link to the past'. Many spiritual and religious beliefs are based on maintaining such links, for example in the ancestor worship of Shintoism (Klass, 1996; Yamamoto *et al.*, 1969). They would also be encouraged and flourish in cultures which emphasise enduring commitment and eternal love, such as the romantic age of the nineteenth century in Britain and North America (M.S. Stroebe *et al.*, 1992; Rosenblatt, 1983).

Goin, Burgoyne and Goin (1979) described the continuing attachment to the dead husband of two widows who otherwise appeared both contented and normal in a psychiatric sense. In one case, the woman had married again, but still maintained an attachment to the first husband 7 years after her remarriage. The other case involved a 49-year-old woman who had been widowed for 6 years, and who was independent and gregarious. She talked to women at work as if her husband were waiting for her to come home, and she did things to please her dead husband.

The crucial aspect of the second task of grief is the changed affective quality of thoughts of the deceased, from negative to positive. Since a lower level of distress is the way in which adjustment is defined in many studies, fully achieving the second task of grief is by definition to meet one common criterion for the resolution of grief. However, some of the examples of a continuing but redefined attachment to the deceased do suggest that, although the affective quality of thoughts towards them has changed, the bereaved cannot be said to be detached from the deceased. Freud (1913, 1917) viewed detachment as the end-point of grieving, a view followed in later accounts (Lindemann, 1944; Bowlby, 1980a), but not by some psychoanalytical writers who emphasised instead that identification enables a healthy representation of the deceased to occur (Klass, 1987–8; Volkan, 1981). These different views parallel the cultural differences in the concept of adjustment discussed in an earlier section.

The third task of grief, gaining a new identity, does imply detachment from the deceased, and yet it can also be viewed as occurring side-by-side with the second task. It involves a change in the person's assumptions about themselves so that these fit with the new reality. The subjective sense of what a change of identity involves is well summed up in Lynne Caine's best-selling personal account of widowhood:

> But today I am someone else. I am stronger, more independent. I have more understanding, more sympathy. A different perspective. I have a quiet love for Martin. I have passionate, poignant memories of him. He will always be part of me. But – if I were to meet Martin today . . .?
> Would I love him?
> I ask myself. Startled. What brought the question to my mind?
> I know. I ask it because I am a different woman.
>
> (Caine, 1974: 222, 1975 edn)

This excerpt describes both the redefinition of attachment to the deceased and gaining a new identity as having been achieved simultaneously. It also portrays positive feelings, raising the related issue of whether bereavement can enable people to feel more positively about themselves and their place in the world. This possibility has been emphasised in connection with a wider range of life changes by Collins, Taylor and Skokan (1990).

Several researchers (Calhoun and Tedeschi, 1989–90; Hogan, personal communication, 1991; Kessler, 1987) have argued that most accounts of grief overlook the potential for personal growth inherent in tragic experiences. Using a rating scale derived from the ways bereaved people talked about their experiences, Hogan found a group of attributes representing 'personal growth', for example a positive outlook on life, becoming more tolerant, more compassionate, and optimistic. Positive features were also common in interviews undertaken by Kessler, and by Calhoun and Tedeschi, for example new freedoms, reaffirming religious faith, enriching the value of life in the present and focusing on the future. Again, these were viewed as signs of personal growth. Similarly, most of a sample of college students who had experienced the death of a parent found positive aspects in the experience which helped their personal development (Schwartzberg and Janoff-Bulman, 1991). Most of another sample of students bereaved over the past 3 years said that they had experienced a positive change in their life goals (Edmonds and Hooker, 1992).

These positive changes occurred alongside the negative aspects of grief, and they could be linked with the gradual change in identity which Parkes and Weiss identified as the third task of grief. There are, however, some other findings that question whether such positive changes are connected with adjustment, measured by lack of distress and negative emotions. Lehman *et al.* (1993) found that people who had lost a spouse or child in a motor vehicle crash 4–7 years before, generally reported (in an interview) more positive than negative life changes. Increased self-confidence was the most common category (in about a third). Others involved enjoying focusing on the present and a greater appreciation of life (about a quarter each). In this study, the numbers of positive changes a person reported were unrelated both to their adjustment and psychological symptoms. Positive changes were also unrelated to either positive or negative emotions, suggesting that the positive emotions sometimes reported in studies of bereavement (Wortman and Silver, 1987, 1992; Bonanno and Keltner, 1997) are different from the experience of positive life changes.

In contrast to these findings, there is a widespread assumption that changes in identity and meaning in life represent an integral part of the resolution of grief. It is inherent in the tasks of grief and in accounts based on these. Harvey *et al.* (1992) viewed losses as forcing people to rethink beliefs about themselves and the world, a process that is achieved by constructing a series of accounts, which gradually provide the loss with meaning, and produce a changed viewpoint of the self and the world. Yet Lehman *et al.* (1993) found that measures that can reasonably be said to reflect the outcome of such a process were not related to the usual measures of adjustment. They have therefore raised the possibility that changes in views of the self and the world may not be as central to the lessening of emotional distress as is widely assumed.

Overall, assessing the three tasks of grief has proved to be difficult. Although concurrent measures indicated that forming an acceptable account was associated with less distress and greater adjustment, evidence from the only longitudinal study suggested that initial attributions to an unacceptable source do not in fact predict greater distress in the long term. The second task, emotional acceptance of the loss, involved a change in affective quality associated with the thoughts of the deceased. In this sense it represents a form of attachment to the memory of the deceased which is no longer painful. Since adjustment following grief is often assessed by the degree of emotional distress, achieving this must, by definition, involve adjustment. Accompanying the decline in distress, and in many accounts central to achieving this, are changes in the person's view of him or herself and the world. Although there is evidence that the positive thoughts likely to be associated with such a process do occur during grieving, the one prospective study found that they did not predict lowered distress.

The concept of grief work

We have already noted that many writers on bereavement have assumed that grief work is central to resolution, and that this belief is derived from psychoanalytic theory. Major therapeutic methods have been devised in order to deal with blocked or frozen grieving in analysis: for example, Volkan (1981) referred to breaking the seal through a procedure called 're-grief theory', which is a brief method of psychotherapy involving an ordered sequence of confronting feelings about the deceased.

A number of writers on the subject of grief have raised a note of caution regarding the assumption that grief work is essential for the resolution of grief (Bonanno and Keltner, 1997; Prigerson *et al.*, 1996b; Rosenblatt, 1983;

Scheper-Hughes, 1992; Shackleton, 1984; M.S. Stroebe, 1992–3; M.S. Stroebe and W. Stroebe, 1990, 1991; Wortman and Silver, 1989, 1992). These are all fairly recent accounts. However, as early as 1957, Volkart and Michael, who examined grief from a cross-cultural perspective, cautioned that 'the extent to which 'grief work' comprises a formidable personal problem must be assessed in terms of context' (pp. 302–3), i.e. the cultural context.

Grief work is difficult to define, making it hard to distinguish from related processes such as yearning (Chapter 5) and rumination. Rumination is the obsessive dwelling upon the loss without any assessment or progression, which is associated with a depressive outcome (see above). Even in those cases where grief work specifically refers to a search for meaning in the loss, there is still the question of whether the outcome is affected by these attributions being negative or positive. Negative attributions are likely to be associated with poor coping (Chapter 8).

M.S. Stroebe (1992–3) argued that these problems make evaluation of whether grief work necessarily facilitates adjustment difficult on the basis of existing empirical evidence. Their own longitudinal study, carried out in Tübingen on a sample of bereaved men and women in their fifties (M.S. Stroebe and W. Stroebe, 1991), did address this problem. They defined grief work as the degree to which their respondents suppressed or confronted grief, measured by a 6-item questionnaire and by interview questions. We should note that the questionnaire statements (M.S. Stroebe and W. Stroebe, 1990) concerned the personal suppression of grief, rather than the extent to which thoughts and feelings were shared with others. As indicated in Chapter 5, this distinction is likely to be crucial in terms of outcome, the expression of negative emotions generally being associated with a poor outcome and sharing experiences with a positive one.

The measures were administered 4–6 months and 14 months after the death. Adjustment was assessed by a rating scale, and also the Beck Depression Inventory, administered at the same times and at 2 years after the death. Among the women, the degree of confronting or suppressing grief bore no relation to the extent of improvement shown between 4–6 months and 2 years after the loss. Among the men, the more they confronted rather than suppressed or distracted themselves from grief, the greater was their increase in adjustment and decrease in depression between 4–6 months and 2 years. This sex difference in the impact of grief work was not associated with any difference in the rate of recovery, nor was there a sex difference in preference for avoidance rather than confrontation.

These results support the view that confronting grief – 'grief work' – is a mediator of better adjustment for men, but the absence of such a relationship for women casts doubt on its generality, and on the assumed general role for grief work in the process of adjustment.

M.S. Stroebe and W. Stroebe (1991) went on to suggest that individual women have different coping styles but, when viewed overall, those involving grief work are no better than those involving suppression. They suggested that the men had more opportunities for distraction (since the sample was derived from a society with traditional values) and that their cultural expectations would discourage disclosure and sharing negative emotions. Both distraction – through work, hobbies or thinking of something else – and seeking privacy if upset, are characteristic ways in which men seek to manage their grief (Cook, 1988; Glick *et al.*, 1974). They can be viewed as stemming from the avoidance of emotional expression associated with the traditional masculine role (Brearley, 1986; Thompson and Pleck, 1986). In terms of the DPM, men are seen as more 'restoration-oriented' whereas women are more 'loss-oriented' (M.S. Stroebe and Schut, 1994, 1995: see also Chapter 13).

M.S. Stroebe (1992–3) speculated that distraction and avoiding sharing emotions represent an extreme lack of grief work, and that when taken this far, they will be detrimental to adjustment. This was later viewed in terms of extreme imbalance in the direction of a restoration-oriented strategy (M.S. Stroebe and Schut, 1994, 1995). To be convincing as an explanation of their particular findings, this argument would need to rest on a difference between the sexes in grief work measures. However, since only non-disclosure was significantly higher for men than women, yet distraction and suppression were the measures most associated with poor adjustment in the men, this was not the case. Acknowledging this, M.S. Stroebe and W. Stroebe (1991) raised the possibility that there are sex differences in the effectiveness of the same strategies. This seems at first sight unconvincing, as it would mean that the same degree of suppression and distraction would be detrimental to adjustment for men, yet have no influence on women's adjustment. Perhaps women endorse these strategies in terms of trying to use them, but through circumstances are unable to do so. Obviously, this research has opened up important questions for the future, and in Chapter 8 I discuss it further in relation to evidence from psychological studies on the consequences of suppressing thoughts.

Another group of researchers measured grief work in a different way and found evidence of an association with better adjustment. In a study of the impact of religious beliefs on coping with the loss resulting from sudden infant death, McIntosh *et al.* (1993) used a measure of 'cognitive processing' which involved the extent to which the person had vivid thoughts about the deceased and the extent to which these had been voluntary, thus implying some form of attempting to work though the loss. This measure was associated with lower concurrent distress and higher well-being, and it predicted a lower level of later distress and a greater sense of well-being 18 months later.

A further research group assessed the grief work hypothesis in two different ways. In their first study (Bonanno *et al.*, 1995), they measured the extent to which a sample of maritally bereaved people reported low negative emotion yet had high measures of heart rate at around 6 months after their loss. Bonanno *et al.* referred to this as negative dissociation, reasoning that such individuals would be avoiding unpleasant feelings of emotion. They found that negative dissociation was associated with minimal signs of grief both at

6 and 14 months, and that although their levels of somatic symptoms were high initially, by 14 months they had dropped to a low level. These results clearly do not support the view that avoidance of emotions following bereavement is associated with poor adjustment. Indeed, they indicate the opposite, that emotional avoidance is an effective way of coping.

The study by Bonanno and Keltner (1997), described in Chapter 5, involved observing the degree of expression of negative emotions among a sample of conjugally bereaved people, and assessing the relation of these emotions to subsequent changes in grief and health. Greater expression of emotions predicted more intense grief and poorer health, when initial grief and emotional feelings were controlled. The researchers concluded that their findings were in the opposite direction to predictions based on the grief work hypothesis. They did, however, add the qualification that their study (like the previous one) did not address the *disclosure* of emotions to others. As indicated above, the two sorts of measures may have very different influences on adjustment.

Both the Bonanno studies cast doubt on a version of the grief work hypothesis that concentrates on the supposed value of outward expression of emotions. However, it is also apparent that the concept of grief work is not always restricted to emotional expression.

A follow-up to the Stroebes' Tübingen study, undertaken in Utrecht (Schut *et al.*, 1994), concentrated on the *disclosure* of emotions. Using a 5-item scale, they examined the pattern of correlations between this and distress at four times after the loss (4, 11, 18 and 25 months). They found that the only earlier measure which predicted later distress was earlier distress, and that the only earlier measure that predicted later disclosure was earlier disclosure. High scores for disclosure initially did not predict later distress, either for men or for women. These results clearly do not support the view that talking to others helps one come to terms with a loss and, by themselves, they cast doubt on a version of the grief work hypothesis that emphasises *disclosure* of feelings and thoughts about grief to others.

However, there are two sets of results which do seem to support an association between disclosure and adjustment. In another analysis of the longitudinal sample of mothers who had experienced the loss of a child from sudden infant death syndrome, Lepore *et al.* (1996) found that mothers who initially reported more intrusive thoughts talked more about the loss at 3 months, and showed lower rates of depression at 18 months than mothers who initially reported fewer intrusive thoughts. These findings, which were reversed if there were social constraints on talking about the loss, suggest that being able to share intrusive thoughts about the loss with others was therapeutic in the long run.

Pennebaker and his colleagues have extensively studied the impact on physical health of suppressing or confronting traumatic thoughts. Pennebaker and O'Heeron (1984) investigated a sample of spouses of suicide and accident victims, and found that the more they discussed the death with friends, the less they ruminated over it, i.e. constantly thought about the spouse and were unable to put him or her out of mind. More confiding and less rumination was also associated with fewer health-related problems, irrespective of the number of close friends.

Further experimental studies (Pennebaker and Beall, 1986; Pennebaker, Kiecolt-Glaser and Glaser, 1988) showed that students who disclosed traumatic experiences and their feelings about them in a written form had fewer subsequent visits to the health centre, a decline in systolic blood pressure and indications of more efficient immune system functioning than students who disclosed less, or wrote about trivial events. It is also interesting to note that writing a 'continuous letter' to the deceased forms an important part of a therapeutic procedure aimed to replace traditional mourning rituals (van der Hart and Goossens, 1987).

Murray and Segal (1994) used Pennebaker's procedure to compare written with vocal expression of feelings about traumatic events. They found that both methods had equivalent moderate positive therapeutic effects in terms of being associated with a subsequent reduction in the painfulness of the topic concerned. However, we should note that in this study there were no long-term effects on health, as assessed by a health questionnaire. A similar lack of impact of disclosure on health measures was reported by Greenberg and Stone (1990, 1992), although they did find greater improvement in health 2 months later for people who had written about severe traumas.

Pennebaker (1988) initially explained his findings in terms of the effort ('inhibition work') required to actively suppress ongoing thoughts and feelings. This effort is reflected in the short term by phasic autonomic changes such as blood pressure and heart-rate increases, and in the long term by stress-related diseases. Reducing the inhibition by disclosure therefore reduces physiological activity. However, as later became apparent (Pennebaker, 1997), equivalent benefits are derived from writing about previously disclosed traumas and those which remain undisclosed. In fact Greenberg and Stone (1990, 1992) found that their participants experienced *more* distress when they wrote about previously disclosed traumas than when they wrote about undisclosed ones, suggesting that in this case talking to others had intensified the negative feelings associated with the event.

Pennebaker's later research, involving linguistic analysis (see below), suggested that it is the integration and cognitive reorganisation of the event that expression enables which leads to the health changes. Pennebaker (1988) suggested that the important feature – for physiological regulation anyway – is a reframing of the event, and finding meaning in it. We have already noted that the construction of meaning is frequently regarded as important in the resolution of grief. Pennebaker added that disclosure of thoughts in the form of spoken or written language is important because it converts the experience into a symbolic form which aids its reorganisation and assimilation.

Pennebaker's more recent research has involved precise linguistic analysis of writing about personal events. A reanalysis of six of his previous studies

(Pennebaker, Mayne and Francis, 1997), found that people whose writings were characterised by an increase in the level of insight or words about causes over the writing period showed an improvement in health. The researchers concluded that it was the *change* in thinking patterns over time, not simply thinking about the loss, that predicted improved health. Indeed, they characterised thinking without cognitive restructuring as equivalent to rumination, which is associated with poor recovery (see above and Chapters 8 and 13).

There is, however, a problem in applying Pennebaker's research to the resolution of grief, and that is that his outcome measures have mainly involved physiological and health measures. Pennebaker *et al.* (1997) found that the same thinking patterns that predicted better health in the six studies did not predict a decline in self-reported distress. However, in a study of people who had lost partners through AIDS, they did find that four measures from the linguistic analysis which did not predict physical health did predict long-term psychological adjustment. These measures were interpreted as an absence of looking back, and of confronting the bereavement: they involved frequent use of words suggesting death, low use of past-tense verbs, increasing positive affect, and decreasing use of unique words.

Pennebaker's research raises a number of possibilities, principally that there are different cognitive mediators of the psychological adjustment to bereavement and of the accompanying changes in physical health. The implications of their research for the concept of grief work are that they have sought to characterise those cognitive processes which are beneficial following a traumatic event. For health-related changes, these involve the reordering of thoughts that occurs as a result of successful confrontation with memories of the loss. This is consistent with earlier characterisations of the successful resolution of grief: Fisher (1984) emphasised the modification of dominant plans for action (which of course include the deceased). Eliot (1946), who was offering guidelines for aiding recovery from war bereavements, described much the same process in more detail:

> If, whenever a memory arises, it is forced out of mind without being revised, reseen, and revalued, it is not fully reassimilated, and it may continue to obsess the personality by day or by night. If, by contrast, such a memory is spontaneously welcomed, and if after a moment of poignant recognition of loss, it is then put back in its new place as a bit of one's valued past, possessing now the very real reality of an acceptable and indestructible memory, it is possible to relax the tensions associated with it, and to move on into actuality, perhaps strengthened by an extension of previously tied up energies. The prompt, relaxed airing and rehearsal (to oneself) of memories as they arise will give opportunity to reset them in their new context, as objects of the past, with appropriate sentiments associated, but not as fears or fetishes or fixations.
>
> (Eliot, 1946: 5)

This description attempts to get to the heart of what the process of resolution involves, by breaking it down into a series of assimilations of discrete memories associated with the deceased and the former life, and changing their personal and emotional significance. These individual assimilations provide the building-blocks for the overall change in identity that the process of grief involves. Whether this process is inevitably successful in bringing about the overall change which can be seen as resolution, and whether the same end-point can be achieved in different ways, are crucial questions needing to be answered by future research. A number of researchers whose work is reviewed in this section have made important contributions to defining what is and is not involved, and have helped to move away from the concept of grief work to a clearer analysis of exactly what may be helpful, and what may be detrimental, for future recovery. The Stroebes' findings also raise the possibility of alternative routes to the resolution of grief. We discuss one likely candidate in the next section.

Can a new relationship resolve grief?

W. Stroebe and M.S. Stroebe (1987a) noted that grief is more short-lived in societies where others are available as a replacement for the dead spouse. For example, in an account of life in the central African Ubena tribes, Culwick and Culwick (1935) referred to very transient grief, with the widow taking up life where she left it but in the home of her next husband. Wrigley (1969), commenting on the parish records of early nineteenth-century Britain, remarked that remarriages within weeks rather than months of a wife's death were not uncommon. Similar observations are made in other historical accounts (Pearson, 1980; Mitterauer and Sieder, 1982: 61). In an anthropological study of the Siriono Indians, Holmberg (1950) found that a widow or widower would remarry within a few days of the former spouse's death. In two out of three cases this was the eldest brother, which is reminiscent of the Hebrew custom of the widow marrying the dead husband's brother (Averill and Nunley, 1988), referred to in the Old Testament:

> If bretheren dwell together, and one of them die, and have no child, the wife of the dead shall not marry without unto a stranger: her husband's brother shall go in unto her, and take her to him to wife, and perform the duty of an husband's brother unto her.
>
> (Deuteronomy 25:5; *The Holy Bible*, 1949)

In this case, remarriage is an obligation for the widow. In other cultures it is strongly encouraged: for example, in the US Samoan community (Ablon, 1971), even those women badly scarred in a community dance-hall fire were remarried a year later.

These examples are all taken from traditional, collectivist societies, and it is likely that it is here that we should find the strongest pressure from kin and others to replace the lost spouse (Lofland, 1985). In western societies, although there is not such explicit encouragement, there are many instances in which the lost relationship is voluntarily replaced fairly soon after the loss. In the first San Diego study (Shuchter, 1986; Zisook *et al.*, 1987a) there was a 10 per cent remarriage rate after 13 months, rising to about a quarter in the third and fourth years. When asked about dating, 47 per cent of the sample expressed an interest 1 month after the loss, and this increased (but not significantly so) over the course of 4 years (Zisook *et al.*, 1987a). About half the sample said that they still enjoyed sex 1 month after the loss, and this rose to 70 per cent by 4 years (Shuchter, 1986). Comparable results were reported in the second San Diego study, although the questions were slightly different: a quarter reported having positive thoughts about remarriage at 2 months, rising to 43 per cent at 7 and 13 months (Shuchter and Zisook, 1993). These findings indicate that an appreciable proportion of the sample were at least interested in the possibility of another relationship.

These studies did not separate the figures for men and women. Bowlby (1980a) commented on the much higher rate of remarriage among widowers than widows: he pointed out that in the Harvard study of Glick *et al.* (1974), by the end of a year after bereavement, half the men had remarried or were likely to do so but that this applied to only 18 per cent of the widows. Other evidence supports the general trend for men to remarry sooner than women. A later analysis of the second San Diego study (Schneider *et al.*, 1996) reported that 61 per cent of the men and 19 per cent of the women were either remarried or involved in a serious relationship by 25 months after the death. Two earlier studies reported the average or median times for remarriage: this was 3 years for men and 7 years for women among a middle-aged sample (Schlesinger and Macrae, 1971) and 1.7 years for men and 3.5 years for women among a wider age range from 20 to over 65 years (Cleveland and Gianturco, 1976).

Although remarriage cannot replace the person who has died, it can replace many of the features of the married state which might be particularly missed – the status it confers, sexual relations, companionship, and in traditional societies a domestic or a provider role. Such cases highlight the distinction between loss of a role, which can be replaced, and loss of an individual, which cannot. It is likely that replacements will be more likely to shorten the grief process in societies where social attachments are more diverse, i.e. are to the extended family or the group, rather than restricted to the nuclear family as they tend to be in the individualistic societies of the west (Volkart and Michael, 1957). There may also be sex differences in the importance placed on individual rather than role-related characteristics. A qualitative analysis of bereavement among older people in South Wales (Pickard, 1994) indicated that widows tended to report a loyalty to their former husbands which prevented many of them contemplating remarriage, whereas men tended to miss the state of being married – the function that a wife fulfilled.

Similarly, in relation to perinatal death, Peppers and Knapp (1980) argued that producing a subsequent healthy baby after an appropriate interval may largely resolve their previous grief. In a prospective study of women who had miscarried, Cuisinier *et al.* (1996) found that both a subsequent pregnancy, and the birth of a new baby predicted lower levels of grief, as did the speed with which a new pregnancy was achieved.

The two-process theory of grief (Hofer, 1984) involves a passive depressive response caused by the lack of a particular type of relationship. Providing the active grief response has reached a low level, this passive one can be curtailed by a new relationship. An alternative explanation (derived from the DPM) was outlined at the beginning of this chapter: according to this, the new relationship enables the person to distract him or herself from loss-related thoughts, allowing the gradual fading of memories associated with the deceased.

We also noted that, according to the grief work hypothesis, this should not lead to resolution. There is little empirical evidence on which to assess whether remarriage does enable or facilitate resolution of grief. Sable (1991) reported that older bereaved people who had new partners 1–3 years after their loss showed fewer physical and psychological symptoms than those who were without new partners. Similarly, Lund *et al.* (1993) reported that remarried widows and widowers (mostly the latter), from their longitudinal sample of older people, showed a greater reduction in stress, better grief resolution and greater life satisfaction, than those who remained unmarried. Schneider *et al.* (1996) found that higher levels of well-being were associated with being married or in a new relationship at 25 months in the second San Diego study.

Burks *et al.* (1988) compared 15 people who had remarried with 15 who had not, from a sample of 192 bereaved individuals, on a variety of measures of stress and adjustment. Initially, they differed little from one another, but by 4–5 years later those who were married showed significantly higher self-esteem, life satisfaction, resolution of grief and social support.

Of course, in all these studies, it is difficult to identify exactly what caused the differences. Those who marry or form new relationships are a self-selected sample, and they may have a more positive outlook on life and higher self-esteem early on. But the finding in one study (Burks *et al.*, 1988) that there were no differences soon after the loss would suggest that this was not the cause. Another possibility is that the social support provided by being married was crucial: to test this we would have to compare the remarried sample with those who received a high degree of social support from other sources, for example from living with close relatives, as was the case in Ablon's Samoan study.

We can also find individual cases where it is clear that remarriage has not resolved grief. Goin *et al.* (1979) described a 64-year-old woman who remarried a year after she was widowed and found that her second husband compared unfavourably with her first: for example, he did not share her interests, and he was mean with money. The woman reported that she felt a continuing relationship with her first husband, who seemed to be saying things to her.

She experienced a sense of comfort from this and did not show any signs of depression or anxiety. In a personal account of his feelings during the 4 years following the sudden death of his young wife Becky, Lichtenberg (1990) described his remarriage after 2 years or so as at first being full of joy compared to the past, but containing an undercurrent of grief. He became irritable, and nothing his second wife did was good enough for him. He finally had a bad quarrel with her on the anniversary of Becky's birthday, and then sought professional help. He realised that he had been blaming Becky for abandoning him, and finally managed to cease doing so and to look to the present and his future with his second wife.

Continued ties to the former spouse may be fostered by personal memories, and also by family influences and pressures, as outlined by Moss and Moss (1980). They referred to triadic bonds between the widow or widower, the former spouse and the present one. Their experiences of counselling remarried older widows and widowers led them to identify a number of potential problems: the social network left by the former spouse, poignant reminders such as anniversaries, and comparison with the dead spouse.

These examples suggest that there is a careful balance to be achieved between reconciling the new relationship and dealing with the continued attachment to the former spouse. They again lead us back to the DPM, which involves the need in most cases for both loss-oriented and restoration-oriented processes for resolution. Even a new relationship, which I have suggested forms an extreme restoration-oriented strategy, may not be enough by itself to resolve grief without some attention to loss-oriented processes.

Conclusions

The earlier parts of this chapter concerned the resolution of grief. Some cultural beliefs emphasise the acceptability of maintaining continuing attachments to the deceased whereas others regard this as abnormal. From a Darwinian viewpoint, grief is resolved when there is a return to normal functioning in everyday tasks, when intrusive thoughts and distress are absent, and when the person has mentally accommodated the changed reality. This corresponds with detachment from the deceased, which forms the basis of definitions of resolution from the writings of Freud through to the present day. An alternative view, that resolution involves a change in the nature of the attachment to the deceased, is found in other psychoanalytically derived writings.

It was apparent that grief can be maintained for long periods and is not resolved in either of the senses outlined above. There were several possible reasons for this – continued loneliness and deprivation, a lack of ways in which to express thoughts and feelings of loss, and extreme rumination. Grief can also last a relatively short time, so that the means through which it is resolved can be by-passed or speeded up.

One approach to defining the end-point of grief was as a series of tasks that need to be accomplished before resolution can be achieved. The first of these, creating an acceptable account of the loss, was associated with lower distress in several studies, but the single prospective study found that it did not predict a greater decline in distress at a later time. The other tasks, memories of the deceased no longer being painful and gaining a new sense of identity, correspond to the two definitions of resolution outlined above. In practice, resolution of grief is generally measured by the absence of distress or depression, which would be associated with achieving either or both of these tasks.

The dominant explanation for how resolution is achieved, the grief work hypothesis, was scrutinised in the later parts of the chapter. There were difficulties defining exactly what grief work involved. Two studies concerning the expression of emotions during grief found that, contrary to predictions, greater emotional expression predicted more intense grief. If grief work was defined more in terms of confronting the loss in thought, or expressing it to others in words or writing, the findings were mixed. It was clear that actively confronting a loss did not always predict more effective resolution. However, it did so under some circumstances, for the men (but not the women) in the Stroebes' study, among the bereaved parents assessed by McIntosh *et al.*, and for physiological and health measures, but not for psychological distress, in Pennebaker's studies of writing about distressing events.

One older description of the cognitive processes that are beneficial following a loss or trauma involves the continued assimilation of particular memories associated with the past life and the deceased, so that their emotional and personal significance are changed. More recent characterisations likewise identify reordering of thoughts associated with the loss as central, particularly for health-related changes. The issue still remains of whether resolution can only be achieved in this way, but the mixed findings in support of the grief work hypothesis would suggest that there are alternative routes. In terms of the Stroebes' DPM, these can be specified as engaging in something sufficiently powerful to replace the memory of the lost loved one, for example a new relationship, or an oscillation between attending to other areas of life and confronting the loss. I examined the evidence for the first of these and concluded that there were indications that this was usually helpful, although in some cases attachment to the deceased continued. In terms of the DPM, this would indicate the occurrence of some loss-oriented processes within the restoration-oriented process of forming a new relationship.

8   The mental processes of grief

> My husband was asleep. All of a sudden I woke up and saw this light beaming
> into the bedroom. It was a beautiful, really bright, white light. I opened up my
> eyes, I saw it, and I saw a vision of Allan. I saw his little cherub face, round
> and darling, and he said 'Yvonne, don't grieve. I am in ecstasy.'
>
> (Laura Palmer, 1987, *Shrapnel in the Heart*: 32)

Introduction

Hallucinations are perhaps the most bizarre manifestations of the altered
patterns of perception and thought that characterise grief. In this quotation,
the sister of a young man killed in the Vietnam War describes waking up and
seeing a vision of her dead brother who has come back to reassure her. As to
its reality, she goes on to say 'I know what I saw' (ibid.). The generation of
these perceptual changes as part of the grief process can be understood by
referring to research on hallucinations under other circumstances.

Similarly, other psychological research and theory can be used to understand the mental processes that are characteristic of grief. In this chapter, we
also consider slips of action (absent-mindedness), the generation of intrusive
thoughts, thoughts that undo the loss, the suppression of unwanted thoughts,
causal attributions (which are closely linked with blame) and beliefs in one's
ability to control events.

Hallucinations

Hallucinations occur under a variety of circumstances, notably under conditions of sensory deprivation (Bexton, Heron and Scott, 1954), after ingesting
certain drugs and in the case of schizophrenia. Several theories have been
proposed to account for hallucinations (Slade and Benthall, 1988; Benthall,
1992). Perhaps the most convincing is that they simply represent mental
events which are misattributed to an external source. People routinely discriminate between experiences that are externally or internally based, and
usually the decision is straightforward. But when it becomes difficult, some
people show a greater readiness than others to misattribute the source of

their experiences. This theory is supported by experimental findings, for example that people who report more frequent hallucinatory experiences show a greater bias towards detecting voices when these are absent in a signal-detection task which involves discriminating the presence or absence of voices (Benthall and Slade, 1985).

This type of research was designed principally to distinguish between different degrees of hallucination-proneness among individuals. The overall theory also predicts that different situations will vary in terms of the likelihood of hallucinations being experienced, because of differences in the ease of making the necessary attribution about the source of stimulation. After a bereavement, intrusive thoughts and a clear visual image of the deceased will both provide a much stronger source of internal stimulation than is usually experienced. This, combined with the minimisation of other forms of stimulation, for example while lying or sitting in a darkened room late at night, will make misattribution more likely. As indicated in Chapter 5, these are the conditions under which hallucinations are most commonly reported by bereaved people.

Those individuals who do see these visions are likely to be those who are more hallucination-prone in terms of Benthall and Slade's measures of individual differences (although this has not yet been tested). If so, hallucinations would be produced by a combination of the three factors – poorer discrimination between internal and external sources of stimulation, heightened internal stimulation, and the specific conditions of reduced sensory input present when the hallucinations are most likely to be experienced.

Slips of action

Bereaved people find that many of their habitual actions – such as laying the table for two, or calling out on arriving home – are no longer appropriate, yet are maintained involuntarily. William James (1892) pointed out that when any commonly repeated sequence of actions is learned, its conscious control gradually diminishes. We all go through many of our routine activities without consciously being involved in them. Reason (1984) viewed this process in terms of a central processor (conscious control) downgrading habitual actions to the control of sub-routines (automatic control).

Research on slips of action, or 'absent-mindedness' (Reason, 1979, 1984), has identified the circumstances under which these automatic sequences become used inappropriately. In most cases, preoccupation or distraction results in conscious attention being absent at a point where it needs to be substituted for automatic control. Most slips involve one of four categories: repetition of an inappropriate action; using the wrong object for the current action; intrusion of a sequence in the wrong place; and omission of a part of the sequence.

The persistence of habitual actions shown by bereaved people involves the first of these, an established pattern that is no longer appropriate because of changed circumstances. Consequently, conscious control is necessary in order to learn a new pattern. However, the bereaved person is more likely to be preoccupied with thoughts in some way connected with the deceased or with past events, so that conscious control will be less likely to be directed towards the routine task at hand. They are, therefore, more likely to be in what Reason (1984) called the wrong control mode, using a strongly learned habit under automatic control at a time when such an old plan for action is inappropriate. Therefore, activities such as laying the table for two, calling a partner from the garden, and turning to them in bed will commonly occur (Parkes, 1972). When such a slip occurs, its consequences will be registered as inappropriate at some point, and perception of the discrepancy provides a signal to return to the conscious level of involvement. In the case of the more usual everyday slips, this will simply entail realisation that a mistake has been made. For a bereaved person, it will also involve returning conscious thought to awareness of the reality of the loss, and to further thoughts and memories of the deceased, thus keeping his or her image in mind repeatedly.

A very perceptive description of this process was provided by C.S. Lewis in his personal account of grief:

> I think I am beginning to understand why grief feels so much like suspense. It comes from the frustration of so many impulses that have become habitual. Thought after thought, feeling after feeling, action after action had H. for their object. Now their target is gone. I keep on through habit fitting an arrow to the string; then I remember and have to lay the bow down. So many roads lead thought to H. I set out on one of them. But now there's an impassable frontier-post across it. So many roads once; now so many *culs de sac*.
>
> (Lewis, 1961: 39)

In other words, the downgrading of habitual actions to non-conscious control, which works so well in a familiar world, does not work in the changed world of the bereaved because the automatic plans for these actions are out of date. Yet they are still executed. But when they are, they set off an alarm bell which drags the reality of the loss back into the conscious mind.

Intrusive thoughts

Intrusive thoughts about the loss and its implications form a central feature of the grief process. These thoughts form a pattern over time, which is also known as preoccupation with the deceased, a phrase which emphasises its obsessional nature. The problem with the obsessional thinking of bereaved people is that it is associated with painful negative emotions about the loss.

Parkes (1971) set out in general terms how grief can be understood in terms of people forming models of their own personal worlds ('the assumptive world') which are used as the basis for everyday thoughts and actions, providing that the accuracy of such models receives confirmation from external reality. However, when an important part of the assumptive world no longer corresponds to reality – as in the case of the loss of a significant relationship – this confirmation is lacking, and the source of the discrepancy is repeatedly brought to mind again. This process occurs because people's assumptive worlds are stable, as a result of learning processes that underlie attachment to significant others (and to other stable aspects of people's lives). One result of this, as we saw in the previous section, is inappropriate plans for actions. Another is that the bereaved person will be dominated by 'inappropriate' thoughts: they – like the actions – are derived from a model of the world which no longer exists.

Parkes' framework can illuminate the generation of intrusive thoughts in the context of grief. However, intrusive thoughts are not confined to grieving, and we can gain a more complete understanding of the processes giving rise to them by examining research and theory on intrusive thoughts in general.

Most theories of the generation of intrusive thoughts – like that of Parkes – involve a discrepancy between internal models and events in the world (Martin and Tesser, 1996). Some, notably Klinger's theory of disengagement (Chapter 5), refer more specifically to unattained goals. Klinger (1975, 1977) argued that whenever someone perceives a block to attaining a goal, recurrent thoughts associated with that unattained goal are generated.

Martin and Tesser (1989, 1996) also suggested that unattained goals are responsible for the generation of intrusive thoughts. They viewed the persistence of a pattern of unwanted thoughts over a period of time, termed rumination, as an attempt to continue goal-directed action when this is prevented in the outside world. It either continues until the goal is attained or until the person no longer seeks that goal. In the case of grief, the first of these is impossible. How the second – resolution – is achieved was the subject of the previous two chapters.

Nolen-Hoeksema (1996) offered a counter-view, that much ruminative thinking does not achieve problem-solving: as its name suggests, it involves going over the same theme, and often the same material, again and again without much goal-directed progress. Nolen-Hoeksema's own studies have shown that rumination accentuates the depressed mood of already depressed people but does not have this effect on people who are not depressed.

The two approaches can be reconciled by supposing that rumination is indeed generated by a major discrepancy, but that in its prototypical form it is maintained precisely because no solution is forthcoming. In this formulation, achieving the goal or changing internal models so as to produce new goals would not be regarded as rumination, which is best reserved for going over the *same* material again and again. This distinction is implicit in the distinction between grief work and rumination noted in the previous chapter.

Thoughts which are independent of current environmental demands include trauma-related intrusive thoughts, daydreaming and worrying. A series of laboratory experiments have shown that there is a reduction of all forms of such 'stimulus-independent thoughts' (SITs) if the external demand is high, but it is difficult to eliminate them entirely (Singer, 1978). Teasdale *et al.* (1993, 1995) demonstrated that SITs were numerous when participants were in a quiet condition with no imposed cognitive demands. When their cognitive resources were deployed by a competing task which demanded continuous attention, there was more interference with the SITs. The competing task had to be one that built in unpredictability, but did not need to be demanding in terms of amount or complexity of information required. Repetitive tasks similar to meditation techniques would be effective. As indicated in a later section, these findings suggest that a high external task demand would be one way of seeking to reduce preoccupation after a loss.

Rumination also varies between individuals in the extent to which it is instigated by loss and other negative life events. For some people, not attaining a relatively minor goal will set off a chain of ruminative thinking that would not occur in another person. This variation is likely to be related to the extent to which people view their minor goals as important for their overall sense of self – in other words, the extent to which not attaining a lower-level goal is linked to higher-order goals (Martin and Tesser, 1996). However, bereavement will be linked to higher-order goals for most people, so that these considerations are unlikely to apply. Nevertheless, there will be individual differences in rumination for other reasons. Some people readily summon up positive thoughts, such as happy memories, in the face of unpleasant events (Boden and Baumeister, 1997). They are therefore more easily able to distract themselves from unpleasant thoughts and emotions. However, even when pleasant distracting activities were provided, Lyubomirsky and Nolen-Hoeksema (1993) found that people with higher depression levels were less likely to engage in them, and were more likely to report that ruminating about their problems provided them with insights into themselves. This interesting finding suggests that a subjective sense of having insight into oneself may be misleading in terms of psychological well-being.

Counterfactuals

One important component of the recurrent thoughts people have about a major unwanted event such as a bereavement concerns the mental undoing of events leading up to the loss. Such 'if only' thoughts are referred to as 'counterfactuals' (Miller and Turnbull, 1992). There have been many laboratory studies of this topic, mostly involving people engaged in role-playing. However, the one study which has concerned real events (Davis *et al.*, 1995) involved two forms of bereavement. In this investigation, undoing thoughts were carefully distinguished from thinking about the event as it *had* occurred, and attributing responsibility to oneself or others (causal attributions: see below).

The first form of bereavement involved parents and spouses bereaved through a motor vehicle crash, interviewed on one occasion 4–7 years later

(Lehman *et al.*, 1987). Davis *et al.* found that most people had engaged in rumination, and just over half of those who had done so had engaged in undoing thoughts. Of these, 55 per cent said that these thoughts involved trying to change their own behaviour. Yet few blamed themselves for the crash, supporting the view that 'if only' thoughts are not the same as blame or causal attributions.

Although ruminations were associated with distress in this study, when undoing thoughts were controlled for, this was not the case – indicating that it was the undoing thoughts that were associated with distress. This finding also raises the question of whether distress causes the person to examine the event and to seek to change it in thought, or whether the undoing thoughts generate the distress.

The second form of bereavement involved a longitudinal sample of parents bereaved through a sudden infant death (Downey, Silver and Wortman, 1990; Lepore *et al.*, 1996). Davis *et al.* considered measures taken at 3 weeks and 18 months after the death, and found that 76 per cent and 42 per cent of the sample reported undoing thoughts at these times. As in the first study, the more undoing thoughts there were the greater was the distress, at both times, and when the level of rumination was controlled. At 3 weeks, guilt was the feeling most closely associated with undoing, but guilt was much less frequent at 18 months.

The longitudinal design of this study enabled it to answer questions about the direction of causality. Distress at 3 weeks predicted the frequency of undoing at 18 months. This occurred when the level of undoing at the first time was controlled, and irrespective of the type of undoing involved, the focus of most people's undoing involving their own actions. Thus it is the higher level of distress that leads to the undoing thoughts, rather than the reverse.

Therefore, the important conclusions from this study are that undoing thoughts follow the distress experienced after a loss, and that they are the aspect of ruminative or intrusive thoughts most strongly linked to distress. 'If only' thoughts are generally distinct from attributions of cause or blame, discussed in a later section, but the two were linked in the second study (see later section on causal attributions).

Suppression and distraction as strategies for coping with unwanted thoughts

In Chapter 7, I considered the concept of 'grief work' – the view that by confronting and going over thoughts associated with the loss, resolution will be achieved. M.S. Stroebe and W. Stroebe (1990, 1991) evaluated this by examining the association between measures of grief work at one time (4–6 months after the death) and relative adjustment at a later time (2 years). Their grief work measures assessed the degree to which the loss was confronted or avoided: specific measures were suppression, distraction, avoidance of reminders, emotional control and non-disclosure. Although these were all positively correlated (M.S. Stroebe and W. Stroebe, 1991), individual figures (M.S. Stroebe and W. Stroebe, 1990) indicate that many of the values were low: only four out of ten were statistically significant for the men,[1] and two out of ten for the women;[2] four values were near to zero, and one was zero. It would be reasonable to conclude from these low correlations and from the low internal consistency of the scale,[3] that the measures do not constitute a single scale representing avoidance of grief work. Furthermore, only two of the six measures (suppression and distraction) were found to be related to lack of improvement in depression scores over time for the men (no measures were related for women). Suppression and distraction were moderately related to one another.[4]

From these detailed findings, it would be reasonable to conclude that there are several ways of avoiding the thoughts and feelings associated with grief, and that these may differ in terms of their associations (if any) with resolution.

Other evidence suggests that distraction of thoughts is associated with improved well-being compared to dwelling on thoughts of a stressor. Nolen-Hoeksema and Morrow (1991) obtained measures of emotional health and styles of responding to negative moods from students before and after the 1989 San Francisco (Loma Prieta) earthquake. They found, amongst other things, that those who tended to focus on their feelings and thoughts, and the possible causes and implications of these, showed negative emotions for longer than those who tended to distract themselves from doing so by engaging in other activities. Nolen-Hoeksema and Morrow were careful to distinguish between distraction and suppression (which they did not measure in their study), regarding this as maintaining a negative mood. In studies of grief, it is consistently found that rumination is associated with poor adjustment (Nolen-Hoeksema *et al.*, 1994; Remondet *et al.*, 1987; Videka-Sherman, 1982), and distraction strategies, such as helping others and keeping busy, are associated with decreased depression and better adjustment following bereavement (Videka-Sherman, 1982; Lund *et al.*, 1993). On the other hand, suppression of thoughts is associated with more psychological distress (Gass, 1987), depression and anxiety (Wegner and Zanakos, 1994).

Further evidence on the associations between suppression or distraction and resolution comes from experimental studies on the consequences of suppressing unwanted thoughts. Wegner *et al.* (1987) asked volunteers (who were alone) to verbalise their stream of thoughts into a tape recorder for 5-minute sessions. During one session they were asked to try not to think about a white bear, and in the second they were asked to try to think about it; for half the

1 The significant values were $r = .35$ to $.47$, and the non-significant ones $r = .01$ to $.30$.
2 The significant values were $r = .38$ to $.55$, and the non-significant ones $r = .00$ to $.30$.
3 The Cronbach's alpha (coefficient alpha) was $.60$ (M.S. Stroebe and W. Stroebe, 1991).
4 $r = .42$ for men and $r = .38$ for women.

participants the order of the sessions was reversed. Those who were initially asked not to think about the bear successfully suppressed thinking about it, but in the subsequent session they showed more thoughts about the bear than the people who had not had the suppression condition first. It seemed that even suppression of as innocuous a stimulus as a white bear led to thoughts of it returning at a higher level when the suppression was released.

A second experiment involved the same two conditions with the addition of one involving 'focused distraction'. In this, participants were asked to distract themselves during the initial suppression by directing attention to a red Volkswagen. This distraction procedure was found to moderate the later emergence of the suppressed thought. Wegner *et al.* concluded that distraction was an effective strategy for reducing the later resurgence of a suppressed thought, therefore supporting the distinction made by Nolen-Hoeksema and Morrow (1991) and the evidence from studies of grief that distraction strategies are associated with better resolution.

Wenzlaff, Wegner and Klein (1991) investigated whether later reactivation of a suppressed thought also reinstated the mood that surrounded the original thought. They experimentally induced positive and negative moods in the volunteers by playing two different types of music. As before, the task was to think or not to think about a white bear. Later, all the participants were asked to think about the white bear, and music was again used to induce a positive or negative mood. As in the earlier study (Wegner *et al.*, 1987), people who initially suppressed thoughts of the bear showed more frequent subsequent thoughts of it. Those who were in a similar mood during thought suppression and subsequent expression showed a stronger rebound of the suppressed thought.

A second experiment investigated the participants' moods following suppression or expression of the thought. Those who initially tried to suppress their thoughts experienced a reinstatement of the initial mood that surrounded the thought suppression. Wenzlaff *et al.* suggested that the process of thought suppression has the effect of linking that thought with the person's mood, so that both will return together at a later time. Since most of the thoughts that people try to suppress are negative ones, the strategy of thought suppression will therefore not only lead to thought reinstatement at a later time, but will also produce reinstatement of the original negative mood.

A different explanation, that the act of suppression itself generates the emotion associated with an emotional thought, was advanced by Wegner and Gold (1995). This hypothesis better accounts for the results of two studies examining both cognitive and autonomic nervous system responses to suppressing thoughts about an 'old flame' – a former romantic partner who was still desired (Wegner and Gold, 1995). A rebound of emotions (measured by physiological changes), but not of thoughts, occurred following suppression of such thoughts, and the two measures were not associated. The researchers suggested that the absence of a rebound of suppressed thoughts in this case was attributable to the participants continuing to suppress such painful thoughts anyway. Participants' comments and the presence of a rebound when the former partner was not still desired, make this explanation plausible.

All the studies which found the rebound effect involved a new thought presented to participants by the experimenter (note that Wegner and Gold's did not). Kelly and Kahn (1994) investigated whether the rebound effect occurred when people were asked to suppress their own intrusive thoughts, and found that it did not. They explained this in terms of people being able to develop strategies to prevent the rebound for their own frequently occurring thoughts, but not for new ones. These findings, and those of Wegner and Gold, do suggest that the original white bear rebound effect is limited to a new set of intrusive thoughts – such as those occurring immediately after a bereavement or a stress-inducing event. It is likely that people find ways of keeping familiar intrusive thoughts out of consciousness. However, Wegner and Gold's physiological measures also suggest that the feelings associated with the intrusive thoughts are not suppressed.

We can conclude that both experimental studies and those of real-life stressors indicate that distraction is a more effective strategy than suppression for avoiding thinking about painful thoughts. However, there may be additional problems with distraction for already depressed people. First, they are less likely to use distraction, preferring rumination instead, which they associate with gaining understanding of themselves (Lyubomirsky and Nolen-Hoeksema, 1993). Second, when they do distract themselves, they tend to use negative thoughts to do so (Wenzlaff, Wegner and Roper, 1988).

However, Teasdale (1989a,b) found that providing depressed participants with a complex distraction task led to a marked reduction in the frequency of depressing thoughts, compared with participants provided only with a blank wall and a white light. Distraction also decreased the depressed mood, which is consistent with the findings that negative thoughts are tied to negative mood (Wenzlaff et al., 1991). In Teasdale's study, distraction was generated from outside, rather than by relying on the person's own distraction strategies as it was in the experiments by Wenzlaff et al. (1988).

Some meditation techniques (De Silva, 1985, 1990) involve focusing attention on alternative stimuli, and are therefore similar to distraction tasks. They will have the same result of stopping the flow of unwanted thoughts. In this case, the experiments by Teasdale et al. (1993, 1995) on the effectiveness of repetitive but unpredictable tasks in blocking intrusive (SIT) thoughts demonstrate experimentally the effectiveness of this technique.

A further possible cognitive strategy is to focus attention on the unwanted thought. This is very different from thinking *about* the unwanted thought, and it forms the basis of other forms of meditation exercise. The aim is to concentrate on a single object or experience in order to reduce the habitual flow of thought connections (Crook, 1980: 337–351). Seeking to place the centre of attention on the unwanted thought itself has parallels with some behaviour therapy techniques (De Silva, 1985, 1990) and with the technique of 'paradoxical intention', described by Frankl (1960, 1964). Here, a phobic or obsessive-compulsive patient focuses attention directly towards the *source* of the anxiety, rather than thinking *about* it.

Causal attributions: self-blame and blaming others

Negative events are especially likely to evoke causal reasoning (Weiner, 1985; Taylor, 1991). This is made more difficult by certain circumstances, for example where someone is missing presumed dead (Hunter, 1986; Figure 8.1), or the cause of death is unknown, as these both involve insufficient grounding in reality. Where there is clearly someone to blame, as in the case of murder or a drunk-driver vehicle crash (Lord, 1987; Rynearson, 1987; Range and Niss, 1990), extreme forms of blame are encouraged by the clear identification of someone whose intentional or negligent action caused the death.

There are individual differences in the way people attribute causes for events, and these will influence how an individual constructs his or her meaningful account of a loss. There is research on both the causal attributions for

Figure 8.1 The grave of an unknown soldier from the Second World War. Where a person is missing, presumed dead, it becomes difficult for the bereaved to form a meaningful account of the loss.

Source: Photograph by the author, taken at the War Cemetery on the Greek island of Leros, 1994

a major loss, and on their association with different levels of distress follow-ing such a loss. The first (known as attribution research) is considered in this section, and the second (attributional research) is covered in the next.

One way of attributing responsibility for a bereavement is self-blame, and this is found to be much more likely in cases of deaths resulting from a sudden or traumatic cause, such as a motor vehicle crash or suicide, than one resulting from illness (Miles and Demi, 1983–4; Weinberg, 1994). Even in other cases, when someone asks why their particular loved one has been taken from them, they may search for reasons in their own behaviour or personality for the death. A tendency towards self-blame has also been found among victims of rape (Roth and Lebowitz, 1988; Frazier and Schauben, 1994), cancer patients (Wortman, 1976), and those paralysed by an accident (Bulman and Wortman, 1977). Self-blame is consistent with experimental evidence that people exaggerate their ability to influence outside events in general, and particularly those with serious negative consequences (Taylor and Brown, 1988; Wortman, 1976). As indicated in the section on counterfac-tual thoughts, Davis *et al.* (1995) found a link between such self-blame and undoing thoughts among bereaved parents who had lost a child through a sudden infant death: this suggests that thinking about ways in which one *could* have prevented the death may encourage thinking that one *should* have done so.

An alternative dispositional bias is to blame others for negative events. Several social-psychological theories have emphasised the importance of maintaining the belief in a controllable, consistent world, and how this influ-ences the way people attribute causality (Wortman, 1976). Perhaps the best known of these is the Just World Theory (Lerner, 1965; Furnham and Procter, 1989). This refers to a belief that people generally get what they deserve, i.e. merit and fate are closely aligned. It stems from a need to view the world as an orderly place, so that plans and long-term goals can be under-taken. In order to maintain this belief in the face of negative events that happen to others, many people will be motivated to attribute blame for the event to the victim or to denigrate them so that they can be seen as deserving their fate. Since serious negative consequences are more threatening to the just world belief than minor ones, there will be an increase in the tendency to attribute responsibility as the event increases in significance.

Beliefs about a just world are held to a greater degree by some people than by than others, and this is likely to influence how they view unwanted events. Rubin and Peplau (1975) designed a scale to measure differences in such beliefs, with items such as 'By and large people deserve what they get' and the negative item 'Careful drivers are just as likely to get hurt in traffic accidents as careless ones'. People who believe strongly in a just world are more likely to be religious and authoritarian than non-believers (Furnham and Procter, 1989).

If a bereaved person focuses attention on the fate of the deceased, belief in a just world may lead to the deceased being viewed as the cause of their own death, by negligence or omission. Obviously the circumstances will be important, some lending themselves to being readily attributed to the deceased's own actions, as in the case of suicide (van der Wal, 1989–90) or a heavy smoker dying of lung cancer. But it is important to emphasise that just world attributions are not rational: where suffering occurs, it is minimised, or else the victim is blamed for it.

Just world beliefs may alternatively lead to the bereaved person looking for another individual to hold responsible for the death, even when there is no rational basis for it. This may help to explain the readiness of some bereaved people – particularly parents (Chapter 6) – to blame medical staff or a hospital for the death. Their reasoning would appear to involve the following: 'In a just world, our child wouldn't die: therefore it was someone's actions or inactions that caused it'. In the case of cot death, there is no apparent medical cause of death, and therefore someone close to hand within the family, such as an older sibling, may be blamed (Halpern, 1972; Tooley, 1975). Again, there is usually no apparent rational basis. These are, however, speculations as there is at present no research on the suggested link between just world beliefs and attributions of responsibility for the death among bereaved people.

Blame and resolution

Attributions of responsibility assume importance in relation to grief because of their suggested link to resolution. Excessive self-blame has long been identified as being associated with poor outcome. Shand (1920) stated that suffering was increased when people saw their misfortunes as caused by their own folly, and a similar view was advanced by Parkes (1985). The available evidence does largely support a link between self-blame and recovery from bereavement. For example, Gass (1987, 1989a) found that self-blame and poor psychological health were positively correlated[5] among older widows and widowers; van der Wal *et al.* (1988) found that feelings of guilt were positively correlated with depression at 4 months after the loss among people bereaved by suicide; and Weinberg (1994) found that self-blame was associated with poorer adjustment among a miscellaneous sample of bereaved people.

In contrast, studies of a wider range of negative events indicate mixed findings for an association between self-blame and adjustment (Montada, 1992). Among one sample of patients who were paralysed as a result of accidents, self-blame was found to be *positively* related to adjustment, based on social workers' ratings (Bulman and Wortman, 1977). Among a sample of stroke patients, attributions of self-responsibility were associated with poorer adjustment (Thompson, 1991). Montada (1992) found that it was specifically

5 r = .41 for widowers and .28 for widows.

the negative emotions of guilt, and of hostile feelings towards others, that were associated with poor adjustment among a sample of spinal injury patients. Adjustment was not related to thoughts about causal attributions for the event in the absence of these emotions.

Although most of the evidence points to blaming oneself being associated with a poor outcome, Averill (1968) and others have argued that self-blame can provide a meaning for the loss, which is preferable to viewing the world as a random place. A similar argument has been advanced to account for the occurrence of self-blame by rape victims (Wortman, 1976), and presumably it could account for the positive association between self-blame and adjustment found in the first sample of spinal injury patients.

Janoff-Bulman (1979) made a distinction between two sorts of self-blame for negative life events, which has been influential in subsequent research. Behavioural self-blame involves attributions about the person's own actions, i.e. a source which is potentially modifiable and is therefore likely to be associated with a belief that similar actions can be avoided in the future. Characterological self-blame involves attributions about the person's own character, i.e. a source which cannot easily be modified and is therefore unlikely to be associated with a belief that similar actions can be avoided in the future. This form of self-blame is therefore likely to be associated with lowered self-esteem and higher rates of depression. Janoff-Bulman (1979) found support for this link, in that characterological self-blame was more prevalent among depressed than non-depressed college students.

The evidence that has accumulated since this initial study has been mixed. Some studies have found a link between behavioural self-blame and lack of distress, although a number of others have not (Anderson *et al.*, 1994; Janoff-Bulman, 1993). Frazier and Schauben (1994) found that in the case of both bereavement and relationship break-up, behavioural self-blame was associated with *more* psychological distress and that it showed no relation with perceived future control over such events, among a sample of women college students. In fact, the two forms of self-blame were closely associated, indicating that these respondents did not make a clear distinction.

One difficulty in assessing Janoff-Bulman's self-blame distinction is that different methods have been used to assess attributional styles. Studies such as that of Frazier (1990) and Frazier and Schauben (1994) used a rating scale which enabled the two sorts of self-blame to overlap. Where a clear distinction is made between the two sorts of self-blame, and in particular between the degree of control involved, results tend to be more consistent with the association between characterological self-blame and depression predicted by Janoff-Bulman, at least as far as general reactions to failure are concerned (Anderson *et al.*, 1994). Whether these results generalise to bereavement is another matter.

In evaluating all studies that have found a general link between distress and self-blame, or ones with a specific type of self-blame, we should bear in mind that it is not necessarily the self-blame that causes the distress. It is possible that being more distressed may generate more self-blame or a particular way of thinking about the loss. This possibility has to be taken seriously in view of evidence that, among bereaved parents, initial attributions of responsibility did not predict later distress even though at one particular time measures of responsibility and distress were associated (Downey *et al.*, 1990; Chapter 7).

There is no evidence on the possible impact on subsequent resolution of blaming the deceased. In other contexts, a tendency to blame the victims of losses and illnesses is associated with perceived invulnerability and optimism, and with just world beliefs (Montada, 1992). These findings are consistent with the view that such attributions have a defensive function (Shaver, 1970).

Parkes (1985) suggested that blaming other people for a loss is associated with more intense or prolonged grieving. However, the evidence on this point is mixed. Blaming others was related to poorer coping among the sample of paralysed patients investigated by Bulman and Wortman (1977). In a study of bereavement, Weinberg (1994) found that blaming others was not associated with poorer recovery, except in the case of a sudden traumatic death where there was also a desire for revenge (which is likely to keep the person thinking about the loss for longer).

Blame that involves a deity is likely to be more complex, since it challenges previously accepted beliefs about the world. C.S. Lewis (1961) questioned the nature and 'goodness' of God, inquiring whether He was shown to be a 'cosmic sadist' by allowing unwarranted suffering. For many bereaved people, belief in a just world or a just God may be shattered or tested by the experience of grief. Anger towards God was found to be associated with more intense grief at a later time in a study of bereavement by Barrett and Larson (1977, cited in Silver and Wortman, 1980). Other religious beliefs may aid the acceptance of the loss: a belief that how one lives in this life determines where one goes in the next, as in the Hindu and Buddhist notions of Karma (Long, 1977), and the traditional Christian emphasis on sin, may counter tendencies to examine God's workings solely in terms of present sufferings.

As indicated in Chapter 7, there is evidence that not being able to attribute *any* cause for the loss is *associated* with more intense grief and more distress, but as in the case of self-blame, this may not be a *causal* relationship between the attribution and later resolution (Downey *et al.*, 1990).

Perceived control

Janoff-Bulman's distinction between behavioural and characterological self-blame involved implications about a person's perceived ability to control their own actions, those with behavioural self-blame apparently seeing themselves as more in control. There are a number of influential theories which have focused specifically on the degree to which individuals believe that their own actions can affect the outcome of events. A strong belief in the efficacy of one's own actions will counter the feeling of an uncontrollable world which is subject to chance forces. As indicated earlier, people tend to exaggerate the degree to which their behaviour influences uncontrollable outside events (Taylor and Brown, 1988; Wortman, 1976), and they tend to view their own behaviour as more subject to personal control than that of others. However, some people do this to a greater extent than others.

A famous distinction between people's perceived degree of self-control for outside events is that of Rotter (1966), who proposed a dimension along which people differed in terms of their tendency to attribute events to internal forces which they feel they can control, or to outside forces (such as fate, luck or God), which they cannot. This distinction parallels the Just World Theory, the tendency to attribute events to outside forces ('external locus of control') being highly correlated with just world beliefs (Furnham and Procter, 1989). However, the emphasis in Rotter's distinction was on perceived control rather than a generalised belief in stability.

People showing an external locus of control generally cope less effectively with a variety of life stresses than those showing an internal locus of control, i.e. those who assume that they have control over the outcomes of events in their lives (Wortman, 1976; K.R. Parkes, 1984). Lower levels of depression are associated with perceived control, at least under situations where it is possible to exercise control (Wortman, 1976). Wortman argued that where the loss was irrevocable, it would be more advantageous to accept what has happened, and therefore a strong belief in personal control may prove maladaptive.

Subsequent evidence from a large-scale prospective study initiated by Wortman *et al.* (1993) provided striking support for this earlier suggestion. People who showed a greater sense of mastery, measured *beforehand*, were hardest hit by the death of their spouse. Also supporting Wortman's suggestion is the finding by Joseph *et al.* (1991), that, among victims of a major North Sea ferry disaster, those who showed more internal and controllable attributions reported higher levels of distress.

In contrast to these results are others from bereaved samples linking perception of control with better adjustment. Gass (1989a) found that a greater feeling of control over bereavement was associated with lower physical and psychosocial dysfunction among older widows and widowers. In their Tübingen bereavement study, W. Stroebe and M.S. Stroebe (1992, 1993, 1994) found that in cases of unexpected loss (which is generally more distressing) people who believed in their own ability to control events were less depressed and showed fewer physical symptoms than those who believed in the influence of outside events. These two findings are more consistent with those for potentially controllable stressors. It is possible that what is involved here is a belief that one can control one's general circumstances and responses to the loss, rather than a belief that one can control a loss which has already happened. In support of this are findings by Remondet *et al.* (1987), who studied response styles among a sample of widows and found that the one they called 'behavioural rehearsal', that is, making plans and decisions about the future and trying to do things for oneself, was associated with better adjustment and negatively related to emotional distress.

These findings also fit with an analysis of traumatic victimisation by Janoff-Bulman (1993). In line with the view of Wortman (1976), she stated that 'It is those with the most positive pre-existing assumptions whose core schemas are most deeply violated' (p. 88). She went on to suggest that although this would lead to greater initial distress, over the longer term, resolution would be facilitated by a more optimistic view of life. Her view was therefore that positive assumptions about the world may be a risk factor for initial psychological distress after an uncontrollable traumatic event, but that in the long term they will aid adjustment.

In addition to studies of general beliefs about a sense of control or mastery, others have concerned a more specific belief – the degree to which people thought that they could do something to alleviate a negative mood once it had occurred (Cantanzaro and Mearns, 1990). This was found to be positively related to the use of active, problem-solving strategies and negatively associated with avoidance strategies among a sample of under-graduates (Kirsh, Mearns and Catanzaro, 1990). It also predicted a more positive mood and the absence of somatic symptoms, even when coping behaviour and other variables were controlled, indicating both a direct effect on mood and an indirect one via coping strategies. We must again note that this study was concerned with how people cope with negative feelings once they arise, and also that it was not concerned with reactions to major losses.

Hardiness

Another concept related to whether people feel that they can control events in their lives is hardiness, identified by Kobasa (1979) as an important variable for predicting whether people become ill or not in the face of a stressor. It involves commitment to activities, a sense of control over one's life and a view of life as a series of challenges. A striking example of a person possessing these characteristics to an unusual degree was the British Second World War fighter pilot Douglas Bader (Brickhill, 1957). Eight years before the war, at the age of 21, he was involved in a flying accident following an act of bravado, in which he lost both legs. He determinedly mastered walking on artificial legs, refusing to use a stick and rejecting help when he fell. He had his car modified so that he could drive it again, and painstakingly learned to play golf. Bader was soon flying again, but the services regulations counted him as 100 per cent disabled and not allowed further solo flying. Throughout the 1930s, he kept trying to get back to the RAF as a pilot, and it was only the outbreak of war combined with his persistence that enabled him to do so. According to his biographer, he became an outstanding leader

and pilot in the Battle of Britain, and afterwards in the raids over occupied France.[6]

Summing up the way that 21-year-old Bader emerged from the months
after he had lost his legs – a time not unnaturally of self-doubt and moodi-
ness – his biographer Paul Brickhill wrote:

> The greatest and most constant factor in his endurance and resilience all
> through the months since December lay in his eternal and aggressive
> response to any challenge, the quality in him that is least elegantly and
> most effectively expressed as guts.
>
> (Brickhill, 1957: 75)

Although it is not clear exactly how hardiness mediates the impact of
stressful events on health (Wiebe and Williams, 1992), there is evidence from
one study that it is associated with a lower intensity of grief. Campbell,
Swank and Vincent (1991) investigated whether hardiness, measured by the
questionnaire developed by Kobasa, was associated with grieving among a
wide-aged sample of North American widows. They found that hardiness
was negatively correlated with grief intensity, and that it significantly predicted grief when other variables such as age and time since the death had
been controlled. They also found that 'time competence' – a measure of living
life in the present, derived from Maslow's description of the self-actualising
personality – was an additional important influence on the intensity of grief.
This would be expected, since it indicates, by definition, a lack of preoccupation with the loss.

These findings show that a personality characteristic which involves being
able to face the consequences of a loss and meet them as a challenge in a
determined and optimistic way is associated with a positive outcome. Again,
we should distinguish between this and the belief that one can control or alter
events once they have happened.

Purpose in life

The attribution of meaning assumes central importance in a further concept,
'meaning in life', which refers to the degree to which people see purpose
and order in their lives, and pursue and obtain worthwhile goals. It is related
to central ideas set out in existential therapy, notably the work of Frankl
(1964) and Meddi (1967). From his concentration camp experiences, Frankl

---

6 A BBC television programme in 1997 questioned many of the judgements of Bader's character
made in his biography and portrayed in the 1950s film *Reach for the Sky* in which he was
played by Kenneth More. These do not affect the present use of him as an example of
hardiness, but relate more to his lack of consideration for others that apparently accompanied
this characteristic in his case.

derived a technique of therapy ('logotherapy'), based on Nietzche's statement 'He who has the *why* to live can bear with almost any *how*'.

Meaning in life has since been measured using a 20-item scale called the Purpose in Life Test (Crumbaugh and Maholick, 1964). These and related scales measuring aspects of meaning in life are found to be strongly associated with well-being, particularly with the presence of positive aspects rather than the absence of negative ones (Zika and Chamberlain, 1992), and are negatively related to depression (Klinger, 1977).

Pfost, Stevens and Wessels (1989) found that bereaved students who reported low scores on the Purpose in Life Test showed more anger than those with high scores. Although there were no significant differences in other aspects of their grief (measured on Sanders' GEI scale), the sample size was small and would therefore only have detected a large effect. Using a larger sample of people bereaved through both natural or traumatic causes, Ulmer, Range and Smith (1991) found that those with greater purpose in life showed lower intensity of grief, assessed by Horowitz's Impact of Events scale (IES: see Chapter 2). Purpose in Life scores were also associated with other measures such as stronger reasons for living, and greater life satisfaction. Similarly, Edmonds and Hooker (1992) found an inverse association between grief, again measured by the IES, and Purpose in Life among a sample of bereaved students. Wheeler (1993–4) also found negative correlations between Purpose in Life and some of Sanders' GEI scales, among 203 bereaved parents recruited from self-help groups.

Two other studies found that samples of bereaved people saw the world as less meaningful, and as more controlled by chance, than did their non-bereaved counterparts (Schwartzberg and Janoff-Bulman, 1991; W. Stroebe and M.S. Stroebe, 1992). In the first case, there was an inverse relationship among the bereaved sample between intensity of grief and their tendency to view the world as meaningful. The comparisons with control samples suggests that it is the experience of bereavement which influences the person's general view of meaningfulness and control.

Conclusions

In this chapter, we have covered a range of psychological research which has implications for the mental processes involved in grief. Some of this research has already been applied to grief to a limited extent, whereas in other cases the links have yet to be made.

Hallucinations tend to occur late in the evening in conditions of poor light. This low level of sensory input corresponds to one condition identified by research on the generation of hallucinations. The other two involved heightened internal stimulation, which clearly applies in the case of grief, and poor discrimination between this and external events, which applies more to some individuals than others.

In a familiar world, many of people's habitual actions are subject to non-conscious control and this only occasionally produces problems, in the form of slips of action. However, the world of the bereaved is a changed one, making the automatic plans used for habitual actions no longer appropriate. They are still used but, when they are, the person is pulled back into conscious thinking by the lack of fit with current reality.

The mismatch between redundant internal models and the changed world without the deceased was also used to explain the generation of the intrusive thoughts which follow bereavement and other traumatic events. Again, the mismatch keeps bringing thoughts of the deceased into the conscious mind. Some psychologists have viewed unintended thoughts as generated by unsolved problems, although it does not follow that prolonged unintended thoughts actually solve the problems generating them. In fact when such thoughts are consistently about the same theme ('ruminations') they clearly do not do so. A high demand in terms of external stimulation lessened unintended thoughts. Individual differences in the extent to which people ruminate following a trauma or loss were associated with the ease with which they can summon up happy memories and whether rumination is regarded as producing insights.

One important aspect of ruminative thoughts is the undoing of past events, 'if only' or counterfactual thoughts, which are distinct from causal attributions or blame (although they may encourage self-blame). A study of bereavement found that they were the part of ruminative thinking that was most closely linked with distress, and that they follow the distress rather than generating it.

Suppression and distraction are two principal ways of seeking to avoid thinking the distressing thoughts of grief. There is some evidence that suppression is associated with higher levels of depression whereas distraction is associated with lower levels and with better adjustment. Experiments involving instructions to suppress an arbitrary neutral thought showed a rebound of this thought which was not found for a distracted thought. Other evidence indicated that the rebound effect was only clearly shown for new thoughts rather than habitual intrusive ones. In addition, distraction may not be helpful to already depressed people, unless a compelling outside source is the distracter.

Self-blame is common among bereaved people. Generally, people exaggerate their ability to influence unwanted events. Self-blame is also more likely if the person can identify any of their own actions that might have altered events preceding the death. Blaming others, either the deceased, or someone prominent in their care, fits a general disposition which involves belief in a just world, although there is no evidence linking the two from studies of bereavement.

Overall, self-blame is likely to be associated with poorer adjustment following bereavement, but there was no clear evidence regarding blaming others. The single longitudinal study found that initial attributions of self-blame did not predict greater distress at a later time, although the two measures taken at the same time were linked.

A related group of attributes involving a belief in personal control, hardiness and meaning in life, influence how grief is experienced, as well as being themselves influenced by the experience of bereavement. A strong belief in personal control is generally found to lessen the impact of negative events, but in the case of bereavement such a belief may lead to more initial distress since any attempt to cope by seeking to change what has happened will be futile. But in the longer term, being able to face the consequences of a loss in a determined and optimistic way is associated with a positive outcome, as is a belief in being in control of everyday events in the aftermath of a loss.

9 An evolutionary view of individual differences in grief

Specifically, parental devotion should grow until around early adolescence, when reproductive potential peaks, and then begin to drop. Just as a horse breeder is more disappointed by the death of a thoroughbred the day before its first race than the day after its birth, a parent should be more heartbroken by the death of an adolescent than by the death of an infant. Both the adolescent and the mature racehorse are assets on the brink of bringing rewards, and in both cases it will take much time and effort, starting from scratch, to get another asset to that point.

(Robert Wright, 1994, *The Moral Animal: Evolutionary Psychology and Everyday Life*: 174, 1995 UK edn)

Introduction

Most of the research considered in the previous four chapters concerned spousal bereavement. The concentration on this form of grief in research undertaken in western industrialised societies such as the US and Britain may be linked to the central importance of the bonds between marriage partners in these 'individualistic' societies (Triandis, 1995; Chapter 3). In 'collectivist' societies, where family and collective responsibilities are seen as more important, bonds between spouses are weaker whereas those between parents and children, and between other relatives, tend to be stronger: attachments are more likely to be more dispersed among a number of kin (Volkart and Michael, 1957).

To begin the examination of differences in grief following the loss of different types of relationship, and at different times in the life cycle, we return to evolutionary psychology (Chapter 4). From this perspective, it is apparent that sexual partners are only one class of biologically important relationships (in this case because they share parenting). Equally important, or more so, are the primary relationships based on kinship, between parent and child and between other members of an extended family, which are given greater emphasis in collectivist societies.

An evolutionary analysis recognises not only kinship but age: 'How warm and generous we feel toward kin depends, theoretically, both on our age and on the kin's age' (Wright, 1994: 174). The ultimate evolutionary reason, as outlined in the opening quotation, is because children of different ages vary in terms of the time and effort put into rearing them and in terms of their potential for producing future offspring: thus a child at adolescence has had a greater investment than has one of a year. The adolescent is also statistically more likely to produce offspring because (throughout human evolutionary history) a one-year-old would have had a much lower chance of survival. However, this calculation is also complicated by the parents' age. Parents will tend to value their existing offspring more (irrespective of the offspring's age) as they become less likely to be able to produce further offspring themselves.

In evolutionary terms, the parent–offspring relationship is a special case of any relationship based on close kinship. Many important insights arose from the realisation that this was the case, first set out by Hamilton (1964) in his theory of inclusive fitness.

Thus the evolutionary analysis of grief following the loss of different types of individual will be based on considerations of kinship, age of the bereaved and age of the deceased. It will also be based on the sex of the two individuals concerned since this is the other major biological variable besides kinship and age. In the next few sections, we consider the evolutionary principles which might enable us to predict how these three variables will affect close relationships, and hence the intensity and pattern of grief.

Kinship and mutual benefit

Kinship is perhaps *the* most important consideration underlying the social relationships of all sexually reproducing animals. I shall first consider the evolutionary principles which enable us to predict the pattern of relations between kin, as a prelude to examining differences in grief for different kin from this perspective.

The realisation that kinship was crucially important for understanding the social behaviour of animals followed from the important insight which is at the heart of modern evolutionary theory, that it is the gene, rather than the group or the species (or even the individual) which is the true unit on which natural selection works. Although this was clear to some of the older evolutionary theorists (Fisher, 1930), and to some of the pioneers of the modern study of animal behaviour (Lack, 1954; Tinbergen, 1953), it was not until the 1960s that it was widely recognised as an important principle underlying the evolution of social behaviour. This came about through the writings of Hamilton (1964), Maynard Smith (1964) and Williams (1966).

The reasoning behind Hamilton's concept of inclusive fitness was as follows. Parents care for their own offspring because offspring are the primary means of passing on parental genes. Even so, a sexually reproducing parent only shares with its offspring, on average, 50 per cent of those genes that are rare in the population as a whole. For convenience, and to follow convention (Dawkins, 1976), I shall refer to this as an index of relatedness of .5 or 50 per cent.[1] Brothers and sisters also show a 50 per cent relatedness. From the point of view of passing on genes, which provides the variation on which natural selection works, an individual who helped younger siblings to survive would be in the same position as one which helped its similar-aged offspring to survive. Inclusive fitness refers to the total fitness or reproductive success of an individual when we add the fitness derived from helping relatives to that derived from producing and caring for its own offspring (although such a calculation must take into account any decrease in care to the offspring that results from helping other relatives).

The principle of inclusive fitness predicts that natural selection will have resulted in individuals showing co-operative and helpful behaviour to others to the extent that they are related to them and in relation to the costs and benefits of that help. It may not, for example, be worthwhile for a bird to lay down its life to save a cousin when it could have brought up a brood of its own (since cousins show an index of relatedness of an eighth).

The implication of the principle of inclusive fitness for relationships between animals is that they will be formed mainly between close relatives. Other cases of close relationships require additional features, particularly deriving benefit from one another, for example achieving a task which either one alone could not achieve. Relationships between parents come into this category. Care by both the mother and the father occurs among species where offspring survival would be much poorer without such care. It is widespread among birds but less frequent among mammals, although humans are among this minority.

Animals also form alliances based on other forms of mutual benefit, such as shared hunting, providing food or defending the group. These are particularly important in non-human primate groups, as they are of course in humans. Relationships can also be based on one animal helping another at one time and their roles being reversed at a later time, a situation termed reciprocal altruism by Trivers (1971). Following Williams (1966), he set out the circumstances under which this could have arisen through natural selection. Help had to be repaid at a later time and there must be ways of recognising freeloading and avoiding individuals who practice it. Reciprocal altruism is an important principle that can explain the evolutionary origins of many features of human friendships (Chapter 9 in Wright, 1994). We intuitively recognise it as 'I'll scratch your back if you'll scratch mine', a saying that implicitly recognises the importance of reciprocal grooming in non-human primates.

Applying these principles to relationships among intelligent social mammals such as primates indicates that we should expect the closest attachments,

---

1 This index therefore discounts the large degree of genetic similarity that there would be between members of the same species drawn from the same population, and concentrates on those genes which are found in common as a result of kinship.

emotional bonds, to be between parents and offspring, and (for a different reason) between sexual partners where shared parental care is essential for offspring survival: this applies to humans but not to some of our close animal relatives (the chimpanzee, bonobo and orang-utan). We should also expect close relationships to occur between other relatives, notably siblings (index of relatedness 50 per cent), uncles or aunts and nieces or nephews (25 per cent relatedness), and grandparents and grandchildren (also 25 per cent relatedness). In species where genetically identical individuals are produced we should expect even closer mutual aid and, underlying it, closer emotional relationships. Whether this applies to human twins depends on whether cases of identical (monozygotic) twins were sufficiently common to have been acted upon by natural selection.

These principles enable us to outline a broad framework for when we should expect close attachments between humans. Grief – in its most basic form – represents an alarm reaction set off by a deficit signal in the behavioural system underlying attachment. The strength of this signal is likely to parallel to some extent the strength of the attachment. The reasoning behind this involves a link between evolutionary principles (either kinship or the net mutual benefit from a relationship) and a behavioural mechanism (the strength of attachment) and a reaction set off by the behavioural mechanism (the intensity of grief). How well this reasoning fits the empirical evidence will be explored in later sections and in Chapters 11–13.

Age

Age introduces a complication into the principles outlined in the previous section. As indicated there, a net contribution to the evolutionary task of passing on one's own genes lies behind all social relationships. However, the usefulness of any other individual, whether offspring, other kin, a sexual partner, or an ally, is dependent on their age. More precisely, it is dependent on their *reproductive value*, a concept put forward by the pioneering evolutionary biologist Ronald Fisher (1930).

In its original form, reproductive value described the expected contribution of a child to its parents' fitness. Except in modern western societies, where infant and child mortality are low, it increases from the beginning of life to an optimal value in young adulthood, thereafter declining to zero when reproduction ceases (Figure 9.1 shows Fisher's original graph based on Australian women in 1911). Reproductive value can be used to describe the degree to which individuals of a particular age will on average contribute to the ancestry of future generations (Archer, 1991a, 1992a; Daly and Wilson, 1988a). From this it can be inferred how useful (in terms of fitness) they are likely to be to relatives, which in turn will predict a range of different types of response tendencies to them. For example, the predictions that as offspring get older, parents will value them more, but as the parents get older they will be valued less by their offspring, has been used by Daly and Wilson (1988a) to

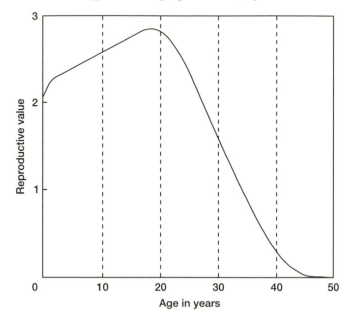

Figure 9.1 Reproductive value of Australian women in 1911.

Source: From Fisher, 1930; 1958 edn, p. 38, Figure 2

predict changes in homicide rates with age between parents and their offspring.

As indicated in the opening quotation for this chapter, we could use the same principles to predict the degree of feeling underlying the relationship, i.e. the strength of attachment, and as a consequence, the intensity of grief. In doing so, we have to consider both the age of the individual who died and the age of the bereaved person. The general prediction in the first instance will be that, for a given class of relationship, the higher the reproductive value, the more intense the grief. Thus, we should expect grief for a child to become more intense with increasing age up to adulthood when reproductive value starts to decline. On the other hand, the reproductive value of the parents declines during their adult life, so that they will increasingly invest in kin, such as sons and daughters, nieces and nephews, and grandchildren, who have a higher reproductive value than the parents. This consideration should lead to an increase with age in parents' attachment to their adult offspring.

Similar reasoning can be applied to spouses. The reproductive value of a long-term sexual partner will decline with age, leading (by itself) to the prediction of less intense grief for older-age partners. However, this has to be balanced against considerations not included in this evolutionary analysis, such as the fewer alternatives available, the length of the attachment and the impact of social isolation.

Sex

Whether an individual is male or female crucially affects what evolutionary biologists call its reproductive strategy, the consistent pattern of behavioural dispositions leading to reproductive success. Trivers (1972) set out the evolutionary principles which underlie the important ways in which we should expect males and females to differ in their behaviour. The specialisation involved in producing either eggs or sperm means that the costs of mating are generally greater for females than males, since they have to produce the nutritive material that surrounds the egg cell. Higher costs of mating for females involve having to produce another batch of eggs if she has mated with a poor-quality male and, where parental care is necessary for survival, being left to rear the offspring. In mammals, females have an additional cost of parenthood, that involved in carrying and nurturing the offspring. These considerations have led to a number of predictions about widespread sex differences in mate choice, sexual behaviour and parenting, as well as other topics such as aggression and risk-taking (see Archer, 1996a,b, for more detailed discussions). For example, females will generally be more discriminating in their choice of a mate, although here there are complications according to whether a short- or long-term relationship is involved (Buss and Schmitt, 1993).

The implications of an evolutionary analysis of sex differences for the study of grief are much less clear than in the case of age differences. There is some suggestion that men become attached to a new partner more readily than women do, i.e. they fall in love sooner, a finding that would be consistent with their greater capacity for superficial sexual relations (Buss, 1994). This may be relevant to the situation of the bereaved spouse in middle age, where remarriage fairly soon after the death is more likely for a man than a woman. However, as noted in Chapter 7, there are also more potential partners available for a bereaved middle-aged man.

Other aspects of sex differences in grief may be indirect consequences of the different reproductive strategies of men and women. In Chapter 6, it was suggested that men and women show different ways of coping with grief. Men are likely to be less expressive and more concerned with maintaining other aspects of their lives, whereas women tend to concentrate more on their feelings. These coping styles can be seen as part of a general tendency towards suppressing rather than expressing negative emotions by men, resulting from a widespread pattern of training boys not to express negative emotions, which are seen as a sign of weakness (Archer, 1996b). I have suggested that this widespread pattern is a consequence of the greater between-sex competition between males than females. It can be seen as functional for competitive dealings with other men, but it can also cause problems both in close relationships with women and in dealing with a loss.

A further aspect of the evolutionary analysis of sex differences concerns the relationship of fathers and mothers with their children. There are two considerations. First, there is greater investment in the foetus and the infant by the mother than the father. This would, typically, bring about a closer emotional bond early in life for the mother than the father. Second, one of the consequences of internal fertilisation is that paternity is never completely certain (whereas maternity is). There might, therefore, be more resistance to forming a bond with an infant by the father than the mother, especially where there are cues indicating that the child may not be his. Reassurances by relatives regarding the paternal (but not the maternal) resemblance of a new infant have been interpreted as following from these evolutionary principles (Daly and Wilson, 1982; Regalski and Gaulin, 1993). Both considerations suggest that at younger ages, the mother should generally show a closer bond with the child than is the case for the father. Therefore, we should expect greater maternal than paternal grief after the death of a foetus or young infant. At later ages, we should expect the investment by the two parents to be more balanced and therefore for the difference to be smaller.

Other principles

Other principles which might be relevant to understanding individual differences in grieving concern the evolutionary conflict of interests that is inherent in most relationships. Trivers (1974) set out the principles underlying the conflict between parents' and offspring's interests. The first principle is that offspring are totally dependent on parents for protection and for resources such as food. For this reason, parents provide their most important relationship. Offspring can also increase their inclusive fitness by aiding siblings (50 per cent index of relatedness). But if the choice is between taking scarce resources for itself or giving them to a sibling, the sibling will lose out. The evolutionary agenda of an offspring is to divert scarce resources to itself rather than sharing them with an existing sibling. The same applies in relation to a future possible sibling: offspring will tend to take what the parent can provide now irrespective of any influence on the parent's capacity to produce and raise further offspring.

Parents, on the other hand, have a different evolutionary agenda, which is to maximise their inclusive fitness by producing as many viable offspring as possible, and to provide sufficient resources for each of them to survive to maturity. This involves ensuring a roughly equal distribution to existing offspring of the same age, and a lessening of provisioning as offspring become able to fend for themselves, leading eventually to abandoning provisioning in favour of younger offspring.

The resulting interplay of the different evolutionary agendas of siblings and parents produces a radically different portrayal of their relationships from that derived from traditional developmental psychology (Archer, 1992a). For example, instead of only involving the transmission of information from parents to offspring, the process of socialisation now becomes a process whereby parents seek to impose their interests at the expense of those of their offspring.

We should expect grief to be particularly strong when a young child loses its parent, since this is *the* important relationship for its survival and hence its future fitness. Loss of a sibling would be expected to be secondary: although on average the index of relatedness is the same as to a parent (50 per cent), siblings are not – like parents – crucial for survival. When a parent loses a young child, the strength of grief will depend on the extent to which there are other avenues for enhancing inclusive fitness available. This will depend on variables such as the number of other children, the age of the parents and the available resources.

These considerations involve viewing the parent to offspring relationship in terms of the available alternatives. In the case of grief, the general issue of the replacement of a relationship was considered in Chapter 4 in terms of Hofer's two-process model of grief, and in Chapter 7 in relation to the reso-lution of grief. The existence of alternatives is probably an important but neglected consideration in grief research, perhaps because the dominant approach has centred on the individual's experience rather than on categories of relationship.

The parent–offspring conflict model examined one type of relationship conflict from an evolutionary perspective. Inherent in any analysis of the two sexes in terms of their different reproductive strategies is the possibility of a conflict of interests. Long-term relationships between mates only exist because of the necessity of shared parenting for those animals with a long vulnerable developmental phase. The two parents are not united through kinship. In evolutionary terms, they co-operate as a consequence of mutual interest in their shared offspring. But in other respects, males and females have different evolutionary agendas: we should therefore expect sources of conflict to arise as a result of unfaithfulness, inequality of resources and exploitation of one sex by the other (Smuts, 1995). There are, however, no clear predictions from an evolutionary viewpoint on the consequences for grief of a conflict-ridden relationship.

How should evolutionary principles be applied to individual differences in grief?

Having considered the evolutionary principles that are relevant for under-standing individual differences in grief, there is still a fundamental problem to be resolved concerning the way they might operate. It arises partly from a general need to consider mechanisms when applying evolutionary principles and partly from the indirect connection between grief and fitness.

The first issue can be summarised as follows. An evolutionary explanation only tells us why a pattern of responding led to reproductive success in the ancestral environment. However, some recent statements about the applica-tion of Darwinian thinking to psychology (Buss, 1995) have emphasised the point that this can also inform us about the mechanisms involved: the past is seen as telling us about the workings of present-day mechanisms. This may be true up to a point, but it is not necessarily the case. The older ethological approach to animal behaviour (Chapters 1 and 4), which predates modern evolutionary psychology, always emphasised the separation of functional (evolutionary) and causal (mechanistic) explanations (Tinbergen, 1963). There is no direct line from genes to behaviour: the reason why something has evolved does not necessarily tell us how it now operates.

This point can be illustrated in relation to kin recognition. Following Hamilton's principle of inclusive fitness, it was soon realised that kinship was an important variable underlying animal behaviour, and that animals bene-fited (in terms of fitness) from being able to recognise kin. The mechanism for recognising kin could be relatively direct, i.e. related to detection of actual genetic relatedness; or it could be indirect, unrelated to this, for example by being based on shared rearing – in other words, 'treat all those with whom you have been brought up as kin' becomes an effective rule. As long as a specific mechanism produces an end product that is favoured by natural selection, it does not matter whether this mechanism is direct or indirect.

Modern evolutionary psychology often seems to assume a relatively direct correspondence between natural selection and mechanism, between func-tional and causal explanations. This certainly applies to the few existing evo-lutionarily based discussions of individual differences in grief. Littlefield and Rushton (1986) derived a set of hypotheses about the relative severity of grief among relatives when a child dies directly from functionally relevant variables such as the sex and age of the bereaved, their kinship with the deceased, and the sex, health and age of the child (Figure 9.2). Similarly, Thornhill and Thornhill (1989) argued that the intensity of grief follows the loss of future fitness that the particular bereavement represents for the individual, in the case of a relative, sexual partner or friend. Both sources seem to have assumed a direct link between genes and behaviour.

In a reply to Littlefield and Rushton's paper (Archer, 1988), I argued an alternative view that differences in the severity of grief reactions between different relatives are likely to follow more accurately the closeness of per-sonal relationships (the strength of attachment) than anything that directly results from the degree of genetic relatedness. In practice, the two will often parallel one another. Indeed, that is why one is a good practical indication of the other. However, I argued that it is variables such as the duration and quality of the relationship that will most closely predict individual differences in grief, rather than the more distant functional considerations. (Although Littlefield and Rushton did distinguish between the two types of explanation, they were seen as alternatives rather than one working through the other.)

It is, therefore, possible to state two alternative evolutionary views of indi-vidual differences in grief. One is that individuals are able to detect variables such as kinship directly and they adjust their relationships accordingly. The other is that although the strength of attachment parallels evolutionarily important variables, such as kinship, sex and reproductive value, it does so through indirect mechanisms such as individuals who are important for one

Figure 9.2 Relatives surrounding a dead infant at a funeral in the Italian village of
         Calabria. Littlefield and Rushton's theory proposes that we can predict the
         degree of grief experienced by relatives directly from their degree of kin-
         ship with the deceased, and from the age, sex and health of the infant.

Source: Photograph by Thomas Höpker

another's inclusive fitness spending more time together and hence tending to
form closer relationships.

A second issue concerns the indirect connection between grief and fitness.
As indicated in Chapter 4, grief itself is maladaptive, but is connected to
features which are adaptive, i.e. ways in which a relationship is maintained
and separation reactions. The connection between fitness and grief therefore
occurs via the strength of the relationship. The implications of such an
indirect link might be that the strength of the relationship only bears a very
general relationship to the intensity of grief, which is influenced by all sorts
of other situational variables (such as personality and ways of coping with
stress). This would mean that the basis for inferences made from the degree of
kinship and other fitness-related variables is further weakened. Again, existing applications of evolutionary principles to individual differences in grief
have not addressed this issue. Littlefield and Rushton (1986) simply
commented that in the process of bereavement we are 'hearing the wail of
frustrated genes', a colourful but ultimately empty phrase derived from
Barash (1979).

Applications of natural selection to individual differences in grief

Using changes in the reproductive value of offspring with age as a basis for their predictions, Crawford, Salter and Jang (1989) asked a wide age range of Canadian adults to rate the relative intensity of grief by parents following the death of ten different age categories of offspring. Overall, they found a substantial correlation (r = .64) between estimated grief intensity and the general curve of reproductive value for the Canadian population (which would have a much flatter curve from birth to 18 years than that in Figure 9.1). Interestingly, they found an even higher correlation (r = .92) with the curve for reproductive value in !Kung hunter-gatherers, whose way of life – and mortality pattern – is more comparable with that inferred for evolving hominids. This suggests that the participants were making intuitive judgements which incorporated adaptive assumptions from the evolutionary past, rather using than those operating today. It is always important to bear in mind this distinction when applying adaptive principles to human behaviour under contemporary conditions (Caro and Borgorhoff Mulder, 1987; Archer, 1991a, 1992a). In effect, these respondents were judging the grief of other individuals as if these individuals were from a traditional or pre-industrial society where infant mortality was still high.

This study was based on the empathy felt by others towards bereaved parents. It also involved the assumption that grief – which is not itself adaptive – indirectly reflects the value of the relationship. In view of these assumptions, it is remarkable that such a clear link with reproductive value was found. It suggests that considerations of reproductive value have been incorporated into the brain mechanisms underlying these intuitive judgements. It is therefore important to look for similar evidence in studies that have examined parental grief more directly. As indicated in the previous section, Littlefield and Rushton (1986) set out a series of hypotheses based on evolutionary principles, each assuming a direct link from functional variables to behaviour.

The findings from this study were limited by a number of methodological problems (Archer, 1988), such as the use of a single-item scale to measure grief severity (but see Chapter 6), low inter-rater reliabilities and the inflation of the sample size by counting both self-ratings and partner ratings for each respondent.

There are also doubts about whether Littlefield and Rushton made the best use of evolutionary principles to derive their specific hypotheses (Archer, 1988). They did not, for example, investigate reproductive value but instead used chronological age, predicting that parents would grieve more for older children than they would for younger children, because older children had had more time and energy invested in them. No difference was found between grief for older and younger children, although a very small correlation (r = .11) with age was found when parent's age was controlled. In another study (Fish, 1986), no association was found between grief and parental age.

However, as indicated in Chapter 11, several studies found an association between gestational age and grief for perinatal deaths: Toedter *et al.* (1988) reported a partial correlation of .47, which indicates that there was a considerable effect over this restricted age range. To be consistent with the strong association found by Crawford *et al.* (1989), we would expect this association to be found over the wider age range from infancy to young adulthood.

An alternative hypothesis – that there is no association between grief and a child's age – is illustrated by the following quotation based on experience of counselling bereaved mothers:

> There seems to be no 'good' age at which a child dies, at least not in the eyes of a bereaved mother. Her investment in the child, at any age, her hopes and plans for the future, and her memories of the past all contribute to a deep sense of loss and longing for 'just a few more years'.
>
> (Schatz, 1986: 307)

Implicit in this quotation is the view that once attachment to the offspring has reached a particular level, grief will occur at a more or less constant strength. In modern societies where infant mortality is low and mothers have few infants in whom they invest heavily, emotional attachment is likely to be high from early in life. Only in societies with a high mortality and high birthrate would we expect a delay in forming attachment which would correspond with the traditional curve for reproductive value. This is of course what Scheper-Hughes (1992) found among shanty-town mothers in Brazil (Chapter 3). Therefore it is possible that there is no automatic linking of grief to reproductive value, but an approximate association mediated by the level of attachment, which is less clearly apparent in societies where there is low mortality and high parental investment in infants from soon after birth.

We can therefore surmise that there will always be a link between grief and attachment (the proximate mechanism) but only under some conditions will there be one between grief and reproductive value (the ultimate adaptive origin). The reasons they might become uncoupled are: (1) the mechanism only has to be good enough to generally deliver the adaptive ends; (2) the mechanism will not necessarily produce adaptive ends under modern conditions; and (3) the link with an adaptive character is in the case of grief an indirect one: therefore there may have been no selection pressure for matching very precisely the strength of grief to the level of attachment.

As parents become older, their own residual reproductive value declines: if grief were susceptible to these changes, we should expect increased grief intensity with parental age for any offspring who had died. This would operate in the same direction as the offspring's reproductive value during their childhood and in the opposite direction during their adulthood, when their reproductive value declines (Figure 9.1). In Littlefield and Rushton's study, when the offspring's age was controlled, no association was found between grief and parental age. Fish (1986) also found little difference in the extent of grief between older and younger mothers; however, older fathers did show a stronger grief reaction, but we cannot in this case separate the influence of parental and offspring age. However, other evidence, reviewed in Chapter 11, does suggest that grief for offspring is stronger among older than younger women, in line with the prediction from their declining reproductive value.

Littlefield and Rushton predicted that mothers would show a higher level of grief than fathers would, reflecting the greater investment required by the female to produce a replacement, and the less than 100 per cent certainty of paternity by fathers. Their results supported this prediction, mothers grieving more intensely than fathers, a finding which has been confirmed in other studies described in Chapter 13. However, the same prediction regarding the relative grief of mothers and fathers can be derived from the closer attachment of mothers to their young children (Archer, 1988), and also from the different coping styles of men and women in the face of any form of bereavement (M.S. Stroebe and Schut, 1995; Schut *et al.*, 1997). In the first case, this could be regarded as the proximate mechanism underlying the evolutionary explanation (Archer, 1988); in the second, the evolutionary explanation would involve an indirect effect of male inexpressiveness, arising in evolutionary terms from male socialisation for competitiveness (Archer, 1996b).

Littlefield and Rushton also predicted that parents would grieve more intensely for boys than for girls. Although there was an effect (high in magnitude but low in terms of probability) in this direction, it is not clear why this hypothesis was made in the first place. It seems to be based on an observation from the ethnographic record of a preference for sons rather than daughters, rather than a prediction from evolutionary theory. Indeed, the authors state that 'The almost universal preference for sons is not readily explainable from a sociobiological perspective' (p. 798). In fact, predictions regarding the sex of the parent and the sex of the offspring would depend on the reproductive strategies of both, which are dependent on developmental and current environmental conditions (Archer, 1988, 1991a, 1992a).

However, as Littlefield and Rushton also indicated, the value of male and female children is dependent on social status. This is a reference to the hypothesis of Trivers and Willard (1973) that the ratio of males and females can be altered according to the status of the parents. One might extend this hypothesis to predict that the less valued sex (males if status is low) would be grieved over less intensely when they die. However, Littlefield and Rushton transposed health for social status in their study when investigating this issue (and they did not find the predicted interaction).

Littlefield and Rushton's study contained some other hypotheses derived from evolutionary principles, concerning the influence of the child's health and its perceived resemblance to the parent (presumed to be indicative of genetic relatedness). They also examined parents' ratings of how they thought various grandparents would react to the death of a grandchild. As predicted on the basis of paternity uncertainty, maternal grandmothers were rated as showing more intense grief than other types of grandparents, and paternal grandfathers the least, although the sizes of these differences were not large ones. These findings are consistent with those from a later study investigating perceived solicitude or care received from the four different types of grandparent (Euler and Weitzel, 1996). Also consistent with the findings for grandparents, Littlefield and Rushton found that ratings for paternal aunts and uncles were lower than those for maternal aunts and uncles. Nevertheless, we are again left with the question of whether these influences arise because people are sensitive to genetic relatedness, or to the closeness of relationships which generally parallels this.

The most impressive evidence of a possible direct link between grief intensity and genetic relatedness comes from studies comparing grief following death of a twin – a topic almost completely overlooked in studies of grief. In two studies (Woodward, 1988; Segal and Bouchard, 1993, followed up in Segal *et al.*, 1995), involving samples of 219 and 279 twins respectively, from the UK and from the US, monozygotic (identical) twins showed significantly greater grief following the death of their co-twin than did dizygotic twins. Since monozygotic twins share the same genes, the survival and reproductive chances of the co-twin will be as valuable for enhancing fitness as those of the person him- or herself. This does not apply to dizygotic twins who are only as closely related as other siblings. This argument, which is based on inclusive fitness theory (Hamilton, 1964), would depend on humans being sensitive to genetic relatedness even outside the normal range, which involves an index of relatedness ranging from zero to $.6^2$ (Wilson, 1995). Studies of reunited monozygotic twins who were reared apart show that they form close relationships, suggesting that there is more to this than shared upbringing and similar treatment by others (Segal, 1988, 1993).

Segal and Bouchard (1993) also found that grief following the twin's death was rated as stronger than that following death of the person's mother and of their spouse (although in this case the sample's average age was high). Unfortunately, these comparisons used both types of twins combined, instead of only monozygotic twins (although monozygotic twins did make up approximately 70 per cent of the sample). The study also relied on the single-item rating scale used by Littlefield and Rushton (1986), but the findings were later confirmed using Sanders' GEI (Segal *et al.*, 1993, 1995). Despite their positive finding for twins, Segal and Bouchard (1993) did not find any differences in the intensity of grief expressed for other relatives – mothers, fathers, grandparents, aunts and uncles – which is again inconsistent with the view that there is detailed shadowing of genetic relatedness by grief intensity. Other results (McIntosh and Wrobleski, 1988) are consistent with this finding.

Segal and Bouchard (1993) and Segal *et al.* (1995) did find that grief

---

2 Full siblings where there was inbreeding.

following loss of a twin declined with age among samples of adult twins. This is therefore consistent with the hypothesis that grief severity decreases with the age-related decline in reproductive value of the deceased.

Conclusions

The limited research reviewed in the previous section provides limited, but inconsistent, evidence of an association between grief and reproductive value, although in one case this involved estimates of others' perceived grief. The evidence for differences according to sex were more in accord with predictions, but could be accounted for in other ways. Findings for kinship were mixed.

Of course, there is little doubt that in general terms we should expect the intensity of grief to reflect the biological importance of a relationship, for example for it to be more intense for a child or a spouse than for an aged parent or friend. It is the detailed shadowing of genetic relationship or reproductive value by grief intensity about which there is uncertainty. As indicated above, there are two problems with expecting such an association: the first is that grief is not itself adaptive, and therefore it may not have been subject to selection to make it closely match functional variables in the relationship which was lost; second, any psychological disposition reflecting the functional benefits of a relationship will act through intermediate mechanisms – such as those underlying attachment – which are themselves subject to other constraints and situational influences.

Having made these reservations, the impressively high correlations found by Crawford and his colleagues and the positive evidence found in the twin studies does make the general approach warrant further investigation. Such studies may benefit from taking a more ethological view, by being aware that functional explanations require mediating mechanisms.

In the next chapter, I again examine the issue of whether there is a close association between characteristics of the relationship with the deceased and the pattern of grief, as is assumed by the evolutionary perspective, but this time from the perspective of attachment theory. I also examine research on individual differences in attachment styles, and their implications for grief. This leads on to the application of another type of evolutionary-based theory, which holds that different types of attachment are adaptations to different environmental conditions.

10 The relationship with the deceased

Uncle Unwin
lived unwed
died unmourned
our tears unshed
his chin unshaved
his soul unsaved
his feet unwashed
his cat unfed
        (Philip Gross, 'Dirge for
Unwin', in Duffy, 1996: 44)

Introduction

According to Parkes (1972, 1986, 1996), grief represents 'the cost of commitment'. If you are unloved, you will – like uncle Unwin – be unmourned. In
evolutionary terms, grief represents the trade-off for being able to maintain
stable relationships (Chapter 4). As indicated in Chapter 9, a general consequence of this would be for the intensity of grief to follow the strength of the
relationship which was lost, which in turn should follow adaptive aspects of
that relationship. But, in view of the indirect way in which grief is related to
fitness, the question was raised as to what extent there is detailed shadowing
of adaptive aspects of the relationship such as kinship and reproductive value.

An alternative approach to predicting individual differences in grieving is
that derived from attachment theory (Chapter 4), where the emphasis is on
the proximate or immediate aspects of the particular relationship (as opposed
to the distal or ultimate aspects which have been shaped by natural selection).
In this chapter, I assess the view, derived from attachment theory, that the
features of grief can be predicted by the characteristics of the relationship. I
begin by examining evidence for a general link between the intensity of grief
and strength of attachment to the deceased, and then consider the association between variations in the quality of relationships and subsequent
grieving.

Although it should be possible to consider the issue of relationship quality in relation attachment theory applied to adults (Berman and Sperling, 1994; Field, 1996; Hazan and Shaver, 1992; Weiss, 1988), most of the current research on bereavement has not come from this perspective. Instead, it has been generated by psychiatric issues. Yet there is a growing body of evidence on individual differences in adult attachment styles and their impact on relationships, including some on reactions to their break-up and loss. This research can be related to some extent to grief.

Finally, I consider an evolutionary approach to attachment styles which has linked them to environmental variations, and hence has viewed them as alternative ways of enhancing fitness. Although new and speculative, this has some implications for individual differences in grief.

The general link between attachment and grief

It is clear that, in general terms, people only grieve strongly for close relationships, those they have built up over a period of time or which have for other reasons assumed importance for them. There are, however, few systematic comparisons over a wide range of relationships differing in their strength of attachment. Standardised rating scales (Chapter 2) are ideal for making such comparisons, but the evidence available at present is relatively limited. Using the GEI (Grief Experience Inventory), Sanders (1979–80) compared people who were newly bereaved following loss of a spouse, an offspring (in the age range 6–49 years), or a parent. People who had lost a son or daughter showed the highest levels of grief whereas those who had lost a parent during adulthood showed the lowest levels. Burnett *et al.* (1997) also found that samples of bereaved parents grieved more intensely than bereaved spouses who in turn grieved more strongly than adult offspring who had lost a parent. Leahy (1992–3) found similar results for a female sample, measuring depression levels.

Studies of specific forms of grief that have included measures of the attachment to the deceased generally find an association between such measures and the strength of grief. For example, in a study of adolescents' reactions to the death of a classmate from leukaemia, McNeil, Silliman and Swihart (1991) found that the intensity of grief followed the closeness of the relationship with the deceased and the frequency of interactions with him. Three studies on grief following death of a pet that retrospectively measured the owners' strength of attachment all found an association between this and the intensity of grief (Archer and Winchester, 1994; Gerwolls and Labott, 1994; Gosse and Barnes, 1994).

Cross-cultural evidence indicates that in many of those cases where grief is, relatively speaking, less intense or even absent, relationships are likely to have been either more widespread or weakened for other reasons. In a far-sighted article written before the concept of attachment was developed, Volkart and Michael (1957) suggested that grief should vary according to the intensity and breadth of family relations, which would in turn vary cross-culturally. In a discussion which parallels Triandis' later distinction between collectivist and individualistic societies, they argued that in societies where the emotional ties are dispersed among many kin, the impact of the loss of one of them will be much less than in societies such as the US where family ties are concentrated on a few individuals. Here emotional ties will be more concentrated, and therefore grief will be more intense when the individual dies. Volkart and Michael further suggested that the pattern of family life in modern western societies fosters over-dependence, whereas that from a more collectivist society produces individuals who are less vulnerable to bereavement. In modern societies we 'may . . . be building persons up for the big letdown by exacerbating vulnerability' (Volkart and Michael, 1957: 304).

In another innovative discussion of the nature of loss, Lofland (1982) sought to identify the different aspects of the ties that bind people together in relationships. Significant others provide us with not only partners in social roles and assistance in everyday tasks, but also linkages to others and a sense of self, and support for a private world-view, a sense of reality and a vision of the future. Lofland outlined instances where these functions are spread across a variety of others, and instances where they are all directed towards one person. Such different patterns correspond to the diversity of attachment relations in different cultures, which are associated with the structural diversity of human societies. They result in different patterns of relationships, and different intensities of grief according to the extent to which all these different functions are fulfilled by one person.

A different reason for little or no grieving, but also one which follows the degree of attachment, is described in the work of Scheper-Hughes (1992) on the women of the shanty-towns of Brazil. As indicated in earlier chapters, her observations showed that these women only very gradually develop attachments to their infants, whose chances of survival are very poor by the standards of the middle class in western societies: 'On the inhospitable rocky outcrop of the Alto de Cruzeiro mother love grows slowly, tentatively and fearfully' (Scheper-Hughes, 1992: 359). The women show restraint and emotional distance towards their young infants, and if such an infant should die, they do not appear to show sorrow. This contrasts with the grief that is shown for older children and significant adults, and the grief shown for children in other non-western societies such as Egypt (Wikan, 1988).

This avoidance of making strong attachments to young infants who are in the vulnerable age for mortality is reminiscent of descriptions of people deliberately avoiding making friends with others in order to spare themselves the pain of grief in circumstances where death is likely to occur. In Pat Barker's novel about the First World War, *The Ghost Road*, she described the reactions of the main character, Prior, an officer who has been to the front three times, when he meets a new officer who has not yet been to war: 'Ghosts everywhere. Even the living were only ghosts in the making. You learned to ration your commitment to them' (Barker, 1995: 46).

Dependency

The previous section was concerned with the general link between the strength of attachment and the intensity of grieving. However, grief resulting from the loss of a particular type of relationship, such as death of a spouse, may be shown in a weak or strong form, it may begin immediately or be delayed, and particular aspects of the process may be distorted. Such individual variations were first studied from a psychiatric perspective (following Freud, 1917) as atypical patterns of grief which resulted from problems in the relationship, notably dependency and conflict.

Dependency is important in attachment theory because it forms the basis of one of two types of insecure attachment identified among infants, the anxious-ambivalent (or preoccupied) style (Ainsworth, 1979). Hazan and Shaver (1987) applied Ainsworth's scheme to adults, and it has since been modified by other investigators of adult attachment (see below). Insecure attachments are generally associated with more intense distress following separation. As indicated above, when one takes a cross-cultural perspective, individualistic societies can be viewed as fostering dependency by encouraging extreme and exclusive relationships.

One of the earliest studies to emphasise dependency was that of Parkes (1964a), who investigated a small number of psychiatric patients whose presenting illness had begun within 6 months of the death of their spouse, parent, sibling, or child. Atypical patterns of grief included prolonged, intense or delayed forms, and grief accompanied by hypochondria. Following Freud (1926), Parkes suggested that prolonged grief, with pronounced anxiety and pining, is associated with a dependent relationship. Thirty years later, Prigerson *et al.* (1997b,c) made a similar connection in relation to case studies of traumatic grief that involved pronounced separation distress, suggesting that for people with dependent attachment styles, marriage to a supportive spouse serves a compensatory function. Therefore, the loss of a spouse who fulfils such a function may rekindle early attachment conflicts, leading to a greater sense of loss of self and loss of safety than would be the case for a securely attached individual. In this sense, the person's reaction is similar to that shown to a loss sustained under traumatic circumstances (see below).

In their long-term study of widows and widowers in Boston (US), Parkes and Weiss (1983) examined evidence for an association between the type of marital relationship and the pattern of grief shown by the survivor. From an initial long list of possible antecedent and demographic influences, they identified two aspects of marital relationships that were associated with poor outcome. One of these was dependency. In their study, it was assessed indirectly by asking, 3 weeks after the death, whether the bereaved person could function in everyday roles without the emotional support or help of the partner. Inability to do so was strongly associated with the extent of preoccupation and yearning for the spouse evident at this first interview.

The sample was divided into people showing high and low yearning: those from the first group showed more intense and prolonged grief 5 weeks later, and at 13 months and 2 4 years. Typical of the early reaction of the high-yearning group was a feeling of 'what shall I do now?', doubting their mental health, and a wish for someone to take over. Emptiness and loneliness were more often reported by this group; signs of grief were still pronounced at 13 months, and depression was more common than in the low-yearning group at the 2–4 year interview.[1]

From their findings, Parkes and Weiss suggested that a more dependent marital relationship led to more severe and prolonged grief. Although this is the most likely interpretation, such a conclusion should be based on measures taken while the partner is alive, rather than on the early response to loss by the survivor. Strictly speaking, the study only tells us that intense yearning and poor functioning early in bereavement is associated with poorer recovery. Nevertheless, this particular finding has proved a robust one (Nolen-Hoeksema *et al.*, 1994; Prigerson *et al.*, 1994, 1997a).

Some other studies have assessed people's relationships retrospectively. Sable (1989) investigated the quality of past relationships among a sample of widows, using a questionnaire designed to assess people's histories of close relationships throughout their lives. Widows who reported more anxious attachments during childhood showed higher distress following their adult bereavement. Those who were more dependent on their husbands also showed greater distress and depression, and fewer signs of recovery, than those who were less dependent. Schwartzberg and Janoff-Bulman (1991) found, among young adults who had lost a parent during the past three years, that their grief intensity was strongly associated with retrospective measures of parental over-protectiveness in childhood.

Although the evidence does suggest a link between a dependent relationship with the spouse or an earlier dependent relationship and subsequent intense and prolonged grieving, it is all based on assessments of dependency made after the bereavement. There are two problems with drawing firm conclusions from such studies: first, the loss of a partner may affect how a person portrays their relationship with them and also earlier relationships; and second, people who show high levels of distress following the loss of a dependent relationship may have shown high levels of distress before the loss. Only a prospective study would enable us to rule out this possibility, and to show that the distress is specific to the *loss* of a dependent relationship.

Some bereaved people deliberately dwell on reminders, places and things associated with the dead person (Chapter 5). However, this tends to maintain preoccupation with the deceased for a long time through the process of rumination (Chapter 8). Parkes and Weiss suggested that this provides a way of maintaining attachment in the case of a dependent relationship, thereby

---

1 About half the high-yearning group showed signs of depression, compared with only one-sixth of the low-yearning group.

prolonging grief, in some cases for many years. An often-cited example of this is Queen Victoria (Jalland, 1989; Parkes and Weiss, 1983). After Prince Albert's death, the Queen instructed that nothing in his room was to be moved, and she had statues of him erected throughout Britain. A photograph of him on his deathbed surrounded by an evergreen wreath was hung a foot above the unoccupied side of every bed in which the queen would sleep, a routine which was kept up for the 30 or so years until her own death. A less extreme practice is to keep some aspect of the dead spouse's belongings or clothing as they were in his or her lifetime. In the film *This Sporting Life* (Lindsay Anderson, 1963), the widow Mrs Hammond (Rachel Roberts) kept her husband's boots by the fireside and polished them regularly.

The suggested link between a dependent relationship and intense grieving is also consistent with the view that the more a person's attachments are concentrated on one person, and the more that person fulfils all the functions of human bonds (Lofland, 1982), the greater will be the grief for them when they die. Individual variations in dependency within a culture can therefore be connected with cross-cultural and historical variations in attachment. Many of the complications of grief which are of particular interest to psychiatrists in modern western societies may be viewed as extreme consequences of an exclusive pattern of attachment, which is a dominant form encouraged in individualistic societies. They are the result of people being encouraged to place 'all their eggs in one basket' (Lofland, 1982). When the loved one dies, the person's whole familiar world – and their sense of self – has been shattered (Prigerson *et al.*, 1997c). This is similar to what happens when someone is subject to a traumatic or sudden loss (Parkes, 1981; Parkes and Weiss, 1983; Rynearson, 1987), or to multiple losses (Kastenbaum, 1969).

Ambivalence and conflict

Freud (1917) suggested that an ambivalent relationship would lead to pathological grief in the form of clinical depression, a view echoed by Abraham (1924). Others in the psychoanalytic tradition (Volkan, 1981) have emphasised the connection between ambivalence and pathological mourning, which involves a conflict between both yearning for the deceased and dreading their return, leading to reactive depression. Becker (1932–3: 398) described the grief of a man who 'had lost all real love for his wife because she had erred sexually with another man', and whose life and death (by suicide) held painful memories for him. He sought to avoid all thoughts and reminders of her. We are not told of the eventual outcome in this case, but one more recent study suggests that his grief may have been prolonged.

Parkes and Weiss (1983) made a retrospective assessment of marital happiness among their sample of bereaved people, by enquiring about eleven different areas of potential marital disagreement, and on the basis of the answers dividing the sample into low- and high-*conflict* groups. The high-conflict group were numerically more common (45 out of 68 respondents).

Their reaction at 6 weeks after the death was one of relatively little upset (or even relief), more social activity and less anxiety, than the low-conflict group. Yet by 13 months, those from the low-conflict group were significantly more likely to have returned to effective functioning, and by 2–4 years they showed better recovery, and lower anxiety, guilt and depression, than did the high-conflict group.

Parkes and Weiss concluded that ambivalence in a relationship produces both blame and a desire to escape, which initially results in a more positive reaction to the loss. This reaction is, however, relatively short-lived and gives way to delayed grief, which is essentially a response to the degree to which the couple have shared their lives together, rather than to the quality of their relationship in terms of happiness. As a woman serving a life sentence for killing her husband (apparently after years of ill-treatment) put it: 'I miss my husband. We were together for so many years. It's easy to remember the good times and forget the bad' (Tracey Williamson in Campbell, 1993: 12). There are also parallels between delayed grief after a conflict-ridden relationship and the continued signs of attachment shown by couples after marital separation (Weiss, 1976, 1982).

Other studies linking marital conflict or an ambivalent relationship with subsequent grief have generally not detected the pattern of delayed grief found by Parkes and Weiss. Admittedly, most have assessed grief at one time only, but even so the findings generally do not fit the pattern expected from their study. One study which is at least *consistent* with the notion of delayed grief is that of Shanfield and Swain (1984). They studied a small sample of parents whose adult sons or daughters had been killed in a motor vehicle crash, and found that those who looked back on their relationships as having been ambivalent showed more guilt and more psychological distress 2 years after the death. However, delayed grief cannot be inferred, since no measures were taken soon after the loss. Zisook *et al.* (1987b) did take measures only 2 months after the death of a spouse, and found poorer outcomes among those who rated their relationships as having been more tense, unsupportive, distant and incompatible. However, these measures may not have captured either ambivalence or conflict. Beutel *et al.* (1995) found that those women who showed the strongest depressive reactions following a miscarriage, and 6 and 12 months later, were more likely to have indicated an ambivalent reaction to the lost foetus, assessed retrospectively during an interview. Taken together, these three studies more support the Freudian notion of a prolonged depressive reaction following loss of an ambivalent relationship than they do a delayed grief reaction. One other study (Lund *et al.*, 1993), of older widows and widowers, found no influence of marital happiness on adjustment measures.

The picture is further complicated when we examine studies that have considered men and women separately. In their Tübingen study, W. Stroebe and M.S. Stroebe (1993) found that although widowers showed more depression and somatic symptoms after losing a less happy marriage, the reverse was the case for widows and the effect was larger in their case. This report did not indicate when the measures were taken, so they are difficult to reconcile with Parkes and Weiss' interpretation of delayed grief. The findings for the men in the Stroebes' study are broadly consistent with those of Gass (1989a,b), who found that older widowers who characterised their former relationship as ambivalent reported more psychosocial problems during the first year of bereavement (assessed at one time only). The findings for women in the Stroebes' study are consistent with those of Dillenburger and Keenan (1994), who studied a sample of widows bereaved through sectarian violence in Northern Ireland. Those who reported more marital happiness showed higher levels of distress after the loss.

In contrast to these studies which all assessed marital quality retro-spectively, Wortman *et al.* (1993) measured marital satisfaction *before* the loss. They found that when changes in depression from before to after bereavement were measured, it was those people with more satisfactory and less conflict-ridden relationships who showed a greater increase in depres-sion. This study involved a variety of measures at time 1 (1985) for a large community sample, and time 2 (1989) measures on 92 people who had been bereaved in the meantime. On average therefore, the second set of mea-sures were taken around 18 months following the loss. This would mean that the pattern of a smaller increase in depression for those who had more conflict-ridden marriages could not be attributable to delayed grief. The findings are, however, consistent with the two sets of findings for widows described above (Dillenburger and Keenan, 1994; W. Stroebe and M.S. Stroebe, 1993).

By taking measures of marital satisfaction before the loss, and by using the *change* in depression scores as the dependent variable, Wortman *et al.* have introduced the two important controls which were absent from the other studies of ambivalence (and those on dependency). Existing studies also dif-fer in other ways, for example the measures of the marital compatibility, the outcome measures, the time since the loss occurred when these were taken, and the statistical procedures. Which of these are important must await further investigation.

Attachment styles

Parkes and Weiss identified the two relationship variables which influenced the course of grief by initially setting up a longer list of possible variables, and concentrating on those which seemed to influence outcome measures. Another possible approach is to concentrate on those aspects of relationships which are likely to prove problematic both for the relationship itself and for adjustment to its loss. This is made possible through the study of attachment styles among adults, based on the earlier classification of relationships between infants and their caregivers by Ainsworth (1979), outlined above. The classifications of adult attachment seem to relate more to individuals rather than to the relationships (as was Ainsworth's), but this should make them more rather than less relevant to bereavement.

The initial scheme applied to adults was that of Hazan and Shaver (1987), which followed Ainsworth's in distinguishing secure, anxious-ambivalent (or preoccupied) and anxious-avoidant forms of attachment. Anxious-ambivalent involves the person wanting to be closer to others than they want them to be, and anxious-avoidant involves others wanting to be closer than the person wants. Hazan and Shaver based their classification on a choice between three prototypical descriptions of the three attachment styles, which were later reformulated as a 13-item questionnaire (Simpson, 1990). There is also an observational method for measuring adult attachment (Rothbard and Shaver, 1994).

Hazan and Shaver found that there were the same proportions of each attachment type among college students and among samples of adults from the general public as there were in Ainsworth's studies of infant attachment. They also found that the relationships of securely attached people lasted considerably longer than those of the other two types, and that there were a number of other differences, for example in notions of romantic love. Securely attached people also reported warmer relationships with both of their parents, and that their parents had warmer relationships with one another.

Keelan, Dion and Dion (1994) studied the relationships of college students over a 4-month period. They found that those who were securely attached showed more commitment to their relationship, more trust in their partner and more relationship satisfaction than insecurely attached students did. Other studies have shown that secure adults – like secure children – are more emotionally positive, have longer relationships and experience fewer break-ups than insecurely attached adults (Rothbard and Shaver, 1994). They also show more baby-talk to their partners (Bombar and Littig, 1996).

Bartholomew and Horowitz (1991) revised the original three-category classification of attachment style. They proposed a 2×2 classification along two dimensions, concerning the people's evaluation of themselves and of others as positive or negative, i.e. as worthy or unworthy. People who regard themselves and others positively will possess a 'secure' attachment style, enabling them to be comfortable with both intimacy and autonomy. If, instead, they regard themselves as unworthy, but others as worthy, this will produce a 'dependent' attachment style and a preoccupation with relationships (equivalent to the original anxious-ambivalent style). Those who are negative about both themselves and others will show a 'fearful' attachment style (equivalent to the original anxious-avoidant style). Finally, people who are positive about themselves but negative about others will show a 'dismissing' style, which creates a category not included in Hazan and Shaver's classification (Brennan, Shaver and Tobey, 1991): they will be wary about other people, who will not live up to their expectations.

It is important to note that this classification, like that of Hazan and Shaver, provides only prototypes (Baldwin *et al.*, 1996; Griffin and

Bartholomew, 1994a). In reality, people do not uniquely fit one category. Instead, they show a mixture of styles across time and relationships (thus indicating that the classification does to some extent describe relationship rather than individual features). Bartholomew and Horowitz (1991) based their classification on a structured interview about people's friendships, romantic relationships and their feelings about relationships. Different statistical procedures[2] confirmed the prototypical styles, and showed that each was associated with particular interpersonal problems. For example, styles nearest to the preoccupied and fearful prototypes (involving negative self-evaluations) were characterised by more interpersonal distress than were the other two styles.

The validity of this scheme was further demonstrated in three studies applying the statistical technique of confirmatory factor analysis to the earlier data and to measures taken from a new sample (Griffin and Bartholomew, 1994b). Confirmatory factor analysis involves testing whether the underlying structure of people's answers fits a particular theoretical model, in this case the two dimensions of evaluating the self and others in terms of a dimension from positive to negative. Overall, there was a good fit with the model, which applied irrespective of whether measures were obtained by self-reports, or interview ratings or peer assessments. Measures intended to assess the dimensions directly, such as self-esteem scales and interpersonal orientation, also confirmed the validity of the two dimensions.[3]

We now come to the question of how these different attachment styles might produce different patterns of grieving. Parkes and Weiss' study suggested that a dependent attachment style – assessed by intensity of yearning – was associated with severe and prolonged grief. Dependency is presumably equivalent to the anxious-ambivalent style of Hazan and Shaver, and to Bartholomew's preoccupied style. As indicated above, the problem with establishing a link between research on attachment styles and on grief is that most studies of grief rely on retrospective measures of relationship styles.

Longitudinal studies which involve measures of attachment taken before the loss are of course more feasible when they are concerned with relationship break-up than with bereavement. Simpson (1990) found that young men who showed an anxious-avoidant relationship style (on Hazan and Shaver's classification), that is, they tended to maintain an emotional distance, also tended to show less emotional upset when the relationship had broken-up. Keelan *et al.* (1994) found that, compared to the insecure categories, securely attached students viewed a former relationship and partner in more positive terms once the relationship had ended. Hindy and Schwarz (1994) found that college students who scored highly on an anxious-attachment scale had a

---

2 Correlations and multi-dimensional scaling.
3 For a more detailed report of measurement theory and research relating to adult attachment, see Griffin and Bartholomew (1994a).

difficult time coping with loss. In another sample, they found that the scale consisted of two components, one describing anxiety about the relationship, and the other an obsessional preoccupation with the partner and the relationship (comparable with Bartholomew's preoccupied style). The second of these was associated with pronounced depression when the relationship had ended.

At present, it is difficult to tell the extent to which findings linking attachment style and reactions to relationship break-up might apply to bereavement. However, there do seem to be parallels between Hindy and Schwarz's results and the suggested link between dependency and pronounced and prolonged grieving.

Sex differences might be worth examining in future studies. More men than women are found in the dismissing category and more women than men in the fearful category (Bartholomew and Horowitz, 1991; Brennan *et al.*, 1991). These differences seem to be associated with wider-ranging differences in the confrontation and disclosure of emotions (Archer, 1996b), which also affect patterns of coping with bereavement (Chapter 13).

An evolutionary approach to attachment styles

Bowlby and Ainsworth made the clear assumption that the normal attachment style is the secure one – 'nature's prototype' as Chisholm (1996) put it. The two (or more) insecure styles were seen as deviations from this prototype. Over recent years there have been a number of challenges to this view from an evolutionary perspective which emphasises adaptive flexibility in development (Hinde, 1986; Lamb *et al.*, 1985; Main, 1990). The different attachment styles are viewed as adaptations to different parenting styles, which in turn are linked to different environmental conditions.

This view of individual differences in attachment has been elaborated by Chisholm (1996) in relation to the evolutionary study of life cycles known as 'life history theory'. Underlying this is the principle that a developing organism selectively allocates its scarce resources to the competing demands of survival, growth and development, and reproduction, all of which are necessary for fitness when considered over the individual's lifespan.

At different times in development, there are different priorities in terms of the allocation of resources. For example, in birds and mammals, sexual maturity is delayed until the organism is sufficiently well developed to be likely to reproduce successfully. At younger ages, survival, growth and development take priority over reproduction. All of these are necessary for fitness when the whole lifespan is considered. Life history theory assumes that the different priorities at different ages lead overall to an optimal level of fitness for the organism, given the restrictions of the environment and the way the organism is constructed. The same principle can be extended to consider optimisation over several generations. One strategy may lead to increased fitness in that more great-grandchildren are produced than would otherwise be the case: selection would favour this option over simply maximising the numbers of offspring within a single generation.

The reasoning behind life history theory also leads us to consider the case of individuals with similar genetic make-up ('genotypes') developing in different environmental conditions. Their responses to these different environments may involve different priorities at different stages of development. Furthermore, different environments early in life can be considered as good predictors of what the organism is likely to encounter later in life. It is these principles that have been applied to different attachment styles (Chisholm, 1996). Some environments will be safer and more predictable than others, and the long-term optimal strategy in such cases will be to produce consistently fewer children over many generations. Other environments will be relatively unsafe and unpredictable, and the optimal strategy in these cases will be the shorter-term one of producing children as quickly as possible. Reproduction rather than parenting becomes the priority in life history decisions.

This theoretical analysis fits the contrasting reproductive strategies of women in modern western societies and those in the Third World today described by Scheper-Hughes (1992). She applied a different theoretical perspective, one which concentrates on the mothers' attachments to their offspring rather than the offspring's attachment style. Scheper-Hughes argued that in pre-demographic transition societies, an older strategy is enacted, one which involves giving birth to many children and investing selectively in those who seem to be 'best bets' for survival. This strategy demands different maternal attachments, sentiments and feelings:

> In a world of great uncertainty about life and death it makes no sense at all to put any *one* person – not a parent, not a husband or lover, and certainly not a sickly toddler or fragile infant – at the center of anything.
> (Scheper-Hughes, 1992: 403)

Chisholm's analysis concentrated on the implications for the child's (rather than the mother's) attachment style. He argued that the way in which young humans sense what their environment is like in terms of it being safe or unsafe is derived from their parents. Parental responses to the environment are signalled to the offspring through the parents' behaviour towards them, and the young react emotionally to this behaviour so as to establish a particular way of relating to their parents. The two insecure attachment styles are viewed as adaptations to parental behaviour which in the evolutionary environment signalled either parental inability to invest in the offspring (anxious-avoidant style) or parental unwillingness to invest (anxious-ambivalent), usually because the priority was the production of other offspring. Secure attachment occurs when the parents are investing in few high-quality young as a response to low risk and low uncertainty in the environment.

These different responses are seen both as rational reactions to the immediate parenting style and ways in which optimal future relationship styles might be predicted. In the first case, the anxious-ambivalent style is a strategy for extracting resources from a mother who is preoccupied with survival, whereas the anxious-avoidant style is a strategy for coping with rejecting mothers. In the long term, the attachment styles are seen as 'socioassays' (Chisholm, 1996) of future relationship characteristics.

The evidence from North American studies does indeed show that adults with an anxious-avoidant style are most likely to report childhood separation from their mothers (Feeney and Noller, 1990), and the anxious-ambivalent style is associated with low or inconsistent maternal involvement (Cassidy and Berlin, 1994).

Adults with secure attachment histories have more stable and longer-term romantic relationships than those with insecure attachment histories, and also tend to be more sensitive to their children (Rothbard and Shaver, 1994). Those with insecure attachment histories tended to marry or cohabit at younger ages with shorter courtships. There is also evidence that women with the anxious-ambivalent style are more likely to be unfaithful to their main partner (Gangestad and Thornhill, 1997).

Attachment styles can therefore be seen as evolved developmental systems through which children are disposed (indirectly) to monitor their environment, so as to be able to make decisions about future allocation of resources to survival and earlier reproduction versus longer-term investment in the growth, development and learning of their offspring.

The life history perspective on attachment is fairly new and much of it is speculative. Its implications for individual differences in bereavement have not been considered. However, it could be extended to view differences in reactions to losses as part of a consistent pattern in the way the person approached relationships, which was originally rooted in his or her response to parenting experiences. Since the reaction to separation is a distinctive part of the attachment style, and grief is an extension of this separation reaction, we should be able to predict different types of grief reactions from different attachment styles, which in turn reflect different reactions to parenting.

Attachment-based and evolutionary views of individual differences

The approach to individual differences in grief taken in this chapter was based on attachment theory, and it therefore emphasised the characteristics of the prior relationship in terms of the overall strength and style of attachment. Within a single type of relationship, for example between a husband and wife, different strengths of attachment and different styles will predict different intensities and forms of grieving.

The evolutionary-based view considered in the previous chapter was also concerned with individual differences in grief. However, here the emphasis was on different categories of relationships, particularly those based on kinship, age or sex. This approach involved predictions based on ultimate or functional considerations. The way in which these mediate the pattern of grief has in the past not always been made specific. It is, however, clear that the intensity of grief is the variable under consideration, and that this in turn is related to different strengths (but not styles) of attachment. This would apply, for example, to grief for different degrees of relatedness, or for offspring of different ages.

In the following three chapters I consider in more detail studies which involve the individual differences highlighted by the evolutionary analysis, that is kinship, age and sex, and wherever possible assess the extent to which they fit the pattern predicted by, first, evolutionary analyses, and second the mediating variable of strength of attachment. As indicated in this chapter, there are usually no very precise predictions from attachment theory about these sorts of individual differences, beyond the general one linking strength of attachment with intensity of bereavement. However, by linking the two approaches, a more complete understanding can be achieved. By examining ultimate explanations, it is possible to specify why certain relationships usually involve different strengths of attachment. By examining strength of attachment, it is possible to examine the degree to which this is the mechanism through which evolutionarily important variables manifest themselves in relationships.

11 Loss of a son or daughter

Perfect little body, without fault or stain on thee,
With promise of strength and manhood full and fair!
Though cold and stark and bare,
The bloom and the charm of life doth awhile remain on thee.

Thy mother's treasure wert thou; – alas! no longer
To visit her heart with wondrous joy; to be
Thy father's pride: – ah, he
Must gather his faith together, and his strength make stronger'.
(Robert Bridges, 'On a dead child', in Quiller-Couch, 1919: 1015)

Introduction

This chapter extends our consideration of bereavement beyond the marital relationship (which has informed existing theories of grief) to the death of a son or daughter at various ages. As indicated in the previous chapters, the type of relationship with the deceased will be the most important predictor of the severity and course of grief. Studies carried out in several western societies show that marital bereavement is often viewed as producing the most severe form of grief. Questionnaire ratings show that it is perceived by most people as the life crisis from which it would take longest to recover (Holmes and Rahe, 1967). Despite this finding, a form of loss that has been found to evoke more intense grief – at least in modern western societies (cf. Scheper-Hughes, 1992) – is death of a son or daughter during infancy or childhood (Burnett *et al.*, 1997; Klass, 1988; Leahy, 1992–3; Middleton *et al.*, 1996; Sanders, 1979–80, 1989; Singh and Raphael, 1981). One crucial feature is that parents lose all their associated hopes and dreams for the future, the 'promise' recognised in the second line of Robert Bridges' poem. What Klass (1988: 13) described as 'an empty historical track' is set up. Grief can be very long lasting, staying with the parents for the rest of their lives – as in the case of Charles and Emma Darwin's grief for their daughter Annie (Chapter 7). Parents become reminded at various times what their child would have been doing years later (Klass, 1988), thus accentuating the impact of anniversaries described for marital grief.

Two evolutionary considerations determine the importance of offspring to their parents. First, they are genetically similar: the index of relatedness is 50 per cent (Chapter 9), i.e. they share on average half the genes that are rare in the whole population. This is the same degree of relatedness as for full siblings. The second consideration is that parents are older and offspring are particularly vulnerable in their younger years. We belong to a species for whom parental care is both essential for survival and is prolonged. The close attachment bonds formed by parents to their children can be understood as a result of an interaction between these two features. With the exception of aiding an identical twin, offspring provide the best available way for humans to perpetuate their genes in the future.

In Chapter 9, I considered the prediction that grief varies with the age of the child according to its reproductive value, that is, its likely contribution to offspring in succeeding generations. This involves a steady increase in parental grief as the child matures, from conception until young adulthood. The development of attachment involves a form of exposure learning derived from a continued mutually satisfying interaction over time (Bowlby, 1969). We should expect an increase in attachment for the first few years of a child's life, but thereafter it is not clear whether there would be increasing strength of parental attachment with the age of the child, or a levelling off after the early childhood years. A further issue concerns the development of attachment before birth. Based on the maternal-bonding research of Klaus and Kennell (1976),[1] which concerned the mother's postnatal attachment, Peppers and Knapp (1980) emphasised the gradual development of a bond before this time through the mental events associated with pregnancy. These begin with planning the pregnancy, its acceptance, and the gradual development of the pregnancy itself, and culminate in early postnatal life. This account also emphasised a disparity in attachment formation between mothers and fathers.

If parental grief does vary according to the child's reproductive value and other variables identified by the evolutionary perspective, it is necessary to look again at the mechanisms which influence the strength of attachment. In addition to its gradual development through the mental plans and representations built up during pregnancy, and subsequent interactions with the infant, attachment strength would also be influenced by cues related to evolutionarily important variables. Daly and Wilson (1988b) introduced the term 'discriminative parental solicitude' to describe the extent to which parents' attentiveness and willingness to care for offspring varies in relation to cues indicating the net fitness advantages of doing so. These include whether the parents were natural or step-parents, the maternal age at which the offspring were born (reflecting the mother's reproductive value), how many other

---

1 The original research was associated with a rigid view of maternal bond formation, but Peppers and Knapp's development of it did not have these features (Archer, 1992a: 68).

children there are, the health of the offspring, and the age of the child (reflecting its reproductive value). In the case of grief, any links with evolutionarily important variables would have to be indirectly mediated via aspects of the relationship, such as attachment strength, which reflected these variables. The precise mechanism whereby cues related to fitness influence variables such as the strength of attachment is not clear at present – the term discriminative parental solicitude is useful up to a point, but it does not tell us *how* parents are influenced by such cues.

Daly and Wilson (1988a,b) used homicide and child abuse rates as negative indices of discriminative parental solicitude, and knowledge of offspring attitudes and beliefs (Daly, McConnell and Glugosh, 1996) as positive indices. Parental grief might profitably be studied from this perspective, but so far it has not been, at least explicitly. Although there is some evidence on how variables such as parents' and offspring's ages, and numbers of other children, affect parents' grief, there are no studies comparing step-parents', adopted parents' and natural parents' grief, and none that specifically relate the reproductive value of parents and offspring to parental grief.

The concept of discriminative parental solicitude can also be applied to some cross-cultural differences. Where parental grief is absent, for example among mothers from parts of the Third World (Scheper-Hughes, 1992), this is associated with a belief-system that minimises the individuality of infants and which does not pin hopes and dreams for the future on a single baby: 'Infants, like husbands and boyfriends, are best thought of as temporary attachments. Both tend to disappoint women' (Scheper-Hughes, 1992: 410). Under these circumstances, the mother is responding to indications of the offspring's likelihood of survival, both generally because of the scarce resources, and individually in terms of assessing whether a particular infant seems robust or fragile. This represents an important variable we should expect to be associated with strength of attachment, and hence the intensity of grief.

Considering the impact of parental age, we should expect a stronger grief reaction at older ages (particularly for women), since reproductive value declines throughout adult life. There would be no parallel prediction from attachment theory, and the mechanism through which this might occur is not immediately apparent.

One other evolutionary prediction is that parents who have lost an only child should be more strongly affected than those with other surviving children, since they have lost their only existing means of passing on their genes. A possible mechanism in this case would be the breadth or narrowness of parental attachments, which would be more narrowly focused for a parent with a single offspring. This parallels the argument that grief will be more intense when the range of family relations is narrow (Volkart and Michael, 1957; Chapter 10).

Another prediction is that fathers would in general be expected to grieve less intensely than mothers, at least for early losses (Figure 11.1). As indicated

Figure 11.1 A father mourning the death of his child in eastern Peru: the prediction from evolutionary theory is that the grief of fathers will generally be less than that of mothers for losses of very young children.

Source: Photograph by Federico Patellani

in Chapter 9, this is derived from the relative parental investment of the two sexes which is, initially anyway, higher in the mother than the father, since she is carrying and feeding the offspring throughout pregnancy and feeding it following birth. Fathers generally begin to show appreciable parental investment only later in development. Based on this consideration, and on paternity uncertainty, we should expect lower paternal than maternal grief, particularly at younger offspring ages. In this case, the mechanism is easily understood in terms of attachment, mothers beginning to bond with the offspring much earlier in its life than is the case for the fathers (Peppers and Knapp, 1980).

The existing studies of parental grief have been informed by very different agendas than these theoretical concerns, often beginning with the practical need for health professionals to recognise grief for offspring who had died at early stages in their development. Such studies tend to be located in the medical literature dealing with pregnancy, birth and early childhood. They are nearly all undertaken within Anglo-American cultures, so that important cross-cultural comparisons can seldom be made.

We can order the available studies according to the age of the child who has died, first examining the impact of miscarriage and induced abortion, second stillbirth and sudden infant death, and finally death of an older child and of adult offspring. This should enable an assessment of the general impact of the child's age to be made. We can therefore begin to address the issue of whether grief does closely follow the child's reproductive value or whether, once parents have fully developed a bond with the child, they feel a high intensity of grief for any loss irrespective of age. We can also examine some of the other variables outlined above, such as the impact of other children, maternal age and the sex of the parent, where they have been studied.

Miscarriage

Death of a child is widely recognised as a severe and difficult form of loss. However, many deaths occur early in the child's development, before the parents have been able to form a relationship based on the individuality of that child. Miscarriages occur in up to 15 per cent of pregnancies in the US (Seibel and Graves, 1980) and Australia (Frost and Condon, 1996), and up to 20 per cent in the UK (Iles, 1989; Lee and Slade, 1996). There have been many reports of reactions such as guilt, depression and anxiety, which are consistent with grieving, occurring following miscarriage among women from the western world (Friedman and Gath, 1989; Gold, 1985; Lee, Slade and Lygo, 1996; Lietar, 1986; Seibel and Graves, 1980; reviews by Frost and Condon, 1996, Lee and Slade, 1996). The attention to the subject of pregnancy loss in western psychology contrasts with the lack of anthropological writing on the subject, which is mostly concerned with cultural attributions for why the loss occurred (Cecil, 1996).

There are several reservations about using reports of depression and anxiety following a miscarriage as evidence of grief. One is that simply noting their occurrence does not demonstrate whether there has been an increase in these measures from before to after the miscarriage. With the exception of some recent studies, most reports include neither measures taken before the miscarriage nor the use of control comparison groups. Even studies which do allow such comparisons contain two further confounds. First, it is known that the rate of miscarriage is increased by stressful circumstances (Sapolsky, 1994), which are themselves likely to raise the levels of depression and anxiety. Second, the physical trauma of a miscarriage constitutes a further stressor contributing to such reactions (Lee and Slade, 1996). These considerations are difficult to control for when looking for evidence of grief.

Bearing in mind these reservations, some studies have used questionnaires which concern grief reactions. Grief intensity scores are usually high immediately after the miscarriage, but generally decline fairly soon afterwards (Beutel *et al.* 1995; Janssen *et al.*, 1996, 1997). Reactions to the loss may last for several months, and years in some cases (Hunfeld, Wladimiroff and Passchier, 1997b), although a long-term retrospective study (Rosenblatt and Burns, 1986) found little indication of long-lasting effects (2–46 years later) in most cases.

The nature and form of any grief reaction is likely to depend on the woman's circumstances, for example whether the pregnancy was planned or not (Seibel and Graves, 1980; Neugebauer *et al.*, 1992a), the existence of recognition and support, uncertainties over future pregnancy prospects, and family pressures to have children (Gannon, 1992). The book by Peppers and Knapp (1980) was based on letters and interviews with parents who had experienced miscarriages, stillbirths and neonatal death in the US. The authors emphasised the social isolation experienced by the parents under all these circumstances, owing to the lack of recognition of their grief by others, especially if the loss occurred early in pregnancy. To an outsider, the foetus is not seen as a person, and both hospital practice (particularly in the past), and wider societal reactions reflect this perception. All this will contribute to social surroundings which constrain talking about the loss, and may prevent or delay its eventual resolution (Lepore *et al.*, 1996; Chapter 8). Similarly, accounts from other cultures indicate little societal recognition of the psychological consequences of pregnancy loss (Cecil, 1996).

To the mother (and to a lesser extent the father), the inner experience may involve a person to whom an attachment begins to be felt right from the beginning of pregnancy, based on plans and hopes for the future (Peppers and Knapp, 1980; Peppers, 1987–8). There may be grief for 'the passing of a dream', as one woman expressed it (Lietar, 1986). This highlights the point made in general models of the generation of grief (Janoff-Bulman, 1989, 1993; Parkes, 1971), that it is the discrepancy between the outside world and the person's inner experience, their cherished ideas and plans, that evokes grief, rather than a loss defined in any objective terms (see Chapter 1). We should, however, also note evidence from retrospective reports (Rosenblatt and Burns, 1986) that some women do not experience a sense that they have lost a person, and are more distressed by the physical and medical aspects of the experience.

Nevertheless, psychological distress unrecognised by others has been sufficiently widespread in the past for the UK Stillbirth and Neonatal Death Society (SANDS) to publish, in 1992, guidelines for hospitals dealing with miscarriages. They called for them to treat the remains with dignity, and to offer parents the opportunity for a burial or cremation. The guidelines acknowledged the importance of the loss to most parents, and they tried to avoid the repetition of past instances of staff acting insensitively when disposing of the remains 'like a piece of rubbish', as one parent put it (Kohner, 1992). In the US, changes in hospital practice, reflecting increasing awareness of parents' grief, have also taken place (Lasker and Toedter, 1994).

On average, we should expect grief to be less pronounced for foetal loss than for stillbirth or neonatal death, from the standpoint of the increasing reproductive value of the offspring mediated by the progressive development of maternal attachment during pregnancy and beyond. We should expect a general increase in grief with the length of the pregnancy, for the same reasons; also a stronger grief reaction as the mother's age increases, and for childless women to be more strongly affected by their loss than women with other children.

These variables have been studied in several longitudinal studies which have included control samples (ideally, both women at comparable stages of pregnancy to control for psychological changes during pregnancy, and also women who are not pregnant). Neugebauer *et al.* (1992b) interviewed nearly 400 women at 2 weeks, 6 weeks and 6 months after a miscarriage. At 2 weeks, they found symptoms of depression to be four times that of a community sample and three times that of a pregnant sample, but the levels were comparable with those of the community sample at the other two times. Interestingly, women first interviewed at 6 weeks or at 6 months also showed elevated depression rates, about three times that of a community sample, suggesting that the intervention (a telephone interview) was therapeutic.

In another report based on some of the same sample assessed within 4 weeks of miscarriage, Neugebauer *et al.* (1992a) found that women who were childless had greatly elevated depression levels, 11 times those of community controls and 7.5 times those of pregnant women. Women with several children did not show higher symptom levels than community women. In this study, neither the length of gestation nor the mother's age had significant influences on depression levels (although women with late pregnancy loss did experience stronger depressive reactions).

In a later study, Neugebauer *et al.* (1997) examined the incidence of major depressive disorder (using DSM-IIIR[2] criteria) among a sample of women who had experienced a miscarriage, and compared them to a matched control sample from the community. Overall, they found that the relative risk (RR) of a depressive disorder was elevated by 2.5 among the women who had had a miscarriage. Again, the risk was greater (RR = 5.0) among childless women compared with those who had children (RR = 1.3). Neither the mothers' age nor their experience of prior reproductive loss affected the risk.

The findings for childless women are consistent with the Darwinian prediction outlined in the Introduction, but those for maternal age were not (the prediction being that older mothers, who have lower reproductive value, would be more affected than younger ones).

A study carried out in Munich by Beutel *et al.* (1995) examined grief and other reactions among 125 women who had miscarried during the first 20 weeks of gestation, at three separate times, after the loss, 6 months and 12 months later. They also compared these women with two matched control groups, one from the community and the other at the same stage during uncomplicated pregnancies. Overall, women who had miscarried showed higher scores on a perinatal grief scale (Toedter *et al.*, 1988; Potvin *et al.*,

2 American Psychiatric Association (1987).

1989), and higher depression and anxiety levels than controls. Depression was still higher than in controls at 6 and 12 months, but anxiety was no different.

When the depression and grief levels of the women who had miscarried were used to divide up the sample, it was found that initial depression (but not initial grief) predicted long-term health problems, and that an ambivalent reaction to the foetus, as well as a previous history of depression, characterised those who were prone to depression. Overall, those without a depressive or grief response showed signs of having not developed a strong attachment to the foetus, which is consistent with the view that attachment strength mediates the grief reaction.

Another longitudinal study (Janssen *et al.*, 1996), undertaken in Nijmegen in the Netherlands, had the additional feature of being prospective: the 227 women who had experienced a miscarriage were derived from an initial sample of 2140 pregnant women. This enabled the researchers to establish that a pre-loss personality variable (neuroticism) strongly predicted higher grief intensity (Janssen *et al.*, 1997). In other studies (Friedman and Gath, 1989) it had been difficult to tell whether this was the case or whether the neurotic characteristics were the result of the loss. Janssen *et al.* (1996, 1997) also found that gestational age was a strong predictor of grief intensity – which is consistent with the earlier study of Kirkley Best (1981), but not that of Neugebauer *et al.* (1992a) described above.

Absence of living children was also (but less strongly) associated with grief intensity (Janssen *et al.*, 1997), as it was in the studies of Kirkley Best (1981) and Neugebauer *et al.* (1992a, 1997). Although maternal age was not overall a significant predictor of grief intensity, older women did show significantly higher scores on the subscale which indicated difficulties coping with the loss. In another study from the same sample, Cuisinier *et al.* (1996) reported that both conceiving again and giving birth to a subsequent healthy child significantly reduced the level of grief. In only a small minority of women was grief reactivated by a subsequent birth.

There is little evidence on fathers' grief following a miscarriage. On the basis of evolutionary theory, we would expect this to be considerably less than that of the mother. The majority of studies that considered fathers indicates that this is the case. For example, Goldbach *et al.* (1991), Theut *et al.* (1989) and Thomas *et al.* (1997) all found that mothers had significantly higher scores than fathers on standardised grief questionnaires and on measures of depression and stress, taken at various times after the loss. However, no control groups were included in these studies, so that the intended measures of reactions to loss may have incorporated pre-existing sex differences in measures of distress and well-being. The importance of making this distinction is discussed further in Chapter 13.

One study produced results apparently at odds with the other findings. Johnson and Puddifoot (1996) administered a perinatal grief scale and the Impact of Events Scale (Horowitz *et al.*, 1980) to male partners of women who had recently experienced a miscarriage in north-east England. They found high levels for both measures, showing that grief levels were similar to norms reported for women soon after experiencing a miscarriage. Although these findings, and reports of interviews with some of the men (Puddifoot and Johnson, 1997) do seem to indicate a stronger than expected grief reaction, there is a problem in interpreting the scale scores without any comparison groups. An additional interesting finding from this study was that the men's grief scores increased with the gestational age at the time of miscarriage, thus paralleling the findings reported above for women.

Induced abortion

There are different views about whether a grief reaction occurs following induced abortion. The debate has mostly concerned the situation in the United States, where abortion was legalised in 1973 and became a matter of private decision. In other countries there are a variety of laws, from complete prohibition to a situation similar to that in the US.

A review of about 250 articles by Doane and Quigley (1981) on psychiatric and related aspects of abortion pointed out the difficulties of drawing conclusions from these studies owing to deficiencies in their design and other methodological problems, a view endorsed by later reviewers (Posavac and Miller, 1990; Wilmoth, De Alteriis and Bussell, 1992). The findings available to Doane and Quigley indicated that only a small percentage of women reported feeling worse than before in the months after an induced abortion. Among these, the commonest feeling was depression, sometimes accompanied by indications of grief. Some women reported positive emotional responses. Other reviews (Adler, 1992) have likewise concluded that only a minority of women experience problems after an induced abortion. A meta-analysis by Posavac and Miller (1990) found an overall improvement in emotional state when pre- and post-abortion measures were compared (see below).

Yet other commentators (Speckhard, 1997; Speckhard and Rue, 1992; Raphael, 1983) have suggested that a pattern of grief not dissimilar to that following a miscarriage commonly occurs, but that it is often suppressed or inhibited, for example because the woman is grateful for the termination and seeks to deny any feelings of attachment to the foetus (Speckhard and Rue, 1992). The absence of any socially acknowledged pattern of mourning under these circumstances would also mitigate against full expression of grieving.

Clearly this claim is difficult to evaluate. It is, however, consistent with some personal accounts, such as that of Kesselman (1990). She wrote of her experiences following three induced abortions, one occurring at a young age and the others following the end of marriage. She noticed a pattern of reactions following each one, and she wrote down her experiences in order to struggle with what in retrospect she viewed as unacknowledged grief. Taking a class on death and dying also helped her come to terms with her experiences. Kesselman argued that the possibility of grieving should be acknowledged in cases of abortion, and that grief therapy should be part of abortion counselling. A similar view was taken by Harris (1986), although she emphasised that only a minority – perhaps 1 per cent – are likely to show grief that raises the sort of problems Kesselman described. Nevertheless, even this incidence would involve many women, given the numbers of induced abortions that have been carried out (in the US it was about 1.5 million per year in the early 1990s, according to Brown, Elkins and Larson, 1993).

Harris (1986) discussed the reasons why a woman would be at a higher risk of post-abortion reactions. She referred to poor emotional adjustment prior to pregnancy, a young age, pressures to have an abortion that might conflict with wanting to continue the pregnancy, religious beliefs incompatible with abortion and, perhaps most importantly, having an abortion for medical reasons rather than as a personal decision to end an unwanted pregnancy. The meta-analytic review of Posavac and Miller (1990) found that only in the case of therapeutic abortions was there lower well-being than in comparison groups. For elective abortions, psychological well-being was higher than among comparison groups.

Another important influence on the outcome is when the abortion was undertaken. Women undergoing later (second trimester) abortions are often younger, they tend to show more denial, and to refer to 'the baby' or 'the child' rather than to 'the pregnancy' or 'the foetus' (Harris, 1986). Abortions carried out at this time are also more like giving birth, the foetus sometimes being delivered alive and viewed by the mother. The woman will also have been pregnant for longer. Although there is evidence of pronounced grief later in pregnancy among women who had undergone elective abortions by amniocentesis (induced miscarriage) at 16–20 weeks (Pasnau and Farash, 1977), there were no comparison groups undergoing earlier abortions in this study. Peppers (1987–8) did find that grief was lowest when a pregnancy was terminated at 7–12 weeks rather than at 13–16 weeks, which in turn was lower than one undertaken at 17–24 weeks. It should be noted that in these comparisons abortion procedures and the foetal age are confounded, so that they cannot be used to assess a possible link between gestational age and grief intensity.

In Peppers' study, grief was measured (by Sanders' GEI) before the termination, when the decision had been made, as well as afterwards. Grief was more intense when the decision had been made, and the comparisons referred to above concern these times. There was a marked decline after the abortion, suggesting that resolution of any grief is rapid. A later meta-analysis of a number of studies comparing pre- and post-abortion levels of grief supported Peppers' findings (Posavac and Miller, 1990).

Adler (1992) reviewed studies of abortion which met certain criteria, notably the use of standard quantitative methods of assessment and having been carried out in the US. From 20 such studies she confirmed that rates of depression, anxiety and other negative emotions decline from before to shortly after the abortion, and that the absolute levels of distress are relatively low. Two types of negative reaction were identified, one socially based, which was most strongly related to religious attendance, and the other more concerned with internal concerns, which was most strongly related to difficulties in making the decision. Clearly, abortion is not necessarily experienced as a loss but various attributional processes associated with social pressures and individual decision-making mediate between the event and any psychological feelings of grief. These were further investigated by Major and her colleagues (Major *et al.*, 1990, Major and Cozzarelli, 1992), who concluded that influences such as blaming the pregnancy on one's character, coping poorly with stressful events in general, perceiving others as unsupportive and unhelpful and difficulties making the abortion decision were all likely to increase distress and lower adjustment after the abortion.

Since abortion is such a highly charged religious and political issue, the existence of grief or trauma reactions has been used to support the anti-abortion case. Some advocates have gone further and accused researchers of denying the negative effects of abortion (Speckhard and Rue, 1992). However, a more even-handed assessment of the quality of the research cited by both sides (Wilmoth *et al.*, 1992) concluded that both were biased, but that the evidence cited by pro-choice advocates was of better quality than that cited by anti-abortion campaigners.

Whatever one's views about the morality of abortion, it is still important to recognise the possibility of grief or trauma reactions, and to provide appropriate counselling (Harris, 1986; Kesselman, 1990), even if severe reactions are uncommon and are only associated with certain risk-factors. At the same time, we should be wary of accounts that seek to exaggerate the reactions for political ends.

When viewing abortion in terms of social policy, it is also important to take a wider view and to balance the possibility of a grief-like reaction following abortion with the severe and prolonged grief often shown by women who have given up a child for adoption (Roll, Millen and Backlund, 1986) or the difficulties entailed in rearing an unwanted child under disadvantageous circumstances (Handy, 1982; Iles, 1989). Such comparisons raise the difficult issue of what is an appropriate control group when considering induced abortion. In the previous section, I referred to two types of comparison used in studies of miscarriage, with pregnant women and with women in the general population. In the case of abortion, it would seem important also to make comparisons with women who carried an unwanted pregnancy to term (Handy, 1982; Wilmoth *et al.*, 1992).

Finally, there is one report which takes the context of abortion away from the politically driven agenda in the US and other western nations. Klass and Heath (1996–7) considered abortion in Japan in relation to the *mizuko jizo*, which is ritualised mourning involving small figures representing the spirits of the aborted foetus. The spiritual background to the ceremony is the widespread (but private) persistence of traditional ancestor worship in modern

Japan. *Mizuko jizo* is a similar process but is complicated because it involves someone who has not been born and therefore is seen as suffering a state of ill-will and enmity, which the ritual seeks to alleviate. The secular background to these rituals is the widespread use of abortion as a form of birth control in modern Japan. A conservative figure (Klass and Heath, 1996–7) is that over a million women have induced abortions each year. In contrast to the US, they tend to be older women who already have children (about three-quarters are 25–39 years of age). The existence of an established ritual suggests that it is recognised that many women will feel grief-like reactions associated with ambivalent feelings following an abortion.

Abortion in Japan fits into a long-established pattern of reproductive restraint, which in earlier times took the form of infanticide. Infanticide has traditionally been carried out by parents when the offspring's prospects were poor, either because of deformities or poor health, or because the parents had few resources (Daly and Wilson, 1988a: 37). In doing so, parents were responding to adaptive cues 'to terminate parental investment' (Hill and Ball, 1996). The modern-day use of abortion in Japan to regulate the numbers of children in the family, so as to value each one and maximise its life prospects, can be viewed as an extension of the traditional use of infanticide. Parents are responding to cues from the complex society in which they live, indicating that their offspring will require a great deal of parental investment to be successful. This leads to the decision to limit family size, which in their society is more readily attained by abortion than by contraception (Klass and Heath, 1996–7): yet it still produces ambivalent feelings about the offspring that are aborted and grief for what they might have been. From an evolutionary perspective, these feelings would arise out of the existing parental investment in the foetus, and would be mediated by the internalisation of feelings of attachment to it. Overall, the decision to abort can be considered as weighing the current parental investment against the perceived future costs of raising that child.

We can use this perspective to make two general predictions about the intensity of grief following an induced abortion. First, we would expect it to be greater at older maternal ages (associated with the decline in reproductive value). Here, we should note that there is evidence from traditional societies for a decline in the number of births leading to infanticide with increasing maternal age (Daly and Wilson, 1988a: 53). There is, at present, little evidence to test this prediction for abortion in the US, but the small-scale study of Pasnau and Farash (1977) did find evidence consistent with it. The grief shown by mothers in Japan, whose average age tends to be considerably greater than those in the US, would also be consistent with this view. We should, however, note that no systematic comparisons have been made between reactions to abortion in the two nations.

A second prediction is that grief following an induced abortion would be greater with increasing age of the foetus, as its reproductive value increases. The limited evidence from the US reviewed earlier in this section was consistent with this but, as previously noted, it is confounded by the more complex and stressful abortion procedures necessary as foetal age increases.

Stillbirth

Although not as common as miscarriages, stillbirths are experienced by a large number of mothers each year (about 1 per cent of deliveries in the US, according to 1985 figures: DeFrain *et al.*, 1990–1). The tragic intermingling of birth and death was expressed in a poem by Charles Lamb:

> I saw where in the shroud did lurk
> A curious frame of nature's work;
> A flower crush'd in the bud,
> A nameless piece of Babyhood
> Was in her cradle coffin lying;
> Extinct, with scarce the sense of dying
> So soon to exchange the imprisoning womb
> For darker closets of the tomb!
> She did but ope an eye, and put
> A clear beam forth, then straight up shut
> For the long dark: ne'er more to see
> Through glasses of mortality.
>   (Charles Lamb, 'On an Infant Dying as Soon
>   as Born', in Quiller-Couch, 1919: 670)

People other than the parents find it hard to appreciate the existence of a stillborn baby as a person: to them it is Lamb's 'nameless piece of Baby-hood', and although it may cause them to stop and think, they will seldom appreciate the emotional impact of the death for the parents. Because still-birth has so seldom been acknowledged in western culture (and indeed in many others), it has been called 'the forgotten grief' (Kirkley Best, 1981; Kirkley Best and Kellner, 1982).

Even though stillbirth entails the loss of the *anticipated* future rather than of an established relationship, the general features of grief are still essentially those described in Chapter 5 for marital bereavement (Giles, 1970; Kennell, Slyter and Klaus, 1970; Kirkley Best and Kellner, 1982; Hutchins, 1986; Smith and Borgers, 1988–9). There is initial disbelief, preoccupation with thoughts of the deceased, guilt, despair, appetite and sleeping disorders, hal-lucinations, illusions of the presence of the deceased, anger and self-blame (especially if no discrete cause of death can be provided). The unexpectedness of the loss may make grief more intense.

There is a consensus in studies of stillbirth that it is helpful for parents to see or hold their baby. Kirkley Best and Kellner (1982) commented that parents who did not do so experienced heightened yearning, a strong impulse to search for the dead baby, jealousy of other babies and hearing phantom crying when there was no infant around, although the evidence on which these conclusions was based is not clear. Whether or not the mother should see or hold the dead baby became a controversial issue for a time, but most authorities now agree that it is helpful if the parents so wish.

Murray and Callan (1988) found greater well-being and lower depression rates among perinatally bereaved parents who expressed most satisfaction with the support they received from the hospital staff. Those reporting greater well-being were also more likely to have been satisfied with the opportunities they had had to create special memories of the baby. These might include having photographs of the dead baby, thus helping to focus the mourning process on his or her individuality. It is interesting to note in this connection that the tradition of post-mortem photography was socially accepted and publicly acknowledged in Victorian times (Ruby, 1988–9): Figure 11.2 shows one of the photographs from Jay Ruby's collection, a baby on a bed from around 1900. This custom is only maintained to the present time through families' own efforts (Hagan, 1974). Figure 11.3 shows a contemporary photograph of a mother holding her baby who had suffered a sudden infant death. Other photographs like this one were subsequently used, along with objects connected with the baby, to maintain memories of her.

There is a large measure of agreement among practitioners (Oglethorpe,

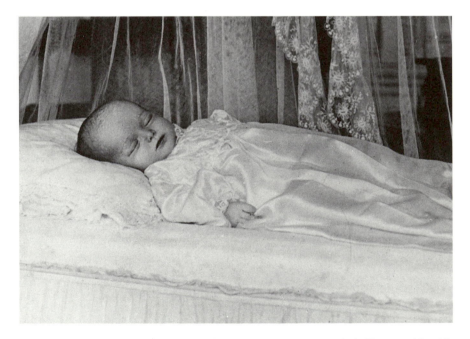

Figure 11.2 The Victorian tradition of post-mortem photography is illustrated by this photograph of a dead infant on a bed, from around 1900.

Source: Reproduced by courtesy of Jay Ruby of the Center for Visual Communication, Mifflintown, Pennsylvania

Figure 11.3 A contemporary photograph of mother Amanda holding her baby Karia
who had died from SIDS, aged 3 months.

Source: Photograph supplied by Odile Archer and reproduced by kind permission of Amanda
Hodgson

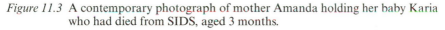

1989) that the mother needs a period of time to come to terms with the loss,
and to move from preoccupation, anger or blame, before beginning another
pregnancy. It has been argued from case studies that if this does not occur, a
new child may come to live in the shadow of the dead infant, or to be held
responsible for the death (Kirkley-Best and Kellner, 1982). Oglethorpe (1989)
referred to a 'replacement child syndrome', where a child is specifically con-
ceived to replace a dead sibling. Associated problems of phobic reactions and
confusion of identity were identified. However, the identification of this condition was largely based on a case study of the replacement of an older child
(Cain and Cain, 1964). This has to be balanced against findings that many
women interviewed after a stillbirth said that they did not want to become
pregnant again (Wolff, Neilson and Schiller, 1970). For other parents, producing a subsequent healthy child after a suitable length of time is likely to
aid resolution of the previously experienced grief (Chapter 8). We should also

note the similar findings for miscarriage, indicating that grief was lessened among women who had a subsequent live birth.

There is very little evidence of changes in grief over time after a stillbirth, or of the relative distress compared to control samples. One exception is the study by Boyle *et al.* (1996), whose study of grief following neonatal death included a sample of mothers who had lost a child through stillbirth. Compared to controls (mothers with a surviving infant), their relative risk for depression was 5.5 at 2 months after the loss, falling to 1.7 at 8 months, although there was a slight increase (to around 2.7) at 15 and 30 months. Anxiety showed a similar trend over time although the initial rate was relatively lower (RR = 4.3).

DeFrain *et al.* (1990–1) measured perceived happiness among mothers, 6 months before a stillbirth, just afterwards, and over the next four years. Happiness was reported to be highest beforehand (near to maximum on the 5-point scale), it fell to near the lowest possible level after the loss, and gradually increased to near the previous high point after 4 years. Although we should be cautious because of the limited measurement, this study, along with the previous one, does suggest that resolution is relatively slow in the case of a stillbirth and that it is generally experienced as a much greater loss than is miscarriage. This is what we would expect intuitively, and is of course predicted by both the reproductive value of the infant and by the gradual development of attachment during the pregnancy.

The same study (DeFrain *et al.*, 1990–1) also found a comparable decline in happiness for fathers immediately after the loss, but a slightly more rapid increase over the next two years. This is consistent with the prediction of a lesser intensity of grief by fathers than mothers for deaths occurring early in life. As with other forms of offspring death, we should expect grief to be more pronounced for mothers who were older and those who had fewer other children, but there is no evidence on these issues for stillbirth.

Perinatal death

Several studies cover the general period of perinatal or neonatal death, that is they include both stillbirths and deaths occurring in infancy (and some include miscarriages as well). Jensen and Zahourek (1972) found that the levels of depression among 25 mothers shortly after a stillbirth or the loss of a baby were significantly higher than normal levels or those among a group of 12 mothers at the time of birth. Levels were still elevated among the bereaved group 6 weeks after the loss, and the mean scores were still above those of controls one year after the loss.[3]

Benfield, Leib and Vollman (1978) studied the grief responses of pairs of parents whose infants had died soon after birth. At an average of 40 days

---

3 By this time the sample was so small that the differences were not statistically significant.

after the loss, they obtained composite grief scores from seven items indicative of the main grief reactions. Grief was significantly higher for mothers than fathers, which is consistent with the limited evidence for miscarriage and stillbirth. Other studies have reported stronger grief reactions or a slower decline in grief by mothers than fathers. Forrest, Standish and Baum (1982) found that the majority of a sample of fathers had recovered by 6 months (as assessed by measures of somatic symptoms, depression and anxiety, in relation to psychiatric norms). In contrast, half the mothers still showed an appreciable reaction 6 months after the loss. Smith and Borgers (1988–9) used Sanders' GEI scale (Chapter 2), to investigate grief following various forms of perinatal death. Mothers showed more intense grief overall than fathers did, a difference which declined with increasing age of the child at death, which is consistent with the view that fathers catch up in terms of their attachment to the infant (Peppers and Knapp, 1980).

Hughes and Page-Lieberman (1989) studied the impact of losses from the 28th week of pregnancy to neonatal death on fathers only. Although intense grief was experienced at first, it soon diminished so that it could be characterised as being of a low intensity. Two other studies, already referred to in the section on miscarriage, also compared mothers and fathers following perinatal losses, and found more pronounced grief by mothers than fathers (Goldbach *et al.*, 1991; Theut *et al.*, 1989).

One problem with nearly all these comparisons between mothers' and fathers' grief is the lack of a comparison group. As indicated in the section on miscarriage, this is necessary in order to identify whether sex differences measured after the loss arise solely from different reactions to it, or whether they incorporate pre-existing differences in levels of psychological distress, depression and anxiety.

The study by Lang and Gottlieb (1991, 1993), involving 57 couples who had experienced a perinatal loss over the previous 2 years, did include a comparison group. They used a 67-item Bereavement Experience Questionnaire, consisting of eight subscales measuring aspects of grief and responses to it, a measure of physical symptoms, and an assessment of the degree of intimacy in their relationship. Mothers showed higher ratings than fathers did for a number of the grief measures, and for physical symptoms. A comparison group of couples who were not bereaved, using only those items which were not specific to the experience of grief, indicated that women reported more physical and psychological symptoms than men, but that the differences were smaller than for the bereaved couples. These findings suggest that some of the differences between bereaved mothers and fathers do indeed arise from pre-existing differences in their reported levels of physical and psychological well-being.

Lang and Gottlieb (1993) found that older offspring ages were associated[4]

---

4 In a series of stepwise regression analyses.

with mothers reporting more morbid fears and fathers reporting greater yearning (which included seeing the deceased). Older fathers' age was associated with a greater sense that life was meaningless. These two findings are consistent with predictions based on the reproductive value of the offspring and the father respectively. However, a third finding, that mothers reported more anger at younger ages, is not consistent with evolutionary predictions.

A follow-up with 35 couples from the same sample 2 years later again found lower scores for husbands than wives on a number of the grief sub-scales (Lang, Gottlieb and Amsel, 1996), although the levels had declined so that only one subscale was different from the control group. Wives whose social intimacy with their husbands had previously been low showed higher grief scores at the follow-up. There was also an influence in the opposite direction: wives whose initial grief reaction was high reported lower intimacy at the follow-up – whereas men's initial grief intensity did not predict their later marital intimacy (Gottlieb, Lang and Amsel, 1996).

Toedter *et al.* (1988) used the Revised Texas Grief Inventory (Chapter 2) to devise a detailed rating-scale measure suitable for perinatal grief. In a study of bereaved mothers, around 60 per cent of whom had suffered their loss during pregnancy, they found that several variables predicted stronger grief 6–8 weeks after the loss. Gestational age was positively associated with grief at this time and in follow-ups around one and two years later (Goldbach *et al.*, 1991). This is consistent with other evidence (Theut *et al.*, 1989) and with predictions based on the offspring's reproductive value.

Toedter *et al.* (1988) found no association between the mother's age and grief intensity – which does not support the prediction based on the mother's reproductive value. However, as the researchers noted, this variable was confounded with higher socioeconomic status and more previous births, both of which were associated with lower grief intensities. It may also be confounded with the clinically referred sample used in this study (Janssen *et al.*, 1997).

Longitudinal studies of perinatal loss in Australia, the US and the Netherlands (Boyle *et al.*, 1996; Goldbach *et al.*, 1991; Hunfield *et al.*, 1997a) all show higher levels of distress and grief soon after the loss and a steady decline thereafter, with measures being taken at various times from 2 weeks to 4 years after the loss. In one study (Hunfield *et al.*, 1997a) distress was still apparent after 4 years in over a third of the women.

We have noted in various places the important observations by Scheper-Hughes (1992) of the lack of grief for their infants among women in a Brazilian shanty-town. These findings can be explained in terms of low maternal grief being associated with the infant's low reproductive value (associated with high infant mortality), mediated by discriminative parental solicitude, which is also selectively directed towards infants showing signs of good survival prospects (Scheper-Hughes, 1992). Thus cues associated with fitness direct the mothers to form attachments to these infants and away from forming attachments to infants with signs of poor viability.

Sudden infant death

Sudden infant death syndrome (SIDS), or 'cot death' as it is called in the UK, occurs without warning and without a discernible medical condition. These features combine to make it particularly difficult to accept since they are generally associated with more distress.

Several small-scale studies of SIDS in the 1970s and early 1980s outlined features of the grief reactions experienced by the parents. An early report of case studies (Halpern, 1972) concluded that an older child may initially become the target of the mother's aggression (cf. Tooley, 1975). One mother threw her daughter out of the house, convinced that she was responsible for the death. The child subsequently developed behaviour problems and the dead infant became a forbidden topic.

Turning on another child following a childhood death is seldom mentioned in studies of other forms of parental bereavement. It is interesting to note that the biography of James Barrie, author of *Peter Pan* (Birkin, 1979), shows that he was in the shadow of his older brother David, who died at the age of 14, when James was 6. His mother subsequently entered a prolonged period of grief and illness, disregarding James, who tried hard to act as much like his dead brother as possible.

Cornwell, Nurcombe and Stevens (1977) provided a good description of the features of grief associated with SIDS, based on a longitudinal study of 11 families from Sydney, following them up from shortly after the death until 13–16 months later. Searching was represented by wandering into the baby's room looking for it. Hallucinations of the baby's face were common and so was a perceptual set for the sight of babies. These reactions were reported by mothers more than a year after the death. Consistent with findings for other types of perinatal death, fathers made much shorter estimates than mothers of the time it would take to recover.[5]

Lewis (1981) interviewed 36 bereaved mothers who all had had another baby during the previous 3 months. These mothers were intensely anxious about the new baby: they were very protective and vigilant, as well as feeling guilty and blaming themselves. Some mothers blamed doctors and health professionals for supposedly advising them incorrectly, and some reported victimisation and accusations from neighbours.

A questionnaire study of 32 US parents who had experienced SIDS during the previous 1–3 years found they viewed it as the most severe crisis they had encountered, and most of them showed psychological and physical reactions (DeFrain and Ernst, 1978). As in other studies, the parents typically took well over a year to return to a level of well-being comparable to that shown before the death.

A few studies of SIDS have included comparison groups. Rubin (1981)

---

5 The mean values were 3.6 and 10.3 months respectively.

found higher levels of anxiety and health-related symptoms among women who had lost a baby through SIDS during the past 10 months, compared with women who had lost a baby in this way 2–6 years before, or with those who were not bereaved. Dyregrov and Matthiesen (1987b) compared parents who had experienced stillbirth, neonatal death or sudden infant death, 1–4 years after the death. Parents who had experienced SIDS initially showed higher levels of anxiety, intrusive thoughts, anger and restlessness than the other two groups. Boyle *et al.* (1996) found that the relative risks for depression and anxiety among mothers who had lost a baby through SIDS were substantially higher than those resulting from other forms of neonatal death or from stillbirth: for example, at 2 months afterwards, the RR for depression was 7.9 for SIDS compared with 4.3 for neonatal death; but 30 months after the loss, it was 6.8 for SIDS and 1.5 for neonatal death. Both these findings support the view that sudden infant death is generally a more traumatic experience than are other forms of infant losses.

There are several interconnected reasons why SIDS might be more difficult to accept and why there might be more intense grief than with other forms of infant death. First, there is no forewarning, which is a feature generally associated with greater difficulties in accepting the death and with more intense and prolonged grieving (Ball, 1976–7; Faletti *et al.*, 1989; Parkes and Weiss, 1983; Vachon *et al.*, 1982b). Second, a SIDS death shares some of the features of traumatic deaths such as suicide (Rynearson, 1987), notably in that there is difficulty in providing an adequate account or explanation of the death. Third, because of the ambiguity over its cause, SIDS may be associated with negative social reactions directed towards the grieving parents. This is likely to be exacerbated by the involvement of the legal system – for example, the parents may be interrogated or even taken into custody by the police (Markusen *et al.*, 1977–8).

Taken together, these features may lead to problems in constructing an account of the loss, and to intrusive thoughts which are difficult to reconcile with assumptions the bereaved person had about the world before the death occurred. Also, the circumstances of SIDS do not help the bereaved to discuss their feelings. A series of studies based on a longitudinal investigation of parents bereaved by SIDS has addressed these issues.

The initial findings from the study (Wortman and Silver, 1992; Chapter 8) were that levels of negative emotional states such as depression and anxiety declined over the study period (3 weeks, 3 months and 18 months after the death), whereas positive emotions increased. As indicated in Chapter 7 (p. 116), Downey *et al.* (1990) found that many parents were not concerned with constructing an account of the loss, and even that those who made attributions of blame to themselves or others were *more* distressed at any one time than those who did not make attributions of responsibility. They also found that the presence or absence of an account of the loss did not predict long-term adjustment. Any link between attributional processes and levels of distress measured at the same time was probably the result of both measures reflecting the overall strength of grief.

Lepore *et al.* (1996) measured the perceived degree of constraint on talking about their loss in mothers whose infants had died from SIDS. Among those who experienced a high degree of constraint, the more intrusive thoughts they experienced shortly after the loss, the greater was their increase in depression at 3 months and 18 months. However, for those mothers who experienced few social constraints, more intrusive thoughts immediately after the loss were not associated with relative depression levels at 3 months after the loss. Indeed, there was even a negative relationship between earlier intrusive thoughts and relative levels of depression at 18 months: those with initially high levels of intrusive thoughts had relatively lower levels of depression 18 months later (the measures of depression being assessed as change scores). As indicated in Chapter 7, this suggests that there may be some long-term benefits of a high initial level of intrusive thoughts in a social environment which was supportive in terms of facilitating talking about these thoughts and feelings.

Most studies of SIDS have focused on the parents. Burns, House and Ankenbauer (1986) studied the grief reactions of 50 children from 43 families in which a SIDS death had occurred during the previous few years (in most cases 2 or 3 years), using a parental questionnaire which asked about the children's grief. Over half of the children were reported to have grieved for longer than a year, and 40 per cent for less than 6 months.

Few studies of SIDS have examined variables affecting the intensity of grief in the way that those of other forms of perinatal death have. Carroll and Shaefer (1993–4) did examine the influence of other children on the coping responses shown by parents following SIDS. In a sample, most of whom had had another child since the death or who were pregnant, they found that mothers with more surviving children sought less support from others and that this declined with the time since the loss. This single piece of evidence is consistent with predictions based on evolutionary reasoning and also on the breadth of maternal attachments.

Death of a child

As indicated in the Introduction, loss of a child is generally regarded as the most difficult loss to bear. Wordsworth's famous poem 'Surprised by Joy', written two years after his 4-year-old daughter died, captures the loss of 'my heart's best treasure':

> – That thought's return
> Was the worst pang that sorrow ever bore,
> Save one, one only, when I stood forlorn,
> Knowing my heart's best treasure was no more;
> That neither present time, nor years unborn

Could to my sight that heavenly face restore.
(Wordsworth, *Desideria*,
in Quiller-Couch, 1919: 616)

In Wordsworth's time, death of a child through disease was much more common than it is now. In Chapter 3, I mentioned the 'consolation literature' of the nineteenth century, written usually by clergymen who were themselves bereaved. In one of these (*The Empty Crib*), Theodore Cuyler (1873: 81–2) referred to one of the thousands of letters he had received from parents in a similar position. It describes three little graves in Allegheny cemetery, for Anna aged 7, Sadie aged 5, and Lillie aged 3, all of whom died within 6 days of scarlet fever. Many other sources describe such multiple losses which were common until relatively recent times (Cressy, 1997; Silverman, 1997).

In many parts of the word today, child and infant mortality is still high: for example, figures for India in early 1992 were around 15 per cent for under-5s (Laungani, 1994). In the western world, we are collectively fortunate in having overcome the ravages of childhood infectious diseases. In the late twentieth century, about 45 per cent of the deaths of older children in the US occur as a result of accidents, whereas leukaemia and other cancers account for about 18 per cent (Osterweis, Solomon and Green, 1984). Studies reviewed by Bowlby (1980a), mainly of parents of children who died from leukaemia, showed that the grief of individual parents has many of the features of conjugal grief, without the experience of loneliness. He also noted that there is a high incidence of psychosomatic and psychiatric symptoms, and behavioural problems such as heavy drinking, under these circumstances. There is also the possibility that mothers' and fathers' grief and coping styles will differ, and that this may generate marital conflict (Chapter 13).

Klass (1988) studied the grief experienced by parents who were members of the Compassionate Friends, the self-help organisation for bereaved parents, using an ethnographic approach. Many of the features he described are familiar from the detailed description of marital grief in Chapter 5, for example the urge to search, self-blame and difficulties with routine tasks. Klass emphasised the enduring sense of a change in identity that accompanies the loss of a child. He viewed identification as a central process in grieving (in contrast to its subsidiary role in attachment theory: see Chapter 5). According to Klass, identification involves fusing the representation of the deceased with the self, which enriches the ego and provides a sense of solace. He regarded this process as being particularly difficult in the case of death of a child, and viewed religious rituals or objects associated with the child as facilitating the process.

Sanders (1979–80) used the Grief Experience Inventory (Chapter 2) to measure the intensity of grief among a sample of middle-aged North Americans, 2 months after the death of their spouse or child. She found that the specific grief reactions were all consistently higher in those who had lost a child. It should be noted, however, that the range of ages for the 'child' extended from 6 years to well into adulthood, the oldest being 49 years.

Fish (1986) found high levels of grief present even some years after the death among a sample of parents who had lost an offspring (at ages from infancy to adulthood) 1 to 16 years before. A similar finding was reported by Martinson *et al.* (1991). In Fish's study, as in others (Bohannon, 1990–1; Moriarty, Carroll and Cotroneo, 1996; Rubin, 1991–2; Schwab, 1996; van der Wal, 1988), levels of grief were generally higher for mothers than for fathers, although fathers showed higher levels when the child had died beyond the age of infancy. This finding is consistent with the evolutionary prediction that in the early years mothers will show greater intensity of grief than fathers, as a consequence of their higher initial parental investment and greater parental certainty. As the child grows older, the relative disparity in parental investment is expected to lessen.

As indicated earlier, considerations of inclusive fitness and the breadth of attachments would predict particularly intense grief among parents who have lost an only child. Wheeler (1993–4) found that parents from the Compassionate Friends who had lost an only child showed lower values on a scale measuring their meaning and purpose in life than did bereaved parents with surviving children. This measure is inversely related to grief (Chapter 8). Talbot (1996–7) contacted bereaved mothers through an organisation for bereaved parents with no surviving children, and again used a measure of meaning and purpose in life. Several variables, for example how helpful friends were, the mother's involvement in voluntary activities and how frequently she discussed her grief with others, predicted higher meaning and purpose in life. Interviews with mothers reporting the lowest and highest questionnaire scores indicated that those with the lowest scores regarded their loss as involving the loss of their whole existence. Those with the highest scores viewed their child as just one part of themselves and had more investment in other areas of life.

Death of an adult son or daughter

The bereavement felt by parents who lose an adult offspring has been relatively little studied, although, as indicated above, some studies of 'death of a child' have included adult offspring. In one of the earlier accounts of bereavement, Gorer (1965) suggested that death of an adult offspring is a particularly traumatic form of grief. He referred to it as 'the most distressing and long-lasting of all griefs'. Although others have expressed doubts about whether this is the case, it does highlight some particular difficulties which may be associated with this form of grief. These are principally the untimeliness of such deaths, and the vivid reminder that the world is not a safe and ordered place.

We would also predict a high intensity of grief under these circumstances from the Darwinian perspective in view of the relative reproductive values of older parents and their adult offspring. Parents' own reproductive value declines throughout adult life, and helping their adult offspring and grand-children becomes the main vehicle for inclusive fitness open to them. Loss of an offspring at this time occurs after years of parental investment and at a time when they generally cannot be replaced.

In the study by Sanders described in the previous section, adult offspring were prevalent among the sample designated as having lost a 'child', and this group showed a high intensity of grieving. Similarly, Leahy (1992–3) found that women who had lost a young adult son or daughter showed higher levels of depression than widows or women who had lost a parent. In Fish's study, mothers' grief for an adult offspring was found to be similar to that experienced for younger ages, whereas fathers showed higher grief for adult offspring than for losses at younger ages.

These, albeit limited, findings do lend some support to Gorer's suggestion, and to the similar Darwinian-based prediction, as do studies of death of an adult offspring in combat. Rubin (1989–90) compared 42 Israeli parents who had lost sons in a war, an average of 9 years before, with a sample of 13 bereaved parents who had lost 1-year-old children around the same time. Using a Hebrew version of Sanders' GEI, he found that the bereaved parents of adults showed higher current levels of grief and higher levels of recalled earlier grief than parents who had lost a young child. Even with such a small comparison group, 29 out of 36 measures were significantly higher for the parents who had lost an adult son. In a follow-up study of 102 Israeli parents who had lost sons in wars 4 and 13 years before, Rubin (1991–2) found that they showed higher levels of grief (on Sanders' GEI) and anxiety than a control sample of 73 non-bereaved adults, even after this length of time.

War provides a common cause of the death of adult offspring in the mod-ern world (Figure 11.4). Bao Ninh (1994) portrayed the devastating effects on parents of the losses experienced in the Vietnam War by the North Viet-namese: in many families several sons were killed throughout the 10-year war. Despite such relatively greater mortality, we are more familiar with the impact of that war on bereaved American parents. The following excerpt was written by a single mother, whose only son died in Vietnam in 1969, aged 21:

> I am the one who rocked him as a baby. I am the one who kissed away the hurts. I'm the one who taught him right from wrong. I'm the one who held him for the last time and watched him fly away to war. I'm the one who prayed each night 'Dear God keep him safe.' I'm the goofy mum who sent him a Christmas tree in Vietnam. I'm the one whose heart broke when told my Billy had died in a helicopter crash. And now I'm the one who still cries at night because of all the memories I have that will never die.
>
> (Palmer, 1987: 119)

There are likely to be additional reasons why grief is pronounced following

Figure 11.4 War is a common cause of the death of young men in the modern world: in this cemetery, the ages of most of the men were in the late teens or early twenties.

Source: Photograph by the author, taken at the War Cemetery on the Greek island of Leros, 1994

a bereavement through war, arising from the sudden and violent nature of the death – what Rynearson (1987) referred to as 'unnatural dying'. We should therefore be cautious in concluding from studies such as those of Rubin that death of an adult offspring necessarily produces persisting long-term effects of loss. A more appropriate comparison was made by van der Wal (1988), who found that parents had less difficulty in adjusting to the death of an adult offspring than to the death of a younger child or to the death of a sibling, in cases of death by suicide or motor vehicle crash (Figure 11.5). Although the nature of the death is likely to be traumatic in these cases, the age categories involved similar causes of traumatic death.

DeVries *et al.* (1997) studied an older group of 78 parents whose adult son or daughter had died during the previous 10 years, drawn from a nationally representative sample. These parents showed higher levels of depression than a control group who had not been bereaved, and showed little change in their depression levels when reassessed 2.5 years later. Their health also declined more than that of controls. Both measures indicate the long-term impact of the bereavement in this sample.

Overall the evidence indicates an intense grief reaction among parents who

Figure 11.5 A roadside shrine to commemorate the spot where a young man died in a motor-cycle accident. Motor vehicle crashes are a common cause of death in young men in peacetime. The sudden and traumatic nature of the death interacts with the person's age to make these untimely and unexpected deaths hard for the parents to accept.

Source: Photograph by the author, taken on the Greek island of Leros, 1994

have lost an adult son or daughter, although some studies are complicated by involving a traumatic source of bereavement, notably war.

Conclusions

There is little systematic evidence on the intensity and duration of grieving for a son or daughter lost at different ages. Nevertheless, putting together the findings at specific ages indicates a steady overall increase in the intensity of grief from early pregnancy loss through to loss of an adult. We should qualify this conclusion by noting that much of the evidence for adults comes from studies of bereavement caused by war, which has additional traumatic features.

An increase in grief with age is consistent with the increase in reproductive value of the offspring from conception to early adulthood, and the decline in parental reproductive value, identified by the evolutionary perspective. Consideration of how the process of attachment develops would predict an increase in grief from conception into childhood, and a relatively constant level thereafter. To account for a continuation in the severity of grief beyond this point requires an additional mechanism sensitive to cues related to fitness. This probably involves an aspect of the internal models of these relationships, concerned with their permanency and their centrality to the person's life, built up over the years.

Evidence consistently supported the prediction that grief would be more pronounced for mothers than for fathers early in the child's life, but thereafter as the child grew older this difference would diminish, although it did not altogether disappear. However, we should note that most studies did not include non-bereaved controls, which would enable responses to the loss to be separated from pre-existing sex differences in depression and other signs of distress.

The evidence on parental age was sparse, but what there was (from miscarriage, abortion and loss of a child) did suggest that grief is more pronounced among older than younger mothers, as is predicted from the declining reproductive value of parents. We might expect this to be greater among mothers around middle age, in view of the menopause.

The few studies which concerned losses among women who had no other children indicated stronger reactions to a miscarriage, and to a greater extent to child deaths at later ages. This was consistent with predictions based on inclusive fitness and the breadth of attachment.

Grief following an induced abortion or SIDS is complicated by the specific circumstances of these losses. Two studies indicated that SIDS was indeed more distressing both initially and in the longer term. It has often been stated that the unexplained nature of the loss produces particular difficulties for the bereaved parents. One carefully controlled study of attributions parents made for the death, and the impact of these attributions on the long-term outcome, indicated that there was no relationship between constructing a meaning for the loss and later adjustment as is widely assumed. A supportive social environment for mothers experiencing more intrusive thoughts after the death did seem to be more important. If this was present, later adjustment was better in these parents than among those with fewer intrusive thoughts. If it was absent, mothers with more intrusive thoughts showed poorer long-term adjustment than those with fewer intrusive thoughts.

Overall, we can see that few studies of the loss of a son or daughter have been designed with theoretical concerns – either evolutionary or psychological – in mind. Those by Silver, Wortman and their colleagues provide exceptions from the viewpoint of social psychology, and are particularly valuable because they address issues that are at the heart of widespread (but untested) ideas about resolution.

12 Death of a relative or friend

For the previous eight years, Lewis had been bottling up the emotion which he had most needed to let out: grief for his mother. The experience of boarding school immediately after Flora died and the stiff-upper-lip schoolboy atmosphere in which the emotions were suspected and tears were thought sissy had led to a profound stiffening and hardening throughout his being.

(A.N. Wilson, *C.S. Lewis: A biography*, 1990: 47)

Introduction

In the previous chapter, I considered parents' reactions to death of their offspring at various stages throughout life. In this chapter, I examine the impact of losing, first, another close relative, such as a parent or a sibling, and then friends. I also examine the loss of partners who are not recognised by others, and of a pet, which in the western world is treated as an honorary family member.

Most studies of bereavement have concentrated on loss of a spouse or a child. Indeed, from an evolutionary perspective, with the exception of identical twins (Segal, 1993), they form the most important – and hence the closest – of human ties. One very important outcome of evolutionary thinking was that it highlighted the importance of kinship ties in the animal world (Hamilton, 1964), and hence provided a reason why they assume such importance in human societies. In Chapter 9, I described the view of Littlefield and Rushton (1986) that a direct link could be established between genetic relatedness and severity of grief, and the wider view of Thornhill and Thornhill (1989) that the intensity of grief followed the magnitude of fitness loss. Whilst being sceptical about the close tracking of genetic relatedness or fitness loss, the general points that kin form an important class of human relationships, and that closer relationships are formed with closer kin, are ones that few would dispute. We should generally expect close family members, such as siblings, to show substantial grief reactions, next in severity only to the loss of a spouse or child, reflecting the evolutionary importance of their relationships.

Reactions to the loss of a parent will be influenced by considerations of age. During their early years, offspring rely on parents for care and protection, and this forms the primary relationship an individual has at this time of life. We should therefore expect the early loss of a parent to evoke a particularly severe form of grief. As the individual grows away from having close ties with his or her parents towards independence and adult and parental relationships, considerations of the parents' reproductive value – in this case *for the offspring* – come into play. Since the value declines over the adult years, a comparable decline in the closeness of attachment, and of the severity of grief (Chapter 9), would be expected.

We might expect a similar association between attachment and reproductive value for siblings, producing an increase in intensity of attachment throughout childhood and a decline from puberty onwards. Grief for other family members may follow the closeness of the genetic relatedness to them, mediated by the strength of attachment, which may in turn reflect their association (Chapter 9). The detailed evidence considered in this chapter will enable us to further evaluate how closely the intensity of grief follows kinship and reproductive value.

Grief for sexual partners would be expected to parallel the closeness of the relationship, which in evolutionary terms represents their potential as mates and parents. Homosexual relationships are often regarded as a paradox for Darwinian thinking (Wright, 1994: 384–6), but they can be understood as by-products of the mechanisms through which most people develop sexual preferences which are – in a Darwinian sense – more appropriate (Archer, 1992a: 69–72, 1996c; Bem, 1996). Friends represent, from an evolutionary viewpoint, people who can be relied upon for mutual aid (Trivers, 1971).

People show grief when a pet dies. Attachment to non-human animals – in the form of pets – provides an intriguing challenge for evolutionary views of human behaviour. Pets are substitute family members, to whom people respond because they share a range of characteristics shown by human infants and children, and in some cases by other human companions. I have argued that, in an evolutionary sense, they are manipulating human parenting responses, and that they fall into the category of social parasites (Archer, 1997).

Death of a parent during childhood

In the western world today, adult mortality rates are such that the loss of a parent before the offspring is 18 years of age is relatively uncommon (about 4 per cent in the US). Before 1800, rates were so high in the UK and the US that a 20-year marriage would have been exceptional, and in some cases 10 years would have been a long time (Fox and Quitt, 1980). Consequently, both spousal bereavement and loss of a parent during childhood would have been common events.

The opening quotation for this chapter is from more modern times. It concerns C.S. Lewis, whose perceptive writings about his own grief were cited in earlier chapters. His biographer was referring to the impact of his mother's death when Lewis was 9-years-old, which was followed immediately by him being sent away to boarding school in England from his native Northern Ireland. As A.N. Wilson commented:

> Presumably there is no paediatrician or child psychologist in the world who would recommend that a nine-year-old boy, within a fortnight of his mother's death, should be sent away from home; and not merely sent away from home, but sent to another country, to a school run on harshly unfeeling lines. But this is what happened to C.S. Lewis.
>
> (Wilson, 1990: 22)

A.N. Wilson indicated that the impact of Lewis' mother's death was compounded by the hostile school environment in which the open expression of grief was regarded as a sign of weakness, and that this had a lasting effect on his character. As indicated in Chapters 7 and 13, suppression of grief is more characteristic of men than women.

In considering the impact of parental death at younger ages than C.S. Lewis' 9 years, we need to take account of the developing understanding of death (Chapter 4). The idea that death is irreversible is not understood at younger ages, supporting Bowlby's view that reactions to death and to separation are the same for young children. Between the ages of 5 and 10 years, death is usually attributed to an outside agency, possibly introducing problems if self-blame is involved. Earlier studies of bereaved children at nursery schools and child guidance clinics indicated a variety of disturbances, such as aggression, anxiety, depression, denial of the death, stealing and other behaviour problems (Brown, 1968). These studies involved clinical observations and impressions, but more systematic evidence supports many of their findings (Markusen and Fulton, 1971; Black and Urbanowitz, 1987). The following three longitudinal studies illustrate some of the more recent research evidence on children's reactions to parental death.

The immediate aftermath of the death of a parent during childhood was studied by Elizur and Kaffman (1982) by interviewing mothers and teachers of a sample of 25 Israeli children, aged 2–10 years, whose fathers had been killed in the Yom Kippur war. Initial indications of grief included crying, expressions of longing, anger and protest. There were also attempts to mitigate the loss, for example by pretending that the father was nearby, or denying the death. This was more common among younger children, confirming earlier findings (Brown, 1968). It may reflect problems with understanding that death is permanent at these ages.

In the second year after the death, there were more signs of a realistic perception of the loss, accompanied by reactions such as fear of being left alone, and increased dependency on the mother. Aggressiveness and restlessness were also reported, more often among boys and older children, as were eating problems and regressive symptoms. Similar reactions formed the basis of the behaviour problems reported in earlier studies (Brown, 1968).

Elizur and Kaffman found that grief declined during the third and fourth years after the death (as did Black and Urbanowitz, 1987). There was, however, considerable individual variation in the reactions, some children experiencing marked difficulties which impaired their everyday functioning (again confirming earlier findings), whereas others were better adjusted to the new reality. A follow-up study (Elizur and Kaffman, 1983) showed an association between maternal characteristics, such as a prolonged depressive reaction or suppression of emotion, and behaviour problems among the children. Childhood temperament, particularly low self-control and tolerance of frustration, were also associated with more behaviour problems.

A second longitudinal study (van Eerdewegh *et al.*, 1982, 1985) involved a sample of 2- to 17-year-old children in St Louis, who were compared with a non-bereaved sample. The children's reactions to their parents' death were assessed at 1 and 13 months afterwards, by interviewing the surviving parent. Signs of distress, such as crying, temper tantrums and bed-wetting, and of a depressive reaction, in the form of withdrawal, sadness, sleep troubles and decreased appetite, were all more common among the bereaved than the control children. Sadness and crying declined from the first to the second interview among the bereaved sample, whereas abdominal pain, disinterest in school and fighting with siblings all increased from the first to the second interview. Overall, however, interest in others increased during this time. The bereaved children's school performance was poorer overall.

Both these studies obtained their information indirectly, from the surviving parent. Silverman and Worden (1993) administered questionnaires and interviewed bereaved school-aged children directly, as well as asking the surviving parents. The interviews (carried out at 4 months and 1 year after the death) showed widespread initial distress, for example crying, which declined thereafter. School performance was lower in some cases but in others there was an improvement. Problems with sleeping, concentration and general distress were reported by only a minority (20–30 per cent) of the sample, and overall the children appeared less affected than in the other two studies.

Silverman and Worden also described ways in which the children maintained contact with their dead parents. Besides dreaming that their parents were still alive, the children commonly spoke to them, and just under half felt that they received an answer. Most of the sample felt that the deceased was watching them, and many found this to be frightening – which is reminiscent of fear of the spirits of the dead that is widespread in traditional cultures (Chapter 5). Three-quarters of the sample kept something personal belonging to the parent, which is again similar to bereavement in other contexts (see Chapter 5, section on mementos and linking objects).

Worden and Silverman (1996) analysed further information from the same sample, collected from the parents at 1 and 2 years after the loss, and compared this with a matched control sample who were not bereaved. They confirmed the impression that behavioural and emotional problems were not substantially elevated 1 year after the death compared with the control sample. However, by 2 years, the bereaved children were more socially withdrawn, anxious and depressed (but did not show more delinquent behaviour, aggression, attention-seeking or physical symptoms). More of the bereaved sample showed a serious behaviour disturbance after 2 years, although not after 1 year.

The first two studies, which were based only on parents' reports, gave the impression of a pronounced grief reaction, in many respects similar to that shown by adults. In both cases, the children's grief had a widespread effect on their conduct, health, well-being and school performance. The child's temperament and the surviving parent's severity of grief affected the child's grief. The third study, which also involved direct interviews with the children, found that a severe reaction occurred only in a minority of cases, although most children were initially upset and showed a continuing connection with the dead parent. At 2 years after the death, there were, however, more problems than were apparent earlier.

There are two aspects to the loss of a parent, the grief response and the consequences of the absence of that parent. The second of these has been described by writers and poets long before there was medical or scientific interest in the subject. For example, Homer (in *The Iliad*) referred to the consequences of Hector's death for his son, in terms of the absence of protection and power:

> An orphaned child is cut off from his playmates. He goes about with downcast looks and tear-stained cheeks. In his necessity he looks in at some gathering of his father's friends and plucks a cloak here and a tunic there, till someone out of charity holds up a wine-cup to his mouth, but only for a moment, just enough to wet his lips and leave his palate dry. Then comes another boy, with both his parents living, who beats him with his fists and drives him from the feast and jeers at him. 'Out you go!' he shouts. 'You have no father dining here.' So the child runs off in tears to his widowed mother.
>
> (*The Iliad*, trans. Rieu, 1950: 410)

In this description, the process of grief becomes complicated by the loss of an important role fulfilled by the deceased, which sets in train all sorts of other changes that can alter the person's life course. Evolutionary analysis of human parenting (Buss, 1994) has also emphasised the enormous practical disadvantages associated with death of a father at a young age (Figure 12.1). In a present-day society, that of the Ache people of Paraguay (Hill and Kaplan, 1988), children are deliberately killed when their father dies in a club fight, such are their poor prospects in his absence.

Using the earlier work of psychoanalysts on children separated from their mothers in orphanages, nurseries and hospitals, Bowlby (1951, 1953) put

Figure 12.1 'The Dead Soldier' by Joseph Wright of Derby, 1789. Not only has his wife lost a husband but the infant (who is looking directly at the observer) has lost someone fulfilling an important role, which is likely to disadvantage him or her for many years.

Source: Reproduced by permission of Holburne Museum, Bath

forward the view that early loss of a parent – principally the mother – causes long-term psychological harm, in the form of mental illness and relationship problems. He was concerned with both the effects of loss through death and through long-term separation, which at an early age are seen as indistinguishable (Bowlby, 1960b; Chapter 4). Support for the specific features of Bowlby's theory of maternal deprivation, when other attendant variables are controlled, is not convincing (Rutter, 1972, 1979). There does, however, appear to be a more limited direct effect of separation on temperament or social behaviour (Tizard and Tizard, 1974; Tizard, 1977), and possibly also on adult attachment styles (Feeney and Noller, 1990).

Another line of enquiry concerns the possible association between psychological problems in adulthood (such as depression) and loss of a parent during childhood (Brown, 1968; Bendiksen and Fulton, 1975; Finkelstein, 1988).

Bendiksen and Fulton found that, after controlling for various socio-economic and demographic variables, there was a higher rate of emotional stress and illness in adults whose families had experienced the loss of a parent through death or divorce when they were children. Roberts and Gotlib (1997) reported similar findings for depression. These results could reflect either the long-term consequences of childhood bereavement on personality, as Bowlby suggested, or the indirect consequences of the loss, mediated by attendant circumstances. Tennant, Bebbington and Hurry (1980) concluded, from the evidence available at the time, that when bereaved and control samples are rigorously matched, no association is found between parental bereavement and later depression.

However, there is an accumulation of positive evidence for such a link among samples of working-class women. It was among such samples that associations between early loss and depression had been found in previous studies (Tennant *et al.*, 1980). In a large community sample of women from south-east London, Brown, Harris and Copeland (1977) found that loss of the mother before the age of 11 years was associated with a higher risk of adult depression. Yet loss of a father or sibling before the age of 17 years, or loss of the mother between the ages of 11 and 17, did not increase the likelihood of depression. Although the authors of this study argued for a direct effect of the sort indicated by Bowlby, later research by the same group showed that indirect effects were involved.

Harris, Brown and Bifulco (1986), studying a sample of working-class women in the Walthamstow area of London, found that loss of the mother (but not the father) before the age of 17 years, either by death or prolonged separation, was associated with clinical depression in adulthood. A retrospective examination of the women's former child-care arrangements suggested that it was neglect (rather than abuse) that was the important variable in the Walthamstow sample. Such neglect was more common after loss of the mother than the father. In accordance with the earlier findings, depression was more prevalent among those who had lost their mothers before 11 years of age (Harris and Bifulco, 1991). A life history involving lack of parental control, early pregnancy, unhappy marriage and poor economic prospects, was identified as providing the links between the childhood event of parental loss and depression in adulthood (Brown, Harris and Bifulco, 1986; Harris and Bifulco, 1991).

In addition to influences mediated by the type of family environment which results from the death of the mother, there may be direct effects on the child's personality development. Harris and Bifulco (1991) reported that maternal loss also induces a form of cognitive helplessness. Although later depression was not associated with childhood mourning in this study, Murphy (1986–7) did find that the degree to which a bereaved child had expressed his or her grief, through means such as emotional expression, attending the funeral, asking questions and hearing about the dead person, was associated – to a small extent – with the absence of loneliness in adulthood. These retrospectively collected measures reflect the degree to which the child was able to express and explore grief, and therefore it would be reasonable to suppose that they were mediated by a more direct effect on personality development.

In this section, we have seen that the death of a parent during childhood produces both an initial grief reaction which then may be associated with childhood behaviour problems and later personality, and also indirect effects associated with the lack of that parent during development, which can also have important negative consequences throughout the life course.

Death of a parent during adolescence or young adulthood

The grief of young people who have lost a parent involves some problems particular to this age group. *When Parents Die* is an articulate and intelligent book written by a young British journalist (Abrams, 1992) whose sudden loss of her father and step-father plunged her into the experience of grief at a time of life when she was unprepared for it. The book provides a brief personal account of the author's own experiences but is mainly concerned with providing help and support for young people in similar circumstances.

As Abrams pointed out, the specific problems encountered at this time of life concern the untimely and unexpected nature of the death. Such deaths are always more difficult to cope with because they make the individual's personal world an unsafe and unpredictable place. This happens against a background of a social world which is – among western young people anyway – concerned with the present and with living. It is also a time when young people are feeling their way in the world and have to make decisions that will affect them for years to come. As Abrams (1992: xvi) put it: 'There simply is not enough time, energy, or emotional strength to cope with everything'. Grieving becomes a struggle, one which is made more difficult by a social world which does not readily accommodate it. Counsellors working with bereaved young people have noted difficulties arising from isolation from the peer group, who will generally not have shared the experience (Abrams, 1992, 1993).

The few available studies generally concern a slightly younger age group. Two of these undertaken in the 1980s reported depression, somatic complaints, poor school marks, and sleeping and eating problems, among bereaved adolescent high-school students, but neither involved a comparison group or followed up the sample (Balk, 1991a).

Harris (1991) reported a small-sample longitudinal study of high-school-age adolescents (13–18 years) from immediately after the death of a parent, to 7 and 13 months afterwards. Their initial responses included distress, guilt feelings, intrusive thoughts, inability concentrating and sleeping, sadness, and worries about the surviving parent. At 7 months, depression, delinquency, high alcohol intake and problems with school work, were reported in half the sample. The levels of stress measured in this sample were much higher than among a sample of adults whose parents had died.

The systematic evidence is, therefore, limited but it does indicate a familiar picture of pronounced grieving at these ages, which other reports indicate may be compounded by the reactions of peers to the grief experienced by adolescents and young adults.

Death of a parent during adulthood

The death of a parent in adulthood is to be expected, since it occurs at an age when life has run its course. It is seen as less unfair and tragic than is the death of a younger person. In twentieth-century North America, it tends to be concentrated around the offspring's middle age. Nevertheless, there are many of the familiar features of grief, such as numbness and disbelief, anger, guilt, intrusive thoughts and reminders (Moss and Moss, 1989; Moss, Resch and Moss, 1997).

Grief for loss of a parent in adulthood is generally less intense than that for other forms of bereavement, such as loss of a spouse or a child (Bass *et al.*, 1990; Burnett *et al.*, 1997; Leahy, 1992–3; Owen, Fulton and Markusen,1982–3; Sanders, 1989). Owen *et al.* concluded that 'a striking characteristic of the response of some persons in this group was the absence of grief' (p. 215). Sanders commented that by adulthood, people's close attachments have mostly been redirected to others, usually spouses and children. As expected, she found more distress at younger ages, when there was strong identification with the parent, and when both parents were lost within a short time.

There is, however, evidence that death of a parent *can* result in the levels of distress more usually associated with other forms of bereavement (Douglas, 1990–1; Horowitz *et al.*, 1984; Scharlach and Frederiksen, 1993). Obviously, the reaction will depend on several important variables, such as the type of continued relationship with the parent, their importance in terms of ties to childhood and the past, and their importance in the structure of the extended family. Pickard (1994) found that the death of a mother during old age was particularly salient for daughters among a working-class community in South Wales.

Also important are the implications of the death for the person's own perceptions of ageing and mortality. Scharlach and Frederiksen (1993) found that changes in self-concept were a major theme revealed in interviews with a sample of educated middle-aged people from Los Angeles who had lost either or both parents during the previous 5 years. Most said that the death had contributed to a greater sense of maturity, for example making them feel more self-reliant, and that they were more aware of their own mortality. For most people, these perceived changes were positive and constructive but a minority experienced them as being stressful.

One situation in which a more intense grief reaction might be expected is when a daughter has been caring for her elderly mother. However, Pratt, Walker and Wood (1992) found that some grief was experienced among a sample of women who had cared for their mothers, but it was not overwhelm-ing (depression scores at 6 months were similar to those for the general population).

Moss *et al.* (1997) investigated a sample of people whose last elderly parent had died during the previous 6–12 months, and found that daughters were more emotionally upset and showed more changes in health than sons did. However, in the absence of a control group, it is not possible to attribute these differences to the impact of the bereavement rather than to pre-existing sex differences (Chapter 11).

Doka (1992) has discussed the role of inheritance in complicating grief for an elderly parent. Apart from difficulties and conflicts caused by feelings of unfair distribution, he also suggested that being the executor for such matters can delay feelings of grief in some cases. There are, of course, material bene-fits from such inheritances, which in some cases provide specific and positive memories of the deceased.

Overall, the evidence indicates that grief for parents who were towards the end of their expected life-course is less than that experienced for younger parents, which is what we should expect, both intuitively and from considera-tions of the parent's decline in reproductive value over the adult years. We should perhaps point out that all the limited research evidence was drawn from the US, which as we have noted, is at the extreme end of Triandis' individualistic–collectivist distinction. We may find more pronounced grief for older parents in societies where there are closer social ties between the different generations within a family.

Death of a grandchild

There is very little research – or indeed few anecdotal reports or commentaries – on grief following death of a grandchild. From an evolutionary perspective, the index of relatedness between a grandparent and a grandchild is on aver-age .25. Because of the age disparity we should expect grandchildren to be important (since the reproductive value of the grandparent will be low and that of the grandchild high). In terms of proximal mechanisms, an attach-ment to a grandchild will involve hopes and aspirations for the future. Death of a grandchild will be particularly untimely from the perspective of the grandparent. Attachment will also vary in terms of the proximity and the day-to-day contacts between grandparent and grandchild. We should expect more pronounced grief in communities with extended families, and among collectivist cultures, where there are tight groups of interdependent people (Triandis, 1995).

The limited available evidence confirms expectations of a pronounced grief reaction among grandparents. DeFrain, Jakub and Mendoza (1991–2) stud-ied the impact of a SIDS death on a sample of grandparents in Nebraska. Common reactions included anxiety, anger, depression and bitterness. Half the sample reported vivid flashbacks to the scene of the death, 42 per cent said that they hoped to go to sleep and wake up with the pain removed, and 29 per cent experienced personal guilt. The experience was frequently described as 'devastating', particularly as it involved both personal grief and seeing the parents of the child grieving too. As with parental grief following a SIDS death, there was continued questioning about why it had happened. Self-blame and blaming others were reported by 38 per cent of the sample.

Comparable levels of grief were found among a sample of 152 grand-parents studied by Fry (1997), and in a smaller sample from various parts of the US recruited from support-group newsletters by Ponzetti and Johnson (1991). In this study, over half experienced shock, and a majority needed to talk about the death. Some reported anger and helplessness. Around 20 per cent said that they thought they had heard or seen the deceased. Again there was the mixture of personal pain and feeling pain for the parents. Com-parison with the parents' grief (Ponzetti, 1992) showed that reactions such as numbness, shock and disbelief were less pronounced among the grandparents than the parents, whereas others such as insomnia, were not. The grand-parents' reactions tended to be focused more on the parents than on the deceased child.

In addition to predictions about the general level of grief, more specific differences between the grief experienced by different kinds of grandparent are predicted by evolutionary considerations, in particular the difference in relationship certainty between mothers and fathers. One clear prediction is that maternal grandmothers should show more care for their grandchildren than other types of grandparent and that paternal grandfathers (whose rela-tionship is mediated by two links of paternity uncertainty) will show the least. A test of this hypothesis, involving asking a large sample of German adults to rate the relative care or solicitude of their grandparents during their child-hood (Euler and Weitzel, 1996), supported it and ruled out other possible explanations such as residential proximity.

The study by Littlefield and Rushton (1986), which sought to apply evo-lutionary principles to the death of a child, found that the *perceived* grief of grandparents (rated by the parents) was less than their own grief but higher than the *perceived* grief of aunts and uncles (also with an index of relatedness of .25 but with higher reproductive values themselves). Consistent with the paternity-certainty hypothesis, maternal grandmothers were estimated as showing higher levels of grief than the other three types of grandparent, all of whose relationship with the grandchild was mediated by at least one link involving paternity uncertainty. The only other evidence bearing on this issue is the finding by Cornwell *et al.* (1977) that there was more blame attached to the mother for a sudden infant death by *paternal* grandparents than by other family members. However, if the grief reactions and attributions of blame both follow evolutionary principles, we should expect them to be mediated through mechanisms such as a closer attachment with the child in the case of *maternal* than paternal grandparents (as indeed was found by Euler and Weitzel, 1996).

The limited evidence indicates that grandparents' grief is as intense as we might expect from evolutionary considerations, but there is little evidence that enables a systematic comparison with other forms of grief at present. There is no direct evidence that enables an assessment of more subtle predictions about differences between categories of grandparent, based on considerations of paternity uncertainty.

Sibling death

Brothers and sisters have an index of relatedness of .5 (Chapter 9), and therefore helping them can have considerable advantages for inclusive fitness. We might also expect sibling relationships to grow stronger with increasing reproductive value and then to decline later in life. Most reports of grief following loss of a sibling concern children or adolescents still living in their parental home. Under these circumstances, there is evidence of fairly strong grief reactions which decline over time (Balk, 1991a).

Two studies found that parents reported increased behaviour problems among bereaved children, assessed up to 2 years after a sibling's death. Hutton and Bradley (1994) compared a small sample of Australian children, aged 4–11 years, who had lost a sibling through SIDS (Chapter 11), with a matched control group. They found a considerably higher level of behavioural disturbances, particularly aggression, social withdrawal and depression, among the bereaved children. McCown and Pratt (1985) also found higher levels of behaviour problems, compared to standardised norms, among a sample of 9–10-year-old children who had lost a sibling.

A broad retrospective study of a sample of adults, mostly from the 25–44 age group, who had lost a sibling aged under 19 years (Rosen, 1984–5) found the usual features of grief. Guilt was common, for example for surviving or for wishing the sibling dead at some time. These feelings persisted for a long time, and three-quarters of the sample said that they had been unable to share them with anyone at the time of the loss, or for a long time afterwards.

These reports note there was relatively little discussion of the death with others in the family, and that this was often compounded by unhelpful responses from the wider community. Other evidence (Martinson and Campos, 1991) indicates that adolescent sibling loss is associated with a more positive long-term outcome when the experience can be shared and the family is able to provide support. This is in accord with the generally beneficial consequences of social support (Stylianos and Vachon, 1993).

Most research on sibling death has focused on adolescent grieving among US samples. Balk (1983) interviewed 33 teenagers, aged 14–19 years, about their grief following death of a sibling, at times varying from 4–84 months afterwards. Most of the usual grief reactions (Chapter 5) were found: shock, numbness, preoccupation, anniversary reactions, confusion, hallucinations, depression, anger, sleeping difficulties, lack of concentration and loneliness.

These all occurred in over half the sample. About a third said that they had had suicidal thoughts.

Balk (1990) interviewed another 42 adolescents, aged 14–19 years, whose sibling had died 4 months to 7 years previously. The reactions immediately after the death were again indicative of grieving: shock, anger, preoccupation and depression were reported by three-quarters or more of the sample, and numbness, guilt and sleep disturbances by over a half. Again, a third thought of suicide. These reactions were reported retrospectively, and had lessened by the time of the interview, but about half said that they still felt depressed, about a third were angry, and nearly all still often thought about their sibling.

Hogan and Greenfield (1991) used a questionnaire designed for sibling bereavement (Hogan, 1988b, 1990) to assess the incidence of grief among a community sample of bereaved adolescents. As expected, this tended to be lower after a longer time had elapsed since the death. However, a relatively high level of grief was reported even when the death had occurred over 18 months before.

Martinson and Campos (1991) interviewed 31 adolescents whose brother or sister had died of cancer 7–9 years before, to assess the long-term consequences of the death. Most of the sample regarded the experience as having enhanced their personal or family growth, although a minority saw it as having a continuing negative impact on their lives.

Fanos and Nickerson (1991) examined the impact of sibling death from cystic fibrosis over an even longer time period, through interviews and questionnaires to people who had lost a sibling from the disease in the 1960s and 1970s. The most persistent signs of chronic grief were found among those who were 13–17 years of age at the time of the death. It revealed itself in the form of guilt, both generally and specifically, in terms of survivor guilt, and how they had coped with the sibling's illness and death. This group also showed greater psychological distress, in the form of anxiety, feelings of vulnerability, somatic complaints and sleeping problems, than those who were younger at the time of the death.

Fanos and Nickerson explained their findings in terms of three characteristics of this age group: first, their formal operational level of thinking produced more searching for meaning that at younger ages; second, their relationships with siblings were likely to have been more complex; and third, there was likely to have been a conflict between the needs of the remaining family members to maintain close ties and the need of the adolescents to distance themselves from the family. In addition, we might note that more intense grief at this time would be predicted from considerations of reproductive value.

One circumstance where the loss of a sibling will be particularly difficult is for older people who never married and lived with their siblings. Pickard's (1994) study of older people in a South Wales community indicated that grief could be as intense as for the loss of a spouse under these circumstances.

Finally, we should again note that in two adult samples of bereaved twins

(Woodward, 1988; Segal and Bouchard, 1993; Segal *et al.*, 1995), higher intensities of grief were found among monozygotic than dizygotic twins (Chapter 9). Segal and Bouchard also found higher levels of grief following the twin's death than that of other family members. Using the Grief Experience Inventory (Sanders *et al.*, 1985) to compare the levels of grief for a co-twin with those found in other studies for bereaved children, spouses and parents, Segal *et al.* (1995) again found that the grief of co-twins was the most intense. These findings highlight the special relationship commonly found between twins, particularly those who are genetically identical (Segal, 1993).

Death of a friend

In *The Iliad*, Apollo comments on the intense and prolonged grief shown by Achilles over the death of his friend and comrade Patroclus, remarking that one would expect a man to grieve for a close relative, such as brother or son, but that such a level of grief seemed out of place for a friend. This particular case of friendship is ambiguous since Patroclus and Achilles grew up together and the Athenians of Homer's time also assumed that they were lovers (Shay, 1991). However, there are many other historical examples of intense grief over a close friend. Tennyson's poem 'In Memoriam A.H.H.' was written in response to the sudden death of his close friend Arthur Hallam, and indicates grief as strong as that felt for a spouse. The seventeenth-century poet Abraham Cowley wrote after the death of his friend William Hervey:

> My dearest Friend, would I had died for thee!
> Life and this world henceforth will tedious be:
> Nor shall I know hereafter what to do
>   If once my griefs prove tedious too.
> Silent and sad I walk about all day,
> As sullen ghosts stalk speechless by
> Where their hid treasures lie;
> Alas! my treasure's gone; why do I stay?
>   (Cowley, 'On the death of Mr. William
>   Hervey', in Quiller-Couch, 1919: 377)

In these examples, grief may seem intense compared with that experienced by men after the death of a friend in modern western societies, where intense male friendships are discouraged by homophobia and lack of personal disclosure. Nevertheless, friendship may be increasing in importance among sections of society where family ties have weakened.

Friends are accorded fewer rights as mourners than members of the deceased's family (Deck and Folta, 1989; Sklar, 1991–2). There is also little research on the grief of friends, despite the prevalence of historical examples. Sklar and Hartley (1990) carried out what they acknowledged was an exploratory study, involving a sample of young adults. A number of the familiar features of grief were reported, including anger towards the deceased, feelings of unreality, guilt, hallucinations, dreams about the deceased, and anniversary reactions. However, the value of the study is limited by the inclusion of sexual partners as well as friends, and the lack of quantitative analysis.

McNeil *et al.* (1991) investigated the reactions of a large class of adolescents (aged 14–18 years) when one of them had died of leukaemia. A majority reported sadness, and between a third and a half an initial reaction of shock or numbness or anger. The severity of the reaction was associated with the degree of closeness to the deceased and the frequency of interactions with him. Most of the class reported thinking about him every day during the first week, and 38 per cent said they thought about him more than four times a day. A large proportion of the sample still felt intense feelings of sadness, anger or confusion 18 months later. As expected, close friends thought about him most often. Some respondents were extremely angry with the researchers for bringing up the subject of the death 18 months after it had happened, indicating that it was still a distressing topic.

A further study (Brent *et al.*, 1993) concerned the death of an adolescent friend or acquaintance through suicide, a type of death which is likely to produce additional problems (Henley, 1984; van der Wal, 1988, 1989–90). Friends showed high levels of depression, which were much higher than those of acquaintances and of non-bereaved controls.

These three studies show that grief is experienced by people who are not a partner or an immediate family member. The second study showed that grief was strongest amongst those whose relationship with the deceased was closest. All three are, however, limited in various ways. In one, the definition of friendship was so wide that it included couples, in another only adolescents' schoolfriends were studied, and in the third the bereavement involved suicide, which has its own complications. All three considered males and females together.

Although there are few studies of grief following a friend's death, there are many of adult friendship itself, usually involving same-sex friendships. North American studies typically find that women form closer and more intimate friendships than men. Rubin (1985) found that most of a sample of men could not name a best friend, and did not see this as regrettable. Men who did have close friends avoided speaking about personal matters with them, saying that they did not want another man to know they were vulnerable. Men's friendships were based on shared activities such as work or sport. Women's friendships were closer and more intimate, based on sharing their personal experiences and feelings with a few others. Most of Rubin's sample of women were able to nominate a best friend and those that could not regretted this.

The masculine friendship pattern is illustrated in the following comments made by biographer A.N. Wilson about C.S. Lewis' circle of friends in Oxford:

Few of his friends ever heard Lewis allude to his inner life ... These men knew almost nothing of the Lewis who had emerged in my reading of private letters and diaries. They knew nothing from him of his childhood trauma, little of his two great emotional attachments to women, and next to nothing of his spiritual journey.

(Wilson, 1990: xii–xiii)

The pattern of sex differences in friendship style described by Rubin has been found in other North American studies (Wright, 1988). It can be related to a broader characterisation of men's and women's behaviour, as agentic (or instrumental), and communal (or expressive) respectively (Eagly, 1987). These involve a concern with activities and analysis, or with relationships and feeling. The distinction can encompass many aspects of men's and women's social behaviour, including their coping strategies following bereavement (Chapter 13). It has also been linked to the societal roles of the sexes (Eagly, 1987, 1995; but see Archer, 1996b).

Nevertheless, some researchers have urged caution when applying these generalisations to friendship styles. Based on interactions between same-sex friends in the US, and the stated purposes of their meetings, Duck and Wright (1993) argued that the distinction between men's and women's friendships is less clear than the labels instrumental and expressive indicate. In most cases, friends meet just to talk, and both sexes can either work on a task or deal with a relationship issue. Nevertheless, women were more positive about same-sex friendships in this study, and they did report investing more heavily in their friendships than did men, and getting more from them. Women's friendships did involve more expressive qualities than men's, although there was no difference in the extent of instrumental activities.

These different interpretations have implications for the relative strengths of attachments in men's and women's friendships. That favoured by Duck and Wright (1983) involves only a superficial difference, male inexpressiveness, whereas the alternative involves a greater strength of feeling in women's relationships (Dosser, Balswick and Halverson, 1986). This would have implications for sex differences in grief for a friend.

Other studies show that men can form strong attachments to one another, especially in closed institutions such as prisons and under conditions of danger such as war. They involved mutual aid, and were jealously guarded. Rubin (1985) mentioned the Australian 'mates,' and the US 'buddies' as further examples of this type of close friendship, where each person depends on the other for survival. Studies of bereavement in combat (Glover, 1984; Garb *et al.*, 1987) indicate the importance of these male friendships which, although not involving the disclosure and intimacy of female friends, nevertheless are characterised by close attachment or bonding. Accompanying this is a pronounced grief reaction following a buddy's death (Mead, 1962: 264).

In these cases of close male friendship, affectional bonds are based on association, and are specific to the situation. They occur when harsh conditions dictate that mutual aid is essential or highly advantageous for survival or protection. Evolutionary thinking has identified the advantages of reciprocal altruism under such conditions (Trivers, 1971).

It is clear from the foregoing discussion that the form of men's and women's friendships are very different. Their developmental origin lies in the sex-segregated peer groups of childhood (Archer, 1992b). From an early age, girls tend to form smaller groups or pairs based on sharing secrets and involving best friends, whereas boys form larger groups with less disclosure and more posturing and concern for status. Language and social expectations are different, and it is little exaggeration to say that the two sexes grow up in different cultural contexts. From these, the very different types of adult friendships of men and women develop.

The different friendship patterns of men and women can also be understood in a historical context. Smith-Rosenberg (1975) carried out a detailed analysis of female friendships among the North American middle classes in the eighteenth and nineteenth centuries, from correspondence and diaries. It was clear that female friendships involved physical affection, emotional intensity and feelings of closeness and love. Smith-Rosenberg cautions against imposing upon these friendships present-day dichotomous thinking about relationships – that they are either sexual or platonic, either normal or abnormal. They arose in a social world which involved rigid separation of men and women, even within the family. Relations between the sexes were formal and stiff, whereas there was a continuity in female life which revolved around women and other children, bounded by the home, church and the institution of visiting. Women were also bound together in physical and emotional intimacy by their reproductive life.

A similar pattern of female friendships is likely to develop whenever the social worlds of male and female are rigidly separated, as they are in many cultures today. The modern western pattern of closer ties between the sexes would seem to be superimposed on this older one, and may be responsible for findings of similarities between the sexes' friendships in specific studies (such as Duck and Wright's). Nevertheless, even in modern western states, the early sex-segregation of boys and girls is maintained, and the adult sex difference in friendship patterns shows a partial continuity with the traditional pattern. This theme is also important when considering the impact of moving to a new area for men and women (McCollum, 1990). It is of course a crucially important consideration for any future research on grief following the death of a same-sex friend, and one which has not at present been addressed in this context.

Grieving for an 'unrecognised' partner

Many close relationships are unrecognised by the wider society. This may extend to the exclusion of a sexual partner from the funeral and mourning arrangements by the family of the deceased. It may happen in the case of extra-marital heterosexual relationships, gay partnerships and some unmarried heterosexual couples.

Since extra-marital affairs are a fairly common occurrence in modern western societies, grief following the death of a partner under these circumstances would not be a rare event, and it occasionally comes to the attention of the news media, for example at the time of the funeral of President Mitterrand of France, which was attended by both his wife and long-term mistress. Nevertheless, there appear to be no studies of this subject. Obviously, the secrecy surrounding many of the relationships would inhibit disclosure to researchers. Doka (1989b) has outlined some of the considerations we might expect to be important under these circumstances. Since the form of the relationship can vary in a number of ways, for example in the commitment involved, its secrecy and its acceptability to others, grief reactions will vary accordingly. Guilt may be pronounced, particularly if the surviving partner now has to explain the nature of the relationship. Ambivalent feelings may surface. Above all, there is likely to be exclusion of the bereaved from support for the dying partner, a lack of social support and exclusion of them from the funeral rites. An example of this is described in Milan Kundera's novel *The Unbearable Lightness of Being*. This excerpt describes how the dead man's former wife took over the funeral arrangements to the exclusion of his current lover:

> In death, Franz at last belonged to his wife. He belonged to her as he never belonged to her before. Marie-Claude took care of everything: she saw to the funeral, sent out the announcements, bought the wreaths, and had a black dress made – a wedding dress in reality . . . Somewhere in the back, supported by a friend, stood the girl with big glasses. The combination of many pills and suppressed sobs gave her an attack of cramps before the ceremony came to an end. She lurched forward, clutching her stomach, and her friend had to take her away from the cemetery.
>
> (Kundera, 1984: 275–6)

One type of relationship which often involves problems of recognition by others is that between gay partners. Hostile attitudes to gays, and (for example in the UK until the late 1960s) the illegality of gay sexual acts by men, led to many of these relationships being kept private. This produces severe problems for the bereaved when a partner dies. Christopher Isherwood's novel *A Single Man* concerns a middle-aged British lecturer living in California, called George. In the aftermath of the sudden death of his male partner in a motor vehicle crash, George felt that he could not attend his partner's funeral, since their relationship was not acknowledged by the family, who in such circumstances are, like the widow in Kundera's novel, seen as the rightful mourners:

> An uncle of Jim's whom he'd never met – trying to be sympathetic, even

admitting George's right to a small honorary share in the sacred family grief – but then as they talked, becoming a bit chilled by George's laconic *yes, I see, yes*; his curt *no, thank you*, to the funeral invitation – deciding no doubt that this much talked-of room-mate hadn't been such a close friend, after all . . .

(Isherwood, 1964: 106)

This type of grief has received more public attention following the increased mortality amongst young gay men due to AIDS. Based on their experience as psychotherapists with bereaved gay men in Los Angeles, Klein and Fletcher (1987) summarised the features that distinguish loss of a gay relationship from a recognised heterosexual one. Some of these are familiar from the above quotation, that surviving partners may be excluded from the funeral plans, that people may question intense feelings for someone who was perceived as 'just a friend', and that there is no descriptive title for a gay mourner in cases where they had not 'come out'. Alternatively, if the relationship was known, the family and friends of the deceased may resent and refuse to accept the bereaved partner. Other features concern the social isolation of the bereaved, for whom the deceased may have been the only real 'family'.

The difficulties experienced following death of a gay partner in part stem from the widespread societal hostility towards homosexuals. Thornton, Robertson and Mlecko (1991) assessed the degree to which female undergraduate respondents would like to be associated with a bereaved person, and how much they saw friends and relatives as providing support, under one of six circumstances: these consisted of three supposedly problematic forms of loss and three which would be recognised and induce positive reactions. One of the first group involved a lesbian couple and this was perceived as evoking a low level of social support, respondents giving lower ratings of wanting to be associated with the person than in all other cases except for an induced abortion.

Some people who are not sexual partners share their lives over long periods of time. Companions who lead celibate lives, or obtain their sexual fulfilment elsewhere, are likely to form strong attachments to people with whom they live. This too is often overlooked. The English actor Dirk Bogarde shared his home with Tony Forwood, his manager and male friend, with whom he had been, except for the other's marriage and the war, for 50 years. After Tony Forwood's death in 1988, Dirk Bogarde said:

Ours was a totally platonic relationship; Tony was a rather puritanical figure who happened to hate the idea of homosexuality, but that doesn't make it any easier to live without him . . . We had an instinctive and unusual partnership and I have to say I now find the weekends painfully long.

(Bogarde, 1988: 38)

There are many other instances in which people may live together or develop a close relationship over many years, but without sexual contact. We should not forget that these relationships involve close attachments, and will lead to strongly felt grief.

Death of a princess and other public figures

An interesting and puzzling phenomenon of the modern age of mass communications is the widespread grief shown after the death of certain public figures. An early example was the grief of fans following the death of Rudolph Valentino. More recently, it was highlighted by the public reaction in the UK and elsewhere to the sudden death of Diana, Princess of Wales at the end of August 1997. In 1963, there was similar intense and widespread public grief following the killing of John F. Kennedy. There are many other examples of mass public expressions of grief following the death of a person well known and revered through the modern media.

Why should people queue for many hours to lay flowers or sign a condolence book in memory of someone they did not know? Why did practically every church and workplace throughout Britain feel the need to participate in this mass expression of grief for Princess Diana? After all, grief is a human reaction to the loss of a close personal relationship. By no stretch of imagination did all these people have a personal relationship with the princess.

The modern mass media brings into people's homes images of both fictitious and famous people, together with a feeling that their lives have some personal importance and significance. They become a part of many people's internal social world, alongside those who are known personally. The immediacy of the images generated by the modern media blurs the distinction for some people. In the days before such images, people's social worlds stretched to their kin, friends and acquaintances. Admittedly there would be second-hand knowledge of powerful and famous public figures, but their lives would not have seemed a familiar part of people's everyday world, as is the case for celebrities made familiar by today's intrusive media. The same phenomenon applies to the part played by television soap stars or pop stars in some people's lives. An outpouring of grief, albeit more limited, often accompanies the fictitious death of a character in a radio or TV soap. In a way, the lives of the British royal family – via extensive media coverage – provided the British people with their grandest and longest running soap opera.

The study of non-human primates may provide one clue as to why people show such great interest in famous and glamorous people they have not met. Dominant and confident animals are often a focus of attention for others in the group, and they can be the source of social support in times of stress (Crook, 1980: 126). Following others (Chance and Jolly, 1970; Larsen, 1975), Crook suggested that, in the human case, individuals of high status and restraint in their actions are often given special attention by others, a process which channels the deeply held dependency needs that many people have. The modern popular media have managed to magnify (or manipulate) such widely held, but scarcely recognised, dependency needs by dwelling repeatedly on images of the lives of famous and glamorous individuals, who are said to possess charisma. In a way, it does not matter that they are unknown to people personally, since it is the attention paid to them that is important. This attention is derived from a primitive response to charismatic individuals which in itself is largely a one-way process. Seen in this light, it is less surprising that people show a grief reaction when such a public figure dies, particularly when this individual meets a sudden, violent and untimely death, features which accentuate grief under any circumstances.

In interviews to the British media at the time of Princess Diana's death, many British people said that they had felt more upset than when a member of their own family had died. This was especially the case when some feature of the princess' circumstances paralleled their own experiences, for example if they were the same age as her children when their own mother or father died. It seems likely that the experience of mass distress and shock provided a background for old feelings of grief to be reawakened, as they might be by an anniversary or reminder, and that these were rendered more salient by perceived similarities with the current tragedy. The context of mass distress would also have given some people the feeling of social support for, and acceptance of, the expression of grief over a past loss, features which may not have been forthcoming at the time of the loss itself.

This section was necessarily speculative, since there is – as far as I know – no research on this topic. Yet it is a real and puzzling phenomenon and therefore merits consideration however speculative the analysis.

Loss of a non-human companion

It is well known that many people become emotionally attached to their household pets and are upset when the pet dies. Alexander Pope commented on this form of grief in the eighteenth century:

> Not louder shrieks to pitying heav'n are cast,
> When husbands, or when lap-dogs breathe their last.
> (Pope, 1714, *The Rape of the Lock, III*: 157)

The existence of pet cemeteries has been noted in several countries, but they are perhaps best known in the US and the UK, the most famous fictional one being the 'Happier Hunting Ground' of Evelyn Waugh's novel *The Loved One* (Waugh, 1948). The commercial potential of such enterprises was underlined in 1971 with the formation of the International Society of Pet Cemeteries (Spiegelman and Kastenbaum, 1990), and the numbers in the US reached over 500 by 1979 (Hickrod and Schmitt, 1982).

Questionnaire studies of crying (Lombardo *et al.*, 1983; Williams and

Morris, 1996) found that a quarter of a US male sample, and just under half of a British male sample said that they would be likely to cry after their pet's death. The comparable figures for women were 58 per cent and 75 per cent. Among the British sample, this was substantially higher than for separation from a loved one or feeling lonely.

There are many anecdotal examples of intense grief over the death of a pet. The following two are taken from a British daily newspaper and from an article by a counsellor for bereaved pet owners in San Francisco (Carmack, 1985). The first is particularly unfortunate. It involved the prosecution of a former mayor of a town in Lancashire following the death of her Yorkshire terrier who had been left in a car on a hot day (*The Guardian*, 12th January 1991). The court case was an additional blow to the poor woman whose dog had been her constant companion since her husband died, sleeping on her bed and being taken to work. She was reported as saying: 'After my husband died, Rutherford [the dog] became an emotional crutch for me. When he died, it nearly killed me . . . it was like losing my husband again.'

The second case concerns Mrs M, a widow of 62 years, who lived with her adult son and five cats. When her favourite cat ('Baby') died, Mrs M would not sleep in her own bed any more, since Baby had slept there. Instead she used the sofa in the living room, clutching a photograph of Baby when she retired for the night. Mrs M kept all of Baby's things – even the litter box – the way they were when they were last used. No one was allowed to sit on Baby's chair, and the other cats were not allowed to jump on it. Whenever she tried to talk about her grief, Mrs M cried. She even avoided the number seven, because Baby had died on the seventh day of the month.

Many of the reactions shown in these two cases would not look out of place following the loss of a close human relationship, and they indicate strong attachments to the animals. Many similar examples can be found among psychiatric reports (Keddie, 1977), surveys of veterinary surgeons and reports from counselling services for bereaved pet owners (Carmack, 1985; Weisman, 1990–1). Although card shops do sell sympathy cards for death of a pet (Figure 12.2), it is probably fair to comment that there is generally little social recognition of this form of loss (Stewart, Thrush and Paulus, 1989), a characteristic it shares with other losses, such as unrecognised adult relationships, collectively termed 'disenfranchised' grief by Doka (1989a).

These sources provide interesting descriptive accounts of grief following death of a pet, but it is difficult to tell how representative they are of pet owners in general. Several more systematic studies have now been undertaken.

A study in the UK (Archer and Winchester, 1994; Winchester, 1992) involved 88 participants who had lost a pet during the previous year. They completed a 40-item grief questionnaire, based on the description of grief by Parkes (1986). Items indicating numbness or disbelief, preoccupation, a loss of self, and being drawn towards reminders were endorsed by the majority of the sample. About a quarter reported the urge to search, avoidance or mitigation of grief, anger, anxiety and depression.

All things bright and beautiful
All creatures great and small
All things wise and wonderful
The Lord God made them all.

Frances Alexander
1818-1895

Figure 12.2 Two examples of commercially produced sympathy cards for the loss of a
pet. The inscription inside one is: 'The loss of a beloved creature is the loss
of a loving friend. I want you to know how sorry I am'.

Source: Reproduced by kind permission of Painted Hearts & Friends, Pasadena, California, and
Recycled Paper Greetings, Inc, Chicago (copyright, original design by Audrey Christie, All
Rights Reserved)

Grief was more pronounced among those living alone, owners experiencing a sudden death, and those who were strongly attached to the pet
(judged from descriptions of what it had meant to the owner). These associations, which have been confirmed in other studies (Gerwolls and Labott,
1994; Gosse and Barnes, 1994) all parallel known predictors of the severity of
grief following a human bereavement (Parkes, 1985). The importance of the
intensity of attachment is consistent with the general link between grief and
the strength of the relationship which is lost (Chapter 10).

In this study, only a small proportion of the sample reported feeling particularly depressed or anxious or angry as a result of the loss – which is what
we should expect in the case of what is, to most people, not a central part of
their lives. Similarly, among a large sample of middle-aged couples in the US,
the death of a pet was viewed as less stressful than that of a close friend or an
immediate family member (Gage and Holcomb, 1991). Among another large
sample, of older people in the US, the death of a pet was associated with
lower rates of depression than was the case for death of a close family member (Rajaram *et al.*, 1993). On this evidence, we can conclude that the women
who grieved for Rutherford and Baby were unusual.

In contrast, two US studies using Sanders' GEI, modified for the death of a pet (Drake-Hurst, 1991; Gerwolls and Labott, 1994), found that levels of grief were similar to those reported for death of a parent, child or spouse. These surprising findings may reflect limitations of the measurement (Chapter 2) or that intense grief for a pet is more widespread than expected. Whichever it is, the formation of attachments by people to their pets raises an important issue. The evolutionary view of attachment (Chapter 9) clearly identified it as a mechanism for fostering biologically important relationships. Why, therefore, do people develop similar feelings for members of other species?

This question has been answered in several different ways, for example that benefits for health and well-being result from pet-keeping (Serpell, 1986). My own evolutionary analysis of pet ownership (Archer, 1997) is that pets provide various satisfying signals that enable people to enter into relationships similar to those with human beings. This relies on human parenting reactions being a response to a set of signals that are found generally in the young of mammals, rather than to signals emitted specifically by human infants. The result of establishing bonds with individuals from another species is that we care for them, provision them and feel love for them. Yet from an evolutionary viewpoint, it is the pets which benefit from the attachment. In this sense, they have become a form of social parasite on their human owners, increasing their reproductive fitness at the expense of the time and resources the owners could have been devoting to their own children and relatives.

This analysis highlights one case where the nature and strength of affectional bonds do not coincide with considerations of fitness, as they do when considering bonds formed to other human beings. From a Darwinian perspective, they can only be understood by considering the way in which humans form attachments with their children, and how pets are able to mimic this process. Here we have a case where arguing directly from fitness considerations (Chapter 9) would not work. Grief for a pet can only be understood as a consequence of an attachment which is maladaptive, yet is understandable in terms of mechanisms which are generally adaptive.

Once the interaction between owner and pet has been set in motion, the owner experiences the sort of rewarding feedback that enables a bond to be developed with a human infant, based partly on recognition of the emotional states and playful moods of the pet species. The intellectual and linguistic limitations of the pet are overcome by owners behaving as if the pet understands them, and in some senses filling in the expected feedback. This can lead to some people preferring their relationships with pets to those they have with people, because the pets appear to provide them with the sort of uncritical feedback that is absent from human relationships. It is in such cases that we should expect the sort of intense grief described in the examples of Rutherford and Baby.

Conclusions

In this chapter I considered grief following losses of different types of relationship, the first being the death of a parent at various stages in a person's
life. The impact of the loss appeared to follow the age considerations outlined
in the Introduction. The available evidence for childhood indicated that there
was a pronounced grief reaction, at least according to the parents' reports.
Long-term consequences of early parental loss may be a partial consequence
of early grieving on personality development, but the social consequences for
the child's subsequent life course are likely to be of even greater importance.
The scant evidence on loss of a parent during adolescence and young
adulthood also indicates more severe grief at these times than during later
adulthood when death of a parent appears more timely. There is consistent
evidence that grief is less intense during the offspring's middle life than
at younger ages. Broadly, these findings fit with predictions based on the
declining reproductive value of parents across their lifespan.

The limited evidence on grandparents indicated that they show an intense
form of grief, as expected from an evolutionary analysis, but there were no
systematic comparisons with other forms of grief to confirm this. Likewise,
there were no studies enabling an assessment of evolutionary predictions
based on the paternity uncertainty that mediates some grandparental kinship
ties.

Grief for siblings has only been studied during childhood and adolescence,
and the available studies indicate that it can be severe at these times. However,
there are again no data on which to make systematic comparisons with grief
following the loss of other types of relationship. Interestingly, one study
found that the level of grief was higher for adolescent children than for
younger-aged ones. This is what would be predicted from their relative
reproductive values.

The twin studies, referred to in an earlier chapter, also indicated more
intense grief for a co-twin (the majority of whom were identical) than for
other classes of kin. There was also some evidence of particularly high rates
of grief for monozygotic twins, as predicted on the basis of their kinship.

Studies of grief following death of a friend confirmed its occurrence for
people who were not kin or sexual partners, but the studies were all limited in
various ways. An examination of the pattern of same-sex friendships among
men and women revealed considerable differences which are likely to be deep-
rooted in terms of their developmental and historical origins. The implications of these different friendship patterns for grief have not yet been
explored, although we did note that the close male friendships formed under
conditions of environmental danger or deprivation fitted evolutionary
analyses involving reciprocal altruism, and are likely to be associated with a
pronounced grief reaction.

Consideration of grief for a socially unrecognised relationship focused on
the social situation in which the bereaved person finds him- or herself. This

involved not just the absence of social support, which has been found to be important in many studies of grief, but also being actively excluded from the rituals of mourning.

I also considered grief following death of a pet, which was interesting because it clearly follows the strength of the relationship to the animal, even though this does not represent a biologically significant relationship. I outlined the view that pets manipulate human attachment mechanisms which have evolved to facilitate relationships with human kin, mainly offspring. Here we have an example where the strength of attachment is not related to fitness considerations and where arguing directly from such considerations to predict the strength of grief would be inappropriate. Attachment to pets provides a good example of the necessity always to consider the proximate mechanisms that mediate any evolutionarily relevant variables.

Overall, the evidence reviewed in this chapter provides only a start to the study of grief for relationships other than those involving offspring or spouses. We should expect them all to be mediated by the strength of attachment and for this to vary in relation to considerations of reproductive value and kinship, except of course in the case of pets.

13   The influence of the age and sex of the bereaved

She pass'd away like morning dew
Before the sun was high;
So brief her time, she scarcely knew
The meaning of a sigh.

As round the rose its soft perfume
Sweet love around her floated;
Admired she grew – while mortal doom
Crept on, unfear'd, unnoticed.
> (Hartley Coleridge, 'Early Death', in
> Quiller-Couch, 1919: 751)

Introduction

People have an intuitive sense that a death occurring at a young age is unexpected and untimely. Beyond a certain age, death is expected and viewed as timely. This is a major consideration for differences in grief according to the age of the deceased. Commonly held beliefs are less readily related to differences between men's and women's experience and expression of grief, although women are expected to express grief – and many other emotions – more openly than are men. But does this mean that they *experience* it more strongly?

In this chapter, I consider how the age and sex of the bereaved person affects their grief, continuing the general theme of examining the loss of different types of relationships from the standpoint of evolutionary theory and attachment theory.

The evolutionary framework informs us about changes in an individual's reproductive value with age, in other words how much they are worth for the inclusive fitness of a relative or partner. This approach was applied in the previous two chapters, to the loss of a child, and to the loss of a parent, at different ages. Thus it was predicted that older parents would value their offspring more than younger ones would, and that as parents reach older ages they would be less valued by their offspring: in Chapter 12 we noted that the next generation's grief was greater for younger than for older parents. This reflects the growing asymmetry in their respective reproductive values with increasing parental age (Daly and Wilson, 1988a: 99).

These predictions are relatively straightforward. But in the case of marital grief, the reproductive values of both partners declines with age, and will be zero after the woman's menopause (the husband's reproductive value will effectively be zero for his wife when she can no longer conceive). From this analysis alone, we would predict a decline in grief for a spouse in middle age and beyond. There are, however, several other considerations.

Younger kin, such as adult offspring and younger relatives, will become more valuable in terms of inclusive fitness to older adults who have no reproductive value themselves. Therefore, the *relative* importance of spouses compared to these individuals may decline. From this viewpoint, some decline in attachment to spouses would occur alongside greater concern for the welfare of younger relatives. This would be more evident in collectivist than in individualistic societies where kinship ties are weakened.

These evolutionary considerations all point to the weakening of conjugal ties at older ages. In contrast, viewing the relationship from an attachment perspective leads to different predictions. The impact of the longer duration of the relationship, and the fewer alternative choices, both would lead to an expectation of more intense and prolonged grief at older ages. The loss of practical support and companionship that the marriage partner represented would also be likely to be more strongly felt at older ages. We should therefore expect prolonged signs of grief, and also social isolation and loneliness. These are likely to be more prevalent among women, in view of their lesser prospects of remarriage at older ages. They are also more likely to occur in individualistic societies, where kinship ties are weakened, than in collectivist societies.

One final consideration is that a death occurring at a younger age is more likely to involve no forewarning, which is associated with more intense and prolonged grieving (Ball, 1976–7; Carey, 1979–80; Parkes and Weiss, 1983; Zisook *et al.*, 1987b).

There are, therefore, several considerations which lead to conflicting predictions about changes in spousal grief with age. More pronounced grief is likely at younger ages for two reasons, that the loss involves someone with a greater reproductive value, and is more likely to be sudden and viewed as untimely. Bereavement at a younger age may therefore be perceived more acutely and lead to greater distress. On the other hand, it comes at a time when it is still possible to find an alternative life. At older ages, more pronounced grief is likely because of the longevity of the relationship and the greater difficulties in adjusting to life without a spouse. Although the death may be seen as more timely, there are fewer prospects of a new life at older ages. This may apply more to women, in view of the unequal sex ratio at older ages.

In Chapter 11, we considered sex differences in parental grief, which were related to the higher initial parental investment of the mother. In this chapter, we consider sex differences in grief more generally, first whether husbands or wives are more affected by the loss of a spouse, second, whether men and women show different ways of coping with bereavement, and third whether sex differences in parental grief are linked with general differences in coping styles.

There are no clear predictions from evolutionary theory about sex differences in reactions to spousal bereavement. Power inequality between the sexes is usually central to feminist analyses. In evolutionary terms, this can be viewed as arising from the conflicting reproductive strategies of the sexes (Smuts, 1995). Both analyses lead to the following argument. If men control women's reproductive lives to such an extent that they derive more benefit from marriage than women do, we would expect men to experience greater role deprivation following the loss of a spouse than a woman would. Men would therefore experience greater distress following the loss of a spouse.

An alternative argument is that although men lose someone who has fulfilled the domestic role and was the carer of his children, women lose the source of material support, status and their link with the wider society. Emphasis on the second of these has led to the opposite prediction, that women's grief will be greater than men's. The issues involved in assessing which of the two predictions best fits the evidence is complex.

Sex differences in grief are also likely to be complicated by the different ways in which men and women typically react to stress-inducing events. This has been referred to in connection with the Dual-Process Model (DPM) in Chapters 6 and 7: women typically confront the event and seek to make sense of it, whereas men typically seek to deal with the event by engaging in alternative actions. These different coping styles are important not only for spousal bereavement but also in the cases of parental grief. Here there will be the added complication that the different coping styles of the bereaved parents may act to the detriment of their relationship.

Therefore, the topics considered in this chapter are, first, whether grief is greater at younger than older ages; second, features such as loneliness and the unequal sex ratio, which may complicate bereavement at older ages; third, sex differences in the intensity of grief for a spouse in relation to the conflicting predictions that have been made; fourth, the coping strategies of men and women when faced with a bereavement; fifth, how these might apply to differences between the grief of mothers and fathers, and whether they operate to the detriment of the marital relationship following loss of a child.

Is grief greater at younger than older ages?

On the occasion of the death of his brother Erasmus in 1881, Charles Darwin wrote to Sir J.D. Hooker expressing the view that grief for a young person is felt more strongly and is more long lasting than that for an older one, on account of the loss of a possible future (F. Darwin, 1888: 228). This view is consistent with the evolutionary considerations outlined in the Introduction.

Contemporary studies of spousal bereavement necessarily involve different ages of both the deceased and the bereaved. A number of such studies have compared the impact of grief on a variety of health-related measures among younger and older samples of bereaved spouses.

The earlier studies concentrated on women. Examining the medical records of an unselected sample of widows, Parkes (1964b) found that for those under 65 years, the consultation rate for psychological problems trebled after the bereavement, but that no difference was apparent for widows over 65 years. In a study of patients receiving psychiatric treatment following bereavement, Parkes (1965) identified younger widows as more likely to show problems of atypical grief. Other studies, which are summarised in Table 13.1, generally agree with these two in that they indicate that younger widows and widowers show more intense grief and have more adjustment problems.

However, some of the studies shown in Table 13.1 found no association between age and the level of grief. Sable (1991) found that older people reported more intense grief than younger ones, although the median age was 63 years in this study.

Overall, the findings are mixed, some showing greater severity of grief at younger ages and others showing no age effect. Only one study found greater grief at older ages, and this one concentrated on an older sample. We are therefore probably dealing with a real effect which is absent or too small to show up under some circumstances, and may occasionally be reversed under specific sets of conditions (possibly when concentrating on an older age group). In order to identify the extent and source of the disparity with any certainty, the studies would have to be analysed in a quantitative way, using meta-analytic techniques (Rosenthal, 1984, 1991).

One other study suggests that concentrating on the relative levels of grief may obscure the detection of a different pattern of response over time at different ages. Sanders (1980) compared conjugal bereavement in people over 65 years with those who were younger, using the Grief Experience Inventory (Chapter 2), and interviews, carried out 2 months after the loss and after 18–24 months. The younger respondents showed higher grief intensities at 2 months, including stronger yearning, distress, panic, and guilt. However, at 18–24 months, the older people showed exaggerated reactions. Personal isolation, depersonalisation, death anxiety and loss of vigour were all higher in this group. Sanders interpreted these differences in terms of the older people experiencing greater loneliness and fears of safety than the younger ones. Her results are reminiscent of findings by Parkes and Weiss (1983) of a delayed grief reaction following a conflict-ridden relationship (Chapter 10). To assess whether a similar pattern occurs in the grief of older people will require more extensive longitudinal studies. If found, it would be consistent with Sable's findings (Table 13.1), since her measures were all taken at least 1 year post-bereavement.

Table 13.1 Summary of studies involving the association of age and grief

Study	Sample	Measure	Finding
Maddison and Walker (1967)	widows (45–60*)	psychological and physical ill-health	higher levels at younger ages
Ball (1976–7)	widows (18–75)	intensity of grief	higher levels at younger ages (18–46) than middle (47–59) or old (60–75) ages
Vachon *et al.* (1982b)	widows (22–69)	General Health Questionnaire	higher levels at younger ages
Parkes and Weiss (1983)	both sexes (under 46)	grief	no age effects
Jacobs *et al.* (1986)	both sexes (40–80)	grief	no age effects
Zisook and Shuchter (1986)	widows (26–83)	anxiety and depression	higher levels at younger ages
van der Wal (1988)	both sexes, bereaved by suicide or road accident	grief	higher levels at younger ages
Hershberger and Walsh (1990)	both sexes (24–74)	adjustment to bereavement	no age effects
Campbell *et al.* (1991)	widows (32–72)	grief	no age effects
Sable (1991)	widows (26–82)	grief	higher levels at older ages (median age 63)
Bartrop *et al.* (1992)	both sexes (24–78)	anxiety and depression	no age effects
Lund *et al.* (1993)	both sexes (50–89)	adjustment to bereavement	no age effects
Reed (1993)	both sexes, bereaved by suicide or road accident (15–82)	grief	higher levels at younger ages

* Husbands' ages.

Other features of grief at older ages

There are two further interrelated issues concerning bereavement in older life – loneliness and the unequal sex ratio. Loneliness is likely to be a particular problem where the spouse was the main companion, and where there is no new partner (Lopata, 1993; Lund *et al.*, 1993; Sable, 1991). When an older woman loses her husband, she loses the marital role at a time when there are few opportunities for remarriage. Studies of a large sample of widows in Chicago (Lopata, 1993) showed that the greater the woman's dependence on her husband, or their interdependence, the less she was able to cope with life after he had died. Lopata emphasised the extent to which women's identity is often built around that of their husbands, and argued that this is especially the case for older generations. She also emphasised the isolation caused by the lack of traditional connecting links in a modern individualist society.

Interviews carried out as part of Sable's (1991) study of older bereaved people (see previous section) suggest that severance of a relationship which has been central to the person's whole life, at a time when other options do not seem attractive or possible, could have accounted for the pronounced grief she found in her older participants.

The lower life expectancy of men than women means that as the population gets progressively older, there will be a far greater proportion of widows than widowers. In the US, widows outnumber widowers at all ages from 25 years of age onwards (figures for 1980: M.S. Stroebe, W. Stroebe and Hansson, 1988). By 65 years of age, over 50 per cent of women are widowed, compared with around 10–13 per cent of men (1984 and 1990s figures for the US: Hansson, Remondet and Galusha, 1993; Rosenzweig *et al.*, 1997; similar figures for the UK: Pickard, 1994). At older ages, therefore, grief is increasingly a problem of widowhood.

In most traditional (collectivist) societies there are formal restrictions and obligations associated with widowhood. These are largely absent in modern western individualistic societies such as the US (Balkwell, 1981; Lopata, 1993). Yet the social position the widow finds herself in will nevertheless put her at a disadvantage, owing to the loss of her link with the sources of money and status.

A study of widows from an English town in the early 1960s (Hobson, 1964) found that they had very few social activities owing to the lack of a male companion. Most of them had pronounced financial problems, and had to seek employment, but they had generally not worked outside the home prior to widowhood. Other considerations, such as dependent children, their grief and the few suitable vacancies, also made it difficult for them to seek employment. The wages were also likely to be low, and to result in a reduction of their widow's benefit. Most of the women were unused to claiming benefits and felt awkward about receiving financial help, whether from the state or from relatives.

Similar problems, in the form of loneliness, and substantial losses of income have been found in North American studies of widows, from the 1960s and 1970s (Balkwell, 1981), and more recently (Zisook *et al.*, 1987a; Avis *et al.*, 1991). In their sample, Zisook *et al.* also found that lack of money was linked to unhappiness. Findings from large survey samples of widows indicate that, in the long term, economic deprivation is more associated with poor morale, depression and other negative feelings than widowhood as such

(Harvey and Bahr, 1974; Umberson, Wortman and Kessler, 1992; see also Wortman *et al.*, 1993).

Lopata's (1993) studies of widowhood, based on two large-scale studies in Chicago, indicated the extent to which the urban world where many widows now live differs from the traditional one in which women's lives are more embedded in family and community networks. Support systems, which were once automatically available, now have to be actively sought, often in the form of specialised professionals. This can be a particular problem for women of an older generation, who relied on their husbands as a link with the wider society and its resources. Many of these women become heavily dependent on their offspring, particularly their daughters, and live in restricted social networks.

The importance of kinship ties is supported by the findings of a study by McGloshen and O'Bryant (1988), which involved widows aged 60–89 years (the mean being 72 years), whose husbands had died 7–21 months before. All of them lived alone. The researchers examined various predictors of both positive well-being and emotional distress. Overall, health had an important impact on both measures, but age, income and education did not. Positive well-being was influenced by the frequency of attending religious worship, the numbers of siblings and support from their offspring. Distress was heightened by previous experience with death, dissatisfaction with the home, and – surprisingly – having paid employment.

From the studies discussed above, it is apparent that there are particular problems associated with widowhood, notably economic deprivation and difficulties in relating to the wider society, which are exacerbated by the individualist nature of modern western society. In addition, the ratio of widows to widowers becomes higher as the age of the population increases, as a consequence of the different life expectancies of men and women.

Sex differences in reactions to marital bereavement

Many of the studies of conjugal bereavement described in earlier chapters only involved widows. Of those that also included widowers, some found no substantial differences in the severity or overall course of grief between men and women (Faletti *et al.*, 1989; Glick *et al.*, 1974; Parkes and Weiss, 1983; Lund *et al.*, 1993; Thompson *et al.*, 1989; van Zandt *et al.*, 1989).

Other studies (Jacobs *et al.*, 1986; Sanders, 1979–80) have found a more severe initial reaction by widows than widowers, according to measures such as depression and anxiety. Carey (1979–80) and Zisook *et al.* (1987b) also reported more adjustment problems, and higher anxiety and depression levels, among widows than widowers during the first year of bereavement. Gallagher-Thompson *et al.* (1993) found a higher proportion of clinical depression among older widows than widowers. Broadly similar results were found for close relatives following a bereavement by suicide or accident (Reed, 1993). Bierhals *et al.* (1995–6) reported the same pattern up to 3 years after the death, but a reversal between 3 and 5 years afterwards, in a cross-sectional sample of older bereaved people.

Overall, these findings seem to indicate that women experience more psychological distress than men following bereavement. Carey (1979–80) attributed this to the greater degree to which women build their lives around their spouses, and the consequent greater role change required by a widow than a widower (see Introduction). As indicated above, social isolation is often a severe problem for widows (Bowlby, 1980a; Carey, 1979–80; Stillon, 1985), and it has been argued that they encounter more difficulties by nature of their social position than do widowers. If this were the case, we would expect problems to be persistent rather than encountered early in the grief process – as found by some of the studies reviewed above.

The Stroebes advocated an apparently contrary view – that men suffer more following bereavement (M.S. Stroebe and W. Stroebe, 1983; W. Stroebe and M.S. Stroebe, 1984). They argued that women carry a greater burden during marriage, in terms of undertaking mundane low-prestige tasks, and at the same time are expected to nurture and support their husbands. Therefore, men in effect experience better social support during marriage than women do. On this view, men have more to lose after a bereavement, in terms of what the marital state provided for them. As indicated in the Introduction, this view is compatible with both feminist and evolutionary analyses of women's position in society.

The important point regarding the Stroebes' hypothesis is that the comparisons referred to so far, which have been used to argue the opposite position (Carey, 1979–80) are between measures of depression and distress taken from samples of men and women after a bereavement. As the Stroebes rightly point out, the sexes do not start at the same pre-bereavement levels on the measures used in these studies, particularly depression and somatic disorders, women tending to show higher levels than men (Hood, MacLachlan and Fisher, 1987; Roberts and Gotlib, 1997; Vingerhoets and van Heck, 1990). There may also be differences between the samples of men and women in these studies which affect their levels of distress and depression.

The Stroebes therefore concentrated their analysis on a comparison of measures obtained from widows and widowers with those of married women and men. The results of these comparisons challenge the view that women are affected more strongly than men by marital bereavement. Comparing rates of depression (and also mental illness, physical symptoms, suicide and mortality), larger differences were found between married men and widowers than between married women and widows. The evidence came from cross-sectional studies from the 1970s that had included comparison groups (M.S. Stroebe and W. Stroebe, 1983), and from one longitudinal study (Parkes and Brown, 1972). Similar results were found in a more recent investigation of elderly men and women who had lost a family member (but not a spouse) during the previous 6 months (Siegel and Kuykendall, 1990).

Although this evidence points to a greater deterioration in mental and physical health for men than women following bereavement, it is based on comparatively few studies, and therefore should be treated with caution since it would take only a few null results to overturn it (Rosenthal, 1979). However, we should note that the evidence for greater male mortality following bereavement is much stronger (M.S. Stroebe and W. Stroebe, 1993; Gallagher-Thompson *et al.*, 1993).

There are, however, two studies which do not support the Stroebes' position in that they report no greater impact of bereavement on men than women. A study by Gallagher *et al.* (1983) compared samples of bereaved and non-bereaved older men and women on measures of depression, grief and mental health. Women showed more symptoms overall than men did, and bereaved people showed more symptoms than those who were not bereaved. But there was no interaction between the two effects, in other words the impact of bereavement was comparable for both men and women.

In a large-scale national survey study, Umberson *et al.* (1992) found that being a widow or widower was associated with higher rates of depression than remaining married, but when the length of time since bereavement was controlled, there was no significant difference between widows and widowers. The time that had elapsed since bereavement varied in this sample from 1 to 64 years, and the association between the time since the bereavement and depression was different in the two sexes. Men who had recently lost a spouse were more depressed than bereaved women, but those who had lost a spouse some time ago were less so. The researchers suggested that previous evidence of greater emotional upset for men than women (W. Stroebe and M.S. Stroebe, 1984) was the result of concentrating on the immediate impact of the loss, rather than the very long times after bereavement studied in this sample. However, it would seem reasonable to concentrate on the first 2–3 years following a bereavement in order to study grief. It is doubtful whether Umberson *et al.* were studying continuing grief rather than reactions to subsequent life events among people bereaved many years before. It is therefore not necessarily counter to the Stroebes' position for women to show higher depression levels than widowers many years after their bereavement.

At first sight, data from the Tübingen longitudinal study (W. Stroebe and M.S. Stroebe, 1993) would appear also to show no sex difference in reactions to bereavement.[1] However, when the Stroebes analysed the depression questionnaires completed by some of those who had been unwilling to be interviewed, they found that depression was higher for the men than for the women, the opposite direction to the sex difference among those who had agreed to be interviewed (M.S. Stroebe and W. Stroebe, 1989–90). Presumably, if these additional people were also considered, the results would show higher relative depression levels for widowers than widows.

---

1 Since they also found no significant sex by marital status interaction for measures of depression and somatic symptoms.

W. Stroebe and M.S. Stroebe (1987b, 1994) therefore suggested that sex differences are more likely to be found in questionnaire than interview studies (which according to their analysis should exclude more depressed men). However, this cannot account for the lack of sex differences in the study by Gallagher *et al.* (1983) since they used questionnaires. Nevertheless, studies in a range of other areas show that women are generally more willing to complete questionnaires which ask about private feelings and events.

The Stroebes have highlighted two important issues for this type of research, the need to concentrate on changes in measures of psychological distress from before to after bereavement, and the difference between men's and women's willingness to volunteer for studies involving disclosure of negative feelings. Obviously, the studies cited at the beginning of this section (notably Carey, 1979–80) were concerned with another issue, whether the intensity, pattern and time course of grieving is typically different for men and women. Whenever such studies involved measures of general well-being or grief measures which include these, it is not possible to tell whether any sex differences result from the impact of the loss, or from differences present before the loss. An ideal study would involve a longitudinal sample of men and women, for whom data on depression and other health-related variables were available before the bereavement occurred. The practical difficulties of obtaining such samples are considerable, but not insurmountable (see Wortman *et al.*, 1993).

The Stroebes' analysis emphasised the greater social support women typically have available after bereavement, and their later Tübingen study supported this (W. Stroebe and M.S. Stroebe, 1993). On the other hand, the social position of the single woman, and the widow in particular, may involve some longer-term disadvantages, as indicated in the previous section. The survey study of Umberson *et al.*, which involved much longer periods of time since bereavement, found that the primary link between widowhood and depression occurred via financial strain, whereas for men it involved strains concerned with managing the household.

Coping strategies of men and women

A related issue is whether the two sexes cope with grief in different ways. There are sex differences in coping styles to everyday negative events (Billings and Moos, 1981; Folkman and Lazarus, 1980; Lu, 1991; Vingerhoets and van Heck, 1990). Women typically use a form of coping termed 'emotion-focused', which involves concentrating on their feelings and expressing emotions, whereas men tend to use 'problem-focused' coping, which involves thinking about the problem, gathering information about it and acting to solve it. Because these studies all concern everyday problems, the differences could have arisen from different types of stressors being experienced or reported by men and women, especially since the earlier evidence came from retrospective reporting.

Two studies have addressed this issue. Porter and Stone (1995) used a daily coping measure, and did find that women reported more problems concerning interpersonal relations and the self, whereas men reported more work-related problems. Moreover, when the nature of the problems was taken into account, there were no sex differences in coping styles. Porter and Stone concluded that it was the content of everyday problems that was different for men and women, and that it was these differences that caused the different coping styles. An experimental study by Ptacek, Smith and Dodge (1994) led to a rather different conclusion. They found that while male and female undergraduates provided similar ratings of the stressfulness of giving a lecture, they differed in the coping strategies they used, men using problem-focused strategies more often than women did, and women using emotion-focused coping more often than men did. However, we should note that both sexes used problem-focused more often than other forms of coping.

Taken together, these two studies do not resolve the issue of the generality of sex differences in coping strategies and the extent to which they arise from different stressors in the lives of men and women.

Nolen-Hoeksema (1987) applied the hypothesis that there are sex differences in coping styles to depression. She argued that a man's response to a depressive mood is more likely to be a behavioural one, and to have a greater chance of decreasing the source of the depressive mood. Women's responses are more likely to involve rumination, and to have a greater likelihood of prolonging and amplifying the source of the depression. In relation to bereavement, the two coping styles would be represented by engaging in another activity, or repeated thoughts about the loss and the deceased (see also Chapters 7 and 8). Nolen-Hoeksema reviewed a range of evidence supporting these suggested sex differences in response to depressive moods. Even if the source of the different responses was again the different problems of men and women (as indicated above), the theory still applies, since it concerns how men and women cope with a depressive mood once it has arisen.

Subsequent studies have supported Nolen-Hoeksema's position. For example, Butler and Nolen-Hoeksema (1994) used a detailed questionnaire to assess people's response to a depressed mood. As in other studies, two main types of response were found, rumination and distraction. Scores on the rumination scale were the best predictor of depression measured two weeks later, when initial depression levels were taken into account. Although women showed higher depression levels than men at 2 weeks, this difference disappeared when the extent of rumination was taken into account. It was the men's lower rumination scores, as opposed to their higher distraction scores, that accounted for their lower levels of depression. This study indicates the importance of rumination – the persistence of intrusive thoughts (Chapter 8) – in accounting for the level of depression and for sex differences in depression. Similarly, among a sample of bereaved adults, Nolen-Hoeksema *et al.* (1994) found that people with a ruminative coping style 1 month after the death were likely to have higher depression levels 5 months later.

This study also found that women reported more rumination than men, which is consistent with evidence from earlier studies of spousal bereavement. Glick *et al.* (1974) found that widowers were more likely to avoid reminders and memories of the deceased whereas widows were more likely to engage in a prolonged review of the circumstances of the death. Gallagher *et al.* (1989) found that while men tended to prefer keeping busy, women tended to use 'cognitive' coping strategies such as reviewing past memories, and trying to make sense of what had happened. M.S. Stroebe and W. Stroebe (1991) found that men were less likely than women to talk about their loss, but (unexpectedly) women showed a stronger tendency towards suppression.

Based on the evidence for general sex differences in coping, M.S. Stroebe and Schut (1993, 1995) proposed an extension of the DPM, considered in Chapter 6: that women show 'loss-oriented' coping strategies, whereas those of men are 'restoration-oriented'. As indicated in Chapter 6, both terms encompass a range of features, but can be summed up as indicating either facing the loss, or avoiding or denying it. Within each, there is the possibility of both positive and negative coping strategies. From this perspective, Nolen-Hoeksema's view of sex differences in depression focuses only on the possible negative consequences of confronting a loss (i.e. rumination) and not enough on the possible negative consequences of behavioural responding. In support of this view, Schut *et al.* (1997) found that widows showed a greater decline in distress following behaviourally oriented (problem-focused) counselling whereas widowers showed a greater decline following counselling which aided the encouragement of emotional expression. This study involved randomly assigning a small sample of widows and widowers to either type of therapy. Nevertheless, apart from this, there is little direct evidence to test the Stroebes' hypothesis that men and women typically show different coping styles following a bereavement.

These different coping styles can be understood as part of a wider pattern of sex differences involving the inhibition of emotional expression by boys and men. It is a widespread part of male socialisation (Gilmore, 1990; Low, 1989). It is also consistent with social role theory (Eagly, 1987, 1995) which views sex differences in social attributes as arising from the historical roles of men and women, into homemakers and full-time paid employees, and from the unequal power associated with these roles (see also Chapter 12, in relation to men's and women's friendships). Greater connection with the feelings associated with relationships can be viewed as a characteristic suiting women for their traditional role, whereas an emphasis on not showing weakness to other men can be viewed as a characteristic suiting men for the world outside the family and for the pursuit of power.

Men's inexpressiveness can also be viewed as having arisen further back in the evolutionary history of the human race, derived from inter-male competition, and maintained by a consistent socialisation pattern which emphasises a male ideal of fortitude, bravery and suppression of negative feelings such as fear and anxiety (Archer, 1996b).

Sex differences in parental grief

Mothers usually show more intense grief than fathers following death of a son or daughter. Specific findings were reviewed in Chapter 11: the sex difference was found following perinatal death (Hughes and Page-Lieberman, 1989), in infancy (Benfield *et al.*, 1978; Dyregrov and Matthiesen, 1987a), childhood (Moriarty *et al.*, 1996), and following death at older ages by suicide or road accident (van der Wal, 1988) or war (Rubin, 1991–2).

Fish (1986) found that the occurrence and extent of the sex difference depended on the age and sex of the child, and the time since the death had occurred. Fathers grieved more for sons than for daughters, and more for older-aged offspring, and their grief was substantially less than that of mothers after 2 years or more had elapsed (although, overall, grief was maintained at a high level for years). Many specific aspects of grieving were different: for example, mothers experienced more social isolation and much higher levels of anger than did fathers. These differences were very large ones (Cohen, 1977).[2] Similarly, Dyregrov and Matthiesen (1987a) found that mothers reported more intrusive thoughts, bodily symptoms, depression, anxiety, and grief, than did fathers. Smith and Borgers (1988–9) also found higher levels for specific aspects of grief – despair, anger, guilt and rumination – for women than men.

As indicated in Chapter 11, the problem in interpreting these studies arises from their omission of a control sample. Lang and Gottlieb (1993) found that although mothers showed more pronounced grief than fathers following a perinatal loss, women in a control sample also showed higher scores than men on those measures that were not specific to the experience of grief. These differences were smaller than those between the bereaved couples and therefore could only partially account for them. These findings suggest that sex differences in psychological distress not connected to grief also contribute to the sex differences reported in studies of parental grief (Chapter 11). Therefore, there are three possible forms of sex differences which might be intermingled in studies of parental grief. First there are baseline differences in psychological distress, such as depression and anxiety, which will complicate interpretation of most studies which have not included a control group. Second, there is the likelihood that women are more attached to their offspring early in their life than men are (following women's greater initial parental investment). Third, there is the possibility of different coping styles by men and women, as outlined above for marital bereavement.

In relation to the second of these, the less intense grief shown by fathers occurs particularly at younger ages (Fish, 1986; Hughes and Page-Lieberman, 1989; Smith and Borgers, 1988–9): it is therefore likely to be at least partly a consequence of the stronger bond between mother and infant

---

2 Between 1.0 and 1.6 standard deviations in magnitude.

(Klaus and Kennell, 1976; Daly and Wilson, 1988a: 69–72) than between father and infant at these ages. In discussing neonatal death, Peppers and Knapp (1980) attributed differences in grieving between husband and wife to both 'incongruent bonding' with the infant and to gender role expectations. They viewed the bonding of the father as lagging behind that of the mother, from the planning of pregnancy until the caretaking. This view predicts that there will be more disparity the earlier the loss takes place. We should, however, note that there is one finding of pronounced grief by fathers following loss during pregnancy (Johnson and Puddifoot, 1996), which may indicate that fathers do possess the potential to form early attachments to the future child.

There is also clear evidence that the sexes do differ in the *way* they cope with bereavement following death of a child, along the lines suggested by M.S. Stroebe and Schut (1993, 1995). Carroll and Shaefer (1993–4) studied coping styles following Sudden Infant Death Syndrome (SIDS) (Chapter 11) and found that mothers more often sought support as a coping strategy and also relied on communication about the loss within the family. Bohannon (1990–1) found that, although bereaved mothers scored more highly than fathers on most of the subscales of Sanders' Grief Experience Inventory (GEI) (Chapter 2), fathers indicated more intense denial than mothers. Other studies, such as that of Cook (1988) suggest that bereaved fathers try to control or hide their feelings, which they say is to protect their wives. However, wives tend to complain about their husbands' unwillingness to share their feelings.

Further examples can be found in Laura Palmer's book describing the letters and poems left at the Vietnam Veterans Memorial. A striking feature was that among the very many letters left there, there were none from fathers to their sons – some fathers would add 'love, Dad' at the end of their wife's letter (Palmer, 1987). Mothers also reported that their husbands would not cry, or would only do so secretly. Evidence that these different styles of grief begin in childhood comes from a study of children's grief by Silverman and Worden (1993), who found that girls were more likely to share their feelings with another family member, whereas older boys were more likely to be told to act in a grown-up way.

The studies summarised in this section indicate that mothers show more intense grieving than fathers, and that this is particularly marked at younger ages. However, this conclusion has to be qualified because most studies have not controlled for the higher levels of psychological distress among women than men. In addition, there is evidence for the different coping strategies that were found for marital grief. As indicated earlier, this way of responding can be seen as part of a widespread pattern of male inexpressiveness.

Do differences in grieving produce marital problems?

Differences in the reactions and coping styles of mothers and fathers follow-ing death of a child may lead to marital difficulties. Some commentators (Bowlby, 1980a; Sanders, 1989; Schwab, 1992) have suggested that marriages suffer under these circumstances. Sanders claimed that 75–90 per cent of couples have serious problems following death of a child, and that these are a direct result of the incongruent grieving styles of mothers and fathers. In his autobiography, the British politician Dennis Healey wrote of an influential figure in the post-war British government:

> His marriage collapsed with the death of his little daughter Helen, in 1922, when she was only five years old and he was thirty-five. From that moment an essential part of his personality ceased to develop. Peter Pan was never far away. His capacity for human feeling withered, though he tried to revive it by a series of sentimental attachments to younger men.
>
> (Healey, 1989: 78)

Fictional accounts also portray marital difficulties following loss of a child. Ian McEwan's novel *A Child in Time* (McEwan, 1987) concerns the broken relationship between the parents of a child who disappears from a supermarket when in the father's care.

However, the few studies that have compared bereaved and non-bereaved parents find conflicting evidence. Najman *et al.* (1993) found that more of a sample of Australian parents whose infants had died were separated 6 months later than was the case for a matched group of parents with surviving children. For those marriages remaining intact, there was a greater likelihood of parents who had lost an infant expressing dissatisfaction with the relation-ship. Fish (1986) found that 70 per cent of an American sample of bereaved parents reported significant marital stress which was related to the loss, but a substantial minority (24 per cent) reported increased cohesion. Sixty per cent of the wives were aware of sexual problems, and 40 per cent of the husbands complained about a lack of sexual contact since the loss. About a third of the husbands and a tenth of the wives were aware of blaming the other for the child's death.

In contrast to these findings, Mitchell, Scragg and Clements (1996) found that the incidence of marital breakdown among New Zealand parents 3.7 years after a SID was no higher than among a control population. Lang and Gottlieb (1991, 1993) found no differences in marital intimacy between a sample of American bereaved parents and non-bereaved controls. However, as they noted, half of the bereaved parents contacted did not participate, mainly because they did not want to discuss their painful experience. Lang and Gottlieb also found that more of their bereaved sample who did agree to participate had thought about separating than was the case for controls. The

Scandinavian study by Dyregrov and Matthiesen (1987a) found that most parents from a sample who had lost an infant 1–4 years before said that the experience had brought them closer together, although a significant minority reported feeling more distant from their partner. Both this study and that of Fish indicate a degree of variability in the extent to which the grief of husbands and wives is incongruous.

The evidence for detrimental effects of parental grief on the interactions between parents is mixed, and would seem to indicate that it occurs in some marriages but not others. A related issue, which has not as far as I know been systematically studied, concerns the interactions between a surviving marriage partner and the children. Writing of the reaction of Albert Lewis, the father of C.S. Lewis ('Jacks'), to the death of his wife (Flora) and his father and brother in the space of four months, A.N. Wilson (1993) commented:

> Albert's grief over the summer had made him a poor companion to his sons, and he was now in no position, emotionally, to look after them on his own . . . . 'His nerves had never been of the steadiest,' C.S. Lewis mercilessly recalled, 'and his emotions had always been uncontrolled. Under the pressure of anxiety his temper became incalculable; he spoke wildly and acted unjustly.' This disturbing passage in *Surprised by Joy* implies that in the weeks leading up to Flora's death, the survivors all hurt one another in an irremediable way. Albert's outbursts of rage against Jacks were not forgiven. 'During these months the unfortunate man, had he but known it, was really losing his sons as well as his wife.'
>
> (Wilson, 1993: 21)

Conclusions

This chapter completes the consideration of grief following losses of different types of relationship by examining the impact of the age and sex of the deceased. Although these variables are, along with kinship, crucially important ones for evolutionary analyses of social behaviour (Chapter 9), the predictions based on them were not clear, at least as far as grieving for a spouse was concerned. The general expectation was that spouses become relatively less important with age in relation to other, younger kin. However, attachment theory could generate the opposite prediction, that grief would be stronger when a longer-lasting, lifelong relationship was lost in later life than when a shorter-lived one was lost at a younger age. This would be reinforced by the social position of someone bereaved later in life.

The findings mostly showed more intense grief at younger ages, associated with a feeling that such deaths are untimely and unexpected, but there were some studies that showed little association between grief intensity and age. Analyses of grief at older ages were complicated by the different life expectancies of men and women. Spousal bereavement in old age is increasingly likely to involve women, and to be associated with problems associated with widowhood, notably economic deprivation and difficulties relating to the wider society, at least in individualistic cultures.

Two predictions were considered regarding sex differences in grief. The first, derived from the greater societal power of men, was that men have more to lose and will grieve more when their spouse dies. The second, derived from the inhibition of emotional expressiveness by men, was that women will express their feelings about grief more than men will, who will try to cope in more practical ways.

Most of the available evidence was in accord with these predictions. A complication in interpreting the findings on sex differences in grief intensity concerned the higher level of psychological distress found among women than men before bereavement. When this was taken into account, the evidence showed a greater increase in measures such as depression and anxiety for men than for women following bereavement. When measures were taken some time after the loss, there were signs of more adverse effects for widows than widowers, which is probably a consequence of the social position of widows rather than the impact of grief.

The evidence for sex differences in coping strategies following bereavement was limited, but it was in accord with the view that women's coping involved forms of confronting the loss, and that men showed more active and less emotional coping styles.

In the case of parental grief, it was again difficult to tell whether the apparently less intense grief of fathers than mothers could be attributed to pre-existing sex differences, because most studies omitted control groups. However, there was evidence that women and men sought to deal with loss of a child in very different ways, women tending to express their feelings and men tending not to, and that women were more greatly affected by the loss as a result of their earlier developing and stronger attachment.

14 Conclusions

Nothing is commoner than to hear sorrow spoken of by some as vain and useless, and of the source of all that is best in us by others. It is alternately regarded as weakening us both physically and morally; and as strengthening and hardening us. It is held to make us bitter, envious and hateful; and also to make us gentle, sympathetic and pitiful. It is regarded by theologians as a chief instrument of religion, as drawing us to a faith in, and a love of God; and it is shown by others to be the frequent source of impeachments of His providence, justice, and love.

(Alexander Shand, 1914, *The Foundations of Character*: 361)

The process of grief

Confusion about the nature of grief, the impact of different ways of coping with it, and its resolution, have continued to this day. Shand sought to chart a way out of the confusion by setting out 'the laws of sorrow', a series of empirically verifiable statements about the process of grief, derived from the literary sources available at the time. These were largely ignored by later researchers and theorists writing about grief in favour of Freud's speculations, published at about the same time, which were based on psychoanalytically framed interpretations of case studies. Rather than being put to the test by later empirical research, they became entrenched as the orthodox way of understanding grief, an approach which was later expanded to encompass other concepts, such as the stages of grief.

I began the first chapter by referring to three different ways of understanding grief, in terms of its mental suffering, harmful physical effects, and as a natural reaction to the loss of a relationship. The way that research on grief developed over-emphasised the first two approaches, so that psychiatric, counselling and medical perspectives predominated, fuelled by the Freudian interpretative framework.

I have emphasised the third way of looking at grief – as a natural human reaction. This places it in the province of biology and psychology, rather than psychiatry and counselling. Grief can be understood as follows: in terms of its universal occurrence in the human species, whatever the culture; in terms of its derivation from simpler forms in the animal world; and as a product of the process of natural selection. From this perspective, it was possible to identify a basic form of the grief reaction shown by animals and young children.

In Chapter 4, I explored the apparent paradox involved in explaining grief as a result of natural selection: grief involves a set of reactions which are harmful to an individual's survival and reproductive chances, yet natural selection involves selection of attributes with the opposite features. However, modern evolutionary thinking emphasises a trade-off between adaptive costs and benefits. Grief can be regarded as a cost incurred in pursuit of something which has an important adaptive consequence. Previous accounts have varied in identifying what this might be, but the most likely candidate involves the persistence of important social bonds when the other individual is absent. This is required either because most absences involve separations rather than permanent losses, or so that social relations are not built on a transient, 'out of sight, out of mind' foundation. To achieve the continuation of social relations in spite of the long- or short-term absences of the other individual, there must be mechanisms that cause a social bond to persist in the other's absence. This is achieved by having an enduring mental model of the other, which is continually checked with the input from the outside world. When there are signs of a discrepancy between this input and the mental model, an emotional reaction – distress – is generated. This account of the evolutionary significance of grief encompasses three earlier speculations (Badcock, 1990; Bowlby, 1980a; Parkes, 1972) which all differed in emphasis but contained two central ingredients: first, they viewed grief in terms of individual survival (rather than group-level selection); second, they viewed grief as the cost of an important feature necessary for maintaining significant social relationships (i.e. those that aid fitness).

This evolutionary account provides a starting-point for understanding grief, enabling it to be seen as a deficit reaction, set off in an animal or young child when a significant other is absent. The reactions that are then set in train involve searching and protest. These energetic responses are followed by, or intermingled with, a more passive depressive reaction which may represent the beginnings of disengagement from the active separation responses. Both occur at pre-linguistic levels of mental processing, and require little understanding of what is going on.

The grief experienced by adult humans goes way beyond these primitive deficit-driven reactions. Distress, protest and despair are certainly parts of adult human grief, but their form is modified. They are also overlain with other reactions, which can only be understood in terms of mental processes unique to human beings. Human grief therefore involves both primitive emotional reactions and complex mental processes. These plunge the person into a bizarre world of intrusive painful thoughts, heightened perception and memories of the deceased, hallucinations, and difficulties addressing everyday tasks which before were taken for granted. People also seek to attribute meaning to the troubling events, by blaming themselves, others or even the deceased.

Individuals try to cope with grief in different ways. These are included as part of the process of grief in descriptive accounts (Parkes, 1972) but are viewed as separate by researchers from a health psychology perspective. Reactions that serve to limit the amount of distressing information about the loss, including outright denial, immersing oneself in other activities, or allowing oneself comforting fantasies, can be viewed as functioning to avoid the overwhelming pain and distress of the loss. If effective, they maintain some form of equilibrium that will allow everyday activities to be undertaken more effectively. The alternative reactions – that serve to confront the reality of the loss in thought and expression – have traditionally been regarded as necessary for the resolution of grief.

The widespread acceptance of this assumption (the grief work hypothesis) seems to have operated like a straightjacket both on research and theory until fairly recently, and it has also strongly influenced practitioners. Critical examination of the concept of grief work showed that it had been used in several senses, and was often not distinguished from rumination, i.e. going over the same thoughts or themes, which research now shows to be associated with poor resolution. Those more recent studies that have operationally defined grief work have yielded mixed findings in terms of its association with the resolution of grief. Again, definitions prove elusive, so that we have to be careful to distinguish the expression of the emotions associated with grief – which seems to predict *greater* distress – from confronting the loss in thoughts and expression – which does in some cases lead to lessening of distress.

The opposite to confronting a loss involves either distraction or denial. M.S. Stroebe and Schut (1994) suggested that these represent a form of coping that would complement confrontation in achieving effective resolution. Other research has suggested that denial – in the form of actively suppressing unwanted thoughts – may be counterproductive, as such thoughts return later, accompanied by the negative mood associated with them. However, there was evidence that this applied only to new unwanted thoughts: thus, established ones might be better controlled. The current evidence also indicated that distraction may be a more effective strategy. However, finding something sufficiently engaging to avoid the intrusive thoughts of grief is difficult, and concentration on other activities is usually impaired during grieving. Entering into a new relationship of the same type as the one which was lost may be a solution in some cases, but the same general point applies – that it must be sufficiently engaging to avoid thoughts continually returning to the lost loved one. In such a situation, people may be vulnerable to generating adverse comparisons between the new and the old.

Resolution of grief proved difficult to define. Freud identified detachment from the deceased (in modern terminology, the breaking of affectional bonds), and most writings on grief have accepted this. In practice, empirical research has used, as criteria for resolution, the waning of distress associated with memories of the deceased or a return to effective functioning in everyday activities. By implication, the previous bonds with the deceased are severed when these criteria are fulfilled. However, a significant minority view is that the bereaved may form a different relationship with the deceased, which involves feeling their comforting presence, kept alive by pleasant reminiscences, mementos and internal dialogues with them. Using the criteria of a lack of distress and a return to effective everyday functioning, such individuals would have resolved their grief. Yet from the perspective of having achieved detachment and no longer feeling love for the deceased, they will not have achieved resolution. It is likely that a redefinition of the internal attachment to the deceased is a necessary first step before achieving detachment, and that it involves a change from negative to positive emotions experienced when thinking about them. For some people, and in some cultures, this state is maintained as an alternative to detachment from the previous relationship.

Individual differences

The last part of the book concerned individual differences in grief from the perspectives of two approaches derived from biology, evolutionary psychology and attachment theory. The first involves understanding human behaviour in terms of its functional origins in evolutionary history. It presents a challenge to the widespread assumption in psychology and the social sciences that there is no appreciable human nature and that the human psyche can only be understood from an environmentalist standpoint. Evolutionary psychologists view humans as responding selectively to a wide variety of environmental events that are (and have been throughout evolutionary history) cues to fitness-enhancing behaviour. According to this perspective, we selectively identify people who attempt to freeload from us or to cheat us, and respond to them with anger, because there are brain mechanisms specifically evolved to achieve these end-results (Wright, 1994). This view provides a contrast with orthodox psychology's characterisation of both the identification of cheats and the generation of anger as being derived from more general mental processes involving logical reasoning and a response to frustration (i.e. general purpose mechanisms).

   Individual differences in the intensity of grief are, in broad terms, mediated by different strengths of attachment. In most cases, the process underlying the formation of attachment involves mutually satisfying interactions; in some cases, the human imagination makes up for the absence or the poverty of the feedback from the other individual: thus a bond can be formed with a future baby from before conception and throughout pregnancy, and it can also be formed with non-humans that behave like humans in important ways. The end-result is the development of an internal model of the other, which in humans becomes part of the person's sense of self.

This account of the development of attachment fits many of the criteria for a general purpose mechanism of the sort familiar to conventional psychologists. However, there is something missing from it, and this concerns the initial selectivity that starts off the interaction leading to the attachment bond. People prefer their own infants, and infants with certain physical and behavioural features; they prefer individuals of the opposite sex who are sexually attractive; and they prefer pets with certain signals shared with human infants. It is generally more difficult to generate an attachment to someone else's infant, to one that looks and behaves unlike other human infants, or to a sexually unattractive individual, or to love a reptile as one loves a pet dog or cat. In most of these examples, people are selectively responding to cues that will lead to the enhancement of their fitness (in the case of pets they are responding to cues that in other contexts would enhance their fitness).

Daly and Wilson (1988b) applied this reasoning to one type of biologically important variable involved in parent-to-child attachment. They suggested that parents use various cues to discriminate between infants and young that have good or poor prospects in terms of future fitness. How this operates in extreme circumstances was shown in the study of the women from the shanty-towns of Brazil, by Scheper-Hughes (1992), where attachments did not occur to younger infants with poor prospects.

The same reasoning can be applied to the main individual differences that are significant for fitness. Very general cues indicating the sex, kinship and age-category are used to decide which particular type of relationship is appropriate, whether the parental (caregiving), nurturant (receiving parental care), or sexual motivational systems are aroused. The cues Daly and Wilson identified are of the sort that will determine a preference for certain individuals over others within these categories. Similarly, cues associated with small differences in age and in kinship will make the development of relationships easier with some individuals than with others. It is clear what such cues are in the case of age, as appearance changes with age. It is more difficult to identify the cues underlying kinship, although there is a theory that subtle physical resemblances underlie preferential social interactions such as friendships (Rushton, 1989). There are various logical problems with this theory, and the direct evidence bearing on it is fragmentary (Archer, 1989; Daly, 1989; Gangestad, 1989). Nevertheless, the same sort of response to cues indicating subtle degrees of relatedness among kin remains a possibility, and would not involve the same objections to the theory applied to friendship. The other – more general – route to showing preferential interactions with closer kin is of course that people tend to share their upbringing and other parts of their lives with those kin to whom they are most closely related.

The formation and maintenance of an attachment bond is therefore controlled by both a general mechanism, usually involving exposure learning, and a series of specific responses to cues that steer relationships towards those that result in enhancing fitness. Attachment is crucial for understanding grief, because it is the breaking of attachment bonds that produces grief. If there is no attachment, there will be no grief. Grief generally parallels the strength of attachment and, as indicated above, the strength of attachment generally parallels fitness-related variables. However, existing studies did not provide a clear answer to whether grief intensity follows very closely evolutionarily significant cues, such as those indicating age and kinship.

There was evidence for a steady increase in the intensity of grief from early pregnancy loss through to loss of adult offspring, consistent with the increase in offspring reproductive value from conception to early adulthood, and the decline in parental reproductive value with age. Consideration of attachment development in terms of a general-purpose mechanism is consistent with an increase in grief from conception into childhood, but thereafter a relatively constant level would be expected. To account for a continuation in the severity of grief beyond this point requires further processes sensitive to cues related to fitness, in this case associated with the relative ages of parent and offspring. Other evidence from parental grief did indicate that it was more pronounced among older than younger mothers, as predicted from the decline in maternal reproductive value with age.

Differences in grief associated with kinship are clearly to be found, in the sense that close kin such as offspring, parents and siblings evoke the strongest grief and death of a distant relative the least grief. But such an association could be predicted on the basis of a general-purpose mechanism underlying attachment formation without any evolutionary considerations. Here evolutionary theory merely provides a reason why there is, on the whole, a gradation in attachment strength from close kin to those who are unrelated. Whether there are also subtle differences in grief, associated with relatively small differences in kinship, was not answered from the available evidence, but the hypotheses for future studies are clear. For example, in the case of grandchildren, a view of attachment based on a general-purpose mechanism would predict that maternal and paternal grandmothers would generally be attached to their grandchildren to an equal extent. An alternative evolutionary hypothesis would predict a subtle difference, that paternal grandmothers would generally be less strongly attached, and show less intense grief, in view of their less certain relatedness to their grandchildren.

The third important evolutionary variable, sex, produced less clear predictions about individual differences in grief, although it was possible to understand the main differences between men's and women's responses to spousal bereavement in evolutionary terms, albeit indirectly. The initially greater grief of men could be viewed in terms of the loss of a more valuable 'resource', and the lesser use of emotion-focused coping by men could be understood in terms of their greater inhibition of all forms of emotional expressiveness, a feature necessary to compete in all male social settings. Sex differences in parental grief could also be understood in terms of the initial inequality of parental investment.

Overall, an evolutionary framework which encompasses the development of attachment through both general and specific mechanisms enables research on individual differences in grief to be understood in terms of a few basic principles, such as the index of relatedness and reproductive value. Most existing research has not started from broad theoretical principles such as these, but has concerned specific applied issues. The sort of approach outlined in this section enables individual differences in grief to be appreciated from a much wider perspective, that is, it would enable much greater integration of the findings than is at present the case. It would also enable the testing of a series of specific hypotheses about the strength of grief based on evolutionary principles; and it would take the study of attachment formation beyond the general-purpose mechanisms emphasised at present, to include responses to cues related to fitness. Of course, it would not explain every aspect of individual differences in grief. It is important to recognise the limitations as well as the strengths of the evolutionary approach. Variables influencing the circumstances of the death, the ability of the bereaved to cope with any unwanted life event, and the social environment after the bereavement, all have important influences on the nature and course of grief, which are not readily understood in terms of evolutionary principles.

References

Ablon, J. (1971). Bereavement in a Samoan community. *British Journal of Medical Psychology*, 44, 329–337.

Abraham, K. (1924). A short study of the development of the libido, viewed in the light of mental disorder. Reprinted in: *Selected Papers of Karl Abraham* (pp. 418–501), introduced by E. Jones. London: Hogarth, 1927.

Abrams, R. (1992). *When Parents Die*. London: Charles Letts.

Abrams, R. (1993). Helping teenagers and young adults cope with the death of a parent. *Bereavement Care*, 12, 16–18.

Adams, N. (1857a). *Agnes and the Key of her Little Coffin, by Her Father*. Boston, MA: S.K. Whipple.

Adams, N. (1857b). *Bertha and her Baptism*. Boston, MA: S.K. Whipple.

Adams, N. (1859). *Catherine*. Boston, MA: J.E. Tilton.

Adelman, H.M. and Maatsch, J.L. (1956). Learning and extinction based upon frustration, food reward and exploratory tendency. *Journal of Experimental Psychology*, 52, 311–315.

Adler, N.E. (1992). Abortion: a case of crises and loss? An examination of empirical evidence. In L. Montada, S-H. Filipp and M.J. Lerner (eds), *Life Crises and Experiences of Loss in Adulthood* (pp. 65–79). Hillsdale, NJ: Erlbaum.

Ainsworth, M.D.S. (1979). Attachment as related to mother–infant interaction. *Advances in the Study of Behavior*, 9, 2–51.

Ainsworth, M.D.S. (1989). Attachments beyond infancy. *American Psychologist*, 44, 709–716.

Alcott, L.M. (1903). *Good Wives*. London and Glasgow: Blackie and Son.

Alexander, R.D. (1986). Ostracism and indirect reciprocity: the reproductive significance of humour. *Ethology and Sociobiology*, 7, 105–122.

Allen, C. and Hauser, M.D. (1991). Concept attribution in nonhuman animals: theoretical and methodological problems in ascribing complex mental processes. *Philosophy of Science*, 58, 221–240.

Allen, M.J. and Yen, W.M. (1979). *Introduction to Measurement Theory*. Monterey, CA: Brooks-Cole.

Altmann, J. (1980). *Baboon Mothers and Infants*. Cambridge, MA: Harvard University Press.

American Psychiatric Association (1980). *Diagnostic and Statistical Manual of Mental Disorders,* 3rd edn (DSM-III). Washington, DC: American Psychiatric Association.

American Psychiatric Association (1987). *Diagnostic and Statistical Manual of Mental Disorders,* 3rd edn, revised (DSM-III-R). Washington, DC: American Psychiatric Association.

American Psychiatric Association (1994). *Diagnostic and Statistical Manual of Mental Disorders,* 4th edn (DSM-IV). Washington, DC: American Psychiatric Association.

Amsel, A. and Roussel, J. (1952). Motivational properties of frustration: I. Effect on a running response of the addition of frustration to the motivational complex. *Journal of Experimental Psychology*, 43, 363–368.

Anderson, C.A., Miller, R.S., Riger, A.L., Dill, J.C. and Sedikides, C. (1994). Behavioral and characterological attributional styles as predictors of depression and loneliness: review, refinement, and test. *Journal of Personality and Social Psychology*, 66, 549–558.

Andrew, R.J. (1972). Recognition processes and behavior, with special reference to effects of testosterone on persistence. In D.S. Lehrman, R.A. Hinde and E. Shaw (eds), *Advances in the Study of Behavior*, Vol. 4 (pp. 175–208). New York and London: Academic Press.

Anthony, S. (1940). *The Children's Discovery of Death: A Study in Child Psychology.* London: Kegan Paul, Trench and Trubner.

Anthony, Z. and Bhana, K. (1988–9). An exploratory study of Muslim girls' understanding of death. *Omega*, 19, 215–227.

Archer, J. (1974). Testosterone and behaviour during extinction in chicks. *Animal Behaviour*, 22, 650–655.

Archer, J. (1986a). Animal sociobiology and comparative psychology: a review. *Current Psychological Research and Reviews*, 5, 48–61.

Archer, J. (1986b). Ethical issues in psychobiological research on animals. *Bulletin of the British Psychological Society*, 39, 361–364.

Archer, J. (1987). Book review of Rosenblatt, P.C. (1983) 'Bitter Bitter Tears: Nineteenth Century Diarists and Twentieth Century Grief Theories.' Minneapolis: University of Minnesota Press. *Journal of Social and Personal Relationships*, 4, 375–376.

Archer, J. (1988). The sociobiology of bereavement: a reply to Littlefield and Rushton. *Journal of Personality and Social Psychology*, 55, 272–278.

Archer, J. (1989). Why help friends when you can help sisters and brothers? *Behavioral and Brain Sciences*, 12, 519–520. (Commentary on Rushton, 1989.)

Archer, J. (1990). Have animal models contributed to studies of loss and separation? *The Psychologist*, 3 (7), 298–301.

Archer, J. (1991a). Human sociobiology: basic concepts and limitations. *Journal of Social Issues*, 47, 11–26.

Archer, J. (1991b). The process of grief: a selective review. *Journal of Advances in Health and Nursing Care*, 1, 9–37.

Archer, J. (1992a). *Ethology and Human Development.* Hemel Hempstead, UK: Harvester-Wheatsheaf.

Archer, J. (1992b). Childhood gender roles: social context and organisation. In H. McGurk (ed.), *Childhood Social Development: Contemporary Perspectives* (pp. 31–61). Hillsdale, NJ: Erlbaum.

Archer, J. (1996a). Evolutionary social psychology. In M. Hewstone, W. Stroebe and G. Stephenson (eds), *Introduction to Social Psychology: A European Perspective* (pp. 24–45). Oxford: Blackwell.

Archer, J. (1996b). Sex differences in social behavior: are the social role and evolution-ary explanations compatible? *American Psychologist*, 51, 909–917.

Archer, J. (1996c). Attitudes towards homosexuals: an alternative Darwinian view. *Ethology and Sociobiology*, 17, 275–280.

Archer, J. (1997). Why do people love their pets? *Evolution and Human Behavior*, 18, 237–259.

Archer, J. and Rhodes, V. (1987). Bereavement and reactions to job loss: a comparative review. *British Journal of Social Psychology*, 26, 211–224.

Archer, J. and Rhodes, V. (1993). The grief process and job loss: a cross-sectional study. *British Journal of Psychology*, 84, 395–410.

Archer, J. and Rhodes, V. (1995). A longitudinal study of job loss in relation to the grief process. *Journal of Community and Applied Social Psychology*, 183–188.

Archer, J. and Winchester, G. (1994). Bereavement following death of a pet. *British Journal of Psychology*, 85, 259–271.

Averill, J.R. (1968). Grief: its nature and significance. *Psychological Bulletin*, 70, 721–748.

Averill, J.R. and Nunley, E.P. (1988). Grief as an emotion and as a disease: a social-constructionist perspective. *Journal of Social Issues*, 44, 79–95.

Averill, J.R. and Wisocki, P.A. (1981). Some observations on behavioral approaches to the treatment of grief among the elderly. In H.J. Sobel (ed.), *Behavior Therapy in Terminal Care: A Humanistic Approach* (pp. 125–150). Cambridge, MA: Ballinger.

Avis, N.E., Brambilla, D.J., Vass, K. and McKinley, J.B. (1991). The effect of widow-hood on health: a prospective analysis from the Massachusets Women's Health Study. *Social Science and Medicine*, 33, 1063–1070.

Azrin, N.H., Hutchinson, R.R. and Hake, D.F. (1966). Extinction-induced aggres-sion. *Journal of the Experimental Analysis of Behavior*, 9, 191–204.

Badcock, C. (1990). *Oedipus in Evolution: A New Theory of Sex*. Oxford: Blackwell.

Baerends, G.P. (1941). Fortpflanzungsverhalten und orientierung der Gragwespe *Ammophila campestris* Jur. *Tijdschrift voor Entomologie,* 84, 68–275.

Baerends, G.P. (1976). The functional organization of behaviour. *Animal Behaviour*, 24, 726–738.

Bagley, P. (1990–1). The death of a father: the start of a story. Bereavement. In Elisabeth Plessen, Brigitte Schwaiger and Jutta Schutting. *New German Studies*, 16, 21–38.

Bailis, L.A. (1977–8). Death in children's literature: a conceptual analysis. *Omega*, 8, 295–303.

Baldwin, M.W., Keelan, J.P.R., Fehr, B., Enns, V. and Koh-Rangarajoo, E.K. (1996). Social-cognitive conceptualization of attachment working models: availability and accessibility effects. *Journal of Personality and Social Psychology*, 71, 94–109.

Balk, D.E. (1983). Adolescents' grief reactions and self-concept perceptions following sibling death: a study of 33 teenagers. *Journal of Youth and Adolescence*, 12, 137–161.

Balk, D.E. (1990). The self-concept of bereaved adolescents: sibling death and its aftermath. *Journal of Adolescent Research*, 5, 112–132.

Balk, D.E. (1991a). Death and adolescent bereavement: current research and future directions. *Journal of Adolescent Research*, 6, 7–27.

Balk, D.E. (1991b). Death, bereavement, and college students: a description of research at Kansas State University. Paper presented at the Annual Meeting of the American Educational Research Association, Chicago, 4 April.

Balkwell, C. (1981). Transition to widowhood: a review of the literature. *Family Relations*, 30, 117–127.

Ball, J.F. (1976–7). Widow's grief: the impact of age and mode of death. *Omega*, 7, 307–333.

Bao Ninh (1994). *The Sorrow of War*. London: Secker and Warburg. (English version from original translation by Phan Thanh Hao, of *Than Phan Cua Tinh Yeu* by Nha Xuat Ban Hoi Nha Van, Hanoi: Writers' Association Publishing House, 1991.)

Barash, D. (1979). *The Whisperings Within*. New York: Harper and Row.

Barker, P. (1995). *The Ghost Road*. London: Viking. (Quotations from 1996 Penguin edn.)

Barrett, C.J. and Schneweis, K.M. (1980). An empirical search for stages of widowhood. *Omega*, 11, 97–104.

Bartholomew, K. and Horowitz, L.M. (1991). Attachment styles among young adults: a test of a four-category model. *Journal of Personality and Social Psychology*, 61, 226–244.

Bartrop, R.W., Hancock, K., Craig, A. and Porritt, D.W. (1992). Psychological toxicity of bereavement: six months after the event. *Australian Psychologist*, 27, 192–196.

Bass, D.M., Noelker, L.S., Townsend, A.L. and Deimling, G.T. (1990). Losing an aged relative: perceptual differences between spouses and adult children. *Omega*, 21, 21–40.

Bateson, P.P.G. (1986). When to experiment on animals. *New Scientist*, 109 (1496), 30–32.

Becker, H. (1932–3). The sorrows of bereavement. *Journal of Abnormal and Social Psychology*, 27, 391–410.

Bem, D.J. (1996). Exotic becomes erotic: a developmental theory of sexual orientation. *Psychological Review*, 103, 320–335.

Bendiksen, R. and Fulton, R. (1975). Death and the child: an anterospective test of childhood bereavement and later behavior disorder hypothesis. *Omega*, 6, 45–59.

Benfield, D.G., Leib, S.A., and Vollman, J.H. (1978). Grief response of parents to neonatal death and parent participation in deciding care. *Pediatrics*, 62, 171–177.

Benson, J. and Falk, A. (1996). *The Long Pale Corridor: Contemporary Poems of Bereavement.* Newcastle upon Tyne, UK: Bloodaxe Books.

Benthall, R.P. (1992). Reconstructing psychopathology. *The Psychologist*, 5, 61–65.

Benthall, R.P. and Slade, P.D. (1985). Reality testing and auditory hallucinations: a signal detection analysis. *British Journal of Clinical Psychology*, 24, 159–169.

Berman, W.H. (1988). The role of attachment in the post-divorce experience. *Journal of Personality and Social Psychology*, 54, 496–503.

Berman, W.H. and Sperling, M.B. (1994). The structure and function of adult attachment. In M.B. Sperling and W.H. Berman (eds), *Attachment in Adults: Clinical and Developmental Perspectives* (pp. 3–28). New York: Guilford Press.

Beutel, M., Deckardt, R., von Rad, M. and Weiner, H. (1995). Grief and depression after miscarriage: their separation, antecedents, and course. *Psychosomatic Medicine*, 57, 517–526.

Bexton, W.H., Heron, W. and Scott, T.H. (1954). Effects of decreased variation in the sensory environment. *Canadian Journal of Psychology*, 8, 70–76.

Bierhals, A.J., Frank, E., Prigerson, H.G., Miller, M., Fasiczka, A. and Reynolds, C.F.

III (1995–6). Gender differences in complicated grief among the elderly. *Omega*, 32, 303–317.

Billings, A.G. and Moos, R.H. (1981). The role of coping responses and social resources in attenuating the stress of life events. *Journal of Behavioral Medicine*, 4, 139–157.

Bindra, D. (1978). How adaptive behavior is produced: a perceptual-motivational alternative to response-reinforcement. *The Behavioral and Brain Sciences*, 1, 41–92 (including commentaries).

Binyon, L. (1921). 'For the fallen'. In *An Anthology of Modern Verse*. London: Methuen (4th edn).

Biondi, M. and Picardi, A. (1996). Clinical and biological aspects of bereavement and loss-induced depression: a reappraisal. *Psychotherapy and Psychosomatics*, 65, 229–245.

Birkin, A. (1979). *J.M. Barrie and the Lost Boys*. London: Constable.

Black, D. and Urbanowitz, M.A. (1987). Family intervention with bereaved children. *Journal of Child Psychology and Psychiatry*, 28, 467–476.

Blurton Jones, N. (1972). Characteristics of ethological studies of human behaviour. In N. Blurton Jones (ed.), *Ethological Studies of Child Behaviour* (pp. 3–33). London: Cambridge University Press.

Blurton Jones, N. and Leach, G.M. (1972). Behaviour of children and their mothers at separation and greeting. In N. Blurton Jones (ed.), *Ethological Studies of Child Behaviour* (pp. 217–247). London: Cambridge University Press.

Boden, J.M. and Baumeister, R.F. (1997). Repressive coping: distraction using pleasant thoughts and memories. *Journal of Personality and Social Psychology*, 73, 45–62.

Bogarde, D. (1988). Interview with Sheridan Morley, entitled 'Neither foreigner nor dead'. *The Times* (London), 8th Oct., p. 38.

Bohannon, J.R. (1990–1). Grief responses of spouses following the death of a child: a longitudinal study. *Omega*, 22, 109–121.

Bohannon, J.R. (1991). Religiosity related to grief levels of bereaved mothers and fathers. *Omega*, 23, 153–159.

Bombar, M.L. and Littig, L.W. (1996). Babytalk as a communication of intimate attachment: an initial study of adult romances and friendships. *Personal Relationships*, 3, 137–158.

Bonanno, G.A. and Keltner, D. (1997). Facial expression of emotion and the course of conjugal bereavement. *Journal of Abnormal Psychology*, 106, 126–137.

Bonanno, G.A., Keltner, D., Holen, A. and Horowitz, M.J. (1995). When avoiding unpleasant emotions might not be such a bad thing: verbal-autonomic response dissociation and midlife conjugal bereavement. *Journal of Personality and Social Psychology*, 69, 975–989.

Borgquist, A. (1906). Crying. *American Journal of Psychology*, 17, 149–205.

Bornstein, P.E., Clayton, P.J., Halikas, J.A., Maurice, W.L. and Robins, E. (1973). The depression of widowhood after thirteen months. *British Journal of Psychiatry*, 122, 561–566.

Bowcott, O. (1992). RUC man murders three. *The Guardian* (London), 5th Feb., p. 1.

Bowlby, J. (1951). *Maternal Care and Mental Health*. Geneva: World Health Organization.

Bowlby, J. (1953). *Child Care and the Growth of Love*. Harmondsworth: Penguin.

Bowlby, J. (1958). The nature of the child's tie to his mother. *International Journal of Psychoanalysis*, 39, 350–373.

Bowlby, J. (1960a). Separation anxiety. *International Journal of Psychoanalysis*, 41, 89–113.

Bowlby, J. (1960b). Grief and mourning in infancy and early childhood. *The Psychoanalytic Study of the Child*, 15, 9–52.

Bowlby, J. (1961). Processes of mourning. *International Journal of Psychoanalysis*, 42, 317–340.

Bowlby, J. (1969). *Attachment and Loss, Volume 1. Attachment*. London: The Hogarth Press and Institute of Psychoanalysis (Penguin edn, 1971).

Bowlby, J. (1973). *Attachment and Loss, Volume 2. Separation: Anxiety and Anger*. London: The Hogarth Press and Institute of Psychoanalysis (Penguin edn, 1975).

Bowlby, J. (1980a). *Attachment and Loss, Volume 3. Loss: Sadness and Depression*. London: The Hogarth Press and Institute of Psychoanalysis (Penguin edn, 1981).

Bowlby, J. (1980b). By ethology out of psychoanalysis: an experiment in interbreeding. *Animal Behaviour*, 28, 649–656.

Bowlby, J. and Parkes, C.M. (1970). Separation and loss within the family. In E.J. Anthony and C. Koupernik (eds), *The Child and His Family* (pp. 197–216). New York and London: Wiley.

Boyle, F.M., Vance, J.C., Najman, J.M. and Thearle, M.J. (1996). The mental health impact of stillbirth, neonatal death or SIDS: prevalence and patterns of distress among mothers. *Social Science and Medicine*, 43, 1273–1282.

Brasted, W.S. and Callahan, E.J. (1984). A behavioral analysis of the grief process. *Behavior Therapy*, 15, 529–543.

Brearley, M. (1986). Counsellors and clients: men or women. *Marriage Guidance*, 22, 3–9.

Brennan, K.A., Shaver, P.R. and Tobey, A.E. (1991). Attachment styles, gender and parental problem drinking. *Journal of Social and Personal Relationships*, 8, 451–466.

Brent, D.A., Perper, J.A., Moritz, G., Allman, C., Schweers, J., Roth, C., Balach, L., Canobbio, R. and Liotus, L. (1993). Psychiatric sequelae to the loss of an adolescent peer to suicide. *Journal of the American Academy of Child and Adolescent Psychiatry*, 32, 509–517.

Brewster, H.H. (1950). Grief: a disrupted human relationship. *Human Organization*, 9, 19–22.

Brickhill, P. (1957). *Reach for the Sky*. London: Fontana/Collins.

Briscoe, C.W. and Smith, J.B. (1975). Depression in bereavement and divorce. *Archives of General Psychiatry*, 32, 439–443.

Brooke, R. (1921). 'The dead'. In *An Anthology of Modern Verse*. London: Methuen (4th edn).

Brown, D., Elkins, T.E. and Larson, D.B. (1993). Prolonged grieving after abortion: a descriptive study. *The Journal of Clinical Ethics*, 4, 118–123.

Brown, D.E. (1991). *Human Universals*. Philadephia, PA: Temple University Press.

Brown, F. (1968). Bereavement and lack of a parent in childhood. In E. Miller (ed.), *Foundations of Child Psychiatry* (pp. 435–455). Oxford and New York: Pergamon.

Brown, G.W., Harris, T.O. and Bifulco, A. (1986). Long term effects of early loss of parent. In M. Rutter, C. Izard and P. Read (eds), *Depression in Childhood: Developmental Perspectives*. New York: Guilford Press.

Brown, G.W., Harris, T.O. and Copeland, J.R. (1977). Depression and loss. *British Journal of Psychiatry*, 130, 1–18.

Brown, M.J. (1986). *Loss and Grief. Part 1, Experiences Shared*. Videocassette, Tavistock Publications.

Browning, E.B. (1883). *Elizabeth Barrett Browning's Poetical Works, Volume II*. London: Smith, Elder and Co.

Bugen, L.A. (1977). Human grief: a model for prediction and intervention. *American Journal of Orthopsychiatry*, 47, 196–206.

Bulman, R.J. and Wortman, C.B. (1977). Attributions of blame and coping in the 'real world': severe accident victims react to their lot. *Journal of Personality and Social Psychology*, 35, 351–363.

Burks, V.K., Lund, D.A., Gregg, C.H. and Bluhm, H.P. (1988). Bereavement and remarriage for older adults. *Death Studies*, 12, 51–60.

Burnett, P., Middleton, W., Raphael, B. and Martinek, N. (1997). Measuring core bereavement phenomena. *Psychological Medicine*, 27, 49–57.

Burns, E.A., House, J.D. and Ankenbauer, M.R. (1986). Sibling grief in reaction to sudden infant death syndrome. *Paediatrics*, 78, 485–487.

Burton, R. (1651). *The Anatomy of Melancholy*, 6th edn (1938 edn, New York, Tudor Publishing Corporation).

Buss, D.M. (1994). *The Evolution of Desire: Strategies of Human Mating*. New York: Basic Books.

Buss, D.M. (1995). Evolutionary psychology: a new paradigm for psychological science. *Psychological Inquiry*, 6, 1–30.

Buss, D.M. and Schmitt, D.P. (1993). Sexual strategies theory: an evolutionary perspective on human mating. *Psychological Review*, 100, 204–232.

Butler, L.D. and Nolen-Hoeksema, S. (1994). Gender differences in response to depressed mood in a college sample. *Sex Roles*, 30, 331–346.

Butterfield, P.A. (1970). The pair bond in the zebra finch. In J.H. Crook (ed.), *Social Behaviour in Birds and Mammals* (pp. 249–278). London: Academic Press.

Cain, A.C. and Cain, B.S. (1964). On replacing a child. *Journal of the American Academy of Child Psychiatry*, 3, 443–456.

Caine, L. (1974). *Widow*. New York: Morrow (quotation taken from 1975 edn, London: Macdonald and Jane's).

Calhoun, L.G. and Tedeschi, R.G. (1989–90). Positive aspects of critical life problems: recollections of grief. *Omega*, 20, 265–272.

Campbell, J., Swank, P. and Vincent, K. (1991). The role of hardiness in the resolution of grief. *Omega*, 23, 53–65.

Campbell, R. (1993). Prisoner in cell block H. *The Guardian 2*, 11th Jan., pp. 12–13.

Carey, R.G. (1979–80). Weathering widowhood: problems and adjustment of the widowed during the first year. *Omega*, 10, 163–174.

Carey, S. (1985). *Conceptual Change in Childhood*. Cambridge, MA: MIT Press.

Carmack, J. (1985). The effects on family members and functioning after death of a pet. *Marriage and Family Reviews*, 8, 149–161.

Caro, T.M. and Borgerhoff Mulder, M. (1987). The problem of adaptation in the study of human behavior. *Ethology and Sociobiology*, 8, 61–72.

Carroll, R. and Shaefer, S. (1993–4). Similarities and differences in spouses coping with SIDS. *Omega*, 28, 273–284.

Carver, C.S. and Scheier, M.F. (1982). Control theory: a useful conceptual framework for personality-social, clinical and health psychology. *Psychological Bulletin*, 92, 111–135.

Caserta, M.S., Lund, D. A. and Dimond, M.F. (1985). Assessing interviewer effects in a longitudinal study of bereaved elderly adults. *Journal of Gerontology*, 40, 637–640.

Cassidy, J. and Berlin, L.J. (1994). The insecure/ambivalent pattern of attachment: theory and research. *Child Development*, 65, 971–991.

Catanzaro, S.J. and Mearns, J. (1990). Measuring generalized expectancies for negative mood regulation: initial scale development and implications. *Journal of Personality Assessment*, 54, 546–563.

Cecil, R. (1996). Introduction: An insignificant event? Literary and anthropological perspectives on pregnancy loss. In R. Cecil (ed.), *The Anthropology of Pregnancy Loss* (pp. 1–14). Oxford, UK and Washington, DC: Berg.

Chance, M.R.A. and Jolly, C.J. (1970). *Social Groups of Monkeys, Apes and Men*. New York: Dutton.

Charters, S.B. (1961). *The Country Blues*. London: Jazz Book Club/Michael Joseph.

Chiles, R. (1982). Tennyson's thanatology. *Death Education*, 6, 49–60.

Chisholm, J.S. (1996). The evolutionary ecology of attachment organization. *Human Nature*, 7, 1–38.

Clayton, P., Desmarais, L. and Winokur, G. (1968). A study of normal bereavement. *American Journal of Psychiatry*, 125, 168–178.

Clayton, P.J., Halikas, J.A. and Maurice, W.L. (1972). The depression of widowhood. *British Journal of Psychiatry*, 120, 71–78.

Clegg, F. (1988). Bereavement. In S. Fisher and J. Reason (eds), *Handbook of Life Stress, Cognition and Health*. Chichester, UK and New York: Wiley.

Cleiren, M.P.H.D. (1993). *Bereavement and Adaptation: A Comparative Study of the Aftermath of Death*. Washington and London: Hemisphere.

Cleveland, W.P. and Gianturco, D.T. (1976). Remarriage probability after widowhood: a retrospective method. *Journal of Gerontology*, 31, 99–103.

Cobb, S. and Lindemann, E. (1943). Neuropsychiatric observations. *Annals of Surgery*, 117, 814–824.

Cochrane, A.L. (1936). 'A little widow is a dangerous thing'. *International Journal of Psychoanalysis*, 17, 494–509.

Coe, C.L., Rosenberg, L.T., Fischer, M. and Levine, S. (1987). Psychological factors capable of preventing the inhibition of antibody responses in separated infant monkeys. *Child Development*, 58, 1420–1430.

Cohen, J. (1977). *Statistical Power Analysis for the Behavioral Sciences*, rev. edn. New York and London: Academic Press.

Collins, R.L., Taylor, S.E. and Skokan, L.A. (1990). A better world or a shattered vision? Changes in life perspectives following victimization. *Social Cognition*, 8, 263–285.

Conboy-Hill, S. (1991). Grief, loss and people with learning difficulties. In A. Waitman and S. Conboy-Hill (eds), *Psychotherapy and Mental Handicap* (pp. 150–170). London and Newbury Park: Sage.

Conner, R.L., Vernikos-Danellis, J. and Levine, S. (1971). Stress, fighting and neuroendocrine function. *Nature*, 234, 564–566.

Cook, J. (1988). Dad's double binds: rethinking fathers' bereavement from a men's studies perspective. *Journal of Contemporary Ethnography*, 17, 285–308.

Cornwell, J., Nurcombe, B. and Stevens, L. (1977). Family response to loss of a child by sudden infant death syndrome. *Medical Journal of Australia*, 1, 227–244.

Cortina, J.M. (1993). What is coefficient alpha? An examination of theory and applications. *Journal of Applied Psychology*, 78, 98–104.

Crawford, C.B. (1989). The theory of evolution: of what value to comparative psychology? *Journal of Comparative Psychology*, 103, 4–22.

Crawford, C.B., Salter, B.E. and Jang, K.L. (1989). Human grief: is its intensity related to the reproductive value of the deceased? *Ethology and Sociobiology*, 10, 297–307.

Cressy, D. (1997). *Birth, Marriage and Death: Ritual, Religion and the Life Cycle in Tudor and Stuart England*. Oxford: Oxford University Press.

Cronin, H. (1991). *The Ant and the Peacock*. New York and Cambridge: Cambridge University Press.

Crook, J.H. (1980). *The Evolution of Human Consciousness*. Oxford and New York: Oxford University Press.

Crumbaugh, J.C. and Maholick, L.T. (1964). An experimental study in existentilism: the psychometric approach to Frankl's concept of *noogenic* neurosis. *Journal of Clinical Psychology,* 20, 200–207.

Cuisinier, M., Janssen, H., de Graauw, C., Bakker, S. and Hoogduin, C. (1996). Pregnancy following miscarriage: course of grief and some determining factors. *Journal of Psychosomatic Obstetrics and Gynecology*, 17, 168–174.

Culwick, A.T. and Culwick, G.M. (1935). *Ubena of the Rivers*. London: Allen and Unwin.

Cuyler, T.L. (1873). *The Empty Crib*. New York.

Daly, M. (1989). On distinguishing evolved adaptation from epiphenomena. *Behavioral and Brain Sciences*, 12, 520–521. (Commentary on Rushton, 1989.)

Daly, M., McConnell, C. and Glugosh, T. (1996). Parents' knowledge of students' beliefs and attitudes: an indirect assay of parental solicitude? *Ethology and Sociobiology*, 17, 201–210.

Daly, M. and Wilson, M. (1982). Whom are newborn babies said to resemble? *Ethology and Sociobiology*, 3, 69–78.

Daly, M. and Wilson, M. (1988a). *Homicide*. New York: Aldine de Gruyter.

Daly, M. and Wilson, M. (1988b). The Darwinian psychology of discriminative parental solicitude. *Nebraska Symposium on Motivation*, 35, 91–144.

Daly, M. and Wilson, M. (1994). Evolutionary psychology of male violence. In J. Archer (ed.), *Male Violence* (pp. 253–288). London and New York: Routledge.

Daly, M., Wilson, M. and Weghorst, S.J. (1982). Male sexual jealousy. *Ethology and Sociobiology*, 3, 11–27.

Darwin, C. (1843). Letter to W.D. Fox [25 March]. In Burkhardt, F. and Smith, S. (eds), *The Correspondence of Charles Darwin*, Vol. 2. (pp. 352–353). Cambridge: Cambridge University Press, (1986).

Darwin, C. (1872). *The Expression of the Emotions in Man and Animals*. London: Murray (1904 edn).

Darwin, F. (1888). *The Life and Letters of Charles Darwin, Vol. III*, London: John Murray.

Davis, C.G., Lehman, D.R., Wortman, C.B. Silver, R.C., and Thompson, S.C. (1995). The undoing of traumatic life events. *Personality and Social Psychology Bulletin*, 21, 109–124.

Dawkins, R. (1976). *The Selfish Gene*. Oxford: Oxford University Press.

Deck, E.S. and Folta, J.R. (1989). The friend-griever. In K. Doka (ed.), *Disenfranchised Grief: Recognizing Hidden Sorrow* (pp. 77–89). Lexington, MA: Lexington Books (D.C. Heath and Co.).

DeFrain, J.D. and Ernst, L. (1978). The physiological effects of sudden infant death syndrome on surviving family members. *Journal of Family Practice*, 6, 985–989.

DeFrain, J.D., Jakub, D.K. and Mendoza, B.L. (1991–2). The psychological effects of sudden infant death on grandmothers and grandfathers. *Omega*, 24, 165–182.

DeFrain, J.[D.], Martens, L., Stork, J. and Stork, W. (1990–1). The psychological effects of a stillbirth on surviving family members. *Omega*, 22, 81–108.

Dembo, T., Leviton, G.L. and Wright, B.A. (1956). Adjustment to misfortune – a problem of social-psychological rehabilitation. *Artificial Limbs*, 3, 4–62.

Denisoff, R.S. (1972). *Sing a Song of Social Significance*. Bowling Green, Ohio: Bowling Green State University Popular Press.

De Silva, P. (1985). Early Buddhist and modern behavioral strategies for the control of unwanted intrusive cognitions. *Psychological Record*, 35, 437–443.

De Silva, P. (1990). Buddhist psychology: a review of theory and practice. *Current Psychology: Research and Reviews*, 9, 236–254.

Desmond, A. and Moore, J. (1991). *Darwin*. London: Michael Joseph.

Deutsch, D.K. (1982). The development, reliability, and validity of an instrument designed to measure grief. *Dissertation Abstracts*, A3844, Michigan State University.

Deutsch, H. (1937). Absence of grief. *Psychoanalytic Quarterly*, 6, 12–22.

DeVries, B., Davis, C.G., Wortman, C.B. and Lehman, D.R. (1997). Long-term psychological and somatic consequences of later life parental bereavement. *Omega*, 35, 97–117.

Dillenburger, K. and Keenan, M. (1994). Bereavement: a behavioural process. *Irish Journal of Psychology*, 15, 524–539.

Doane, B.K. and Quigley, B.G. (1981). Psychiatric aspects of therapeutic abortion. *Canadian Medical Association Journal*, 125, 427–432.

Doka, K.J. (1989a). Disenfranchised grief. In K. Doka (ed.), *Disenfranchised Grief: Recognizing Hidden Sorrow* (pp. 3–11). Lexington, MA: Lexington Books (D.C. Heath and Co.).

Doka, K.J. (1989b). The left lover: grief in extramarital affairs and cohabitation. In K. Doka (ed.), *Disenfranchised Grief: Recognizing Hidden Sorrow* (pp. 67–76). Lexington, MA: Lexington Books (D.C. Heath and Co.).

Doka, K.J. (1992). The monkey's paw: the role of inheritance in the resolution of grief. *Death Studies*, 16, 45–58.

Dollard, J., Doob, L.W., Miller, N.E., Mowrer, O.H. and Sears, R.R. (1939). *Frustration and Aggression*. New Haven: Yale University Press.

Dosser, D.A., Balswick, J.O. and Halverson, Jr, C.F. (1986). Male inexpressiveness and relationships. *Journal of Social and Personal Relationships,* 3, 241–258.

Dostoyevsky, T.M. (1880). *The Brothers Karamazov*, Vols 1 and 2, 1958 edn, translated from Russian by David Magarshack, Harmondsworth, UK: Penguin.

Douglas, A. (1975). Heaven or home: consolation literature in the Northern United States 1830–1880. In D. Stannard (ed.), *Death in America* (pp. 49–68). Pittsburgh, PA: University of Pennsylvania Press.

Douglas, J.D. (1990–1). Patterns of change following parent death in midlife adults. *Omega*, 22, 123–137.

Downey, G., Silver, R.C. and Wortman, C.B. (1990). Reconsidering the attribution-adjustment relations following a major negative life event: coping with the loss of a child. *Journal of Personality and Social Psychology*, 59, 925–940.

Drake-Hurst, E. (1991). The grieving process and the loss of a beloved pet: a study of clinical relevance. *Dissertation Abstracts International*, 51, 5025-B.

Driscoll, J.W. and Bateson, P.P.G. (1988). Animals in behavioural research. *Animal Behaviour*, 36, 1569–1574.

Duck, S. and Wright, P.H. (1993). Reexamining gender differences in same-gender friendships: a close look at two kinds of data. *Sex Roles*, 28, 709–727.

Duffy, C.A. (ed.) (1996). *Stopping for Death*. London: Viking.

Duncan, I.J.H. and Wood-Gush, D.G. M. (1972). Thwarting of feeding behaviour in the domestic fowl. *Animal Behaviour*, 20, 444–451.

Dyregrov, A. and Matthiesen, S.B. (1987a). Similarities and differences in mothers' and fathers' grief following the death of an infant. *Scandinavian Journal of Psychology*, 28, 1–15.

Dyregrov, A. and Matthiesen, S.B. (1987b). Stillbirth, neonatal death and sudden infant death (SIDS): parental reactions. *Scandinavian Journal of Psychology*, 28, 104–114.

Eagly, A. (1987). *Sex Differences in Social Behavior: a Social Role Interpretation*. Hillsdale, NJ and London: Lawrence Erlbaum.

Eagly, A.H. (1995). The science and politics of comparing women and men. *American Psychologist*, 50, 145–158.

Edmonds, S. and Hooker, K. (1992). Perceived changes in life meaning following bereavement. *Omega*, 25, 307–318.

Eliade, M. (1977). Mythologies of death: an introduction. In F.E. Reynolds and E.H. Waugh (eds), *Religious Encounters With Death: Insights from the History and Anthropology of Religions* (pp. 13–23). University Park, PA: Pennsylvania University Press.

Eliot, T.D. (1930). Bereavement as a problem for family research and technique. *The Family*, 11, 114–115.

Eliot, T.D. (1932). The bereaved family. *Annals of the New York Academy of Political and Social Science*, 160, 184–190.

Eliot, T.D. (1946). War bereavements and their recovery. *Marriage and Family Living*, 8, 1–5, 8.

Elizur, E. and Kaffman, M. (1982). Children's bereavement reactions following death of a father. *Journal of the American Academy of Paediatrics*, 21, 474–480.

Elizur, E. and Kaffman, M. (1983). Factors influencing the severity of childhood bereavement reactions. *American Journal of Orthopsychiatry*, 53, 668–676.

Ellis, R.R. and Dick, L.C. (1992). When our clients sing their blues. *Omega*, 24, 289–300.

Engel, G.L. (1961). Is grief a disease? A challenge for medical research. *Psychosomatic Medicine*, 23, 18–22.

Engel, G.L. (1962). Anxiety and depression-withdrawal: the primary effects of unpleasure. *International Journal of Psychoanalysis*, 43, 89–97.

Engel, G.L. (1964). Grief and grieving. *American Journal of Nursing*, 64, 93–98.

Epstein, S. (1993). Bereavement from the perspective of cognitive-experiental self-theory. In M.S. Stroebe, W. Stroebe and R.O. Hansson (eds), *Handbook of Bereavement: Theory, Research and Intervention* (pp. 112–125). New York: Cambridge University Press.

Euler, H.A. and Weitzel, B. (1996). Discriminative grandparental solicitude as reproductive strategy. *Human Nature*, 7, 39–59.

Faletti, M.V., Gibbs, J.M., Clark, M.C., Pruchno, R.A. and Berman, E.A. (1989).

Longitudinal course of bereavement in older adults. In D.A. Lund (ed.), *Older Bereaved Spouses: Research with Practical Implications* (pp. 37–51). New York: Hemisphere.

Fanos, J.H. and Nickerson, B.G. (1991). Long-term effects of sibling death during adolescence. *Journal of Adolescent Research*, 6, 70–82.

Faschingbauer, T.R., DeVaul, R.A. and Zisook, S. (1977). Development of the Texas Inventory of Grief. *American Journal of Psychiatry*, 134, 696–698.

Faschingbauer, T.R., Zisook, S. and DeVaul, R.A. (1987). The Texas Revised Inventory of Grief. In S. Zisook (ed.), *Biopsychosocial Aspects of Bereavement* (pp. 109–124). Washington, DC: American Psychiatric Press.

Fawzy, F.I., Fawzy, N.W. and Pasnau, R.O. (1991). Bereavement in AIDS. *Psychiatric Medicine*, 9, 469–482.

Feeney, J.A. and Noller, P. (1990). Attachment style as a predictor of adult romantic relationships. *Journal of Personality and Social Psychology,* 58, 281–291.

Feeney, J.A. and Noller, P. (1996). *Adult Attachment*. Thousand Oaks, CA: Sage.

Fenster, L., Katz, D.F., Wyrobek, A.J., Pieper, C., Rempel, D.M., Oman, D. and Swan, S.H. (1997). Effects of psychosocial stress on human semen quality. *Journal of Andrology*, 18, 194–202.

Field, T. (1996). Attachment and separation in young children. *Annual Review of Psychology*, 47, 541–561.

Field, T. and Reite, M. (1984). Children's responses to separation from mother during the birth of another child. *Child Development*, 55, 1308–1316.

Finkelstein, H. (1988). The long-term effects of early parental death: a review. *Journal of Clinical Psychology*, 44, 3–9.

Fish, W.C. (1986). Differences in grief intensity in bereaved parents. In T.A. Rando (ed.), *Parental Loss of a Child* (pp. 415–428). Champaign, IL: Research Press.

Fisher, R.A. (1930). *The Genetical Theory of Natural Selection*. Oxford: Clarendon Press.

Fisher, S. (1984). *Stress and the Perception of Control*. London and Hillsdale, NJ: Erlbaum.

Fisher, S. (1989). *Homesickness, Cognition and Health*. Hove, UK: Erlbaum.

Folkman, S. and Lazarus, R.S. (1980). An analysis of coping in a middle-aged community sample. *Journal of Health and Social Behavior*, 21, 219–239.

Follingstad, D.R., Brennan, A.F., Hause, E.S., Polek, D.S. and Rutledge, L.L. (1991). Factors moderating physical and psychological symptoms of battered women. *Journal of Family Violence*, 6, 81–95.

Forrest, G.C., Standish, E. and Baum, J.D. (1982). Support after perinatal death: a study of support and counselling after perinatal bereavement. *British Medical Journal*, 285, 1475–1479.

Fox, V.C. and Quitt, M.H. (1980). *Loving, Parenting and Dying: the Family Circle in England and America, Past and Present*. New York: Psychohistory Press.

Frankl, V.E. (1960). Paradoxical intentions: a logotherapeutic technique. *American Journal of Psychotherapy*, 14, 520–535.

Frankl, V.E. (1964). *Man's Search for Meaning: an Introduction to Logotherapy*. London: Hodder and Stoughton (trans. I. Lasch).

Frazier, P. (1990). Victim attributions and post-rape trauma. *Journal of Personality and Social Psychology*, 59, 298–304.

Frazier, P. and Schauben, L. (1994). Causal attributions and recovery from rape and other stressful life events. *Journal of Social and Clinical Psychology,* 13, 1–14.

Fredrick, J.F. (1976–7). Grief as a disease process. *Omega*, 7, 297–305.

Fredrick, J.F. (1982–3). Biochemistry of bereavement: possible basis for chemotherapy. *Omega*, 13, 295–303.

Freedman, M. (1970). Notes on grief in literature. In B. Schoenberg, A.C. Carr, D. Peretz and A.H. Kutscher (eds), *Loss and Grief: Psychological Management and Medical Practice* (pp. 339–346). New York and London: Columbia University Press.

Freeman, E.M. (1984). Multiple losses in the elderly: an ecological approach. *Social Casework: The Journal of Contemporary Social Work*, 65, 287–296.

Freud, S. (1913). *Totem and Taboo*. Reprinted as Pelican edn, 1938, trans. by A.A. Brill. Harmondsworth, UK: Penguin.

Freud, S. (1917). *Mourning and Melancholia*. Reprinted in: J. Strachey (trans. and ed.), *Standard Edition of Complete Psychological Works of Sigmund Freud*, Vol. 14 (pp. 239–260). London: Hogarth Press and Institute of Psychoanalysis (1957).

Freud, S. (1926). *Inhibitions, Symptoms and Anxiety*. Reprinted in: J. Strachey (trans. and ed.), *Standard Edition of Complete Psychological Works of Sigmund Freud*, Vol. 20 (pp. 77–175). London: Hogarth Press and Institute of Psychoanalysis (1959).

Freud, S. (1929). [letter] To Ludwig Binswanger. In E.L. Freud (ed.), *Letters of Sigmund Freud 1873–1939*, trans. T. and J. Stern, 1961. London: The Hogarth Press.

Fried, M. (1962). Grieving for a lost home. In L.J. Duhl (ed.). *The Environment of the Metropolis* (pp. 151–171). New York: Basic Books.

Friedman, T. and Gath, D. (1989). The psychiatric consequences of spontaneous abortion. *British Journal of Psychiatry*, 155, 810–813.

Frost, M. and Condon, J.T. (1996). The psychological sequelae of miscarriage: a critical review of the literature. *Australian and New Zealand Journal of Psychiatry*, 30, 54–62.

Fry, P.S. (1997). Grandparents' reactions to the death of a grandchild: an exploratory factor analytic study. *Omega*, 35, 119–140.

Fulconer, D.M. (1942). The adjustive behavior of some recently bereaved spouses: a psycho-sociological study. PhD Dissertation, Northwestern University, Evanston, Ill.

Furnham, A. and Procter, E. (1989). Belief in a just world: review and critique of the individual difference literature. *British Journal of Social Psychology*, 28, 365–384.

Gage, M.G. and Holcomb, R. (1991). Couple's perception of stressfulness of death of the family pet. *Family Relations*, 40, 103–105.

Gallagher, D.E., Breckenbridge, J.N. Thompson, L.W. and Peterson, J.A. (1983). Effects of bereavement on indicators of mental health in elderly widows and widowers. *Journal of Gerontology*, 38, 565–571.

Gallagher, D., Lovett, S., Hanley-Dunn, P. and Thompson, L.W. (1989). Use of select coping strategies during late-life spousal bereavement. In D.A. Lund (ed.), *Older Bereaved Spouses: Research with Practical Implications* (pp. 111–121). New York: Hemisphere.

Gallagher-Thompson, D., Futterman, A., Farberow, N., Thompson, L.W. and Peterson, J. (1993). The impact of spousal bereavement on older widows and widowers. In M.S. Stroebe, W. Stroebe and R.O. Hansson (eds), *Handbook of Bereavement: Theory, Research and Intervention* (pp. 227–239). New York: Cambridge University Press.

Gangestad, S.W. (1989). Uncompelling theory, uncompelling data. *Behavioral and Brain Sciences*, 12, 525–526. (Commentary on Rushton, 1989.)

Gangestad, S.W. and Thornhill, R. (1997). The evolutionary psychology of extrapair sex: the role of fluctuating asymmetry. *Evolution and Human Behavior*, 18, 69–88.

Gannon, K. (1992). Psychological sequelae of recurrent miscarriage. Paper presented at British Psychological Society London conference, City University, 15–16 December.

Garb, R., Bleich, A. and Lerer, B. (1987). Bereavement in combat. *Psychiatric Clinics of North America*, 10, 421–436.

Gardner, A. and Pritchard, M. (1977). Mourning, mummification and living with the dead. *British Journal of Psychiatry*, 130, 23–28.

Gass, K.A. (1987). Coping strategies of widows. *Journal of Gerontological Nursing*, 13, 29–33.

Gass, K.A. (1989a). Appraisal, coping and resources: markers associated with the health of aged widows and widowers. In D.A. Lund (ed.), *Older Bereaved Spouses: Research with Practical Implications* (pp. 79–94). New York: Hemisphere.

Gass, K.A. (1989b). Health of older widowers: role of appraisal, coping, resources and type of spouse's death. In D.A. Lund (ed.), *Older Bereaved Spouses: Research with Practical Implications* (pp. 95–110). New York: Hemisphere.

Gauthier, J. and Pye, C. (1979). Graduated self-exposure in the management of grief. *Behavior Analysis and Modification*, 3, 202–208.

Gerwolls, M.K. and Labott, S.M. (1994). Adjustment to the death of a companion animal. *Anthrozoos*, 7, 172–187.

Giles, P.F.H. (1970). Reactions of women to perinatal death. *Australian and New Zealand Journal of Obstetrics and Gynaecology*, 10, 207–210.

Gilmore, D.D. (1990). *Manhood in the Making*. New Haven, CT: Yale University Press.

Glick, I.O., Weiss, R.S. and Parkes, C.M. (1974). *The First Year of Bereavement*. New York: Wiley.

Glover, H. (1984). Survival guilt and the Vietnam veteran. *Journal of Nervous and Mental Disease*, 172, 393–397.

Gogol, N.V. (1842). *Lost Souls*; trans. 1887, London: Vizetelly and Co; 1961 edn trans. from Russian by David Magarshack, Harmondsworth, UK: Penguin.

Goin, M.K., Burgoyne, R.W. and Goin, J.M. (1979). Timeless attachment to a dead relative. *American Journal of Psychiatry*, 136, 988–989.

Golan, N. (1975). Wife to widow to woman. *Social Work*, 20, 369–374.

Gold, J.H. (1985). The grief process after pregnancy loss. In J.H. Gold (ed.), *The Psychiatric Implications of Menstruation* (pp. 65–74). Washington, DC: American Psychiatric Press.

Goldbach, K.R.C., Dunn, D.S., Toedter, L.J. and Lasker, J.N. (1991). The effects of gestational age and gender on grief after pregnancy loss. *American Journal of Orthopsychiatry*, 61, 461–467.

Goldberg, H.S. (1981–2). Funeral and bereavement rituals of Kota Indians and orthodox Jews. *Omega*, 12, 117–128.

Goodkin, K., Feaster, D.J., Tuttle, R., Blaney, N.T., Kumar, M., Baum, M.K., Shapshak, P. and Fletcher, M.A. (1996). Bereavement is associated with time-dependent decrements in cellular immune function in asymptomatic human immunodeficiency virus type 1-seropositive homosexual men. *Clinical and Diagnostic Laboratory Immunology*, 3, 109–118.

Gorer, G. (1965). *Death, Grief and Mourning in Contemporary Britain*. London: Cresset Press.

Goss, R.E. and Klass, D. (1997). Tibetan Buddhism and the resolution of grief: the *Bardo-Thodol* for the dying and the grieving. *Death Studies,* 21, 377–395.

Gosse, G.H. and Barnes, M.J. (1994). Human grief resulting from death of a pet. *Anthrozoos*, 7, 103–112.

Gottlieb, L.N., Lang, A. and Amsel, R. (1996). The long-term effects of grief on marital intimacy following an infant's death. *Omega*, 33, 1–19.

Greenberg, M.A. and Stone, A.A. (1990). Writing about disclosed versus undisclosed traumas: health and mood effects. *Health Psychology*, 9, 114–115.

Greenberg, M.A. and Stone, A.A. (1992). Emotional disclosure about traumas and its relation to health: effects of previous disclosure and trauma severity. *Journal of Personality and Social Psychology,* 63, 75–84.

Griffin, D. and Bartholomew, K. (1994a). The metaphysics of measurement: the case of adult attachment. In K. Bartholomew and D. Perlman (eds), *Advances in Personal Relationships, Volume 5: Attachment Processes in Adulthood* (pp. 17–52). London: Kingsley.

Griffin, D. and Bartholomew, K. (1994b). Models of the self and other: fundamental dimensions underlying measures of adult attachment. *Journal of Personality and Social Psychology,* 67, 430–445.

Grimby, A. (1993). Bereavement among elderly people: grief reactions, post-bereavement hallucinations and quality of life. *Acta Psychiatrica Scandanavica*, 97, 72–80.

Guiton, P. and Wood-Gush, D.G.M. (1967). Studies on thwarting in the domestic fowl. *Revue de Comparative Animale*, 5, 1–23.

Hagan, J.M. (1974). Infant death: nursing interaction and intervention with grieving families. *Nursing Forum*, 13, 372–385.

Halpern, W.I. (1972). Some psychiatric sequelae to crib death. *American Journal of Psychiatry*, 129, 398–402.

Hamilton, W.D. (1964) The genetical evolution of social behavior, I and II. *Journal of Theoretical Biology*, 7, 1–52.

Handy, J.A. (1982). Psychological and social aspects of induced abortion. *British Journal of Clinical Psychology*, 21, 29–41.

Hansson, R.O., Remondet, J.H. and Galusha, M. (1993). Old age and widowhood: issues of personal control and independence. In M.S. Stroebe, W. Stroebe and R.O. Hansson (eds), *Handbook of Bereavement: Theory, Research and Intervention* (pp. 367–380). New York: Cambridge University Press.

Harlow, H.F. and Harlow, M.K. (1965). The affectional systems. In A.M. Schrier, H.F. Harlow and F. Stollnitz (eds), *Behavior of Nonhuman Primates, Vol. 2* (pp. 287–334). New York and London: Academic Press.

Harris, B.G. (1986). Induced abortion. In T.A. Rando (ed.), *Parental Loss of a Child* (pp. 241–256). Champaign, IL: Research Press.

Harris, E.S. (1991). Adolescent bereavement following the death of a parent: an exploratory study. *Child Psychiatry and Human Development*, 21, 267–281.

Harris, T. and Bifulco, A. (1991). Loss of a parent in childhood, attachment style, and depression in adulthood. In C.M. Parkes, J. Stevenson-Hinde and P. Marris (ed.), *Attachment Across the Life Cycle* (pp. 234–267). London: Routledge.

Harris, T., Brown, G.W. and Bifulco, A. (1986). Loss of parent in childhood and adult psychiatric disorder: the role of lack of adequate parental care. *Psychological Medicine*, 16, 641–659.

Harvey, C.D. and Bahr, H.M. (1974). Widowhood, morale, and affiliation. *Journal of Marriage and the Family*, 36, 97–106.

Harvey, J.H., Orbuch, T.L., Weber, A.L., Merbach, N. and Alt, R. (1992). House of pain and hope: accounts of loss. *Death Studies*, 16, 99–124.

Haworth, J.T. and Hill, S. (1992). Work, leisure, and psychological well-being in a sample of young adults. *Journal of Community and Applied Psychology*, 2, 147–160.

Hazan, C. and Shaver, P.R. (1987). Romantic love conceptualized as an attachment process. *Journal of Personality and Social Psychology*, 52, 511–524.

Hazan, C. and Shaver, P.R. (1992). Broken attachments: relationship loss from the perspective of attachment theory. In T.L. Orbuch (ed.), *Close Relationship Loss: Theoretical Approaches* (pp. 90–108). New York and Berlin: Springer-Verlag.

Healey, D. (1989). *The Time of My Life*. London: Michael Joseph.

Helsing, K.J. and Szklo, M. (1981). Mortality after bereavement. *American Journal of Epidemiology*, 114, 41–52.

Henley, S.H.A. (1984). Bereavement following suicide: a review of the literature. *Current Psychological Research and Reviews*, 3, 53–61.

Herbert, T.B. and Cohen, S. (1993). Depression and immunity: a meta-analytic review. *Psychological Bulletin*, 113, 472–486.

Herman, S.J. (1974). Divorce: a grief process. *Perspectives in Psychiatric Care*, 12, 108–112.

Hershberger, P.L. and Walsh, W.B. (1990). Multiple role involvements and the adjustment to conjugal bereavement: an exploratory study. *Omega*, 21, 91–102.

Hickrod, L.J.H. and Schmitt, R.L. (1982). A naturalistic study of interaction and frame: the pet as 'family member'. *Urban Life*, 11, 55–77.

Higginson, I. (1996). Preface. In J. Benson and A. Falk (eds), *The Long Pale Corridor: Contemporary Poems of Bereavement*. Newcastle upon Tyne, UK: Bloodaxe.

Hill, C.M. and Ball, H.L. (1996). Abnormal births and other 'ill omens': the adaptive case for infanticide. *Human Nature*, 7, 381–401.

Hill, K. and Kaplan, H. (1988). Tradeoffs in male and female reproductive strategies among the Ache: part 2. In L. Betzig, M. Borgerhoff Mulder and P. Turke (eds), *Human Reproductive Behaviour: a Darwinian Perspective* (pp. 291–305). Cambridge, UK and New York: Cambridge University Press.

Hill, S. (1974). *In the Springtime of the Year*. London: Hamish Hamilton. (Penguin edn 1977.)

Hillary, R. (1942). *The Last Enemy*. London: Macmillan. (Pan edn 1956.)

Hinde, R.A. (1970). *Animal Behaviour: a Synthesis of Ethology and Comparative Psychology* (2nd edn). New York: McGraw-Hill.

Hinde, R.A. (1974). *Biological Bases of Human Social Behaviour*. New York: McGraw-Hill.

Hinde, R.A. (1982). *Ethology*. Oxford: Oxford University Press.

Hinde, R.A. (1983). Dialogue with Jonathan Miller. In J. Miller (ed.), *States of Mind* (pp. 174–190). London: BBC.

Hinde, R.A. (1986). Some implications of evolutionary theory and comparative data for the study of human prosocial and aggressive behavior. In D. Olweus, J. Block and M. Radke-Yarrow (eds), *Development of Antisocial and Prosocial Behavior* (pp. 13–32). New York and London: Academic Press.

Hindy, C.G., and Schwarz, J.C. (1994). Anxious romantic attachment in adult relationships. In M.B. Sperling and W.H. Berman (eds), *Attachment in Adults: Clinical and Developmental Perspectives* (pp. 179–203). New York: Guilford Press.

Hobson, C.J. (1964). Widows of Blackton. *New Society*, 24th Sept., 4 (no. 104), 13–16.

Hodgkinson, P.E. and Shepherd, M.A. (1994). The impact of disaster support work. *Journal of Traumatic Stress*, 7, 587–600.

Hofer, M.A. (1984). Relationships as regulators: a psychobiological perspective on bereavement. *Psychosomatic Medicine*, 46, 183–197.

Hofer, M.A. (1996). On the nature and consequences of early loss. *Psychosomatic Medicine*, 58, 570–581.

Hofer, M.A., Wolff, C.T., Friedman, S.B. and Mason, J. (1972). A psychoendocrine study of bereavement: Part 1. 17-hydroxycorticosteroid excretion rates of parents following death of their children from leukemia. *Psychosomatic Medicine*, 34, 481–491.

Hoffman, H.S., Searle, J.L., Toffey, S. and Kozma Jr, F. (1966). Behavioral control by an imprinted stimulus. *Journal of the Experimental Analysis of Behavior*, 9, 177–189.

Hogan, N.S. (1988a). Hogan Grief Reactions Checklist. Miami: University of Miami, School of Nursing.

Hogan, N.S. (1988b). The effects of time on the adolescent sibling bereavement process. *Pediatric Nursing*, 14, 333–335.

Hogan, N.S. (1990). Hogan Sibling Inventory of Bereavement. In T. Touliatos, B. Perlmutter and M.A. Straus (eds), *Handbook of Family Measurement Techniques* (p. 524). Newbury Park, CA and London: Sage.

Hogan, N.S. and Greenfield, D.B. (1991). Adolescent sibling bereavement symptomatology in a large community sample. *Journal of Adolescent Research*, 6, 97–112.

Hojat, M. and Vogel, W.H. (1987). Socioemotional bonding and neurobiochemistry. *Journal of Social Behaviour and Personality*, 2, 135–144.

Hollenbeck, A.R., Susman, E.J., Nannis, E.D., Strope, B.E., Hersh, S.P., Levine, A.S. and Pizzo, P.A. (1980). Children with serious illness: behavioral correlates of separation and isolation. *Child Psychiatry and Human Development*, 11, 3–11.

Holmberg, A.R. (1950). *Nomads of the Long Bow*. Washington, DC: Smithsonian Institute.

Holmes, T.H. and Rahe, R.H. (1967). The social readjustment rating scale. *Journal of Psychosomatic Research*, 11, 213–218.

The Holy Bible (1949). Authorised King James Version. London and New York: Collins.

Hood, B.M, Maclachlan, I.M. and Fisher, S. (1987). The relationship between cognitive failures, psychoneurotic symptoms and sex. *Acta Psychiatrica Scandinavica*, 76, 33–35.

Hopkins, J. and Thompson, E.H. (1984). Loss and mourning in victims of rape and sexual assault. In J. Hopkins (ed.), *Perspectives on Rape and Sexual Assault* (pp. 104–117). London: Harper and Row.

Horacek, B.J. (1991). Toward a more viable model of grieving and consequences for older persons. *Death Studies*, 15, 459–472.

Horowitz, M.J. (1976). *Stress Response Syndromes*. New York: Jason Aronson.

Horowitz, M.J., Bonanno, G.A. and Holen, A. (1993). Pathological grief: diagnosis and explanation. *Psychosomatic Medicine*, 55, 260–273.

Horowitz, M.J., Weiss, D.S., Kaltreider, N., Krupnick, J., Marman, C., Wilner, N. and Dewitt, K. (1984). Reactions to the death of a parent: results from patients and field subjects. *Journal of Nervous and Mental Disease*, 172, 383–392.

Horowitz, M.J., Wilner, N., Kaltreider, N. and Alvarez, W. (1980). Signs and symptoms of posttraumatic stress disorder. *Archives of General Psychiatry*, 37, 85–92.

Hughes, C. B. and Page-Lieberman, J. (1989). Fathers experiencing a perinatal loss. *Death Studies*, 13, 537–556.

Hunfeld, J.A.M., Wladimiroff, J.W. and Passchier, J. (1997a). Prediction and course of grief four years after perinatal loss due to congenital anomolies: a follow-up study. *British Journal of Medical Psychology*, 70, 85–91.

Hunfeld, J.A.M., Wladimiroff, J.W. and Passchier, J. (1997b). The grief of late pregnancy loss. *Patient Education and Counselling*, 31, 57–64.

Hunfeld, J.A.M., Wladimiroff, J.W., Passchier, J., Uniken Venema-van Uden, M.M.A.T., Frets, P.G. and Verhage, F. (1993). Reliability and validity of the prenatal grief scale for women who experienced late pregnancy loss. *British Journal of Medical Psychology*, 66, 295–298.

Hunter, E.J. (1986). Missing in action. In T.A. Rando (ed.), *Parental Loss of a Child* (pp. 277–289). Champaign, IL: Research Press.

Hutchins, S.H. (1986). Stillbirth. In T.A. Rando (ed.), *Parental Loss of a Child* (pp. 129–144). Champaign, IL: Research Press.

Hutton, C.J. and Bradley, B.S. (1994). Effects of sudden infant death on bereaved siblings: a comparative study. *Journal of Child Psychology and Psychiatry*, 35, 723–732.

Iles, S. (1989). The loss of early pregnancy. In M.R. Oates (ed.), *Psychological Aspects of Obstetrics and Gynaecology* (pp. 769–790). London: Baillière Tindall.

Irwin, M. and Pike, J. (1993). Bereavement, depressive symptoms and immune function. In M.S. Stroebe, W. Stroebe and R.O. Hansson (eds), *Handbook of Bereavement: Theory, Research and Intervention* (pp. 175–195). New York: Cambridge University Press.

Isherwood, C. (1932). *The Memorial*. London: Hogarth Press. (Quotations taken from 1988 edn, published by Methuen, London.)

Isherwood, C. (1964). *A Single Man*. London: Methuen. (Quotations taken from 1991 Minerva paperback, published by Mandarin, London.)

Izard, C.E. (1991). *The Psychology of Emotions*. New York and London: Plenum.

Jacobs, S.C. (1987). Measures of the psychological distress of bereavement. In S. Zisook (ed.), *Biopsychosocial Aspects of Bereavement* (pp. 125–138). Washington, DC: American Psychiatric Press.

Jacobs, S., Hansen, F., Kasl, S., Ostfeld, A., Berkman, L. and Kim. K. (1990). Anxiety disorders during acute bereavement: risk and risk factors. *Journal of Clinical Psychiatry*, 51, 269–274.

Jacobs, S., Kasl, S., Ostfeld, A., Berkman, L. and Charpentier, P. (1986). The measurement of grief: age and sex variation. *British Journal of Medical Psychology*, 59, 305–310.

Jacobs, S., Kasl, S., Ostfeld, A., Berkman, L., Kosten, T.R. and Charpentier, P. (1987). The measurement of grief: bereaved versus non-bereaved. *The Hospice Journal*, 2, 21–36.

Jacobs, S.C., Kosten, T.R., Kasl, S.V., Ostfeld, A.M., Berkman, L. and Charpentier, P. (1987–8). Attachment theory and multiple dimensions of grief. *Omega*, 18, 41–52.

Jahoda, M. (1979). The impact of unemployment in the 1930s and 1970s. *Bulletin of the British Psychological Society,* 32, 309–314.

Jahoda, M. (1982). *Employment and Unemployment*. Cambridge: Cambridge University Press.

Jalland, P. (1989). Death, grief, and mourning in the upper-class family, 1860–1914. In R. Houlbrooke (ed.), *Death, Ritual and Bereavement* (pp. 171–187). London and New York: Routledge.

James, W. (1892). *Psychology: the Briefer Course.* New York: Henry Holt. (Harper Torchbook edn, ed. G. Allport, New York: Harper and Row, 1961.)

Jankofsky, K.P. (1981–2). From lion to lamb: exemplary deaths in chronicles of the middle English period. *Omega*, 12, 209–226.

Jankowiak, W.R. and Fischer, E.F. (1992). A cross-cultural perspective on romantic love. *Ethnology*, 31, 149–155.

Janoff-Bulman, R. (1979). Characterological versus behavioral self-blame: inquiries into depression and rape. *Journal of Personality and Social Psychology*, 37, 1798–1809.

Janoff-Bulman, R. (1989). Assumptive worlds and the stress of traumatic events: applications of the schema construct. *Social Cognition*, 7, 113–136.

Janoff-Bulman, R. (1993). *Shattered Assumptions: Towards a New Psychology of Trauma.* New York: Free Press.

Janoff-Bulman, R. and Frieze, I.H. (1983). A theoretical perspective for understanding reactions to victimization. *Journal of Social Issues*, 39, 1–17.

Janssen, H.J.E.M., Cuisinier, M.C.J., de Graauw, K.P.H.M. and Hoogduin, K.A.L. (1997). A prospective study of risk factors predicting grief intensity following pregnancy loss. *Archives of General Psychiatry*, 54, 56–61.

Janssen, H.J.E.M., Cuisinier, M.C.J., Hoogduin, K.A. L., and de Graauw, K.P.H.M. (1996). Controlled prospective study on the mental health of women following pregnancy loss. *American Journal of Psychiatry*, 153, 226–230.

Jenkins, R.A. and Cavanaugh, J.C. (1985–6). Examining the relationship between the development of the concept of death and overall cognitive development. *Omega*, 16, 193–199.

Jensen, J.S. and Zahourek, R. (1972). Depression in mothers who have lost a newborn. *Rocky Mountain Medical Journal*, 69, 61–63.

Johnson, M.P. and Puddifoot, J.E. (1996). The grief response in the partners of women who miscarry. *British Journal of Medical Psychology*, 69, 313–327.

Joseph, S.A., Brewin, C., Yule, W. and Williams, R. (1991). Causal attributions and psychiatric symptoms in survivors of the *Herald of Free Enterprise* disaster. *British Journal of Psychiatry*, 159, 542–546.

Jump, J.D., (ed.) (1974). *Alfred Tennyson: In Memorium and Other Poems.* London: J.M. Dent and Sons.

Kaminer, H. and Lavie, P. (1993). Sleep and dreams in well-adjusted and less adjusted holocaust survivors. In M.S. Stroebe, W. Stroebe and R.O. Hansson (eds), *Handbook of Bereavement: Theory, Research and Intervention* (pp. 331–345). New York: Cambridge University Press.

Kastenbaum, R. (1969). Death and bereavement in later life. In A.H. Kutscher (ed.), *Death and Bereavement* (pp. 28–54). Springfield, IL: Charles C. Thomas.

Kaufman, I.C. and Rosenblum, L.A. (1967). The reaction to separation in infant monkeys: anaclitic depression and consolation-withdrawal. *Psychosomatic Medicine*, 29, 648–675.

Kaufman, I.C. and Rosenblum, L.A. (1969). Effects of separation from mother on the emotional behavior of infant monkeys. *Annals of the New York Academy of Sciences*, 159, 681–695.

Keddie, K.M.G. (1977). Pathological mourning after the death of a domestic pet. *British Journal of Psychiatry*, 131, 21–25.

Keelan, J.P.R., Dion, K.L. and Dion, K.K. (1994). Attachment style and heterosexual relationships among young adults: a short-term panel study. *Journal of Social and Personal Relationships*, 11, 201–214.

Keenan, B. (1992). *An Evil Cradling*. London: Hutchinson. (Quotations taken from 1993 Vintage Edn.)

Kelly, A.E. and Kahn, J.H. (1994). Effects of suppression of personal intrusive thoughts. *Journal of Personality and Social Psychology*, 66, 998–1006.

Kemeny, M.E., Weiner, H., Duran, R., Taylor, S.E., Visscher, B. and Fahey, J.L. (1995). Immune system changes after the death of a partner in HIV-positive gay men. *Psychosomatic Medicine*, 57, 547–554.

Kennell, J.H., Slyter, H. and Klaus, M.H. (1970). The mourning response of parents to the death of a newborn infant. *New England Journal of Medicine*, 283, 344–349.

Kesselman, I. (1990). Grief and loss: issues for abortion. *Omega*, 21, 241–247.

Kessler, B.G. (1987). Bereavement and personal growth. *Journal of Humanistic Psychology*, 27, 228–247.

Kim, K. and Jacobs, S. (1993). Neuroendocrine changes following bereavement. In M.S. Stroebe, W. Stroebe and R.O. Hansson (eds), *Handbook of Bereavement: Theory, Research and Intervention* (pp. 143–159). New York: Cambridge University Press.

Kirkley Best, E. (1981). Grief in response to prenatal loss: an argument for earliest maternal attachment. Unpublished PhD Dissertation, University of Florida.

Kirkley Best, E. and Kellner, K.R. (1982). The forgotten grief: a review of the psychology of stillbirth. *American Journal of Orthopsychiatry*, 52, 420–429.

Kirsch, I., Mearns, J. and Catanzaro, S.J. (1990). Mood-regulation expectancies as determinants of dysphoria in college students. *Journal of Counselling Psychology*, 37, 306–312.

Kissane, D.W., Bloch, S., Dowe, D.L., Snyder, R.D., Onghena, P., McKenzie, D.P. and Wallace, C.S. (1996a). The Melbourne family grief study, I: Perceptions of family functioning in bereavement. *American Journal of Psychiatry*, 153, 650–658.

Kissane, D.W., Bloch, S., Onghena, P., McKenzie, D.P., Snyder, R.D. and Dowe, D.L. (1996b). The Melbourne family grief study, II: Psychosocial morbidity and grief in bereaved families. *American Journal of Psychiatry*, 153, 659–666.

Klass, D. (1987–8). John Bowlby's model of grief and the problem of identification. *Omega*, 18, 13–32.

Klass, D. (1988). *Parental Grief: Solace and Resolution*. New York: Springer.

Klass, D. (1996). Ancestor worship in Japan: dependence and the resolution of grief. *Omega*, 33, 279–302.

Klass, D. and Heath, A.O. (1996–7). Grief and abortion: *Mizuko Kuyo*, the Japanese ritual resolution. *Omega*, 34, 1–14.

Klaus, M.H. and Kennell, J.H. (1976). *Maternal–infant Bonding*. St Louis, MO: Mosby.

Klein, M. (1940). Mourning and its relation to manic-depressive states. *International Journal of Psychoanalysis*, 21, 125–153.

Klein, S.J. and Fletcher, W. III (1986). Gay grief: an examination of its uniqueness brought to light by the AIDS crisis. *Journal of Psychosocial Oncology*, 4, 15–25.

Klinger, E. (1975). Consequences of commitment to and disengagement from incentives. *Psychological Review*, 82, 1–25.

Klinger, E. (1977). *Meaning and Void: Inner Experience and the Incentives in People's Lives*. Minneapolis: University of Minnesota Press.

Kobasa, S.C. (1979). Stressful life events, personality and health: an enquiry into hardiness. *Journal of Personality and Social Psychology*, 37, 1–11.

Kohner, N. (1992). *A Dignified Ending*. London: Stillbirth and Neonatal Death Society.

Koocher, G.P. (1973). Childhood, death and cognitive development. *Developmental Psychology*, 9, 369–375.

Kubler-Ross, E. (1969). *On Death and Dying*. New York: Macmillan.

Kubler-Ross, E. (1971). The five stages of dying. In *Encyclopedia Science Supplement* (pp. 92–97). New York: Grollier.

Kundera, M. (1984). *The Unbearable Lightness of Being*. London: Faber and Faber; New York: Harper and Row. (Paperback edn, 1985). Trans. from the Czech by Michael Henry Heim.

Lack, D. (1954). *The Natural Regulation of Animal Numbers*. Oxford: Clarendon.

Lamb, M.E., Thompson, R.A., Gardner, W. and Charnov, E.L. (1985). *Infant–Mother Attachment*. Hillsdale, NJ: Erlbaum.

Lamprecht, J. (1977). A comparison of the attachment to parents and siblings in juvenile geese (*Branta canadensis* and *Anser indicus*). *Zeitschrift für Tierpsychologie*, 43, 415–424.

Lane, C. and Hobfoll, S.E. (1992). How loss affects anger and alienates potential supporters. *Journal of Consulting and Clinical Psychology*, 60, 935–942.

Lang, A. and Gottlieb, L.[N.] (1991). Marital intimacy in bereaved and nonbereaved couples: a comparative study. In D. Papadatou and C. Papadatos (eds), *Children and Death* (pp. 267–275). New York and London: Hemisphere.

Lang, A. and Gottlieb, L.[N.] (1993). Parental grief reactions and marital intimacy following infant death. *Death Studies*, 17, 233–255.

Lang, A., Gottlieb, L.N. and Amsel, R. (1996). Predictors of husbands' and wives' grief reactions following infant death: the role of marital intimacy. *Death Studies*, 20, 33–57.

Larsen, R.R. (1975). Charisma: a reinterpretation. In M.R.A. Chance and R.R. Larsen (eds), *The Social Structure of Attention* (pp. 253–272). New York: Wiley.

Lasker, J.N. and Toedter, L.J. (1994). Satisfaction with hospital care and interventions after pregnancy loss. *Death Studies*, 18, 41–64.

Laslet, P. (1968). *The World We Have Lost*. London: Methuen.

Lattanzi, M. and Hale, M.E. (1984–5). Giving grief words: writing during bereavement. *Omega*, 15, 45–52.

Laudenslager, M.L. (1988). The psychobiology of loss: lessons from humans and nonhuman primates. *Journal of Social Issues*, 44, 19–36.

Laudenslager, M.L., Boccia, M.L. and Reite, M.L. (1993). Biobehavioral consequences of loss in nonhuman primates: individual differences. In M.S. Stroebe, W. Stroebe and R.O. Hansson (eds), *Handbook of Bereavement: Theory, Research and Intervention* (pp. 129–142). New York: Cambridge University Press.

Laungani, P. (1994). Patterns of bereavement in Indian and English society. Presented at Fourth International Conference on Grief and Bereavement in Contemporary Society, Stockholm, June 12–16.

Laurence, A. (1989). Godly grief: individual responses to death in seventeenth-century Britain. In R. Houlbrooke (ed.), *Death, Ritual and Bereavement* (pp. 62–76). London and New York: Routledge.

Leahy, J.M. (1992–3). A comparison of depression in women bereaved of a spouse, child, or a parent. *Omega*, 26, 207–217.

LeBrun, C. (1734). *A Method to Learn to Design the Passions*. Augustian Reprint Society, nos 200–201. William Andrews Clark Memorial Library, UCLA, 1980. (Trans. by John Williams from 1698 'Conference de M. Le Brun sur l'expression générale et particulière'. Paris: E. Picard.)

Lee, C. and Slade, P. (1996). Miscarriage as a traumatic event: a review of the literature and new implications for intervention. *Journal of Psychosomatic Research*, 40, 235–244.

Lee, C., Slade, P. and Lygo, V. (1996). The influence of psychological debriefing on emotional adaptation in women following early miscarriages. *British Journal of Medical Psychology*, 69, 47–58.

Lehman, D.R., Davis, C.G., Delongis, A., Wortman, C.B., Bluck, S., Mandel, D.R. and Ellard, J.H. (1993). Positive and negative life changes following bereavement and their relations to adjustment. *Journal of Social and Clinical Psychology*, 12, 90–112.

Lehman, D.R., Wortman, C.B. and Williams, A.F. (1987). Long-term effects of losing a spouse or child in a motor vehicle crash. *Journal of Personality and Social Psychology*, 52, 218–231.

Lepore, S.J., Silver, R.C., Wortman, C.B. and Wayment, H.A. (1996). Social constraints, intrusive thoughts, and depressive symptoms among bereaved mothers. *Journal of Personality and Social Psychology*, 70, 271–282.

Lerner, M.J. (1965). Evaluation of performance as a function of performer's reward and attractiveness. *Journal of Personality and Social Psychology*, 1, 355–360.

Lev, E., Munro, B.H. and McCorkle, R. (1993). A shortened version of an instrument measuring bereavement. *International Journal of Nursing Studies*, 30, 213–226.

Lévi-Strauss, C. (1973). *Tristes Tropiques*, trans. by J. and D. Weightman. London: Jonathan Cape. (Original published in 1955 by Librarie Plon, Paris.)

Levine, S., Wiener, S.G., Coe, C.L., Bayart, F.E.S. and Hayashi, K.T. (1987). Primate vocalization: a psychobiological approach. *Child Development*, 58, 1408–1419.

Levy, L.H., Derby, J.F. and Martinkowski, K.S. (1992). The question of who participates in bereavement research and the Bereavement Risk Index. *Omega*, 25, 225–238.

Levy, L.H., Derby, J.F. and Martinkowski, K.S. (1993). Effects of membership in bereavement support groups on adaptation to conjugal bereavement. *American Journal of Community Psychology*, 21, 361–381.

Levy, L.H., Martinkowski K.S. and Derby, J.F., (1994). Differences in patterns of adaptation in conjugal bereavement: their sources and potential significance. *Omega*, 29: 71–87.

Lewis, C.S. (1961). *A Grief Observed*. London: Faber and Faber.

Lewis, S. (1981). Some psychological consequences of bereavement by sudden infant death syndrome. *Health Visitor*, 54, 322–325.

Lichtenberg, P.A. (1990). Remembering Becky. *Omega*, 21, 83–89.

Lieberman, S. (1978). Nineteen cases of morbid grief. *British Journal of Psychiatry*, 132, 159–163.

Lietar, E.F. (1986). Miscarriage. In T.A. Rando (ed.), *Parental Loss of a Child* (pp. 121–127). Champaign, IL: Research Press.

Lindemann, E. (1944). Symptomatology and management of acute grief. *American Journal of Psychiatry*, 101, 141–148.

Littlefield, C,H, and Rushton, J.P. (1986). When a child dies: the sociobiology of bereavement. *Journal of Personality and Social Psychology*, 51, 797–802.

Llewellyn, M. (1991). *The Art of Death*. London: Reaktion Books.

Lloyd, P. (1978–80). A young boy in his first and last suit. *Minneapolis Institute of Arts Bulletin*, 64, 104–111.

Lloyd, P. (1982). A death in the family. *Bulletin of the Philadelphia Museum of Art*, 7 (33), 2–13.

Lofland, L.H. (1982). Loss and human connection: an exploration into the nature of the social bond. In W. Ickes and E.S. Knowles (eds), *Personality, Roles and Social Behavior* (pp. 219–242). New York: Springer-Verlag.

Lofland, L.H. (1985). The social shaping of emotion: the case of grief. *Symbolic Interaction*, 8, 171–190.

Lombardo, W.K., Cretser, G.A., Lombardo, B. and Mathis, S.L. (1983). Fer cryin' out loud – there is a sex difference. *Sex Roles*, 9, 987–995.

Long, J.B. (1977). Death as a neccessity and a gift in Hindu mythology. In F.E. Reynolds and E.H. Waugh (eds), *Religious Encounters with Death: Insights from the History and Anthropology of Religions* (pp. 73–96). University Park, PA: Pennsylvania University Press.

Lopata, H.Z. (1993). The support systems of American urban widows. In M.S. Stroebe, W. Stroebe and R.O. Hansson (eds), *Handbook of Bereavement: Theory, Research and Intervention* (pp. 381–396). New York: Cambridge University Press.

Lord, J.H. (1987). Survivor grief following a drunk-driving crash. *Death Studies*, 11, 413–435.

Low, B.S. (1989). Cross-cultural patterns in the training of children: an evolutionary perspective. *Journal of Comparative Psychology*, 103, 311–319.

Lu, L. (1991). Daily hassles and mental health: a longitudinal study. *British Journal of Psychology*, 82, 441–447.

Lund, D.A. (1989). Conclusions about bereavement in later life and implications for interventions and future research. In D.A. Lund (ed.), *Older Bereaved Spouses: Research with Practical Implications* (pp. 217–231). New York: Hemisphere.

Lund, D.A., Caserta, M.S. and Dimond, M.F. (1986). Gender differences through two years of bereavement among the elderly. *The Gerontologist*, 26, 314–320.

Lund, D.A., Caserta, M.S. and Dimond, M.F. (1989). Impact of spousal bereavement on the subjective well-being of older adults. In D.A. Lund (ed.), *Older Bereaved Spouses: Research with Practical Implications* (pp. 3–15). New York: Hemisphere.

Lund, D.A., Caserta, M.S. and Dimond, M.F. (1993). The course of spousal bereavement in later life. In M.S. Stroebe, W. Stroebe and R.O. Hansson (eds), *Handbook of Bereavement: Theory, Research and Intervention* (pp. 240–254). New York: Cambridge University Press.

Lund, F.W. (1930). Why do we weep? *Journal of Social Psychology*, 1, 136–151.

Lyubomirsky, S. and Nolen-Hoeksema, S. (1993). Self-perpetuating properties of dysphoric rumination. *Journal of Personality and Social Psychology*, 65, 339–349.

McClowry, S.G., Davies, E.B., May, K.A., Kulenkamp, E.J. and Martinson, I.M. (1987). The empty space phenomenon: the process of grief in the bereaved family. *Death Studies*, 11, 361–374.

McCollum, A.T. (1990). *The Trauma of Moving: Psychological Issues for Women*. Newbury Park, CA and London: Sage.

McCown, D.E. and Pratt, C. (1985). Impact of sibling death on children's behavior. *Death Studies*, 9, 323–335.

McDougall, W. (1923). *An Outline of Psychology*. London: Methuen.

McEwan, I. (1987). *A Child in Time*. London: Jonathan Cape.

McEwan, I. (1992). *Black Dogs*. London: Jonathan Cape. (Quotation from 1993 Picador edn.)

McFarland, D.J. (1966a). On the causal and functional significance of displacement activities. *Zeitschrift für Tierpsychologie*, 23, 217–235.

McFarland, D.J. (1966b). The role of attention in the disinhibition of displacement activity. *Quarterly Journal of Experimental Psychology*, 18, 19–30.

Macfarlane, A. (1979). Review essay: *The Family, Sex and Marriage in England 1500–1800* by Lawrence Stone, New York, Harper and Row, 1977. *History and Theory*, 18, 103–126.

McGahern, J. (1990). *Amongst Women*. London and Boston: Faber and Faber.

McGloshen, T.H. and O'Bryant, S.L. (1988). The psychological well-being of older, recent widows. *Psychology of Women Quarterly*, 12, 99–116.

McIntosh, D.N., Silver, R.C. and Wortman, C.B. (1993). Religion's role in adjustment to a negative life event: coping with the loss of a child. *Journal of Personality and Social Psychology*, 65, 812–821.

McIntosh, J.L. and Wrobleski, A. (1988). Grief reactions among suicide survivors: an exploratory comparison of relationships. *Death Studies*, 12, 21–39.

McNeil, J.N., Silliman, B. and Swihart, J.J. (1991). Helping adolescents cope with the death of a peer: a high-school case study. *Journal of Adolescent Research*, 6, 132–145.

Maddison, D. and Viola, A. (1968). The health of widows in the year following bereavement. *Journal of Psychosomatic Research*, 12, 297–306.

Maddison, D. and Walker, W.L. (1967). Factors affecting the outcome of conjugal bereavement. *British Journal of Psychiatry*, 113, 1057–1067.

Mailer, N. (1949). *The Naked and the Dead*. London: Allen Wingate. (Quotation from 1992 Paladin edn.)

Main, M. (1990). Cross-cultural studies of attachment organization: recent studies, changing methodologies, and the concept of conditional strategies. *Human Development*, 33, 48–61.

Major, B. and Cozzarelli, C. (1992). Psychosocial predictors of adjustment to abortion. *Journal of Social Issues*, 48, 121–142.

Major, B., Cozzarelli, C., Sciacchitano, A.M., Cooper, M.L., Testa, M. and Muller, P.M. (1990). Perceived social support, self-efficacy, and adjustment to abortion. *Journal of Personality and Social Psychology*, 59, 452–463.

Malinowski, B. (1926). *Crime and Custom in Savage Society*. London: Kegan Paul, Trench and Trubner; New York: Harcourt Brace.

Mapother, E. (1926). Discussion on manic-depressive psychosis. *British Medical Journal*, II, 872–879.

Markusen, E. and Fulton, R. (1971). Childhood bereavement and behavior disorders: a critical review. *Omega*, 2, 107–117.

Markusen, E., Owen, G., Fulton, R. and Bendiksen, R. (1977–8). SIDS: the survivor as victim. *Omega*, 8, 277–284.

Marris, P. (1958). *Widows and their Families*. London: Routledge and Kegan Paul.

Marris, P. (1974). *Loss and Change*. London: Routledge and Kegan Paul.

Martin, L.L. and Tesser, A. (1989). Toward a motivational and structural theory of ruminative thought. In J.S. Uleman and J.A. Bargh (eds), *Unintended Thought* (pp. 306–325). New York: Guilford Press.

Martin, L.L. and Tesser, A. (1996). Some ruminative thoughts. In R.S. Wyer Jr. (ed.), *Ruminative Thoughts: Advances in Social Cognition Volume IX* (pp. 1–47). Mahwah, NJ: Erlbaum.

Martinson, I.M. and Campos, R.G. (1991). Adolescent bereavement: Long-term responses to a sibling's death from cancer. *Journal of Adolescent Research*, 6, 54–69.

Martinson, I.M., Davies, B. and McClowry, S. (1991). Parental depression following death of a child. *Death Studies*, 15, 259–267.

Marvin, R.S. (1977). An ethological-cognitive model for the attenuation of mother–child attachment behavior. In T. Alloway, P. Pliner and L. Krames (eds), *Attachment Behavior* (pp. 25–60). New York: Plenum.

Marwit, S.J. (1996). Reliability of diagnosing complicated grief: a preliminary investigation. *Journal of Consulting and Clinical Psychology*, 64, 563–568.

Mason, W.A. (1997). Discovering behavior. *American Psychologist*, 52, 713–720.

Masters, R., Friedman, L.N. and Getzel, G. (1988). Helping families of homicide victims: a multidimensional approach. *Journal of Traumatic Stress*, 1, 109–125.

Matchett, W.F. (1972). Repeated hallucinatory experiences as a part of the mourning process among Hopi Indian women. *Psychiatry*, 35, 185–194.

Maynard Smith, J. (1964). Group selection and kin selection. *Nature*, 210, 1145–1147.

Mead, G.M. (1934). *Mind, Self and Society. From the Standpoint of a Social Behaviorist*. Chicago: University of Chicago Press.

Mead, M. (1962). *Male and Female*. Harmondsworth, UK: Penguin. (First published 1950, New York: William Morrow.)

Meddi, S.R. (1967). The existential neurosis. *Journal of Abnormal Psychology*, 72, 311–325.

Melzack, R. and Wall, P. (1982). *The Challenge of Pain*. Harmondsworth, UK: Penguin.

Menig-Peterson, C. and McCabe, A. (1977–8). Children talk about death. *Omega*, 8, 305–317.

Messer, S. (1990). Individual responses to death in Puritan Massachusetts. *Omega*, 21, 155–163.

Middleton, W., Burnett, P., Raphael, B. and Martinek, N. (1996). The bereavement response: a cluster analysis. *British Journal of Psychiatry*, 169, 167–171.

Middleton, W., Moylan, A., Raphael, B., Burnett, P. and Martinek, N. (1993). An international perspective on bereavement-related concepts. *Australian and New Zealand Journal of Psychiatry*, 27, 457–463.

Middleton, W. and Raphael, B. (1987). Bereavement: state of the art and state of the science. *Psychiatric Clinics of North America*, 10, 329–343.

Middleton, W., Raphael, B., Burnett, P. and Martinek, N. (1997). Psychological distress and bereavement. *Journal of Nervous and Mental Disease*, 185, 447–453.

Miles, M.S. and Demi, A.S. (1983–4). Toward the development of a theory of bereavement guilt: sources of guilt in bereaved parents. *Omega*, 14, 299–314.

Miller, D.T. and Turnbull, W. (1992). The counterfactual fallacy: confusing what might have been with what ought to have been. In L. Montada, S-H. Filipp and M.J. Lerner (eds), *Life Crises and Experiences of Loss in Adulthood* (pp. 179–193). Hillsdale, NJ: Erlbaum.

Miller, S.I. and Schoenfeld, L. (1973). Grief in the Navajo: psychodynamics and culture. *International Journal of Social Psychiatry*, 19, 187–191.

Mineka, S. and Suomi, S.J. (1978). Social separation in monkeys. *Psychological Bulletin*, 85, 1376–1400.

Mitchell, E.A., Scragg, L. and Clements, M. (1996). Marital status and births after losing a baby from sudden infant death. *European Journal of Pediatrics*, 155, 712–716.

Mitterauer, M. and Sieder, R. (1982). *The European Family: Patriarchy to Partnership from the Middle Ages to the Present*. Oxford: Blackwell. (Trans. from German by K. Oosterveen and M. Horzinger.)

Montada, L. (1992). Attribution of responsibility for losses and perceived injustice. In L. Montada, S-H. Filipp and M.J. Lerner (eds), *Life Crises and Experiences of Loss in Adulthood* (pp. 133–161). Hillsdale, NJ: Erlbaum.

Morgan, P. (1972). *Child Care: Sense and Fable*. London: Temple Smith.

Moriarty, H.J., Carroll, R. and Cotroneo, M. (1996). Differences in bereavement reactions within couples following death of a child. *Research in Nursing and Health*, 19, 461–469.

Moss, M.S. and Moss, S.Z. (1980). The image of the deceased spouse in remarriage of elderly widow(er)s. *Journal of Gerontological Social Work*, 3, 59–70.

Moss, M.S. and Moss, S.Z. (1984–5). Some aspects of the elderly widow(er)'s persistent tie with the deceased spouse. *Omega*, 15, 195–206.

Moss, M.S. and Moss, S.Z. (1989). The death of a parent. In R.A. Kalish (ed.), *Midlife Loss: Coping Strategies* (pp. 89–114). Newbury Park and London: Sage.

Moss, M.S., Resch, N. and Moss, S.Z. (1997). The role of gender in middle-age children's responses to parental death. *Omega*, 35, 43–65.

Murphy, P.A. (1986–7). Parental death in childhood and loneliness in young adults. *Omega*, 17, 219–228.

Murray, E.J. and Segal, D.L. (1994). Emotional processing in vocal and written expression of feelings about traumatic experiences. *Journal of Traumatic Stress*, 7, 391–405.

Murray, J. and Callan, V.J. (1988). Predicting adjustment to perinatal death. *British Journal of Medical Psychology*, 61, 237–244.

Nagy, M. (1948). The child's theories concerning death. *The Journal of Genetic Psychology*, 73, 3–27.

Najman, J.M., Vance, J.C., Boyle, F., Embleton, G., Foster, B. and Thearle, J. (1993). The impact of child death on marital adjustment. *Social Science and Medicine*, 37, 1005–1010.

Nesse, R.M. (1991). What good is feeling bad? The evolutionary benefits of psychic pain. *The Sciences*, November/December, 30–37.

Neugebauer, R., Kline, J., O'Connor, P., Shrout, P., Johnson, T., Skodol, A., Wicks, J. and Susser, M. (1992a). Determinants of depressive symptoms in the early weeks after miscarriage. *American Journal of Public Health*, 82, 1332–1339.

Neugebauer, R., Kline, J., O'Connor, P., Shrout, P., Johnson, T., Skodol, A., Wicks, J. and Susser, M. (1992b). Depressive symptoms in women in the six months after miscarriage. *American Journal of Obstetrics and Gynecology*, 166, 104–109.

Neugebauer, R., Kline, J., Shrout, P., Skodol, A., O'Connor, P., Geller, P.A., Stein, Z., and and Susser, M. (1997). Major depressive disorder in the six months after miscarriage. *Journal of the American Medical Association*, 277, 383–387.

Nolen-Hoeksema, S. (1987). Sex differences in unipolar depression: evidence and theory. *Psychological Bulletin*, 101, 259–282.

Nolen-Hoeksema, S. (1996). Chewing the cud and other ruminations. In R.S. Wyer Jr (ed.), *Ruminative Thoughts: Advances in Social Cognition Volume IX* (pp. 135–144). Mahwah, NJ: Erlbaum.

Nolen-Hoeksema, S., McBride, A. and Larson, J. (1997). Rumination and psychological distress among bereaved partners. *Journal of Personality and Social Psychology*, 72, 855–862.

Nolen-Hoeksema, S. and Morrow, J. (1991). A prospective study of depression and posttraumatic stress symptoms after a natural disaster: the 1989 Loma Prieta earthquake. *Journal of Personality and Social Psychology*, 61, 115–121.

Nolen-Hoeksema, S., Parker, L.E. and Larson, J. (1994). Ruminative coping with depressed mood following loss. *Journal of Personality and Social Psychology*, 67, 92–104.

O'Brien, T. (1990). *The Things They Carried*. London: HarperCollins (1991 Flamingo edn used for quotes).

Oglethorpe, R.J.L. (1989). Parenting after perinatal bereavement – a review of the literature. *Journal of Reproductive and Infant Psychology*, 7, 227–244.

Osterweis, M., Solomon, F. and Green, M. (1984). *Bereavement: Reactions, Consequences and Care*. Washington, DC: National Academy Press.

Owen, G., Fulton, R. and Markusen, E. (1982–3). Death at a distance: a study of family survivors. *Omega*, 13, 191–225.

Pacholski, R.A. (1986a). Death themes in the visual arts: resources and research opportunities for death educators. *Death Studies*, 10, 59–74.

Pacholski, R.A. (1986b). Death themes in music: resources and research opportunities for death educators. *Death Studies*, 10, 239–263.

Palmer, L. (1987). *Shrapnel in the Heart: Letters and Remembrances from the Vietnam Veterans Memorial*. New York: Random House.

Parkes, C.M. (1964a). Grief as an illness. *New Society*, London, 3, no. 80, 11–12.

Parkes, C.M. (1964b). Effects of bereavement on physical and mental health – a study of the medical records of widows. *British Medical Journal*, 2, 274–279.

Parkes, C.M. (1965). Bereavement and mental illness. *British Journal of Medical Psychology*, 38, 1–16.

Parkes, C.M. (1970). The first year of bereavement: a longitudinal study of the reaction of London widows to the death of their husbands. *Psychiatry*, 33, 444–467.

Parkes, C.M. (1971). Psychosocial transitions: a field for study. *Social Science and Medicine*, 5, 101–115.

Parkes, C.M. (1972). *Bereavement: Studies of Grief in Adult Life*. London and New York: Tavistock. (Penguin edn, 1975.)

Parkes, C.M. (1981). Anticipatory grief. *British Journal of Psychiatry*, 138, 183.

Parkes, C.M. (1985). Bereavement. *British Journal of Psychiatry*, 146, 11–17.

Parkes, C.M. (1986). *Bereavement: Studies of Grief in Adult Life*, 2nd edn London and New York: Tavistock. (Penguin edn, 1986.)

Parkes, C.M. (1988). Bereavement as a psychosocial transition: Processes of adaptation to change. *Journal of Social Issues*, 44, 53–65.

Parkes, C.M. (1995). Attachment and bereavement. In T. Lundin (ed.), *Grief and Bereavement: Proceedings from the Fourth International Conference on Grief and Bereavement in Contemporary Society, Stockholm, 1994*. Stockholm: Swedish Association for Mental Health.

Parkes, C.M. (1996) *Bereavement: Studies of Grief in Adult Life*, 3rd edn. London and New York: Routledge.

Parkes, C.M., Benjamin, B. and Fitzgerald, R.G. (1969). Broken heart: a statistical study of increased mortality among widowers. *British Medical Journal*, part 1, 740–743.

Parkes, C.M. and Brown, R.J. (1972). Health after bereavement: a controlled study of young Boston widows and widowers. *Psychosomatic Medicine*, 34, 499–461.

Parkes, C.M. and Weiss, R.S. (1983). *Recovery from Bereavement*. New York: Basic Books.

Parkes, K.R. (1984). Locus of control, cognitive appraisal, and coping in stressful episodes. *Journal of Personality and Social Psychology*, 46, 655–668.

Pasnau, R.O. and Farash, J.L. (1977). Loss and mourning after abortion. In C.E. Hollingsworth and R.O. Pasnau (ed.), *The Family in Mourning: a Guide for Health Professionals* (pp. 89–94). New York and London: Grune and Stratton.

Pearson, L. (1980) Changes wrought by death. In V.C. Fox and M.H. Quitt (eds), *Loving, Parenting and Dying: The Family Circle in England and America, Past and Present* (pp. 407–421). New York: Psychohistory Press.

Pennebaker, J.W. (1988). Confiding traumatic experiences and health. In S. Fisher and J. Reason (eds), *Handbook of Life Stress, Cognition and Health* (pp. 669–682). Chichester and New York: Wiley.

Pennebaker, J.W. (1997). Writing about emotional experiences as a therapeutic process. *Psychological Science*, 8, 162–166.

Pennebaker, J.W. and Beall, S.K. (1986). Confronting a traumatic event: toward an understanding of inhibition and disease. *Journal of Abnormal Psychology*, 95, 274–281.

Pennebaker, J.W., Kiecolt-Glaser, J.K. and Glaser, R. (1988). Disclosures and immune function: health implications for psychotherapy. *Journal of Consulting and Clinical Psychology*, 56, 239–245.

Pennebaker, J.W., Mayne, T.J. and Francis, M.E. (1997). Linguistic predictors of adaptive bereavement. *Journal of Personality and Social Psychology*, 72, 863–871.

Pennebaker, J.W. and O'Heeron, R.C. (1984). Confiding in others and illness rate among spouses of suicide and accidental-death victims. *Journal of Abnormal Psychology*, 93, 473–476.

Peppers, L.G. (1987–8). Grief and elective abortion: breaking the emotional bond? *Omega*, 18, 1–12.

Peppers, L.G. and Knapp, J. (1980). *Motherhood and Mourning*. New York: Praeger.

Pfeiffer, J.E. (1969). *The Emergence of Man*. New York: Harper and Row.

Pfost, K.S., Stevens, M.J. and Wessels, A.B. (1989). Relation of purpose in life to grief experiences in response to the death of a significant other. *Death Studies*, 13, 371–378.

Pickard, S. (1994). Life and death: the experience of bereavement in South Wales. *Ageing and Society*, 14, 191–217.

Pincus, L. (1976). *Death and the Family: the Importance of Mourning*. London: Faber and Faber.

Pollock, G.H. (1961). Mourning and adaptation. *International Journal of Psychoanalysis*, 42, 341–361.

Pollock, L.A. (1983). *Forgotten Children: Parent–Child Relations from 1500 to 1900*. Cambridge: Cambridge University Press.

Ponzetti, J.J. (1992). Bereaved families: a comparison of parents' and grandparents' reactions to the death of a child. *Omega*, 25, 63–71.

Ponzetti, J.J. and Johnson, M.A. (1991). The forgotten grievers: grandparents' reactions to the death of grandchildren. *Death Studies*, 15, 157–167.

Pope, A. (1714). 'The rape of the lock'. In A.W. Ward (ed.), *The Poetical Works of Alexander Pope*. London: Macmillan, 1964.

Porritt, D. and Bartrop, R.W. (1985). The independence of pleasant and unpleasant affect: the effects of bereavement. *Australian Journal of Psychology*, 37, 205–213.

Porter, L.S. and Stone, A.A. (1995). Are there really gender differences in coping? A reconsideration of previous data and results from a daily study. *Journal of Social and Clinical Psychology*, 14, 184–202.

Posavac, E.J. and Miller, T.Q. (1990). Some problems caused by not having a conceptual foundation for health research: an illustration from studies of the psychological effects of abortion. *Psychology and Health*, 5, 13–23.

Potvin, L., Lasker, J. and Toedter, L. (1989). Measuring grief: a short version of the Perinatal Grief Scale. *Journal of Psychopathology and Behavioral Assessment*, 11, 29–45.

Powers, L.E. and Wampold, B.E. (1994). Cognitive-behavioral factors in adjustment to adult bereavement. *Death Studies*, 18, 1–24.

Powers, W.T. (1978). Quantitative analysis of purposive systems: some spadework at the foundations of scientific psychology. *Psychological Review*, 85, 417–435.

Pratt, C.C., Walker, A.J. and Wood, B.L. (1992). Bereavement among former care-givers to elderly mothers. *Family Relations*, 41, 278–283.

Price, J.S. (1972). Genetic and phylogenetic aspects of mood variation. *International Journal of Mental Health*, 1, 124–144.

Prigerson, H.G., Frank, E., Kasl, S.V., Reynolds, C.F. III, Anderson, B., Zubenko, G.S., Houck, P.R., George, C.J. and Kupfer, D.J. (1994). Complicated grief and bereavement-related depression as distinct disorders: Preliminary empirical validation in elderly bereaved spouses. *American Journal of Psychiatry,* 152, 22–30.

Prigerson, H.G., Maciejewski, P.K., Reynolds, C.F. III, Bierhals, A.J., Newsom, J.T., Faskzka, A., Frank, E., Doman, J. and Miller, M. (1995). Inventory of complicated grief: a scale to measure maladaptive symptoms of loss. *Psychiatry Research,* 59, 65–79.

Prigerson, H.G., Bierhals, A.J., Kasl, S.V., Reynolds, C.F. III, Shear, M.K., Newsom, J.T. and Jacobs, S. (1996a). Complicated grief as a disorder distinct from bereavement-related depression and anxiety: a replication study. *American Journal of Psychiatry,* 153, 1484–1486.

Prigerson, H.G., Shear, M.K., Newsom, J.T., Frank, E., Reynolds, C.F. III, Maciejewski, P.K., Houck, P.R., Bierhals, A.J. and Kupfer, D.J. (1996b). Anxiety among widowed elders: is it distinct from depression and grief? *Anxiety*, 2, 1–12.

Prigerson, H.G., Bierhals, A.J., Kasl, S.V., Reynolds, C.F. III, Shear, M.K., Day, N., Beery, L.C., Newsom, J.T. and Jacobs, S. (1997a). Traumatic grief as a risk factor for mental and physical morbidity. *American Journal of Psychiatry,* 154, 616–623.

Prigerson, H.G., Shear, M.K., Frank, E., Beery, L.C., Silberman, R., Prigerson, J. and Reynolds, C.F. III. (1997b). Traumatic grief: a case of loss-induced trauma. *American Journal of Psychiatry,* 154, 1003–1009.

Prigerson, H.G., Shear, M.K., Bierhals, A.J., Pilkonis, P.A., Wolfson, L., Hall, M., Zonarich, D.L. and Reynolds, C.F. III (1997c). Case histories of complicated grief. *Omega*, 35, 9–24.

Ptacek, J.T., Smith, R.E. and Dodge, K.L. (1994). Gender differences in coping with stress: when stressor and appraisals do not differ. *Personality and Social Psychology Bulletin*, 20, 421–430.

Puddifoot, J.E. and Johnson, M.P. (1997). The legitimacy of grieving: the partner's experience at miscarriage. *Social Science and Medicine*, 45, 837–845.

Quiller-Couch, A. (ed.) (1919). *The Oxford Book of English Verse*. Oxford: Clarendon Press.

Rachman, S. (1974). *The Meanings of Fear*. Harmondsworth, UK: Penguin.

Rajaram, S.S., Garrity, T.F., Stallones, L. and Marx, M.B. (1993). Bereavement – loss of a pet and loss of a human. *Anthrozoös*, 6, 8–16.

Ramsay, R.W. (1977). Behavioural approaches to bereavement. *Behaviour Research and Therapy*, 15, 131–135.

Rando, T.A. (1983). An investigation of grief and adaptation in parents whose children have died from cancer. *Journal of Pediatric Psychology*, 8, 3–20.

Rando, T.A. (1992–3). The increasing prevalence of complicated mourning: the onslaught is just beginning. *Omega*, 26, 43–59.

Range, L.M. and Niss, N.M. (1990). Long-term bereavement from suicide, homicide, accidents and natural deaths. *Death Studies*, 14, 423–433.

Raphael, B. (1983). *The Anatomy of Bereavement*. New York: Basic Books.

Raphael, B. (1995). The measure of grief. In T. Lundin (ed.), *Grief and Bereavement: Proceedings from the Fourth International Conference on Grief and Bereavement in Contemporary Society, Stockholm, 1994.* Stockholm: Swedish Association for Mental Health.

Reason, J. (1979). Actions not as planned: the price of automatization. In G. Underwood and R. Stevens (eds), *Aspects of Consciousness, Volume 1, Psychological Issues* (pp. 67–89). London and New York: Academic Press.

Reason, J. (1984). Lapses of attention in everyday life. In R. Parasuraman and D.R. Davies (eds), *Varieties of Attention* (pp. 515–549). London and New York: Academic Press.

Reed, M.D. (1993). Sudden death and bereavement outcomes: the impact of resources on grief symptomatology and detachment. *Suicide and Life Threatening Behavior*, 23, 204–220.

Rees, W.D. (1971). The hallucinations of widowhood. *British Medical Journal*, 4, 37–41.

Regalski, J.M. and Gaulin, S.J.C. (1993). Whom are Mexican infants said to resemble? Monitoring and fostering paternal confidence in the Yucatan. *Ethology and Sociobiology*, 14, 97–113.

Reite, M., Kaemingk, K. and Boccia, M.L. (1989). Maternal separation in bonnet monkey infants: altered attachment and social support. *Child Development*, 60, 473–480.

Reite, M., Short, R., Seiler, C. and Pauley, J.D. (1981). Attachment, loss and depression. *Journal of Child Psychology and Psychiatry*, 22, 141–169.

Remondet, J.H., Hansson, R.O., Rule, B. and Winfrey, G. (1987). Rehearsal for widowhood. *Journal of Social and Clinical Psychology*, 5, 285–297.

Reynolds, S. (1992). Survivor of the velvet revolution. *The Observer (London)*, 12 January.

Rieu, E.V. (trans. and ed.) (1950). *Homer, The Iliad*. Harmondsworth: Penguin.

Ritchey, R.L. and Hennessy, M.B. (1987). Cortisol and behavioral responses to separation in mother and infant guinea pigs. *Behavioral and Neural Biology*, 48, 1–12.

Roberts, J.E. and Gotlib, I.H. (1997). Lifetime episodes of dysphoria: gender, early childhood loss and personality. *British Journal of Clinical Psychology*, 36, 195–208.

Robertson, A. (1967). *Requiem: Music of Mourning and Consolation*. London: Cassell.

Rogers, M.P. and Reich, P. (1988). On the health consequences of bereavement. *The New England Journal of Medicine*, 319, 510–512.

Rojo, A. (1991). Corpses seemed shrunk by the heat of bunker fire. *The Guardian* (London), 14th Feb., p. 1.

Roll, S., Millen, L. and Backlund, B. (1986). Solomon's mothers: mourning in mothers who relinquish their children for adoption. In T.A. Rando (ed.), *Parental Loss of a Child* (pp. 257–268). Champaign, IL: Research Press.

Rosen, H. (1984–5). Prohibitions against mourning in childhood sibling loss. *Omega*, 15, 307–316.

Rosenblatt, P.C. (1983). *Bitter Bitter Tears: Nineteenth-Century Diarists and Twentieth-Century Grief Theories*. Minneapolis: University of Minnesota Press.

Rosenblatt, P.C. and Burns, L.H. (1986). Long-term effects of perinatal loss. *Journal of Family Issues*, 7, 237–253.

Rosenblatt, P.C., Walsh, R. and Jackson, D.A. (1972). Coping with anger and aggression in mourning. *Omega*, 3, 271–284.

Rosenblatt, P.C., Walsh, R. and Jackson, D.A. (1976). *Grief and Mourning in Cross-cultural Perspective*. Human Relations Area File Press.

Rosenbloom, C.A. and Whittington, F.J. (1993). The effects of bereavement on eating behaviors and nutrient intakes in elderly widowed persons. *Journal of Gerontology*, 48, S223–S229.

Rosenthal, R. (1979). The 'file drawer' problem and tolerance for null results. *Psychological Bulletin*, 86, 638–641.

Rosenthal, R. (1984). *Meta-Analytic Procedures for Social Research*. Beverly Hills, CA and London: Sage.

Rosenthal, R. (1991). Meta-analysis: a review. *Psychosomatic Medicine*, 53, 247–271.

Rosenzweig, A., Prigerson, H., Miller, M.D. and Reynolds, C.F. III (1997). Bereavement and late-life depression: grief and its complications in the elderly. *Annual Review of Medicine*, 48, 421–428.

Roth, S. and Lebowitz, L. (1988). The experience of sexual trauma. *Journal of Traumatic Stress*, 1, 79–107.

Rothbard, J.C. and Shaver, P.R. (1994). Continuity of attachment across the life span. The structure and function of adult attachment. In M.B. Sperling and W.H. Berman (eds), *Attachment in Adults: Clinical and Developmental Perspectives* (pp. 31–71). New York: Guilford Press.

Rotter, J.B. (1966). Generalized expectancies for internal versus external control of reinforcement. *Psychological Monographs*, 80, no. 1 (whole no. 609).

Rubin, L. (1985). *Just Friends: The Role of Friendship in Our Lives*. New York and London: Harper and Row.

Rubin, S. [S.] (1981). A two-track model of bereavement: theory and application in research. *American Journal of Orthopsychiatry*, 51, 101–109.

Rubin, S.S. (1989–90). Death of the future? An outcome study of bereaved parents in Israel. *Omega*, 20, 323–339.

Rubin, S.S. (1991–2). Adult child loss and the two-track model of bereavement. *Omega*, 24, 183–202.

Rubin, Z. and Peplau, L.A. (1975). Who believes in a just world? *Journal of Social Issues*, 31, 65–89.

Ruby, J. (1988–9). Portraying the dead. *Omega*, 19, 1–20.

Rush, B. (1794). *An Account of the Bilious Remitting Yellow Fever as it Appeared in the City of Philadelphia in the Year 1793*. Philadelphia: Thomas Dobson.

Rush, B. (1812). *Medical Inquiries and Observations Upon the Diseases of the Mind*. Philadelphia: Kimber and Richardson.

Rushton, J.P. (1989). Genetic similarity, human altrusim, and group selection. *Behavioral and Brain Sciences*, 12, 503–559 (including commentaries).

Rutter, M. (1972). *Maternal Deprivation Reassessed*. Harmondsworth, UK: Penguin.

Rutter, M. (1979). Maternal Deprivation 1972–1978: new findings, new concepts, new approaches. *Child Development* 50, 283–305.

Rynearson, E.K. (1987). Psychological adjustment to unnatural dying. In S. Zisook (ed.), *Biopsychosocial Aspects of Bereavement* (pp. 77–93). Washington, DC: American Psychiatric Press.

Sable, P. (1989). Attachment, anxiety and loss of a husband. *American Journal of Orthopsychiatry*, 59, 500–506.

Sable, P. (1991). Attachment, loss of a spouse, and grief in elderly adults. *Omega*, 23, 129–142.

Sanders, C.M. (1979–80). A comparison of adult bereavement in the death of a spouse, child and parent. *Omega*, 10, 303–322.

Sanders, C.M. (1980). Comparison of younger and older spouses in bereavement outcome. *Omega*, 11, 217–232.

Sanders, C.M. (1989). *Grief: The Mourning After: Dealing with Adult Bereavement*. New York and Chichester: Wiley.

Sanders, C.M., Mauger, P.A. and Strong, P.N. (1985). *A Manual for the Grief Experience Inventory*. Palo Alto, CA: Consulting Psychologist Press.

Sapolsky, R.M. (1994). *Why Zebras Don't Get Ulcers: a Guide to Stress, Stress-related Diseases, and Coping*. New York: W.H. Freeman.

Sargant, W. and Slater, E. (1940). Acute war neuroses. *The Lancet*, July 6th, 2, 1–2.

Saum, L.O. (1975). Death in the popular mind of pre-Civil War America. In D. Stannard (ed.), *Death in America* (pp. 30–48). Pittsburg, PA: University of Pennsylvania Press.

Schaller, C.B. (1963). *The Mountain Gorilla*. Chicago: University of Chicago Press.

Scharlach, A.E. and Fredriksen, K.I. (1993). Reactions to the death of a parent during middle life. *Omega*, 27, 307–319.

Schatz, B.D. (1986). Grief of fathers. In T.A. Rando (ed.), *Parental Loss of a Child* (pp. 303–314). Champaign, IL: Research Press.

Scheper-Hughes, N. (1992). *Death Without Weeping: the Violence of Everyday Life in Brazil*. Berkeley, CA: University of California Press.

Schleifer, S.J., Keller, S.E., Camerino, M., Thornton, J.C. and Stein, M. (1983). Suppression of lymphocyte stimulation following bereavement. *Journal of the American Medical Association*, 250, 374–377.

Schlesinger, B. and Macrae, A. (1971). The widow and widower and remarriage: selected findings. *Omega*, 2, 10–18.

Schneider, D.S., Sledge, P.A., Shuchter, S.R. and Zisook, S. (1996). Dating and remarriage over the first two years of widowhood. *Annals of Clinical Psychiatry*, 8, 51–57.

Schut, H.A.W., Stroebe, M.S., Stroebe, W., van den Bout, J. and de Keijser, J. (1994). Are accepted ways of coping with loss really efficacious? Presented at Fourth International Conference on Grief and Bereavement in Contemporary Society, Stockholm, June 12–16.

Schut, H.A.W., Stroebe, M.S., van den Bout, J. and de Keijser, J. (1997). Intervention for the bereaved: gender differences in the efficacy of two counselling programmes. *British Journal of Clinical Psychology*, 36, 63–72.

Schwab, R. (1992). Effects of a child's death on the marital relationship: a preliminary study. *Death Studies*, 16, 141–154.

Schwab, R. (1996). Gender differences in parental grief. *Death Studies*, 20, 103–113.

Schwartzberg, S.S. (1992). AIDS-related bereavement among gay men: the inadequacy of current theories of grief. *Psychotherapy*, 29, 422–429.

Schwartzberg, S.S. and Janoff-Bulman, R. (1991). Grief and the search for meaning: exploring the assumptive worlds of bereaved college students. *Journal of Social and Clinical Psychology*, 10, 270–288.

Schwarzer, R. and Weiner, B. (1991). Stigma controlling and coping as predictors of emotions and social support. *Journal of Social and Personal Relations*, 8, 133–140.

Seay, B., Hansen, E. and Harlow, H.F. (1962). Mother–infant separation in monkeys. *Journal of Child Psychology and Psychiatry*, 3, 123–132.

Segal, N.L. (1988). Cooperation, competition, and altruism in human twinships: a sociobiological approach. In K.B. MacDonald (ed.), *Sociobiological Perspectives on Human Development* (pp. 168–206). New York: Springer-Verlag.

Segal, N.L. (1993). Twin, sibling and adoption methods: tests of evolutionary hypotheses. *American Psychologist*, 48, 943–956.

Segal, N.L. and Bouchard, T.J. (1993). Grief intensity following the loss of a twin and other relatives: test of kinship hypotheses. *Human Biology*, 65, 87–105.

Segal, N.L., Bouchard, T.J., Welson, S.M. and Gitlin, D.G. (1993). Grief for deceased twins exceeds grief for other relatives: update and new findings. Paper presented at APS, Chicago, June.

Segal, N.L., Welson, S.M., Bouchard, T.J. and Gitlin, D.G. (1995). Comparative grief experiences of bereaved twins and other bereaved relatives. *Personality and Individual Differences*, 18, 525–534.

Seibel, M. and Graves, W.L. (1980). The psychological implications of spontaneous abortion. *The Journal of Reproductive Medicine*, 25, 161–165.

Seitz, P. and Warrwick, L. (1974). Perinatal death: the grieving mother. *American Journal of Nursing,* 74, 2028–2033.

Seligman, M.E.P. (1975). *Helplessness*. San Francisco: Freeman.

Serpell, J.A. (1986). *In the Company of Animals*. Oxford: Blackwell.

Seyfarth, R. and Cheney, D. (1992). Inside the mind of a monkey. *New Scientist*, 133, 25–29.

Shackleton, C.H. (1984). The psychology of grief: a review. *Advances in Behaviour Research and Therapy*, 6, 153–205.

Shakespeare, W. (1623a). *Macbeth*. 1925 edn, reprint of 1902 new edn, ed. by A.W. Verity. Cambridge: Cambridge University Press.

Shakespeare, W. (1623b). *Julius Caesar*. 1923 edn, reprint of 1900 5th edn, ed. by A.W. Verity. Cambridge: Cambridge University Press.

Shand, A.F. (1914). *The Foundations of Character*. London: Macmillan.

Shand, A.F. (1920). *The Foundations of Character*, 2nd edn. London: Macmillan.

Shanfield, S.B. and Swain, B.J. (1984). Death of adult children in traffic accidents. *Journal of Nervous and Mental Disease*, 172, 533–538.

Shaver, K.G. (1970). Defensive attribution: effects of severity and relevance on the responsibility assigned for an accident. *Journal of Personality and Social Psychology*, 14, 101–113.

Shay, J. (1991). Learning about combat stress from Homer's *Iliad*. *Journal of Traumatic Stress*, 4, 561–579.

Shelley, P.B. (1821). 'Adonais'. In T. Hutchinson (ed.), *Shelley: Poetical Works* (1905 edn). London and New York: Oxford University Press.

Shuchter, S.R. (1986). *Dimensions of Grief: Adjusting to the Death of a Spouse*. San Francisco and New York: Jossey-Bass.

Shuchter, S.R. and Zisook, S. (1988). Widowhood: the continuing relationship with the dead spouse. *Bulletin of the Menninger Clinic*, 52, 269–279.

Shuchter, S.R. and Zisook, S. (1993). The course of normal grief. In M.S. Stroebe, W. Stroebe and R.O. Hansson (eds), *Handbook of Bereavement: Theory, Research and Intervention* (pp. 23–43). New York: Cambridge University Press.

Siegel, J.M. and Kuykendall, D.H. (1990). Loss, widowhood, and psychological distress among the elderly. *Journal of Consulting and Clinical Psychology*, 58, 519–524.

Silver, R.L., Boon, C. and Stones, M.H. (1983). Searching for meaning in misfortune: making sense of incest. *Journal of Social Issues*, 39, 81–101.

Silver, R.L. and Wortman, C.B. (1980). Coping with undesirable life events. In J. Garber and M.E.P. Seligman (eds), *Human Helplessness: Theory and Application* (pp. 279–375). New York: Academic Press.

Silverman, P.R. and Worden, J.W. (1993). Children's reactions to the death of a parent. In M.S. Stroebe, W. Stroebe and R.O. Hansson (eds), *Handbook of Bereavement: Theory, Research and Intervention* (pp. 300–316). New York: Cambridge University Press.

Silverman, S.M. (1997). Justice Joseph Story and death in early 19th-century America. *Death Studies*, 21, 397–416.

Simpson, J.A. (1990). Influence of attachment styles on romantic relationships. *Journal of Personality and Social Psychology*, 59, 971–980.

Singer, J.L. (1978). Experimental studies of daydreaming and the stream of thought. In K.S. Pope and J.L. Singer (eds), *The Stream of Consciousness: Scientific Investigations into the Flow of Human Experience* (pp. 187–223). New York and London: Plenum.

Singer, J.L. and Kolligian, J. (1987). Personality: developments in the study of private experience. *Annual Review of Psychology*, 38, 533–574.

Singh, B. and Raphael, B. (1981). Postdisaster morbidity of the bereaved: a possible role for preventative psychiatry? *Journal of Nervous and Mental Disease*, 169, 203–212.

Sklar, F. (1991–2). Grief as a family affair: property rights, grief rights, and the exclusion of close friends as survivors. *Omega*, 24, 109–121.

Sklar, F. and Hartley, S.F. (1990). Close friends as survivors: bereavement patterns in a 'hidden' population. *Omega*, 21, 103–112.

Slade, P.D. and Benthall, R.P. (1988). *Sensory Deception: A Scientific Analysis of Hallucinations*. London: Croom-Helm.

Slater, E.P. (1972). Some aspects of exploration and learning in three strains of mice. M.Phil Dissertation, University of Sussex.

Smart, L.S. (1993). Parental bereavement in Anglo-American history. *Omega*, 28, 49–61.

Smith, A.C. and Borgers, S.B. (1988–9). Parental grief response to perinatal death. *Omega*, 19, 203–214.

Smith, K.R. and Zick, C.D. (1996). Risk of mortality following widowhood: age and sex differences by mode of death. *Social Biology*, 43, 59–71.

Smith-Rosenberg, C. (1975). The female world of love and ritual: relations between women in nineteenth-century America. *Signs*, 1, 1–29.

Smuts, B. (1995). The evolutionary origins of patriarchy. *Human Nature*, 6, 1–32.

Speckhard, A. (1997). Traumatic death in pregnancy: the significance and meaning of attachment. In C.R. Figley, B.E. Bride and N. Mazza (eds), *Death and Trauma: the Traumatology of Grieving* (pp. 67–100). Washington, DC and London: Taylor and Francis.

Speckhard, A. and Rue, V.N. (1992). Postabortion syndrome: an emerging public health concern. *Journal of Social Issues*, 48, 95–119.

Speece, M.W. and Brent, S.B. (1984). Children's understanding of death: a review of three components of a death concept. *Child Development*, 55, 1671–1686.

Spencer, A.J. (1982). *Death in Ancient Egypt*. Harmondsworth, UK: Penguin.

Spencer, N. (1992). He was wonderful tonight. *The Observer* (London), 9th Feb., p. 59.

Spencer-Booth, Y. and Hinde, R.A. (1971a). Effects of 6 days' separation from mother on 18- to 32-week old rhesus monkeys. *Animal Behaviour*, 19, 174–191.

Spencer-Booth, Y. and Hinde, R.A. (1971b). The effects of 13 days' maternal separation on infant rhesus monkeys compared to those of shorter and repeated separations. *Animal Behaviour*, 19, 595–605.

Spenser, E. (1596). *The Faerie Queene. Books I–III* (1909 edn, ed. by J.C. Smith). Oxford: Clarendon Press.

Spiegelman, V. and Kastenbaum, R. (1990). Pet rest memorial. Is eternity running out of time? *Omega*, 21, 1–13.

Squire, J.C. (1921). 'To a bull-dog'. In *An Anthology of Modern Verse*. London: Methuen (4th edn).

Stambrook, M. and Parker, K.C.H. (1987). The development of the concept of death in childhood: a review of the literature. *Merrill Palmer Quarterly*, 33, 133–157.

Steele, R.L. (1977). Dying, death, and bereavement among the Maya Indians of Mesoamerica: a study in anthropological psychology. *American Psychologist*, 32, 1060–1068.

Stern, K., Williams, G.M. and Prados, M. (1951). Grief reactions in later life. *American Journal of Psychiatry*, 108, 289–294.

Stewart, C.S., Thrush, J.C. and Paulus, G. (1989). Disenfranchised bereavement and loss of a companion animal: implications for caring communities. In K. Doka (ed.), *Disenfranchised Grief: Recognizing Hidden Sorrow* (pp. 147–159). Lexington, MA: Lexington Books (D.C. Heath and Co.).

Stillon, J.M. (1985). *Death and the Sexes*. Washington and London: Hemisphere Publishing Corporation.

Stone, L. (1977). *The Family, Sex and Marriage in England 1500–1800*. New York: Harper and Row.

Stroebe, M.[S] (1992–3). Coping with bereavement: a review of the grief work hypothesis. *Omega*, 26, 19–42.

Stroebe, M.S. (1994a). The broken heart phenomenon: an examination of the mortality of bereavement. *Journal of Community and Applied Social Psychology*, 4, 47–61.

Stroebe, M.S. (1994b). Helping the bereaved to come to terms with loss: what does bereavement research have to offer? Presented at Conference on Bereavement and Counselling, St George's Hospital Medical School, 25 Mar.

Stroebe, M.[S], Gergen, M., Gergen, K.J. and Stroebe, W. (1992). Broken hearts or broken bonds: love and death in historical perspective. *American Psychologist*, 47, 1205–1212.

Stroebe, M.S. and Schut, H.A.W. (1993). Differential patterns of coping with bereavement between widows and widowers. Presented at British Psychological Society Social Psychology Section Conference, Jesus College, Oxford, 22–24 Sept.

Stroebe, M.S., and Schut, H.A.W. (1994). The dual process model of coping with bereavement. Presented at Fourth International Conference on Grief and Bereavement in Contemporary Society, Stockholm, 12–16 June.

Stroebe, M.S., and Schut, H.A.W. (1995). The dual process model of coping with loss. Presented at the International Work Group on Death, Dying and Bereavement, St Catherine's College, Oxford, UK, 26–29 June.

Stroebe, M.S. and Stroebe, W. (1983). Who suffers more? Sex differences in health risks of the widowed. *Psychological Bulletin,* 93, 279–301.

Stroebe, M.S. and Stroebe, W. (1989–90). Who participates in bereavement research? A review and empirical study. *Omega,* 20, 1–29.

Stroebe, M.[S.] and Stroebe, W. (1990). Does 'grief work' work? A review and empirical evidence. *Reports from the Psychological Institute, University of Tübingen,* 31.

Stroebe, M.[S.] and Stroebe, W. (1991). Does 'grief work' work? *Journal of Consulting and Clinical Psychology,* 59, 479–482.

Stroebe, M.S. and Stroebe, W. (1993). The mortality of bereavement: a review. In M.S. Stroebe, W. Stroebe and R.O. Hansson (eds), *Handbook of Bereavement: Theory, Research and Intervention* (pp. 175–195). New York: Cambridge University Press.

Stroebe, M.S., Stroebe, W., Gergen, K.J. and Gergen, M. (1981–2). The broken heart: reality or myth? *Omega,* 12, 87–106.

Stroebe, M.[S], Stroebe, W. and Hansson, R.O. (1988). Bereavement research: an historical introduction. *Journal of Social Issues,* 44, 1–18.

Stroebe, M.S., van den Bout, J. and Schut, H.A.W. (1994). Myths and misconceptions about bereavement: the opening of a debate. *Omega,* 29, 187–203.

Stroebe, W. and Stroebe, M.S. (1984). When love dies: an integration of attraction and bereavement research. In H. Tajfel (ed.), *The Social Dimension: European Developments in Social Psychology,* Vol. 1 (pp. 250–281). Cambridge and New York: Cambridge University Press.

Stroebe, W. and Stroebe, M.S. (1987a). *Bereavement and Health.* Cambridge and New York: Cambridge University Press.

Stroebe, W. and Stroebe, M.[S.] (1987b). Bereavement as a stressful life event: a paradigm for research on the stress–health relationship. In G.R. Semin and B. Krahé (eds), *Issues in Contemporary German Social Psychology: History, Theories and Application* (pp. 258–272). London and Beverly Hills, CA: Sage.

Stroebe, W. and Stroebe, M.S. (1992). Bereavement and health: processes of adjusting to the loss of a partner. In L. Montada, S-H. Filipp and M.J. Lerner (eds), *Life Crises and Experiences of Loss in Adulthood* (pp. 3–22). Hillsdale, NJ: Erlbaum.

Stroebe, W. and Stroebe, M.S. (1993). Determinants of adjustment to bereavement in younger widows and widowers. In M.S. Stroebe, W. Stroebe and R.O. Hansson (eds), *Handbook of Bereavement: Theory, Research and Intervention* (pp. 208–226). New York: Cambridge University Press.

Stroebe, W. and Stroebe, M.S. (1994). The Tübingen longitudinal study of bereavement: what lessons have we learnt? Presented at Fourth International Conference on Grief and Bereavement in Contemporary Society, Stockholm, 12–16 June.

Stroebe, W., Stroebe, M. and Domittner, G. (1988). Individual and situational differences in recovery from bereavement: a risk group identified. *Journal of Social Issues,* 44, 143–158.

Stylianos, S.K. and Vachon, M. (1993). The role of social support in bereavement. In M.S. Stroebe, W. Stroebe and R.O. Hansson (eds), *Handbook of Bereavement: Theory, Research and Intervention* (pp. 397–410). New York: Cambridge University Press.

Tait, R. and Silver, R.C. (1989). Coming to terms with major negative life events. In J.S. Uleman and J.A. Bargh (eds), *Unintended Thought* (pp. 351–382). New York: Guilford Press.

Talbot, K. (1996–7). Mothers now childless: survival after the death of an only child. *Omega,* 34, 177–189.

Taylor, S.E. (1991). Asymmetrical effects of positive and negative events: the mobilization–minimization hypothesis. *Psychological Bulletin*, 110, 67–85.

Taylor, S.E. and Brown, J.D. (1988). Illusions and well-being: a social psychological perspective on mental health. *Psychological Bulletin*, 103, 193–210.

Taylor, S.E. and Brown, J.D. (1994). Positive illusions and well-being revisited: separating fact from fiction. *Psychological Bulletin*, 116, 21–27.

Teasdale, J.D. (1989a).Working memory and the stream of consciousness: daydreaming, depression and distraction. Paper presented to British Psychological Society Annual Conference, St Andrews, 31 March–3 April.

Teasdale, J.D. (1989b). Daydreaming, depression and distraction. *The Psychologist*, 2, 189–90.

Teasdale, J.D., Dritschel, B.H., Taylor, M.J., Proctor, L., Lloyd, C.A., Nimmo-Smith, I. and Baddeley, A.D. (1995). Stimulus-independent thought depends on central executive resources. *Memory and Cognition*, 23, 551–559.

Teasdale, J.D., Proctor, L., Lloyd, C.A. and Baddeley, A.D. (1993). Working memory and stimulus-independent thought: effects of memory load and presentation rate. *European Journal of Cognitive Psychology*, 5, 417–433.

Tennant, C., Bebbington, P. and Hurry, J. (1980). Parental death in childhood and risk of adult depressive disorder: a review. *Psychological Medicine*, 10, 289–299.

Tennes, K., Downey, K. and Vernadakis, A. (1977). Urinary cortisol excretion rates and anxiety in normal 1-year-old infants. *Psychosomatic Medicine*, 39, 178–187.

Tennyson, A. (1847). 'The Princess'. Reprinted in: J.D. Jump (ed.), *Alfred Tennyson: In Memoriam and Other Poems*. London: J.M. Dent and Sons, 1974.

Tennyson, A. (1850). 'In Memoriam A.H.H'. Reprinted in: J.D. Jump (ed.), *Alfred Tennyson: In Memoriam and Other Poems*. London: J.M. Dent and Sons, 1974.

Theut, S.K., Pedersen, F.A., Zaslow, M.J., Cain, R.L., Rabinovich, B.A. and Morihisa, J.M. (1989). Perinatal loss and parental bereavement. *American Journal of Psychiatry* 146, 635–639.

Thomas, V., Striegel, P., Dudley, D., Wilkins, J. and Gibson, D. (1997). Parental grief of a perinatal loss: a comparison of individual and relationship variables. *Journal of Personal and Interpersonal Loss*, 2, 167–187.

Thompson, E.H. Jr and Pleck, J.H. (1986). The structure of male role norms. *American Behavioral Scientist*, 29, 531–543.

Thompson, J. (1985). *Psychological Aspects of Nuclear War*. Leicester: British Psychological Society.

Thompson, L.W., Gallagher, D., Cover, H., Gilewski, M. and Peterson, J. (1989). Effects of bereavement on symptoms of psychopathology in older men and women. In D.A. Lund (ed.), *Older Bereaved Spouses: Research with Practical Implications* (pp. 17–24). New York: Hemisphere.

Thompson, S.C. (1991). The search for meaning following a stroke. *Basic and Applied Social Psychology*, 12, 81–96.

Thornhill, R. and Thornhill, N.W. (1989). The evolution of psychological pain. In R.W. Bell and N.J. Bell (eds), *Sociobiology and the Social Sciences* (pp. 73–103). Lubbock, TX: Texas Technical University Press.

Thornton, G., Robertson, D.U. and Mlecko, M.L. (1991). Disenfranchised grief and evaluations of social support by college students. *Death Studies*, 15, 355–362.

Tinbergen, N. (1942). An objectivistic study of the innate behaviour of animals. *Bibliotheca Biotheoretica, Series D*, 1, 39–98.

Tinbergen, N. (1951). *The Study of Instinct*. London: Oxford University Press.

Tinbergen, N. (1953). *Social Behaviour in Animals*. London: Methuen.

Tinbergen, N. (1963). On the aims and methods of ethology. *Zeitschrift für Tier-psychologie*, 20, 410–413.

Tizard, B. (1977). *Adoption: A Second Chance*. London: Open Books.

Tizard, J. and Tizard, B. (1974). The institution as an environment for development. In M.P.M. Richards (ed.), *The Integration of the Child into a Social World* (pp. 137–152). London and New York: Cambridge University Press.

Tobach, E. (1970). Notes on the comparative psychology of grief. In B. Schoenberg, A.C. Carr, D. Peretz and A.H. Kutscher (eds), *Loss and Grief: Psychological Management in Medical Practice* (pp. 347–354). New York and London: Columbia University Press.

Toedter, L.J., Lasker, J.N. and Alhadeff, J.M. (1988). The Perinatal Grief Scale: development and initial validation. *American Journal of Orthopsychiatry*, 58, 435–449.

Tooley, K. (1975). The choice of a surviving sibling as 'scapegoat' in some cases of maternal bereavement. *Journal of Child Psychology and Psychiatry*, 16, 331–339.

Triandis, H. (1995). *Individualism and Collectivism*. Boulder, CO: Westview.

Trivers, R.L. (1971). The evolution of reciprocal altruism. *Quarterly Review of Biology*, 46, 35–57.

Trivers, R. (1972). Parental investment and sexual selection. In B.B. Campbell (ed.), *Sexual Selection and the Descent of Man* (pp. 136–179). Chicago: Aldine.

Trivers, R. (1974). Parent–offspring conflict. *American Zoologist*, 14, 249–264.

Trivers, R. and Willard, D. (1973). Natural selection of parental ability to vary the sex-ratio of offspring. *Science*, 179, 90–91.

Twain, M. (1893). 'The Californian's Tale'. Reprinted in: C. Neider (ed.), *The Complete Short Stories of Mark Twain* (pp. 266–272). New York: Doubleday, 1957.

Ulmer, A., Range, L.M. and Smith, P.C. (1991). Purpose in life: a moderator of recovery from bereavement. *Omega*, 23, 279–289.

Umberson, D., Wortman, C.B. and Kessler, R.C. (1992). Widowhood and depression: explaining long-term gender differences in vulnerability. *Journal of Health and Social Behavior*, 33, 10–24.

Vachon, M.L.S., Sheldon, A.R., Lancee, W.J., Lyall, W.A.L., Rogers, J. and Freeman, S.J.J. (1982a). Correlates of enduring stress patterns following bereavement: social network, life situation and personality. *Psychological Medicine*, 12, 783–788.

Vachon, M.L.S., Rogers, J., Lyall, W.A., Lancee, W.J., Sheldon, A.R. and Freeman, S.J.J. (1982b). Predictors and correlates of adaptation to conjugal bereavement. *American Journal of Psychiatry*, 139, 998–1002.

van den Bout, J., Schut, H.A.W. and Stroebe, M. (1994). 'Myths of coping with loss': are they endorsed? Presented at Fourth International Conference on Grief and Bereavement in Contemporary Society, Stockholm, 12–16 June.

van der Hart, O. and Goossens, F.A. (1987). Leave-taking rituals in mourning therapy. *Israeli Journal of Psychiatry and Related Sciences*, 24: 87–98.

van der Wal, J. (1988). *De Nasleep van Suicides en Dodelijke verkeersongevallen*. Leiden: DSWO Press.

van der Wal, J. (1989–90). The aftermath of suicide: a review of empirical evidence. *Omega*, 20, 149–171.

van der Wal, J., Cleiren, M.P.H.D., Diekstra, R.F.W. and Morotz, B.J.M. (1988). The early impact of bereavement after suicide or fatal traffic accident. In S.D. Platt and N. Kreitman (eds), *Current Research on Suicide and Parasuicide* (pp. 214–225). Edinburgh: Edinburgh University Press.

van Eerdewegh, M.M., Bieri, M.D., Parrilla, R.H. and Clayton, P.J. (1982). The bereaved child. *British Journal of Psychiatry*, 140, 23–29.

van Eerdewegh, M.M., Clayton, P.J. and van Eerdewegh, P. (1982). The bereaved child: variables influencing early psychopathology. *British Journal of Psychiatry*, 147, 188–194.

van Lawick-Goodall, J. (1968). The behaviour of free-living chimpanzees in the Gombe stream reserve. *Animal Behaviour Monographs*, 1, 161–311.

van Zandt, S., Mou, R. and Abbott, D. (1989). Mental and physical health of rural bereaved and nonbereaved elders: a longitudinal study. In D.A. Lund (ed.), *Older Bereaved Spouses: Research with Practical Implications* (pp. 25–35). New York: Hemisphere.

Videka-Sherman, L. (1982). Coping with death of a child: a study over time. *American Journal of Orthopsychiatry*, 52, 688–698.

Vingerhoets, A. and van Heck, G. (1990). Gender and coping: their relationship to symptoms. *Psychosomatic Medicine*, 52, 239–240.

Volkan, V. (1972). The linking objects of pathological mourners. *Archives of General Psychiatry*, 27, 215–221.

Volkan, V. (1981). *Linking Objects and Linking Phenomena: A Study of the Forms, Symptoms, Metapsychology and Therapy of Complicated Mourning*. New York: International Universities Press.

Volkart, E.H. and Michael, S.T. (1957). Bereavement and mental health. In A.H. Leighton, J.A. Clausen and R.N. Wilson (eds), *Explorations in Social Psychiatry* (pp. 281–307). London: Tavistock.

Vormbrock, J. (1993). Attachment theory as applied to wartime and job-related marital separation. *Psychological Bulletin*, 114, 122–144.

Waugh, E. (1948). *The Loved One*. London: Chapman and Hall.

Wegner, D.M. (1988). Stress and mental control. In S. Fisher and J. Reason (eds), *Handbook of Life Stress, Cognition and Health* (pp. 683–697). London and New York: Wiley.

Wegner, D.M. and Erber, R. (1992). The hyperaccessibility of suppressed thoughts. *Journal of Personality and Social Psychology*, 63, 903–912.

Wegner, D.M. and Gold, D.B. (1995). Fanning old flames: emotional and cognitive effects of suppressing thoughts of past relationships. *Journal of Personality and Social Psychology*, 68, 782–792.

Wegner, D.M., Schneider, D.J., Carter, S.R. and White, T.L. (1987). Paradoxical effects of thought suppression. *Journal of Personality and Social Psychology*, 53, 5–13.

Wegner, D.M. and Zanakos, S. (1994). Chronic thought suppression. *Journal of Personality*, 62, 615–640.

Weinberg, N. (1994). Self-blame, other blame, and desire for revenge: factors in recovery from bereavement. *Death Studies*, 18, 583–593.

Weiner, B. (1985). 'Spontaneous' causal thinking. *Psychological Bulletin*, 97, 74–84.

Weisman, A.S. (1990–1). Bereavement and companion animals. *Omega*, 22, 241–248.

Weiss, R.S. (1976). The emotional impact of marital separation. *Journal of Social Issues*, 32, 135–145.

Weiss, R.S. (1982). Attachment in adult life. In C.M. Parkes and J. Stevenson-Hinde (eds), *The Place of Attachment in Human Behaviour*. (pp. 171–184). London: Tavistock.

Weiss, R.S. (1988). Loss and recovery. *Journal of Social Issues*, 44, 37–52.

Weiss, R.S. (1991). The attachment bond in childhood and adulthood. In C.M.

Parkes, J. Stevenson-Hinde and P. Marris (ed.), *Attachment Across the Life Cycle* (pp. 66–76). London: Routledge.

Wenzlaff, R.M., Wegner, D.M. and Klein, S.B. (1991). The role of thought suppression in the bonding of thought and mood. *Journal of Personality and Social Psychology*, 60, 500–508.

Wenzlaff, R.M., Wegner, D.M. and Roper, D.W. (1988). Depression and mental control: the resurgence of unwanted negative thoughts. *Journal of Personality and Social Psychology*, 55, 882–892.

Westermeyer, J. (1973). Grenade-amok in Laos: a psychosocial perspective. *International Journal of Social Psychiatry*, 19, 251–260.

Wheeler, I. (1993–4). The role of meaning and purpose in life in bereaved parents associated with a self-help group: compassionate friends. *Omega*, 28, 261–271.

Wiebe, D.J. and Williams, P.G. (1992). Hardiness and health: a social psycho-physiological perspective on stress and adaptation. *Journal of Social and Clinical Psychology*, 11, 238–262.

Wiener, S.G., Bayart, F., Faull, K.F. and Levine, S. (1990). Behavioral and physiological responses to maternal separation in squirrel monkeys (*Saimiri sciureus*). *Behavioral Neuroscience*, 104, 108–115.

Wikan, U. (1988). Bereavement and loss in two Muslim communities: Egypt and Bali compared. *Social Science and Medicine*, 27, 451–460.

Wikan, U. (1990). *Managing Turbulent Hearts: A Balinese Formula for Living*. Chicago and London: University of Chicago Press.

Wilde, O. (1905). *De Profundis*. London: Methuen.

Williams, D.G. and Morris, G.H. (1996). Crying, weeping or tearfulness in British and Israeli adults. *British Journal of Psychology*, 87, 479–505.

Williams, G.C. (1966). *Adaptation and Natural Selection: a Critique of Some Current Evolutionary Thought*. Princeton, NJ: Princeton University Press.

Williams, R.B. and Eichelman, B. (1971). Social setting: influence on the physiological response to electric shock in the rat. *Science*, 174, 613–614.

Wilmoth, G.H., De Alteriis, M. and Bussell, D. (1992). Prevalence of psychological risks following legal abortion in the US: limits of the evidence. *Journal of Social Issues*, 48, 37–66.

Wilson, A.N. (1990). *C.S. Lewis: A Biography*. London: William Collins (quotations from 1991 Flamingo edn).

Wilson, D.S. (1995). Commentary on identical twins. *Human Behavior and Evolution Society Electronic List*, 8th Mar.

Winchester, G. (1992). An investigation of the human grief reactions following the death of a pet. Unpublished B.Sc Dissertation, Lancashire Polytechnic, Preston, UK.

Windholz, M.J., Marmar, C.R. and Horowitz, M.J. (1985). A review of the research on conjugal bereavement: impact on health and efficacy of intervention. *Comprehensive Psychiatry*, 26, 433–447.

Wolff, J.R., Nielson, P.E. and Schiller, P. (1970). The emotional reaction to stillbirth. *American Journal of Obstetrics and Gynecology*, 108, 73–76.

Woodward, J. (1988). The bereaved twin. *Acta Geneticae Medicae et Gemellologiae*, 37, 173–180.

Worden, J.W. (1981). *Grief Counselling and Grief Therapy*, 2nd edn. New York: Springer-Verlag; London: Routledge.

Worden, J.W. and Silverman, P.R. (1996). Parental death and the adjustment of school-age children. *Omega*, 33, 91–102.

Wortman, C.B. (1976). Causal attributions and personal control. In J.H. Harvey, W.J. Ickes and R.F. Kidd (eds), *New Directions in Attribution Research*, Vol. 1 (pp. 23–52). Hillsdale, NJ: Erlbaum.

Wortman, C.B. and Silver, R.C. (1987). Coping with irrevocable loss. In G.R. Vanden Bos and B.K. Bryant (eds), *Cataclysms, Crises, and Catastrophes: Psychology in Action* (pp. 189–235). Washington, DC: American Psychological Association.

Wortman, C.B. and Silver, R.C. (1989). The myths of coping with loss. *Journal of Consulting and Clinical Psychology*, 57, 349–357.

Wortman, C.B. and Silver, R.C. (1992). Reconsidering assumptions about coping with loss: an overview of current research. In L. Montada, S-H. Filipp and M.J. Lerner (eds), *Life Crises and Experiences of Loss in Adulthood* (pp. 341–365). Hillsdale, NJ: Erlbaum.

Wortman, C.B., Silver, R.C. and Kessler, R.C. (1993). The meaning of loss and adjustment to bereavement. In M.S. Stroebe, W. Stroebe and R.O. Hansson (eds), *Handbook of Bereavement: Theory, Research and Intervention* (pp. 349–366). New York: Cambridge University Press.

Wretmark, G. (1959). A study in grief reactions. *Acta Psychiatrica et Neurologica Scandanavia Supplement*, 136, 292–299.

Wright, P.H. (1988). Interpreting research on gender differences in friendship: a case for moderation and a plea for caution. *Journal of Social and Personal Relationships*, 5, 367–373.

Wright, R. (1994). *The Moral Animal: Evolutionary Psychology and Everyday Life*. New York: Pantheon. (Quotations taken from 1995 Little Brown edn.)

Wrigley, E.A. (1969). *Population and History*. New York: McGraw-Hill; London: Weidenfeld and Nicholson.

Yamamoto, J., Okonogi, K., Iwasaki, T. and Yoshimura (1969). Mourning in Japan. *American Journal of Psychiatry*, 125, 1660–1665.

Young, M., Benjamin, B. and Wallis, C. (1963). The mortality of widows. *The Lancet*, (no. 7305), 31st Aug., pp. 454–456.

Zika, S. and Chamberlain, K. (1992). On the relation between meaning in life and psychological well-being. *British Journal of Psychology*, 83, 133–145.

Zisook, S., DeVaul, R.A. and Click, M.A. (1982). Measuring symptoms of grief and bereavement. *American Journal of Psychiatry*, 139, 1590–1593.

Zisook, S., Mulvihill, M. and Shuchter, S.R. (1990). Widowhood and anxiety. *Psychiatric Medicine*, 8, 99–116.

Zisook, S. and Shuchter, S.R. (1986). Time course of spousal bereavement. *General Hospital Psychiatry*, 7, 95–100.

Zisook, S. and Shuchter, S.R. (1986). The first four years of widowhood. *Psychiatric Annals*, 15, 288–294.

Zisook, S. and Shuchter, S.R. (1991). Depression through the first year after death of a spouse. *American Journal of Psychiatry*, 148, 1346–1352.

Zisook, S. and Shuchter, S.R. (1993). Uncomplicated bereavement. *Journal of Clinical Psychiatry*, 54, 365–372.

Zisook, S., Shuchter, S.R. and Lyons, L.E. (1987a). Adjustment to widowhood. In S. Zisook (ed.), *Biopsychosocial Aspects of Bereavement* (pp. 49–74). Washington, DC: American Psychiatric Press.

Zisook, S., Shuchter, S.R. and Lyons, L.E. (1987b). Predictions of psychological reactions during early stages of widowhood. *Psychiatric Clinics of North America*, 10, 355–368.

Author index

Subject index

Note: page numbers in italics refer to illustrations or figures where these are separated from their textual reference.